Medieval English Drama

Patterns of Literary Criticism

GENERAL EDITORS

Marshall McLuhan
R. J. Schoeck
Ernest Sirluck

Medieval English Drama

Essays Critical and Contextual

EDITED BY

Jerome Taylor and Alan H. Nelson

The University of Chicago Press

CHICAGO AND LONDON

The University of Chicago Press, Chicago 60637
The University of Chicago Press, Ltd., London

International Standard Book Number: 0–226–79146–7 (clothbound)
Library of Congress Catalog Card Number: 72–77479

Contents

Illustrations

Jerome Taylor

I. Critics, Mutations, and Historians of Medieval English Drama: An Introduction to the Essays That Follow

> Historians undertake to arrange facts,—called stories, or histories—assuming in silence a relation of cause and effect. Their assumptions, hidden in the depths of dusty libraries, have been astounding but commonly unconscious . . . ; so much so that if any captious critic were to drag them to light, historians would probably reply, with one voice, that they had never supposed themselves required to know what they were talking about.
>
> Henry Adams, *The Education of Henry Adams*[1]

> The best actors in the world, either for tragedy, comedy, history, pastoral, pastoral-comical, historical-pastoral, tragical-historical, tragical-comical-historical-pastoral; scene indivisible, or poem unlimited.
>
> Polonius, in *Hamlet*, II.ii

Histories of early English drama and the critical interpretations upon which these rest—the whole corpus of such scholarship since Sharp's *Dissertation*[2] of 1825—must sometimes strike one as illegitimately descended from Polonius and as likely to carry that descent too far. Polonius earned his unenviable reputation by making inferences, moral as well as aesthetic, from inapplicable discriminations indiscriminately combined. Collectively and uncritically taken, modern schol-

1. (New York, 1931), p. 382. O. B. Hardison, Jr., cites the passage in his critique of histories of early medieval drama, which, he charges, have "retained the basic form established in 1903 by E. K. Chambers's *The Medieval Stage*," and of recent scholarship, which "has continued to accumulate new records and to suggest modifications in regard to influences and modes of transmission without seriously questioning the frame within which the new material is to be placed." See *Christian Rite and Christian Drama in the Middle Ages: Essays in the Origin and Early History of Modern Drama* (Baltimore, 1965), Essay I: "Darwin, Mutations, and the Origin of Medieval Drama," pp. 1–2.

2. Thomas Sharp, *A Dissertation on the Pageants or Dramatic Mysteries Anciently Performed at Coventry*, 1825.

arship similarly gives one the impression that medieval drama is a
ritual-dramatical-tragical-comical mystery stretching upwards into the
morality play; at the same time it seems to present medieval drama
as a technically undramatic and disjointed thing which is nonetheless
a veritable tragical-comical-moralistical-ritual miracle, indivisible and
unlimited.

On first rediscovering multiple forms of ritual and drama in medieval
documents, nineteenth-century scholars early applied the term "drama"
to them all. Assorted rites of the medieval church, the Mass in particular,
the *Quem quaeritis* or troped Introit of the Easter Mass, the Latin sung
plays associated with the liturgy, the non-extant Paternoster plays, the
vernacular cycles or *mystères*, the "miracles" or dramatized saints' lives,
the moralities—all were found "dramatic" in some respect, and hence
"drama." The umbrella term seemed the more apt because the diverse
forms were viewed as developmental increments or "links"—sometimes,
for textual scarcity, "missing links"—in the evolution of an ideal drama
from merest germ in the troped "-a" of the Easter Introit "alleluia" to
fullest organic growth in Renaissance tragedy and comedy.

Because E. K. Chambers imagined that "the dramatic tendencies of
Christian worship declared themselves at an early period" and that the
Mass is "an essentially dramatic commemoration of one of the most
critical moments in the life of the Founder," he ventured to propose
that the medieval drama is "of the highest interest as an object lesson
in literary evolution. The historian is not often privileged to isolate a
definite literary form throughout the whole course of its development,
and to trace its beginnings, as may here be done, beyond the very bor-
ders of articulate speech."[3] Karl Young, restricting his studies to the
Latin sung drama, reaffirmed the metaphor of organic evolution of
drama out of ritual;[4] current and more comprehensive histories, ranging

3. *The Medieval Stage* (Oxford, 1903), II, 3. Elsewhere Chambers adds three
genetic factors to the germ of the wordless "alleluia" and its verbalized tropes:
"Modern drama arose, by a fairly well-defined line of evolution, from a threefold
source, the ecclesiastical liturgy, the farce of the mimes, the classical revivals of
humanism. Folk-drama contributed but the tiniest rill to the mighty stream" (I,
182). The biological metaphor appears to become somewhat diluted.

4. His discrimination among the Mass, semidramatic ritual ceremonies, and fully
dramatic liturgical plays does not prevent his speaking of drama as "a spontaneous
new birth and growth within the confines of Christian worship." He echoes Chambers when he says: "Having denounced the plays of others, the Church spontaneously, independently, and gropingly invented a new theatrical product. . . . So
modest were its beginnings, so measured were its innovations, and so ample are the
records of its falterings, that the drama of the medieval Church presents to the
historian a unique opportunity for isolating a literary form and observing its development from almost inarticulate origins, through centuries of earnest experiment,
into firmly conceived results." *The Drama of the Medieval Church* (Oxford, 1933),
I, 1 and 12.

from medieval to Elizabethan times, preserve it.[5] Most recently, O. B. Hardison, Jr., though he attacks what he calls "the organic analogy" and "the evolutionary concept" as such, extends to the point of identity the very likenesses between ritual and drama upon which the evolutionary hypothesis had rested; for, in the Middle Ages, he holds, discrimination "between religious ritual (the services of the Church) and drama did not exist. Religious ritual *was* the drama of the Middle Ages" —though he somewhat inconsistently concedes that there was an "evident shift from ritual to representational modes,"[6] that is, a shift presumably from ritual to drama, as if in the Middle Ages there obtained between these two an essential distinction without an existential difference.

When compared with the achievements of Renaissance drama in which the supposed evolutionary process was said to have culminated, every form of medieval drama has been found to be different from its offspring rather than like them, and not only markedly different from the progeny but far inferior to them. It has been argued that the Corpus Christi plays failed in the expression of something called the tragic spirit

5. Two instances suffice. A. P. Rossiter, *English Drama from Early Times to the Elizabethans: Its Background, Origins, and Development* (London, 1950), who also adds religious dance to the wordless ritual elements from which drama has evolved, retains the "germ" theory: "Beyond the beginnings of recognizable dramatic art lies a world of rituals. The simplest and most primitive is the dance: always at its beginnings a religious act, a wordless rite of temporary physical and emotive dedication. . . . A kind of drama in ecclesiastical Latin and closely connected with the Church liturgy of the great Christian feasts is generally regarded as the restarting-point of dramatic history after the barbarian interregnum of the Dark Ages. . . . Ritual drama is . . . traced from the germ of the *Quem Quaeritis*, as a trope or sung interpolation, in the *Introit*: the chant sung while the celebrant approached the altar. . . . As the trope was interpolated into the service, stretching it (as it were), so further incidents extend the *Quem Quaeritis*. . . . This accretive process altered the Easter trope, changing it to developed playlets" etc. (pp. 15 and 42–44 passim). Arnold Williams, *The Drama of Medieval England* (East Lansing, Mich., 1961), for the most part avoiding the "organic analogy" in tracing the development of drama, nonetheless finds that "all drama whose origins have been studied turns out to have arisen out of ritual. . . . Drama has had two births in Europe, once from the rites of pagan Greece, the second time from those of Christian Rome. How this came about is a fascinating story, conjectural in parts but sufficiently clear in broad outline to afford perhaps the best account anywhere of the rise of a literary form. . . . the liturgy of the Roman Church abounded in materials easily dramatized. Anyone who has ever attended a Catholic mass knows that it teems with elements of drama: the dialogue of antiphons and response, the movements of the priest . . . all is the finest kind of material for the dramatist" (Prologue, pp. 4–6).

6. *Christian Rite and Christian Drama in the Middle Ages*, Preface, pp. viii–ix. For the undoubted value of Hardison's critique of traditional histories and interpretations of medieval drama, yet for problems created by his own critical method, see the review by Arthur Heiserman, *Modern Philology*, 65 (1967–68), 241–44. Examination of Hardison's critique (see especially Essay I, pp. 1–34) is essential for an understanding of the present collection and for this Introduction; it is often cited, but its influence is present even when citation is not explicit.

and hence made no contribution to the medieval heritage of Elizabethan tragedy.[7] Yet, when the Corpus Christi plays allegedly yielded to the seductive advances of secular realism and comic farce, they have been said to have achieved in these alone the best that comedy can attain.[8] And yet, for all its achievement in the comic mode, "the religious drama had no dramatic technique or dramatic purpose, and no artistic self-consciousness." If we would inquire into its dramaturgy, we are warned that "to carry to the study of the medieval religious drama a body of criteria derived from Aristotle, Horace, and their Renaissance followers, or of specialists in the technique of the modern drama or of drama in general is to bring the wrong equipment . . . because we have here the strange case of a drama that was not striving to be dramatic but

7. Willard Farnham, *The Medieval Heritage of Elizabethan Tragedy* (Oxford, 1956; reprinted with corrections from the first edition of 1936), finds that "the tragic spirit must be said to have remained rudimentary among the writers of mysteries" (pp. 173–74), for "fully developed tragedy is possible only where keen desire or high ability to understand human suffering unite with noble capacity for taking pleasure in its artistic representation" (p. 2), whereas the Corpus Christi play, like all "ritualistic" or "religiously commemorative" drama, is "too reverent of tradition to make creative changes in the essential matter of a story handed down from the immemorial past. . . . At most it elaborates the record with a naive realism" (pp. 4–5). But tragic inevitability and tragic irony "do not lie exposed in the raw stuff of life. They are exposed through the artist's perception and are only made plain to us when his hand has so molded life as to bring their lines into high relief. Hence the plot of an artistic tragedy is itself a philosophy of life . . . honestly concerned with the mystery of human suffering" (p. 6). Questionable are Farnham's contentions that the Corpus Christi play is not concerned with the mystery of human suffering; that it is content simply to elaborate with naive realism the record of Scripture without creative changes in the received story; that it lacks a protagonist—man seen in men with imperfections recognizably like our own; that there is no tragic inevitability or irony overseeing the actions men commit; that there is no plot which unites the whole and projects a philosophy of life; and that there is no pleasure in its artistic representation. Of great assistance in removing such misconceptions is V. A. Kolve's *The Play Called Corpus Christi* (Stanford, Calif., 1966). Farnham also denies "the tragic spirit" to miracle plays. Only "in the latest of the major forms evolved by medieval religious drama, namely, the moral play or morality, we may find a tragic spirit definitely developing" (pp. 176–77).

8. See below, the essay by Lawrence J. Ross, "Symbol and Structure in the *Secunda Pastorum*," p. 177 and the references there cited. For identification of "secular" elements and "common humor" with "artistic" impulse hampered by religious demands, see Rossiter, *English Drama from Early Times to the Elizabethans*, pp. 48, 50: "Many reasons are given why drama 'left the Church' to become 'secularized' in streets and markets. Increase in length, interruption of ritual, the growing demand for spectacle, the detachment of episodes from their proper seasons, the intrusion of the common tongue and common humour, and the objections of the strict have all been suggested. But it must be remembered that it was only the evolutional growth-points of drama which came 'out of God's blessing into the warm sun.' . . . The simplest explanation of the 'exit' from the church is that the secular world gave more room for developments which were already pressing on inventive 'literary' minds. The secular world gave freedom, and an impulse we may properly call artistic took the line of least resistance."

to be religious, a drama whose motive was worship and not amusement."[9]

As these representative selections show, medieval drama has been viewed as drama because it is identifiable with ritual, yet it has also been denied all dramatic quality because it is religious. It has been said to excel in instances of comic but not of tragic art, and yet it has been taken as serious in intent and without any aim to amuse. Since its art was allegedly not intended to be thought of as art, it has been denied examination by any canons of art that aesthetic theory has sought to devise. What we find in such allegations are repeated combinations of "disjunctive terms," and they are "critically disabling."[10] In the peculiar pastiche which might be formed from them, some neo-Polonian interpreter of medieval drama, if such a man could exist, might rejoice in having displayed therein the fine and full measure of his wisdom and his wit. What he would have displayed is that, like Polonius, he had merely been eclectic in his conclusions, undiscerning of bad method in his secondary sources, and unaware of any need to search for a more discriminating analysis than his authorities had employed.

Only superficially will the essays selected for this volume seem to follow one another in the order familiar in traditional histories, to condone the evolutionary hypothesis, and to be deservedly suspect for its errors. The three that follow (chaps. 2–4) deal with the liturgical sung drama and with ritual forms from which, it has been said, all modern drama evolved; the next eleven (chaps. 5–15) deal with the subsequent vernacular plays of the fourteenth through the sixteenth centuries, nine of them with English Corpus Christi or cycle plays in particular; and the last three (chaps. 16–18) deal with two exemplary early English moralities. Four of these essays are new: the present Introduction, the essay by E. Catherine Dunn, and the two by Alan H. Nelson have not previously been published. Many have been revised or supplemented by or with the approval of their authors; all rely upon new critical and interpretive insights corrective of older understandings of medieval drama and its development. Each has its own focus, formulates its own terms and questions, and establishes its own conclusions. But when they are taken together, the picture of medieval drama that emerges is not a pastiche of inapplicable discriminations indiscriminately combined. This collection of scholarly criticism reveals, both in itself and in the corpus of medieval drama to which it directs its attention, a systematic unity. Certainly, however, it pretends to reveal no biological or systemic unity;

9. Hardin Craig, *English Religious Drama of the Middle Ages* (Oxford, 1955; reprinted with corrections, 1964), pp. 4–5.
10. The phrases are Ross's, below, p. 180.

holism is not postulated by any essay here.[11] By the selection, re-editing, and ordering of its essays critical and contextual, this volume seeks to build toward a less partial interpretation and a more plausible history of medieval English drama than those offered in interpretations and histories still widely read.

The nature and value of interpretations and histories rest primarily upon the kinds of questions they ask or at least imply, secondarily upon the answers they give. In introducing the essays in this book, it will be well, while summarizing the conclusions to which they come, to survey the questions from which they start and the assumptions and terms which frame them. The essays by Marshall, Dunn, and Smoldon invite special attention at the outset. The questions, assumptions, and definitions which they find essential to their explorations of liturgical sung drama and the ritual within which it appeared prove no less applicable to the later vernacular cycles and moralities. Once these questions, assumptions, and terms have been identified in chapters 2, 3, and 4, that identification will facilitate description of all the rest of the essays.

Historians and interpreter-critics of medieval drama have long been agreed upon one thing: a definition of "drama" is essential to their inquiries. Some have lamented the absence of one and provided none; some have attempted one, casual but self-assured or diffident even in their certainty; all have been subjected to critical review: the problem still remains. Is there a working definition of "drama" which will include all that has conventionally been called medieval drama? Shall the definition be extended to ritual—the Mass, the Divine Office, "semi-dramatic" liturgical ceremonies? Can the term "dramatic" be applied to productions that share common scriptural or liturgical materials and incidental formal likenesses, while the term "drama" is restricted to those

11. Holism is "the philosophic theory first formulated by Jan C. Smuts that the determining factors in nature are wholes (as organisms) which are irreducible to the sum of their parts and that the evolution of the universe is a record of the activity and making of these wholes." *Webster's Third New International Dictionary Unabridged* (1969), s.v. "holism." "Systemic" refers to the kind of unity found in a living organism; "systematic," to a rationally ordered plan, provided, for example, by the integrated points of inquiry in a method of analysis. A work of art, though not systemic, not an organism, is nonetheless a system, "organic" (*like* an organism) by analogy alone: it holds its constituent elements in coinforming tension in a unitary whole. Adequate systematic analysis will not reduce a work of art to a sum of its parts, as if these were discrete subwholes joined by mere accretion or addition. Such analysis is not content to divide a work into physical chunks; it also and especially distinguishes elements active throughout the whole. The form of systematic analysis to be followed here will distinguish among kinds of materials used, the way or ways they are combined, the specific design the combination effects, and what altogether these express or represent, hence invite as felt insight, or aesthetic experience.

which share essential formal differentiae in manner of representation, in experience projected and effect contained? Shall the undifferentiating practice of notable medieval interpreters—their taking of analogies for identities—direct the critical analysis of art products from their time? If to follow their practice is historical criticism, does such historical criticism have universal conceptual merit?

Raised here is a fundamental question: the nature and function of definition in matters of inquiry and inference. On its resolution much depends.

The special value of Mary Hatch Marshall's "Aesthetic Values of the Liturgical Drama" is that it affords a working definition of drama: it both states and implies parameters[12] which, by their presence and changing values, discriminate ritual from drama yet show wherein they are alike. Descriptively rich, the essay re-creates a picture of this drama for those "who almost never have a chance to experience it in performance and are separated from the Middle Ages by centuries of cultural revolution"; it creates this picture by making use of the "valuable hints of movement, mimetic action, costume, and symbolic properties scattered in the rubrics" and inferrable from dialogue in verbal texts of the plays (libretti without music, William Smoldon will complain of modern editions).[13] But the description does not rest with imaginable surface materials; it penetrates to the significance materialized in them, in short to the form which gives them life. In so doing the essay counteracts "false and limited assumptions about the nature of drama and of the liturgical drama in particular," and it elevates to the category of art, to the status of full drama in its own right, each "apparently simple fossilized text" which any cursory reader may too hastily mistake for something "lifeless, a dreary little undifferentiated amoeba of modern drama, without plot, without character, almost without conflict, whose only value is historical," not an achievement of art in itself, at most the "germ" of true drama to come.

12. A parameter is an interpretive and defining measure, "an arbitrary constant characterizing by each of its particular values some particular member of a system," an element "which may have various values each fixed within the limits of a stated case or discussion." *Webster's Third New Int'l Dict. Unabr.*, s.v. "parameter." The set of parameters here are the four terms of systematic analysis noted above, last sentence of n. 11, "constant" in that they are consistently applied to every "member" or product called "medieval drama," their "various values" in each such "particular member" serving to "characterize" it in distinction from others.

13. Marshall's visual description of these will recall, for those fortunate enough to have seen them, the New York Pro Musica productions of *The Play of Herod*, a conflation of two twelfth-century sung dramas from the Fleury Playbook, under the direction of the late Noah Greenberg; or of *The Play of Daniel*, originally written by students at the cathedral of Beauvais and played annually between 1150 and 1250. Both are recorded by Decca, albums DL 79402 and DL 10095–10096.

Likeness between Christian rite and Christian drama begins, for Marshall, with shared materials and stops when one considers the differing manners in which they combined them and the differing effects they thus achieved. Words, allusions, images, music, movement, sacred space and sacred time, "liturgical personages" themselves, remain materially identical in ritual and drama, but in the plays they take on new formal character and identity as dramatic manner informs, indeed transforms, them all—altar into historic sepulcher, corona of candles into the Nativity star, vaulted roof into a dated sky, and deacons into weeping Marys or angels. The audiovisual "language" of the play, symbolic to begin with, thus undergoes a second symbolic reform, becomes symbol resymbolized, "imaginatively fed by centuries of emotional association with sacred seasons and sacred places, the Christian story of salvation through Christ, the beautiful familiar words of the liturgy, and the church's age-old habit of symbolism, but having its own values and its own function as drama."

Materials, or audiovisual "language," form one parameter; as applied to liturgy and liturgical drama the value of that parameter does not change. But impersonation in the representation constitutes another parameter; it is of zero value in the liturgy, of positive and developing value in the plays, and thus it measures the formal difference between Christian rite and Christian drama:

The liturgical plays are distinguished from the many liturgical and extra-liturgical ceremonies of the church which contain dramatic elements in symbolic gesture by the fact that in the plays living actors assume the roles of the characters of sacred story. There is no impersonation in the Mass nor in strictly liturgical observance. . . . With the added elements of mimetic action and dialogue, impersonation is the basic criterion of this drama, as of any, effectually separating it from religious rite.[14]

14. Use of impersonation, impersonational presentation of a story, as the essential criterion of drama was early advocated by John Matthews Manly in his "Literary Forms and the New Theory of the Origin of Species," *Modern Philology*, 4 (1906–7), 576–95: "There were many things which to us seem capable of becoming drama; the only valid test of development is what actually happened. Antiphones [*sic*] might become more antiphonal; sermon, epic, comedy, *estrif*, *débat*, might develop a more lively dialogue; none of them, as a matter of fact, became drama; none of them varied beyond its class. But these things look very much like the drama, and good men and true have been deceived by them. Perhaps the only way in which we can avoid deception is to begin with the mediaeval drama when it was unmistakably drama, and carefully go back to the time when it came into existence. We shall thus be able to see exactly what were the effective changes. . . . The features that seem essential to distinguishing it from other forms of literature, and the only essential features, are: the presentation of a story in action, and the impersonation of the characters concerned in the story. Dialogue, though important and usually present, is not essential; the pantomime makes no use of speech, the monologue develops its situation without the participation of a second actor" (pp. 581–

The distinction is definitive, but the materials which liturgical drama shares with the liturgy limit its visibility. The original symbolic value of the materials which it was fitting to retain conspired with the form which their dramatic transformation might take. The scriptural figures dramatically impersonated, their preset expressions of thought and feeling like the noted melodies in which dialogue was to be sung, the stylized sequence of plotted actions like the stylized gestures and costumes prescribed for their execution, belong, as Marshall tells us, not to "a realistic drama, but a formalized poetic drama . . . filled with symbolism, partly of a direct iconic sort." But only in the symbolic-iconic quality of the materials are liturgical sung plays identifiable with the sacred rites into which they were interpolated. So long as materials remained restricted to such symbolic form they constrained in their projection all development of character in *dramatis personae*, all invention of thought and individuating personality in what was said or sung, and allowed no more than moving tableau for the action to be expressed.

82, 585). On the relative merits of "the differential or difference-dialectic," which proceeds "by the separation of dissimilars," versus "the integral or likeness-dialectic," which "reaches solutions by combinations of like with like," see Elder Olson, "An Outline of Poetic Theory," in R. S. Crane, ed., *Critics and Criticism, Ancient and Modern* (Chicago, 1952), pp. 546–66.

Hardison, *Christian Rite and Christian Drama in the Middle Ages*, pp. 30–33, has made clear the faulty discrimination and shifting meanings of "action," "dialogue," and "impersonation" when used as differentiae of drama by Chambers, Young, Craig, and others. Hardison is wrong, however, to dismiss impersonation as "a nineteenth-century concept . . . in marked contrast to medieval and Renaissance attitudes." As against his contention that "the criterion of impersonation . . . is at odds not only with probable medieval attitudes but with the impassioned testimony of nineteenth- and twentieth-century actors as well," it is here proposed that role-playing, posturing, simulation or mimetic action, while common to all human behavior, acquire special form in the impersonation proper to drama. In the liturgy, even in the Mass, the officiant does not pretend to be Christ. He does not act the part of Christ but *ex parte Christi*, on behalf of Christ, who is conceived as supernaturally present and without surrendering divine identity to his minister. The priest, following his text, commemorates Christ, recalls his words in indirect discourse, and, in doing so, is asked by the rubrics to simulate the posture narrated in the words—to raise his eyes toward heaven as he breaks the bread and lifts the cup. For a priest suddenly to presume that he was Christ, to impersonate Christ, would be imposture. One is reminded of Solon's alleged denunciation of Thespis as an impostor for daring to impersonate Dionysus in the first dramatization of the dithyramb during the course of sacred rites; the story is probably apocryphal, but apt. Three attitudes have been observed in different celebrants of the Mass: pretentious simulation, quietly recognized by the congregation as officious vanity; imaginative absorption, mystically oriented, in contemplation of symbolic act and gesture; and deeply chastened literalism, the simple holiness of a minister of Christ, acting for Christ as his ordained representative. None of these involves "representing" Christ by feigned impersonation. The line between role-playing in life and impersonation in drama is fine; the distinction is essential.

But any icon, through its conventionalized symbolization in matter
and form, has reference to an interpretive thought, a "feeling-idea"[15] to
which one is carried by its means and manner. Symbolic in its materials
and dramatic though restrictedly so in its form, liturgical drama yields,
as one might expect, an iconic yet strictly dramatic plot—a sequence of
iconic actions by dramatically impersonated agents through stage values
of place and time. Whether in one play the actions are those of disconsolate women who, lamenting the death of their lord, discover that
he lives yet among them so that their sorrow is turned to joy; or whether
in another they are those of disconsolate shepherds who, lamenting
man's life and times, discover that salvation has been born among them
so that their sorrow, and the world's, is also turned to joy—whatever
the altered terms of its plotted representation, there is "a dramatic
peripety, the turn from sorrow to joy, present in every one of these
plays, even the simplest," and its communal confirmation is anticipated
in the "Te Deum laudamus" or, in Germany, the "Christ ist erstanden,"
provided for congregation or audience to sing with the cast.[16] Such a
movement in human experience, such an "action" as an interpretive pattern of life, may have archetypal universality as a response to a universal
human wish or need, but in medieval Christian drama it is an "action"
imitated in Christian terms. "Awareness of a familiar archetypal pattern
may enlarge our sense of a relation between the liturgical drama of
the medieval Christian church and long human experience, but comparative anthropology, fascinating as it is, offers little specific aid in comprehending this particular form of art of medieval Christian culture."[17]

15. The phrase is used by Marshall of costumes prescribed in the plays, which
"almost invariably consist of a modification of ecclesiastical vestments, in symbolic
suggestion, not realism," and which hence "often touched upon a whole range of
associated feeling-ideas through the iconographical system of attribute, familiar also
in medieval plastic art."

16. Marshall notes that the "intense preoccupation with re-creating the human
suffering of the crucified Christ in every conceivable realistic detail" such as one
finds in the cycle plays, "belongs to the late days of the medieval system." See
Robinson's essay, below.

17. The criterion used thus far to distinguish liturgical drama from ritual—
essentially the plotted and impersonational representation of an "action" or commonly understood interpretation of life—is denied by John Speirs to the cycle
plays, where we shall shortly see it applies no less than here. See his *Medieval
English Poetry: The Non-Chaucerian Tradition* (London, 1957), pp. 316–17: "If
we agreed that the Mystery Cycle is for the most part not yet art," he says, "but is
still as a whole in the ritual phase, we shall agree that it does not present an 'action'
so as to be fully intelligible to an audience unfamiliar with it. The Mystery Cycle is
not representational or fully self-explanatory of an action; it does not unfold or
expose an action as for an audience who expect to be shown, so as to understand,
what happened and how it happened, how it began, evolved and ended. . . . The
modern reader, who would prefer to see the whole Mystery Cycle as a drama
according to his conception, is naturally baffled by the gaps in what appears to him

The materials and plotted events of this drama, then, for all their corroborative evidential nature, are to be distinguished from the persuasions of overt didactic instruction, even from those of abstract allegory. Represented are " 'the picturable intuitive concrete' rather than 'the rational abstract,' 'story as against dialectical discourse, exposition,' " and the representation has all the effect of mythic drama. The mythopoeic events drawn from Christian history project no panorama or piece of history as such but induce or evoke, through their dramatic representation, an interpretive vision of life and an emotive response which together invite a psychic conversion or confirmation, an affectively experienced insight and metanoia, or change of spirit. They are expressive as lyrics are, and, with the psychic distance art cannot escape, they initiate within audience-participants a psychic experience identical with the experience which the events represent.[18]

This analysis of Marshall's essay prompts an evaluation of distinguishing terms in their application to liturgical drama. "Religious and not didactic" in aim; oriented toward "worship and not amusement": these discriminations do apply, for they characterize correctly the effect achieved by such drama. But "religious, hence not dramatic," or "ritual and therefore drama": these combinations do not apply, for they fail to make essential discrimination between materials and dramatic form. "Serious but without tragic sense," or "comic because farce": neither do these combinations apply, for they ignore the "action" most deeply expressed and the interpretive response to life which that "action," as expressed in diverse plots, invites. Material means, dramatic manner, "action" expressed, effect achieved: such parameters systematize analysis as one measures their changing values. Regulative of critical focus, ap-

---

an imperfect sequence of events. He is accustomed—no doubt rightly—to expect from a drama the apprehensible detailed unity of structure of a complete work of art. . . . But we shall continue to misunderstand the Mystery Cycle if we try to regard it as a blundering effort at art instead of still being, as a whole, at the stage of ritual. We can see from our historical viewpoint that it is in process of becoming art—comedy or tragedy—and we can see that there are individual Cycle plays which we may claim to have become art, to be genuine dramatic poems. It is these few outstanding plays which are properly the object of literary criticism."

18. As Marshall puts it, they effect a "total emotional experience, in which lyricism plays a part intrinsic, not extrinsic, to [this] drama" by which "faith is warmed and confirmed." As a "total emotional experience"—identical in some of the materials used, comparable but not identical in the psychic experience represented and invited, and radically distinct in nondramatic manner of representation—liturgy, even the Mass, resembles liturgical drama. Discrimination between what is identical, what comparable, and what distinct must be kept clearly in mind when reading Marshall's statement that "all dramas and all rituals are symbolic of human activity in a fundamental iconic way, and all dramatic conventions are symbols."

propriate to the texts under scrutiny, and productive of definition, they allow applicable discriminations to be discriminately combined.[19]

Two methodological cautions relating to such discriminations may now be advanced. First, to define or "illuminate" dramatic forms of the Middle Ages in light of some alien form (such as the form, actual or fancied, of Renaissance tragedy, or of Renaissance comedy, or of medieval ritual) which, in some selected aspect, medieval drama is imagined more or less to resemble, is to transport a poetic figure violently into critical discourse—to practice critical metonymy by vesting one thing with the name of another. Again, to limit one's attention to a selected constitutive part of medieval drama (for example, to its materials or "language" with no regard for the representational form in which these appear or the psychically distanced effect which they collaborate to produce) and to take that part as definitive of the nature of the whole, is to practice critical synecdoche, to mistake part for whole in an absurd fashion. In analytic interpretation, poetic metonymy is bad, poetic synecdoche is worse, and conflation of the two is blindness confirmed.[20]

Second, historical criticism may be conceived in two ways, one valid, one not. The practice of notable medieval interpreters like Amalarius of Metz or Honorius of Autun—their taking of analogies for identities to the neglect of formal differences, as when they call the Mass a tragic drama—must be recorded by historians of criticism. Valid historical criticism records all such practices of the past; to exclude such errors from the record of critical efforts would perpetuate our ignorance of mistakes useful to know if only to avoid them. To contend, however,

19. Some will wish to call them "neo-Aristotelian." No absolute merit is claimed for them; they are used here for their pragmatic merit—they prevent inconsistency in discriminating likenesses and differences, hence prevent the mixing of classes in interpreting the products described. See Elder Olson, "The Poetic Method of Aristotle: Its Powers and Limitations," *English Institute Essays, 1952* (New York, 1952), pp. 70–94; reprinted in *Aristotle's "Poetics" and English Literature* (Chicago, 1965), pp. 175–91.

20. The peril of converting poetic figure into critical license is memorialized, ironically, in a well-known nineteenth-century poem—John G. Saxe's "The Blind Men and the Elephant":

> It was six men of Indostan
>   To learning much inclined,
> Who went to see the elephant
>   (Though each of them were blind),
> That each by observation
>   Might satisfy his mind.

When each felt a flank, tusk, trunk, leg, ear, or tail, he "saw" only a wall, spear, snake, tree, fan, or rope. The poem concludes with the observation that

> . . . each was partly in the right,
> And all were in the wrong!

that all critics must follow some undiscriminating critical practice in order to be true to the art produced when that practice existed is to endow bygone critical fashions with a regulative power over art and with a universal conceptual merit that no critical set can claim.[21] This is historical criticism misconceived. To know what men of another period saw in the art they received or made is one thing; to see what they saw as directive of what one should also see may be to "see" with the sages of Indostan (see n. 20 above). Neither ignorance of past errors nor imitation of them will do.

But if metonymy and synecdoche may not set the canons of critical method, there is no question about the need to recognize their purely poetic operation within the works one is examining. Clearly, in medieval drama these figures deliver the meanings of symbolic language, of metaphoric or mythic thought, and the iconic significance of whole plays. They do not apply, however, to impersonational process as mere process, to impersonation as general technique; they will not make drama, which employs impersonation, become ritual nor ritual, which does not employ impersonation, become drama.

Marshall had noted that "Originally, the *Quem quaeritis* trope . . . was attached to the Introit of the Easter Mass; not until it was removed to the conclusion of Easter Matins in the tenth century did it become a play, with impersonation. There is a suggestion here that only at a distance from the heart of the mystery in the sacrificial Mass was drama freshly achieved." E. Catherine Dunn's essay, "Voice Structure in the Liturgical Drama: Sepet Reconsidered," examines exactly where, in what way, and to what extent impersonation, with attendant "dialogic" expression and representational technique, was imposed upon the "language" of the liturgy. Her rehabilitation of a nineteenth-century scholar to whom justice has not been done is refreshing. Both her extension of the perceptive distinctions he made and her correction of his metaphoric use of evolution to describe the changes he saw, will, together with Smoldon's essay, invite a third cautionary observation about histories of drama and the limits of their task.

Addressing itself to materials common to liturgy and liturgical drama, Sepet's *Origines catholiques du théâtre moderne* (a book we have been unwise to neglect, as Dunn makes clear) "probes the voice patterns in the liturgical chant of the Carolingian era for their dramatic potential and places emphasis on the structure of lessons and responsories in the office of Matins." In the nocturns of the Matins office, the lector, or

21. Hardison so contends in *Christian Rite and Christian Drama in the Middle Ages,* Essay II, "The Mass as Sacred Drama," pp. 35–79.

reader, will sing, for example, a passage from the prophet Isaiah. A single cantor or choir leader (precentor) "delivers the initial response to the reading which all have just heard":

The precentor's response may be given, for example, in the words and thus, in effect, in the voice of Isaias, which he appears to assume as his own. Hearing the precentor intone these words (the basic text of the *responsum* or reply), the choir, breaking in to echo a portion of them, is in turn interrupted by the precentor, who adds yet another thought to his responsive address. Continuing in this fashion, precentor and choir, by cumulative extension and repetition of their collective thought, effect a dialogic response both to the reading and to each other in a kind of group meditation . . . a restatement, a commentary, or a lyrical expression of the joy or grief implicit in the passage.

In the *Mystère d'Adam* of the twelfth century with its strange mixture of Latin and the vernacular, of liturgical reading and dramatic representation, one finds "the play that most clearly realizes the potential for dramatic form of the combined lection and responsory." Seen clearly in it, and less clearly but still unmistakably in the lesson-responsory voice pattern of Matins or in the transformation of the "Vos, inquam" lection of Christmas Matins into the Prophet Play, is what Sepet called "a struggle" to escape from "the enveloping monologue," or narrative voice, on the part of "a dialogue enchained within it."

Did the *Quem quaeritis* Introit trope of the Easter Mass become drama when transferred to Matins but not before? In one sense of "become" Dunn finds this is so and draws support from Karl Young, who "took a firm stand against the Introit trope as drama, demonstrating that the surviving texts do not contain rubrics for costume, gesture, or action which would indicate full impersonation of the roles. Only after the removal of the trope from the Introit to the office of Matins are such rubrics present in the manuscripts." Not only with matter, then, do the rubrics always deal, but sometimes with the dramatic form it is to take. Along with dialogue itself, they prescribe impersonation, "fictive assumption of an identity . . . involving both speech and action in imitation of another."

Thus, one may recognize "the various forms of musical dialogue as fundamental to the origins of medieval drama in the sense, at least, that such chanted dialogue provided the context within which genuine drama arose." But "arose" or "become" imply no "strictly chronological or evolutionary progress, and Sepet did little service to his great work by using metaphorical language borrowed from biological evolution. Conscious experimentation was involved, as he well knew, and some of the most advanced stages of the process occurred early (e.g. in the twelfth-century *Mystère d'Adam*) and some of the most awkward solutions of the problem were still visible in the late fourteenth century, as in the pedestrian Expositor of the Chester cycle."

Dealing still with the materials of medieval liturgical drama, with sung melodic lines, William L. Smoldon's "The Melodies of the Medieval Church Dramas and Their Significance" exposes the peril of inquiring into this drama from what Karl Young called "an exclusively literary point of view" and ignoring the music by which, as the critic must find, "the effects of the dramatic texts are often enough considerably enhanced," and by which, as the historian must find, the earliest *Quem quaeritis* dramatizations show close melodic relationship to the wholly nondramatic Introit tropes of the Easter Mass and no relationship whatever to the music of any other rite or ceremony, real or hypothetical.[22] Not only the nondramatic yet "dialogic" Easter trope, but identically nondramatic and "dialogic" Christmas and Ascension tropes are found within the Introits of their respective feasts. In music, they bear relationship only to the different melodies of the Introits themselves, not to each other and not to the melodies of antiphons and responsories of the Divine Office.

But music—like words, allusions, images, even movements, as has been said above—is part of the materials with which an artist can work. Left to the artist's free invention is the form by means of which he will combine all his materials and with which he will clothe them. More than one medieval monastic or priestly artist may have heard his materials call for combination into a form already partly recognizable and familiar to him in the "voice" structure of Matins. Given our knowledge of the *troparium* of the Abbey of St. Martial de Limoges, of "the monastery's

22. Smoldon has in view Hardison's hypothesis of a nonextant vigil ceremony, more dramatically representational than the Easter vigil Mass with which he proposes it could have been associated. See Hardison, Essay V, "The Early History of the *Quem quaeritis*," pp. 178–219, esp. p. 219: "An analysis of *Quem quaeritis* manuscripts in these [literary-textual] terms consistently leads to the conclusion that the dialogue originated not as an Easter trope but as a ceremony associated with the vigil Mass. . . . Enough features of the original may be dimly observed in the texts and rubrics of extant manuscripts to justify a tentative reconstruction, but this reconstruction is offered only as a suggestion. Concerning the date and place of origin of the ceremony there is no evidence at all. Here scholarship must yield to pure speculation." Smoldon admires the ingenuity of the argument but finds "one great flaw in the structure," namely, "a total disregard of music," which "will be found to be just as valuable evidence as are the 'libretti'—and frequently more so." In this case scholarship attentive to musical evidence finds that the tenth-century *troparium* of St. Martial de Limoges supplies place, date, and likely circumstances for dramatic invention. Here literary scholarship yields not to speculation but to musicology. One admires the candor and caution, though equally laments the limits, expressed in Marshall's confession that she "must unhappily exclude [music] from consideration, in blank ignorance" while "the whole subject awaits further study by musicologists." Smoldon supplies a long-felt need.

avant-garde position in the field of musical invention," the "degree of free and unofficial composition" and "new art" encouraged there, one may hazard a probable guess—an *obiter dictum*, no more—that the dramatic combination of musical and verbal elements was first effected there. Even if such a probable guess were put aside and any exchange of influence between art forms denied as unproven, the historian of drama would still have to describe the difference in form between liturgy and liturgical drama. To characterize that difference he would have to discuss the "escape" of the fully realized dramatic "voice" that Dunn has clearly defined.

In their bearing upon evolution or upon some differently conceived development of forms, these remarks now allow a third caution to be inferred. History of medieval drama is possible, but not as once conceived. It is not the story of a change, but the record of changes made. It tells not of the evolution of a form, pretending to analyze a process of reproduction as effected through some "germ" within which genetic factors randomly varied or conserved the shape of each newly engendered thing. Rather, constant in its application of a single systematic analysis, it compares the analyzed constituents of finished products of art, and it leaves to the curiosity of psychologists and sociologists of art all inquiry into the productive process. The products may be classified according to likenesses and differences in respects consistently defined, and in the simplicity or complexity, in this sense the "sophistication,"[23] with which they manifest them. Classification and comparison, of themselves, need imply no causal-sequential line. Likeness and difference are the change among products, and no exchange of influence, even were chronological pinpointing possible,[24] can generally be more than guessed.

23. Complexity does not "evolve" from simplicity; each involves a distinct style in the handling of materials and form. The simple, properly conceived, is the contrary of the simple-minded; the simple is not raw, crude, artless, signifying little, primitive like a childish beginning, but pure in materials and form, spare in their refinement, restrained like classic art, profound in direct appeal, and ultimate in the meaning which contemplation, like childlike play, finds playing in native design. Complexity is often elaborate, overlaid with multiple artistic designs, laced with intricate meanings, and oblique in the edgy scrutiny which its sophistication, like that of some "mature" adults, invites.

24. Hardison rightly criticizes Chambers's view that "disregarding . . . in the main the dates of the manuscripts, it is easy so to classify the available versions as to mark the course of a development." See *Medieval Stage*, II, 28, 32, and Hardison, *Christian Rite* . . . , p. 13. Hardison observes that Chambers's "classification system moves from simple to complex" and leniently allows that "The existence of a spectrum of forms from the *Quem quaeritis* to the enormous Corpus Christi cycles doubtless made the evolutionary hypothesis inevitable" (p. 12). In this Introduction, the necessity of a "spectrum of forms" is being affirmed for histories of medieval drama, and the inevitability, indeed the possibility of an evolutionary hypothesis, denied.

Not some story of how they developed but the story that they developed, the descriptive charting of definitive points of change, is a sufficiently graphic aim for histories of medieval English drama. Points of change are hard enough to calculate; causes guessed at beyond them have always been questionable and may frequently be found not to count.[25]

The aim of this Introduction, like that of an analytic history of art, is not to tell a story, to sleuth out some evolving critical method rebegotten essay by essay as these are ordered in this book. Each essay, like the products of art it discusses, is a production in itself. From the contents of each, one can chart likenesses and differences among the products of medieval drama, and only these need be observed. They can best be seen if one keeps in mind the analytic terms and cautions derived thus far from discussion of Marshall, Dunn, and Smoldon. Comparison among the vernacular cycles, which the next eleven essays treat; comparison between the morality plays with which the last three essays deal; comparison of cycles with moralities in general, or of both with liturgical drama, and of all these with ritual—such comparison may now be drawn with respect to surface materials the plays combine; plots they use as combining forms; interpretations of life, or "action,"

25. Manly sought to refine and correct the evolutionary hypothesis for the history of the drama but not to abandon it; he felt it necessary for literary study to tell the story of a change and saw the hypothesis as essential to the task: "We know that literature and art and social life are not plants or animals, and that they have their own laws of existence; but even if we try to keep steadily before us the fallacy residing in such terms as 'organism' and 'evolution,' it is practically impossible to speak or think of any unified body of facts showing progressive change as men habitually spoke and thought before 1860. That we should still speak and think as if the needs of human thought could be met by a mere chronological record is not to be wished" ("Literary Forms," p. 580). On the other hand, protesting against evolution as commonly conceived, he argued the necessity of analyzing each product ("what actually happened"), classifying the products analyzed, and noting the "effective changes"; see the passages quoted above, n. 14. There is semantic slippage in his term "effective changes": instead of meaning "effective within each product," a meaning consistent with his belief that none of the products "varied beyond its class," it takes on the sense of a change brought about by one class in its effect upon another. Still later, however, he credits "genius" with the invention of a new "class" or "species" of work (p. 583) and warns that "generalizations and theories of sciences may be suggestive and valuable to us, if we use them only to stimulate our own thought and our perception of the facts in our own field; if we are careful not to substitute analogy for explanation of process, the application of a formula for real mastery of the phenomena; if we remember that new combinations of literature are not strictly analogous to those of biology" (p. 594). For profounder analysis of the nature and relationships of history and critical analysis than that offered here, see the essays entitled "History versus Criticism in the Study of Literature," "Criticism as Inquiry; or, The Perils of the 'High Priori Road,'" and "Critical and Historical Principles of Literary History," in Ronald S. Crane, *The Idea of the Humanities and Other Essays Critical and Historical* (Chicago, 1967), II, 3–156.

which the materials and plots represent; and the kind of cognitive-affective release which, together, all these elements contain as their potential effect. That these elements coinform and qualify each other as they coexist within each play becomes clear from each author's discussion: despite different specializations of focus and somewhat different choices of terms, each essay, in discussing primarily one element, has had to imply if not pursue the rest.

No summary here should preempt the reader's privilege to chart likenesses and differences for himself. A few observations, however, will indicate the expectations that the remaining essays, as here ordered, may be counted on to fulfill.

In art as in life, matter is the ground of the end result, and the nature of that result depends much upon the type of combination that the matter will sustain. It has now been seen that the materials of the liturgical drama (the audiovisual "language" not only of the words, allusions, images, movements, props, and costumes but also of the music) deliver iconically stylized characters acting iconically stylized tableaux which corroborate, as does a lyric, the experience of conversion from some form of doubt to some form of new perception and joy. In the vernacular cycle plays of later origin, however, there is a reduction of symbolic references in the very materials with all the results such reduction entails.

Severe reduction of the symbolic reference of materials is evident both in the late cycle plays of France and in fourteenth-century French history plays, in one of which Chaucer's royal master, Richard II, flamboyant throughout his artful life, acted a leading role. Howard M. Brown's "Musicians in the *Mystères* and *Miracles*" and the late Laura Hibbard Loomis's "Secular Dramatics in the Royal Palace, Paris, 1378, 1389, and Chaucer's 'Tregetoures' " supply the grounds of illuminating contrasts with the English cycle plays—the one with respect to music which, in the French plays, "had no leading part in the dramas, but served merely as an adjunct to the often brilliant spectacle . . . one more decorative element . . . in these mélanges of realistic illusion, dazzling display, and pedantic edification"; the other with respect to "the skill of medieval mechanics in producing animated automata and other magic-seeming contrivances" for staging in literal-minded illusions the taking of Jerusalem in the First Crusade, the fall of *Troye la Grant*, or defeat of the sultan Saladin—"excursion into secular history, divorced from all religious legend" and devoid of symbolic intent. When John R. Elliott, Jr., in "The Sacrifice of Isaac as Tragedy and Comedy," compares the symbolic intent and figural relationships of the Abraham-Isaac episode in the English cycle plays with the manner of its representation in *Le Sacrifice de Abraham* (1539) and the *Abraham Sacrifiant* (1550) of Théodore de Bèze, he makes clear that in the French plays, "the whole framework of God's historical design and man's relation to it is thrown out, leaving only the moral issue as the center of interest" and substituting "verbal disquisition for significant action." In all these late French plays, symbolism is replaced by literalism in audiovisual materials. In the newly sophisticated[26] French cycles, spectacular display, ornamental musical concerts, dances, processions, and declamations appear in the now "traditional scenes: celestial, pastoral, demonic, and regal," and the panorama of these does duty for plot, as does panorama of chivalric exploit in the secular history plays. From the sophisticated French *mystère* and its derivatives, the lessons are not deep: one learns that the model human reaction is impassioned ratiocination in situations of stress or vented wit and adroitness when nothing serious impends. Affectation of pathos and cultivation of wit, sheer bedazzlement in sights and sounding brass—these are represented as the final refinement of a life to be admired. Elliott is led to observe:

Between the medieval and Renaissance dramatizations of the Sacrifice of Isaac it is the differences rather than the similarities that stand out. In no sense does the medieval drama in this instance merely pave the way for the emergence of more artistic and sophisticated forms in the sixteenth century. Rather, the Renaissance versions of the story are quite different in kind and reflect new ways of representing the relations between man and God.

In the secular history plays, the relations of man with God are as extrinsic and as pretentious as in the Crusades themselves; the lesson is the spectacle of heroic posture, heroic acclaim, and aspiration for prowess and fame.

About the music, the staging, and the spectacular elements of the English cycle drama (produced in England as late as 1575, at least), we have precious little evidence.[27] Alan H. Nelson's "Some Configurations of Staging in Medieval English Drama" attempts a purely technical reconstruction of physical staging yet makes it possible to see symbolic reference in the configurations he finds. Thus, in the Hegge or N-Town cycle he finds stage clusters which, with their multiple *loca*[28]—a mountain, a hill with fixed tree and posted star, a sepulcher, a "temple"—and the reuse of these for different scenes in the drama, provide an "effi-

26. See n. 23, above.
27. Collected, for example, in Chambers, *Medieval Stage*, II, Appendix E, "Extracts from Account Books," 240–58, and Appendix W, "Representations of Mediaeval Plays," 329–406.
28. Cf. Marshall: "The characteristic medieval dramatic technique of the simultaneous scene and multiple setting and the movement they entailed are iconically symbolic, as any dramatic convention may be" (below, p. 36).

ciency of signification and design" and reinforce the figural or exemplary relationships among the episodes themselves.

It is precisely the figural and the exemplary relationships among the pageants, subsumed within a chronological line of sequential action, that leads me, in the next essay on "The Dramatic Structure of the Middle English Corpus Christi, or Cycle, Plays," to speak of the "polymorphic" nature of the cycle plots and to deny the panoramic looseness with which they have been charged. For Elliott, in the essay following mine, the line of sequential action in whole cycles, indeed in individual pageants as well, is "comic" in the medieval sense of movement from adversity to joy: "By this definition, the form of Christian history, and hence of any drama imitating it, was clearly comic rather than tragic." Not with the medieval definition in mind[29] but with the merits of persons in the drama, especially in the Judgment plays, I prefer to speak of the plot as "a melodramatic tragedy in the confirmation of disaster for the wicked who are deservedly damned, and a tragedy of narrowly averted disaster for the rest of mankind, even for the saints, since God's interventions, while expected, given his promise, are beyond all men's expectations and deserts." Despite different meanings critics may prefer for "tragic" and "comic," on one point they will doubtless agree. As in the liturgical drama, the "action" in the English cycles is a metaphoric interpretation of life, life as an exchange of psychic states to be effected or lost—a "redemption" (term of commercial exchange, a "buying back"), a "salvation" ("health" or "security") offered by God and, by the measure of man's cooperation, rejected or received.

Painting, unlike ritual, has never been mistaken for drama, though the materials of painting and ritual and drama are in one respect alike. Things which ritual and drama will say with words or use as properties for their respective performers, painting will show with colors and graphic design, and in all three, as Marshall reminds us, the projections are frequently symbolic, touching upon "a whole range of associated feeling-ideas through the iconographical symbolism of attribute, familiar also in medieval plastic art." Lawrence J. Ross, in "Symbol and Structure in the *Secunda Pastorum*," examines the unity this play achieves through a "charged realism," better, a naturalism of the kind Panofsky speaks of in his *Early Netherlandish Painting*—a naturalism, as Panofsky puts it, "not as yet wholly secular," indeed "still rooted in the conviction that physical objects are, to quote St. Thomas Aquinas . . . 'corporeal metaphors of things spiritual.' " Panofsky uses metonymy to recover the meaning of a symbolic "language" in painting that unmistakably

29. See discussion of "historical criticism," above.

employed it. Ross proposes that "the English playwright too moves through created things—the rustic characters, their speech, and homely offerings—in the representation of man's relation to spiritual mystery." He holds that the Adoration scene, "by its fusion of affectively rendered homely realism and symbolism," is typical of the "mode of representation" in the entire play, throughout which the playwright's "lively sense of the actual, everywhere evident in his awareness of the social scene, in his responsiveness to gesture, and in his mastery of idiom, is like the inspired meticulous observation of Van Eyck in that he also sees, and makes us perceive, that 'all reality is saturated with meaning.' " In light of this mode of representation, the sheep-stealing scene is not "realistic" and "comic" and the Adoration scene a religious afterthought; rather, "the heart of the Wakefield Master's symbolic design is that the two parts of his play are truly analogous actions"—"the recovery, at the birth of a child, of what was lost." Thus, "a simply theologic reading of the play can be no more critically adequate than celebrations of it for its farce alone." Here, in a "dramaturgy of analogical action," are no "immiscible juxtapositions," no "uncombinable antinomies of the medieval mind," as Rossiter once held. By such analogical dramaturgy, "clowning and adoration, mystery and nescience and boorishness" are "brought into the context of one vision," in which the effect is not disjunction but an enlightening "aesthetic jar," a constructive dissonance. Attention to the significance of a ball, a bird, a bunch of cherries—materials found in paintings as in this play—have led Ross to discover a form of symbolic naturalism common to the art of both. In Nan Cooke Carpenter's "Music in the *Secunda Pastorum*," along with the technical knowledge and purely functional use of the music in the play, are shown the symbolic references of music to character, evil as opposed to good, earthly cacophony against celestial song, a use of music which deserves comparison with that which Brown finds in the French *mystères*.

The symbolic projection of materials shown in Alan H. Nelson's "The Temptation of Christ; or, The Temptation of Satan" is of yet another kind. The Temptation plays in the York, N-Town, and Chester cycles are literal dramatizations of an allegedly historic event in Christ's life. That "historic" event nonetheless wears the guise of a parable and uses the materials of allegory: the stones, if changed to bread, mean concession to sensual indulgence; the pinnacle of the Temple, if Christ were to leap from it but save himself, means seeking public acclaim; the mountain view embracing all the kingdoms of the world, if Christ were to gain these through worship of Satan, would mean abdication of his divinity for worldly power. The temptations, Nelson observes, "have a significance which is to be understood partly from explications presented within the play or implicit in the dialogue, and partly from a wider context of theological exposition and pictorial symbol." Noting that the N-Town play in particular "imitates the morality tradition," he supplies the doctrinal knowledge which allegorical form and matter always presuppose and employ.

The "realism" discussed in J. W. Robinson's "The Art of the York Realist" and Hans-Jürgen Diller's "The Craftsmanship of the Wakefield Master" belongs to two different styles of dramaturgy. Neither wholly excludes figural or exemplary interconnections among characters and scenes; but both transcend mere typology and develop a high degree of individuation in *dramatis personae* and the words, thoughts, and deeds they invent for them. The single playwright who seems to have written eight plays on Christ's passion (and perhaps others besides) in the York cycle and whom others have called "the York realist" is in fact, Robinson observes, "more of a naturalistic playwright than a realist, and he is misnamed." The naturalism Robinson has in mind, however, is not the symbolic naturalism Ross finds in the Wakefield *Second Shepherds' Play*. Says Robinson: "Other medieval dramatists (and more learned medieval exegetes, too) would not normally concern themselves with the temperature of the water in which Pilate washed his hands—the allegorical meaning, perhaps, but not the temperature." This playwright "elaborated on the given story by pursuing its matter into the places to which (with some art) it naturally led—to "Herod's fastidious vanity, the soldiers' bestiality, Pilate's love of upper-class comforts, and the obsequiousness of his train." Such individuation of character and scene led, if Robinson is right, to an individuation of each of these pageants from the others in a manner that may approach the panoramic display of discrete units of spectacle in the French *mystères* with some loss of unitary spiritual meaning in the whole.

"Realism" as mere "depiction of contemporary life," Diller notes, has been used as an epithet of praise for certain of the cycle plays; but an epithet of praise is not a critical concept, an attribute of dramatic craft. He proposes that "realism" more properly obtains when dramatized "actions and emotions are subject to the same general laws as our own" —when dialogue is made to build a psychological reality behind the overt physical action it accompanies, when processes of thought are created to account for motives that are not merely assigned, when interpersonal relationships are made to shade in intensity and depth as character reacts with character in a developing situation: "it is in this kind of realism that the Wakefield Master excels," and Diller's references to the six plays attributed to the Master abound. In this analysis of the Master's "realism," Ross's case for his symbolic naturalism is extended, not contravened, and a further dimension of his craft is explored.

Ernst Cassirer, in *An Essay on Man*,[30] tells us that man begins by extrovert interest in the physical universe, partly because need for survival demands that he come to terms with his environment, partly because he is forever curious about "things." Yet man's curiosity, Cassirer says, forever terminates in an introvert interest in himself. "In the first mythological explanations of the universe we always find a primitive *anthropology* side by side with a primitive *cosmology*. The question of the origin of the world is inextricably interwoven with the question of the origin of man. Religion does not destroy these first mythological explanations. On the contrary, it preserves the mythological cosmology and anthropology by giving them new shape and new depth." And yet, "In all the higher forms of religious life the maxim 'Know thyself' is regarded as a categorical imperative, as an ultimate moral and religious law."[31]

If something like this is so, it is not surprising that in the early cycle plays "action" combines a Christian theological cosmology (supernatural forces that create and direct the universe) with a theologized, a teleologized human history, mythic or metaphoric in form, the biblical story of interactions between God and aberrant man. And it is not surprising that in the morality plays, though the metaphoric form of the vision remains, the "action" focuses not upon universal history but upon psychic forces within the life of universalized aberrant "man."

David J. Leigh's "The Doomsday Mystery Play: An Eschatological Morality" forms a perfect bridge between the cycle plays and the early moralities. Last pageant in all four extant cycles, the Doomsday or Judgment play offers an analogous dramatic solution of the same problem faced by the morality playwrights: "the symbolic representation by means of allegory of nonhistorical events directly related to the moral lives of their audience." As against the historically, temporally, and geographically localized events of the preceding pageants (exceptions: the Creation pageant, the Parliament of Heaven in the N-Town cycle; to which one must add, in specific respects, the pageants of Christ's Temptation and his Descent into Hell), the Judgment play deals with "events" in nonhistorical, nontemporal, and nonspatial terms. Its *dramatis personae* are supernatural agencies subdivided and anthropomorphized and human agents personified by "anonymous crowds of 'good' or 'evil' souls" or by "universal social types." As Nelson finds doctrinal knowl-

30. Subtitled *An Introduction to a Philosophy of Human Culture* (New Haven, 1944: here cited from the Yale Paperbound edition, sixteenth printing, 1966). See chap. I, "The Crisis in Man's Knowledge of Himself," and for the distinction between "symbol" and "sign" applicable to symbolization in the cycle plays and the moralities, chap. II, "A Clue to the Nature of Man: The Symbol," and chap. III, "From Animal Reactions to Human Responses," pp. 1–41.

31. Ibid., p. 8.

edge essential in explicating the allegory of the Temptation, Leigh finds that the Judgment plays require the same, and he supplies it in an appendix remarkable for its illumination of "the nonrepresentative events," which he calls anagogic in form, hence "beyond the grasp of human experience except through the medium" which moralities also employ. Discriminating in observing likenesses between the Judgment play and the moralities, Leigh is no less discriminating in observing likenesses between the Judgment play and the twelfth-century Tegernsee *Ludus de Antichristo* with its allegorical personification of Church, Synagogue, Justice, Mercy, Heresy, Hypocrisy, and "kings" of the nations—discussed by Marshall too as a rare exception to the "presentational" symbolism of the liturgical sung drama. Definition—description of dramatic form—is the limit of Leigh's endeavor; with no assumption that formal likenesses provide documentary proof of "chronological causality" or evolution of a form, he concludes, discretion preserved, that "the eschatological allegory of the Last Judgment as performed in the fourteenth and fifteenth centuries held within itself the conditions for the development of a full-fledged morality play."

Of the remaining three essays, Edgar T. Schell's "On the Imitation of Life's Pilgrimage in *The Castle of Perseverance*" and V. A. Kolve's "*Everyman* and the Parable of the Talents" direct attention in the first place to the psychic "action" which these two moralities imitate and to the specific metaphors or parables in which that "action" was expressed in received tradition, assumed in the plays. Beyond this, they are concerned with transformations or mutations which dramatic manner requires such "action" to undergo as it is translated from the descriptive openness of narrative to the spatiotemporal limits of drama which reinterprets them for stage. Natalie Crohn Schmitt's "Was There a Medieval Theatre in the Round? A Re-examination of the Evidence," intending a technical reconstruction of the staging of *The Castle of Perseverance* in correction of Richard Southern's *Medieval Theatre in the Round* (1957), must begin, like the other two essays, with the verbal texture of the play, but from this is inevitably led to the metaphoric thought which the "language" represents and the symbolic stage sustains.

Schell presents a case against indiscriminate application to the moralities of a critical formula which "sees" their action as a psychomachia, "an ethical debate between personified Virtues and Vices." *Everyman* provides an example of "the violence necessary to fit at least one dramatic fact under this critical formula," for in *Everyman* there are no personified Vices, hence Vices meet no Virtues, much less engage them in ethical debate. In *Everyman* the plot is constructed as a progress, not a debate. Schell builds his argument not around *Everyman* but around *The Castle of Perseverance* because the siege of the Castle which occurs well along in the play "is closest in form to the battle in Prudentius' poem"; if he can prove that even here such a psychomachia is incidental to a larger metaphor, his thesis applies the more strongly to moralities lacking any overt psychomachia at all.

The progress or pilgrimage metaphor which Schell finds central to the play is common to innumerable narrative poems about the journey of life. The plots of the narrative poems "serve to imitate the same spiritual sequence . . . , each quite different from the others but all demonstrably related to the same stock." That "stock" and metaphoric view of life is most succinctly expressed in a pseudo-Bernardine parable which calls man a king's son *(filius regis)* who is at first needy and foolish *(egens et insipiens)*, then impulsive and rash in prosperity *(praeceps et temerarius in prosperis)*, next trembling and desperate in adversity *(trepidus et pusilanimus in adversis)* and finally insightful and informed and perfected in the kingdom of charity *(providus et eruditus et perfectus in regno charitatis)*. "If we can find the same sequence at the heart of *The Castle of Perseverance*, we can conclude that the *Castle* imitates the same model of human experience, and we can assign the differences in the mode of imitation to the different demands made on theater and the different opportunities it offers."

In the *Castle*, the *platea* surrounded by its five "mansions" and with its central fortification, "physical indices of Mankind's moral state," "realizes in theatrical terms the moral landscapes of the narrative pilgrimages." "The *platea* itself, the neutral ground between, is the place of moral change where the first stirrings of the spirit toward God or the world are given physical form in movements toward the symbolic scaffolds." In drama, "the physical representation of action onstage enforces a stricter separation of modes of being than the imaginative representations of narrative poetry, which take place in the more elastic theater of the mind, and in [any case] a sustained journey is at best awkwardly represented on stage," whereas a sustained journey "is part of the 'language' of narrative poetry." The "language" appropriate to drama, then, requires that the imitated action of a spiritual journey or pilgrimage be translated from geographic movement across literal time to movement across psychically symbolic space (the scaffolds), only partially sustained "in the metaphors of travel." Important for its fuller visualization of the stage of this play, Schmitt's essay relocates the "ditch," more properly, "moat," within the stage set and establishes its proper symbolic meaning on historical grounds. One learns "that crossing over the water in *The Castell of Perseverance* signifies a transformation of the soul" as it returns to or departs from the castellated center of its morally fortified "salvation" or security in a world hardly secular.

Like Schell, Kolve faults the silence of scholarship on the metaphor of journey or pilgrimage in *Everyman*, this time, however, not "the pilgrimage of life," which *Everyman* does not compass, but "the death-journey of the soul to Judgment." He discovers that "the meaning of the action" lies within the metaphoric reference of the play's "language": "words like 'reckoning,' 'account making,' 'lending,' and 'spending' compose the essential verbal matrix of the play," and, together with the account book which Everyman is required to "clear" and to bring with him as "a literal stage property," these establish "what the play is most urgently about." These verbal-visual materials mark "the intellectual structure just below the surface of the play," "the covered logic of an action that made that action coherent and inevitable"—they bring one, in short, to the Parable of the Talents, Jesus' symbolic expression of the reckoning which the Lord, "greedy" for all he can bring his servants to gain, will exact from every man, summoning each to render an account of capital gains on the talents (weight of gold) entrusted to his care. But when summoned one must "come" or "travel," and another "verbal matrix" must materialize in the play. Words like "pylgrymage," "vyage," "journey," refer to the final act of life, the ascent of the soul into the "far country." Together, the metaphoric terms of final journey make "consecutive, spatial, linear" the "extremely complex process of how a man dies." For "the desertions—friends, kin, goods, beauty, strength, the five senses—are in some sense simultaneous, for none of these is irretrievably lost until they are lost altogether, at the moment of extinction." Thus, "the 'longe journey'—all those desperate wanderings in the *platea*, the search for companionship into the grave—is really born of the allegorical mode itself." Symbolic "language" and a universal "action" of life metaphorically expressed provide "less a new 'source' for *Everyman*, than the source behind the sources."

The essays in this volume, when more fully examined than in this sketch, delineate likenesses and differences more revealing of the nature and history of medieval drama than much that has elsewhere and generally been said. Yet the essays are not polemical. They do not attack previous scholarly attempts but, in evaluating them, support the revision of insight at which those attempts themselves had aimed and which scholarship can never neglect. They are not doctrinaire: they do not follow a fixed critical methodology. If a system has been used, even proposed, in this Introduction, it is for its value as a practical tool. For in taking data as one finds them one must still make something out of what one takes, or, rather, one must have a lens through which to see what the data would make of themselves. Much remains to be made out of the essays of this book; the reader has now been offered a lens through which to see what they make of themselves.

Mary H. Marshall

2. Aesthetic Values of the Liturgical Drama

The Latin drama of the medieval church had a hold on men's imaginations for approximately six hundred years, from the tenth century to the sixteenth, although its creative phase was briefer, from the tenth to the thirteenth century; yet to readers of our day, who almost never have a chance to experience it in performance and are separated from the Middle Ages by centuries of cultural revolution, the liturgical drama often seems lifeless, a dreary little undifferentiated amoeba of modern drama, without plot, without character, almost without conflict, whose only value is historical. Of the hundreds of surviving Latin church plays, a score or so, chiefly products of the schools in the twelfth and thirteenth centuries, have a relatively high value as entertainment, in sophisticated and independent versification, variety of episode and spectacle, freedom in dealing with biblical and legendary narrative, occasional humor, a slight sense of character types; and some critics would reserve the term "drama" only for this small group. I think the view which excludes from the category of art the hundreds of simpler and more uniformly serious liturgical plays rests on false and limited assumptions about the nature of drama and of the liturgical drama in particular, and I want to suggest what seem to me the values of the genre as a whole, while recognizing the variety within it.

The liturgical plays are distinguished from the many liturgical and extraliturgical ceremonies of the church which contain dramatic elements in symbolic gesture by the fact that in the plays living actors assume the roles of the characters of sacred story. There is no impersonation in the Mass nor in strictly liturgical observance. But in the plays clerical actors speak and move as the Marys and the angels at the tomb, the apostles and the Magi. With the added elements of mimetic action and dialogue, impersonation is the basic criterion of this drama, as of any, effectually separating it from religious rite.[1]

[Reprinted from *English Institute Essays, 1950* (New York: Columbia University Press, 1951), pp. 89–115, by permission of the author and the publisher. Copyright 1951 by the Columbia University Press.]
1. [For a recent challenge to the traditional acceptance of impersonation, imper-

Critically, we are in a good position to understand them now, these hundreds of little plays, through the editorial work of several generations of scholars, culminating in Karl Young's masterly book *The Drama of the Medieval Church* (Oxford, 1933), and through two recently developed lines of thought: one is contemporary interpretive criticism of the whole experience created by a poetic nonrealistic drama, a method which has been applied chiefly to the Elizabethans; the other is the study of myth in relation to ritual and to deeply felt beliefs of a homogeneous society. Analogies between the origin of Greek drama in religious rite and the origin of medieval drama are inescapable and profoundly suggestive, but only in general. In its details the origin of Greek drama is still a matter of controversy between the anthropological school represented by Jane Harrison, Gilbert Murray, F. M. Cornford, and skeptical philologist-historians such as Pickard-Cambridge.

The liturgical plays of the Middle Ages deserve more critical attention than they have received. Most of the past studies have concentrated on making available more texts, on developmental descriptions of the genre, problems of interrelation and transmission of texts, regional differences within the similarities of an international drama in an international language, matters of influence, including the influence of the liturgical plays on late medieval popular drama in the vernaculars, and examination of the milieux which fostered them. Karl Young's whole presentation, the classic in the field, is built on a logical organization, ordering the plays on a specific subject according to a progress from simple to complex forms, for a chronological organization would run into impossible diffi-

---

sonational dialogue, and mimetic action as effecting a formal difference between liturgical drama and ritual, see O. B. Hardison, Jr., *Christian Rite and Christian Drama in the Middle Ages* (Baltimore: Johns Hopkins Press, 1965), which has "attempted to show that in the ninth century the boundary that Chambers and Young posited between religious ritual (the services of the Church) and drama did not exist," that "ritual *was* the drama of the early Middle Ages," that "the Mass was consciously interpreted as drama during the ninth century," and that "representational ceremonies were common in the Roman liturgy long before the earliest manuscripts of the *Quem quaeritis* play" (p. viii). On the other hand, distinguishing between "ritual," "representational," and "dramatic," Hardison also speaks of "the evident shift from ritual to representational modes" in the eleventh and twelfth centuries (p. ix); in Essay VI, "From *Quem quaeritis* to Resurrection Play," he concludes that "liturgical drama is the outcome of a search for representational modes which preserve a vital relation to ritual" (p. 252); and elsewhere he observes that "the Easter cycle," like the Mass, "is dramatic in structure and nonrepresentational in mode" (p. 176). Discussions of medieval drama continue to use terms like "ritual," "representational," and "dramatic" equivocally, at one moment to lump together things materially comparable but totally different in form, at another moment to differentiate between things different either in matter, in form, or in both. The problem is one of clarity and consistency of definition. Miss Marshall gives to the term "drama" a single formal reference and insists upon applying the term to all, and only to all, compositions meeting the formal criterion.]

culties of dating. Young made many cogent critical judgments, noting hundreds of small dramatic successes in order and phrasing and effectiveness, and small incongruities and ineptitudes in adapting the given material to dramatic form. Many of the various amplifications of the basic dialogue he considered enlargements on the side of liturgical festal rejoicing, rather than on the side of drama. I am indebted to him at every turn, but I think we must consider each of these texts as a whole, seeking as well as we may to apprehend the total emotional experience, in which lyricism plays a part intrinsic, not extrinsic, to drama.

The essential element of music in these plays I must unhappily exclude from consideration, in blank ignorance. Yet this was almost entirely a sung drama, a lyric drama in the primary sense that the words were carried by melody. How great a part the music played in the effect is evident to anyone who has heard one of the rare modern renditions. The music of only a few of the plays has been printed, and the whole subject awaits further study by musicologists. But even a discussion of the texts alone and the valuable hints of movement, mimetic action, costume, and symbolic properties scattered in the rubrics which accompany them in the manuscripts may avail something. I shall not always pause to identify or to date the texts from which I draw illustrations; the references can usually be found through Karl Young's index and bibliography.

The anonymity and imitativeness of these plays, in which formulas of phrasing are repeated from one version to another in the midst of small fresh inventions, make of them a genre to which developmental and evolutionary metaphors are more plausibly relevant than to most. Yet their individual clerical authors existed, although we know the name of only one of them. With some informed adjustment of the focus we habitually turn on the art of our own contemporary culture, we may see artistic achievement of many kinds in the Latin church plays—a drama physically sustained by a great institution and imaginatively fed by centuries of emotional associations with sacred seasons and sacred places, the Christian story of salvation through Christ, the beautiful familiar words and music of the liturgy, and the church's age-old habit of symbolism, but having its own values and its own function as drama.

In the first place, with few minor exceptions this is not a didactic drama in any overt sense; it is too deeply rooted in belief for intellectual didacticism. Belief is often stated as assertion, but in simple terms of feeling. By an understandable paradox, medieval religious drama became explicitly didactic as it became secular. The liturgical drama, like most art, is a "presentational" rather than a "discursive" form, in Susanne Langer's terminology. Austin Warren describes communally accepted myth in terms which are as applicable to the liturgical plays which dramatize the Christian story. They represent "the picturable intuitive concrete," rather than "the rational abstract," "story, as against dialectical discourse, exposition."[2] Physically and visually they re-create the narrative episodes upon which the Christian faith rests—above all, in more than four hundred versions the visit of the Marys to the sepulcher on Easter morning, the primary episode which bears witness to the Resurrection of Christ. The language is characteristically the familiar language of the liturgy, and the embroideries upon it called tropes, which themselves became traditional, like the well-known central kernel of this drama, the *Quem quaeritis;* and lyric passages were frequently incorporated from hymns and that large class of religious compositions called sequences, especially in the twelfth century and later. There are often other lyric additions of lament or rejoicing and occasionally invented dialogue. But supporting all is the scriptural narrative. Frequent enlargements of the scope of the Easter play multiply the evidences of the Resurrection by the display of the grave-cloths to the congregation, by the race of Peter and John to the empty tomb, by Christ's appearance to Mary Magdalene, according to the Gospel of John, more rarely Christ's appearance to Cleophas and his companion on the road to Emmaus, according to the Gospel of Luke, to the disciples gathered together in an upper room, and to doubting Thomas. Hennig Brinkmann has drawn attention to the corroborative evidential nature of the episodes drawn from the gospels for dramatization—episodes familiarly emphasized in the gospel readings of the Mass in the Easter season—and sees the same basic motive in liturgical plays of seasons other than Easter: "Seeing we are compassed about with so great a cloud of witnesses."[3]

The Latin Easter play, never a part of the authorized liturgy, but in hundreds of churches inserted at the end of Easter Matins—the symbolic anniversary of the very moment of the Resurrection—characteristically concludes with the triumphant affirmation with which Matins always ends, the Te Deum—"We praise Thee, O God, we acknowledge Thee to be the Lord."

The teaching is implicit, through emotional experience, through literal story and the feeling it engenders by centuries of association; the telling episodes of the gospels are re-created by physical impersonation, and faith is warmed and confirmed. Only the slightest overt didacticism enters, and that of an elementary sort, in allusion.

The simple concreteness of the liturgical Easter plays is utterly re-

2. René Wellek and Austin Warren, *Theory of Literature* [new rev. ed. (New York, 1956), pp. 190, 191].
3. H. Brinkmann, "Zum Ursprung des liturgischen Spieles," in *Xenia Bonnensia* (Bonn, 1929), pp. 106–43.

moved from one characteristic medieval form of discursive thought often applied to scripture, and makes no use of abstract allegory. Compare any of these dramatic versions of the Visit to the Sepulcher with Dante's interpretation of Mark's story of Easter morning as an allegory of the active and the contemplative life. In the *Convivio* (IV. 22) Dante suggests that the three Marys stand for the sects urging the active life, the Epicureans, the Stoics, and the Peripatetics, who seek blessedness in the tomb, that is, in the present world, only to be told that it is not there, but has gone before them into Galilee—Galilee, which stands for speculation, contemplation, spiritual light. Only one Latin church play known to me employs anything like this familiar sort of medieval allegorical interpretation, and that is a unique fragment of the late twelfth century from the monastery of Vorau in Austria, a play about Isaac and Rebecca, in which static allegorical comment distributed through the action proves a method as unhandy for drama as one would expect. Moreover, in the Latin church plays as a whole there are almost no personified abstractions. The only major example is a unique twelfth-century play from the monastery of Tegernsee, which uses the legend of Antichrist for German political and moral propaganda, and introduces the symbolic pair of figures Synagoga and Ecclesia, as well as Justice and Mercy, Gentiledom, Heresy, and Hypocrisy. Precursors of later medieval dramatic abstractions of good and evil appear in two of the sophisticated scholastic plays of the famous thirteenth-century Benedictbeuern manuscript, with the devil and the angel who contest for influence over the minds of the Christmas shepherds and of the unregenerate Mary Magdalene. There are, of course, occasional allusions in the liturgical drama to familiar symbolic typology—to Christ as the new Adam, for example, the bridegroom of the parable of the wise and foolish virgins, in the play called the *Sponsus*. In the play of the Slaughter of the Innocents, Rachel appears as the prototype of all maternal grief, as she does in the Gospel of Matthew. But these types are symbols, not pure intellectual abstractions.

One medieval play of the Christmas season, of which only four Latin versions within the church exist, presents a series of Old Testament prophets and a few pagans, summoned to bear their witness to Christ, to convince the unbelieving Jews and gentiles. It stands alone in the church drama as having a primary source in sermon, not in scriptural narrative and liturgy or legend. Lacking their mythic quality, it has no such deep roots in feeling about the central Christian story as does the main body of liturgical plays, and dramatically it is a poor and static thing, in spite of lavish verse in some texts and a few concretely developed episodes of Nebuchadnezzar and Simeon and Balaam and the speaking ass, or the bitter anti-Semitic comedy of the prophet scene in the comprehensive Christmas play from Benedictbeuern. The prophet play almost alone in the liturgical drama is insistently didactic, but here, too, the emphasis is on simple evidence of Christ's divinity, not on abstract doctrine. As a whole the genre of the liturgical drama is a direct presentational form which represents sacred story concretely by dramatic methods, without allegory or theology or didacticism.

But if the liturgical drama is not didactic or allegorical, neither is it ritual drama. It does not mythologize or explain ritual practices, although it shared with rite its "punctual" nature, in Gaster's phrase,[4] an annual repetitive performance at a certain time and season. It had no supernatural efficacy, no authority imposed by the cult; it was never obligatory. It is rather a Christian mythic drama, representing the major episodes of the sacred narrative upon which belief in the divinity of Christ rests, created in close association with Christian rite, but distinct from it, although the ecclesiastical authors of the plays make natural use of familiar liturgical language and liturgical personages, the liturgical chorus and liturgical music, the church and often the altar.

Originally the *Quem quaeritis* trope which supplies the dialogue at the sepulcher was attached to the Introit of Easter Mass; not until it was removed to the conclusion of Easter Matins in the tenth century did it become a play, with impersonation. There is a suggestion here that only at a distance from the heart of the mystery in the sacrificial Mass was drama freshly achieved.

The characteristic emotion of the liturgical drama is joy. The Passion of Christ, his human suffering, was rarely dramatized within the church. Besides a number of semidramatic laments of Mary, only three complete medieval Latin versions of a Passion play are known, and a fragment of a fourth; the earliest, from Monte Cassino, first printed by Dom Mauro Inguanez in 1936, is of the twelfth century.[5] In general, an intense preoccupation with re-creating the human suffering of the crucified Christ in every conceivable realistic detail belongs to the late days of the medieval system. The emotional nexus of the great mass of liturgical plays lies in joy in the assurance implied by the divine Resurrection, secondarily the divine Birth. The plays crystallized in simple objective form the joy of the high moments of the Christian year, above all Easter.

4. [See below, n. 7; title given in body of text.]
5. Dom Mauro Inguanez, "Un Dramma della Passione del secolo XII," in *Miscellanea Cassinese*, No. 12 (1936), pp. 7–38. [For a recent full-length study, see Sandro Sticca, *The Origins and Development of the Latin Passion Play* (Albany: State University of New York Press, 1969).]

I know only two thoroughgoing attempts to analyze the emotional genesis and function of the *Visitatio sepulchri*, by Julius Schwietering and Hennig Brinkmann.[6] With certain differences, both suggest the Latin play as in its origin a climax of the monastic observances from Good Friday to Easter, after the dark preparatory days of Lent: the sad penitential commemoration of the Crucifixion in the liturgical Adoration of the Cross in the Mass of Good Friday, followed by the ceremony of the Deposition of the Cross or Host in symbolic commemoration of the burial; and very early on Easter morning, before Matins, the private and devotional ceremony of raising the cross and restoring it to the altar. Then, after Matins, came the play of the Visit to the Sepulcher, a public release of joy in art, though art of a simple formal kind. It is probably fair to call it public, even though sometimes we must infer from rubrics that it was presented primarily for the monastic community in choir. Often a much larger congregation of the people is indicated as audience.

In the view of Schwietering and Brinkmann, the emotional action of the *Visitatio*, the "plot," is a dramatic peripety, the turn from sorrow to joy, present in every one of the plays, even the simplest. The mourning women approach the tomb and receive the glad angelic announcement. In play after play they turn to the congregation with songs of joy, and the choir bursts into the Te Deum. The action may be extended, the witnesses may be multiplied, the risen Christ may or may not appear, but the essential peripety is always there. The climax of joy was often reinforced by ringing all the bells of the church, and in Germany the people themselves had their moment of participation and release in singing their famous song "Christ ist erstanden." Even those who share the same faith now may not be able to recapture the way in which Easter was experienced in the Middle Ages, in monasteries and ecclesiastical communities whose daily life and devotions were governed by the commemorative and symbolic ecclesiastical calendar, but some effort of the imagination may lead us to approach it.

How deep in the primitive experience of Near Eastern and European people was such a pattern of emotion, ritually expressed in seasons of austerity and mortification ending in the release of joy and revitalization is made abundantly clear in *The Golden Bough* and in Theodor H. Gaster's recent book, *Thespis: Ritual, Myth and Drama in the Ancient Near East*.[7] Awareness of a familiar archetypal pattern may enlarge our

6. J. Schwietering, "Über den liturgischen Ursprung des mittelalterlichen geistlichen Spiels," in *Zeitschrift für deutsches Altertum*, LXII (1925), 1–20. [For Brinkmann's work, see n. 3, above.]
7. New York: Henry Schuman, 1950.

sense of a relation between the liturgical drama of the medieval Christian church and long human experience, but comparative anthropology, fascinating as it is, offers little specific aid in comprehending this particular form of art of medieval Christian culture.

What I have said about the concrete but evidential nature of the Latin Easter plays applies also in general to the far fewer liturgical plays of seasons other than Easter—the Christmas plays, for instance. Not Nativity but Epiphany is the center here, the coming of the Magi, those gentile witnesses. Some dozen plays on this subject exist, as compared with upwards of four hundred plays of the Visit to the Sepulcher; and those which include scenes of Herod are often very spirited indeed, in versions of the eleventh and twelfth centuries, with hexameter verse, tags from Vergil and Sallust, with a tyrant's pomp and the movement of messengers and lively gestures by the angry Herod. Very occasionally the slaughter of the Innocents was dramatized too, and the adoration of the shepherds, though in more narrowly localized uses; the prophet plays of the Christian season I have already mentioned. A few other episodes of Christian and Old Testament story received occasional dramatizations within the church, more independent of the liturgy, but all illustrating the power of God and of faith—for example, the raising of Lazarus, the conversion of Saint Paul, the lively stories of Joseph and his brethren, of Daniel under Belshazzar and Darius, and legends of Saint Nicholas. The saints' plays, too, are evidential. Every central myth generates its peripheral and supporting myths, as Malinowski has pointed out for more primitive cultures.[8]

Brinkmann suggests that though the profound impulse to create drama came from the emotional tension of the high point of the Christian year at Easter, a distance from that solemn joy with its ritual and liturgical associations offered a freer opportunity, less weighted with religious tradition, for subsequent dramatic creation. Most of the few extant plays dealing with subject matter less central and sacred than the Resurrection, like those I have just mentioned, show relatively great literary skill in versification, invention, and spectacle, a tendency toward entertainment. Little or no use is made of the liturgical chorus; the attachment to the regular liturgy is tenuous, sometimes not indicated at all. Performance may have taken place in hall or refectory instead of in church. But some liturgical connection may remain, in a final Te Deum suggesting that the play was given at Matins, or a Magnificat if it was given at Vespers. And like the more traditional liturgical plays, these

8. [See Bronislaw Malinowski, *Magic, Science, and Religion, and Other Essays* (Garden City: Doubleday Anchor Books, 1955), p. 132; for discussion of "Myth in Primitive Society," see pp. 92–148.]

too, with their wider use of literary resources, belong in the general category of a medieval Christian mythic drama; they rest on the Christian story and were supported by an ecclesiastical community on its festal occasions.

In form the liturgical plays have certain further methods and techniques in common which play a great part in the emotional effect—notably symbolism and lyricism.

With all its concreteness, this is not a realistic drama, but a formalized poetic drama, whether its language happens to be prose or verse or some mixture of the two. It is filled with symbolism, partly of a direct iconic sort, when the symbol bears some resemblance to the thing symbolized, and partly of a richer kind with more extension in meaning through Christian tradition. In a sense, of course, all dramas and all rituals are symbolic of human activity in a fundamental iconic way, and all dramatic conventions are symbols.

The characteristic dramatic convention of the liturgical plays is a symbolic use of place and space and movement within the church. In many an Easter play the altar—itself in some sense a tomb with its relics—stands for the sepulcher of Christ. Or the sepulcher may be represented by something especially constructed or adapted for Easter observances—a canopied niche in the wall, or an ark or chest, or a structure large enough to shelter an angel, sometimes large enough for the Marys and two apostles to enter. Christmas angels may sing from high up in the roof. The castle of Emmaus, with a practicable table set with bread and wine, the Christmas manger, the throne of Herod, set up in the nave or at one of the doors or at the entrance of the choir or at any convenient place, all have the elementary iconic quality natural to art, dramatic art in particular, in any age. The characteristic movement of the liturgical plays necessitated by the symbolic representation of place, which was already familiar in church processions, is a foreshortened conventionalized symbol of journeying. So the Magi approach, each from his separate corner as from his region, pointing out the star, or the two disciples journey down the aisle to Emmaus. The characteristic medieval dramatic technique of the simultaneous scene and multiple setting and the movement they entailed are iconically symbolic, as any dramatic convention may be.

The properties give a formalized suggestion of what they are to represent. The star may be a corona of candles let down from the roof and moving before the Magi. The lightning at the Resurrection in a play from Coutances is represented by two angels bearing candelabra of ten lighted candles, at the sight of which the soldiers at the tomb fall terrified as if dead. In the thirteenth-century Easter play from Benedictbeuern, the soldiers are frightened by a mighty sound of thunder and by two angels, one in red bearing a flaming sword, who strikes, and one in white bearing a cross. In countless plays the Marys carry thuribles of incense to represent their spices and unguents, and in some plays they liturgically cense the sepulcher. More rarely, they carry other sacred vessels. When the iconic symbolism of things and properties has deep familiarity in sacred uses, emotions may be touched by their very appearance—the altar, or the cross itself, as elevated at the final moment of rejoicing in a *Visitatio* from Fritzlar.

The costumes worn by the monastic and clerical actors almost invariably consist of a modification of ecclesiastical vestments, in symbolic suggestion, not realism—usually dalmatics or albs or copes. The clerics representing the Marys may wear amices drawn over their heads to suggest women's garb. All roles, of course, were taken by men, except in a convent, and except that the Christmas angels and the Innocents slaughtered by Herod and sometimes the angels at the tomb were represented by boys, with their high clear voices.

This nonrealistic formal costuming often touched upon a whole range of associated feeling-ideas through the iconographical symbolism of attribute, familiar also in medieval plastic art. The angel at the tomb, white-clad, may carry a palm, as in the tenth-century *Visitatio* from Winchester. The risen Christ may appear to Mary Magdalene, not realistically as a gardener, but holding a cross or crowned. In a play of the thirteenth century from Fleury, after appearing to Mary in the likeness of a gardener, he returns to all three holy women at the joyous conclusion as Christ in glory, in a white dalmatic and white priestly dress, with a precious phylactery on his head, carrying a cross with the sacred standard in his right hand and a gospel-book adorned with gold in his left, saying, "Fear not." In the Dublin Easter play John wears a white tunic and carries a palm, while Peter wears a red tunic and carries the keys. The prophets of a thirteenth-century play from Laon are as iconographically represented as the prophets in contemporary stained-glass windows—Moses, bearded, in a dalmatic, bearing the tablets of the law; David in kingly habit; John the Baptist, long-haired, bearded, in a fur garment, bearing a palm; Balaam spurred, riding on an ass.

The occasional suggestions of a realism of common life are almost equally iconographical, in the staffs carried by the ecclesiastically dressed shepherds of a Christmas play from Rouen, and the pilgrim staffs and wallets and caps of Cleophas and his companion in plays of the journey to Emmaus, at the same time that their basic dress is ecclesiastical. The risen Christ who appears to them in the Fleury *Peregrinus* play is barefoot, dressed in a tunic, wearing a pilgrim cap and carrying a wallet, but in one hand he bears a symbolic palm.

Sometimes we are told that costumes were highly colored as with the red-clad Peter of the Dublin Easter play, or a late *Visitatio* from Meissen, in which the Marys and Peter and John wear red, and the angels white. The three kings of the Besançon procession of the Magi were crowned and wore tunics of different colors. The angels of a late Easter play from Narbonne were winged and clad in white and violet and red.

It is difficult to be sure about gesture, on the ground of rubrics alone, but that, too, was probably formalized and iconographical, as when, for instance, the Marys or two apostles display the grave-cloths to the congregation, or Cleophas and Luke recognize Christ at Emmaus in the breaking of the bread. The height of formalized gesture appears in a fourteenth-century dramatic lament from Cividale, to be sung by the Virgin and others at the foot of the cross, in which every line is accompanied by a rubric: "Here she strikes her hands together"; "Here she points to Christ"; "Here she turns to the people"; "Here she strikes her breast."

In the liturgical drama, action and word follow a decorous order. When the three Marys are individualized at all, their speeches follow an exact succession, with Mary Magdalene usually given a major position as first or third speaker. When the Magi gather, each points out the star, and they may exchange a formal kiss of peace. They speak in due succession, sometimes first the one in the middle, then the one on the right, then the one on the left. Their adoration at the manger, as each makes his gift with brief allusion to its traditional mystic significance, was probably highly formal. And as they sleep before the manger in a Fleury play, one may visualize them in terms of stained glass and miniature as three parallel forms, crowned, lying in a regal row. The ceremonious pomp of Herod, with his messengers and armed men, may have reflected the forms of a feudal society.

In the freer representations of the Herod episodes, gesture was also obvious and strongly marked. In one play the bearded scribes assiduously turn the pages of the prophetic book and point out with their fingers the significant passage to the incredulous king. And when the angry Herod hurls away the book, throws swords about, and makes threatening gestures, presumably the clerical actor had a free field open to talent. Always we must assume individual variations of gesture within the formal tradition by men with more than usual ability as actors, especially on occasions of not-too-solemn joy. There is no need to assume that in the Middle Ages the mimetic gift was confined to professional entertainers.

The lyricism of the liturgical drama is another aspect of its formal structure, not only in that all speeches are sung, but also in that the dialogue is variously extended by specifically lyric passages, whether liturgical pieces, religious songs, or invented expressions of feeling. Those assigned to personages of the play are usually expressions of grief or of gladness, and represent one way of intensifying dramatic emotion, no more and no less artificial a convention than operatic arias, though simpler.

The role of the liturgical chorus, slight or nonexistent in a few school plays which have their own forms of more conscious and sophisticated lyricism, contributes greatly to the form of most liturgical plays, especially those of Easter. It provides the link with ritual, with the authorized cult, and with deep associative habit, and serves several purposes within the plays.

Liturgical pieces sung by the choir create a frame of introduction and conclusion which helps to give the plays their formal entity. The third and last responsory of Easter Matins, sung by the choir, appropriately introduces the Easter play: "When the sabbath was past, Mary Magdalene and Mary the mother of James, and Salome, bought spices, that they might come and anoint him, alleluia. And very early on the first day of the week, they came to the tomb when the sun was risen." The play of the journey to Emmaus, given in the middle of the processional Vespers of Easter Monday or Tuesday, often begins with the hymn, "Jesus, our redemption," sung by the choir or the two apostles, and ends with an outburst of glad liturgical pieces on the risen Christ. And as we have seen, the play of the Visit to the Sepulcher rounds off similar liturgical rejoicing with the Te Deum. The choral lyric conclusion which gives the final release of emotion is an integral part of the whole experience.

Liturgical pieces sung by the choir provide accompaniment for movement during the play. The characters of the Easter play sometimes take their stations while the last responsory of Matins is being sung. The race of Peter and John to the tomb is often accompanied by the choir singing the antiphon "And they ran both together." In a play from Bilsen, while Herod ascends his throne, the choir sings an antiphon of Advent, "Upon the throne of David." In school plays which give no evidence of using the liturgical choir, processional movement is sometimes accompanied by elaborate choral pieces called *conductus*, as in two fine plays about Daniel, of the twelfth century.

Perhaps the most important contribution of the liturgy to the substance of many plays, and one which has hardly been noted in quite these terms, is that liturgical pieces extend the frame of reference and the significance of the simple Christian story represented in the action, by scriptural Judaic-Christian metaphor, infinitely familiar to the clergy through the daily cursus of devotions, and perhaps in more limited fashion to the people too, especially when reenforced by the experience of ecclesastical sculpture and stained glass, in which traditional metaphor and description often become iconography. The instantaneous emotional response in those who are deeply familiar with this language is far more reverberant than a cursory modern reading of an apparently simple fossilized text may suggest.

To illustrate, in conclusion, the values of the liturgical drama, I should like to describe one play particularly rich in these significant images and symbols, and beautiful in the unified formal simplicity of its means, the play of the Slaughter of the Innocents from the famous thirteenth-century playbook of the monastery of Saint-Bénoit-sur-Loire at Fleury, near Orléans.

Fundamentally, it is a concrete representation of the literal story from Matthew, of Herod's wrath and the flight into Egypt, of the slaughter of the young children of Bethlehem, and the safe return of Joseph and Mary and the child—a complete action. It is symbolic in the typological figure of the lamenting Rachel, suggested by Matthew's account, remembering Jeremiah: "A voice was heard in Ramah, weeping and great mourning, Rachel weeping for her children, and she would not be comforted, because they are not." Still deeper in symbolism is the association of the slain children of Bethlehem with the army of virgin saints about the throne of the Lamb in the Apocalypse, and the visual image of the Lamb itself, reinforced by John's account of the baptism of Christ and the liturgical Agnus Dei: "O Lamb of God, who takest away the sins of the world." These associations, made again and again in the regular liturgy of Innocents' Day, were naturally available to the imagination of the unknown author of the Fleury play, as to a good part of his audience.

The language, beyond what is supplied by Matthew and lyric laments in preexisting religious poetry and in other church plays, consists largely of antiphons and responsories of All Saints, Advent, Innocents' Day, the Assumption, even Good Friday, and the Agnus Dei of the Mass. A moving part of the dialogue is supplied by a responsory of Matins on Innocents' Day, *Sub altare Dei*, based on the apocalyptic image (Rev. 5:9–11) of the souls of them that had been slain for the word of God or the testimony which they held: "Under the altar of God I have heard the voices of the slain: Why dost thou not defend our blood? And they received the divine response: Endure yet a little while, until the number of your brethren is fulfilled." Here is the eternal human question: How can such things as the murder of the innocent be allowed by a just God? and a response of reassurance in the divine plan. Through the wealth of symbolic Christian reference in the liturgical pieces, and through the laments of Rachel, which generalize from the immediate experience to universal maternal grief, the play is given extension in significance. And the symbolic treatment of the children's death and their comforting summons to Paradise relate the central episode to the Christian hope.

The method of the play is formalized symbolic suggestion, not realism. Herod's human wrath, the physical slaughter, the grieving mothers are concrete enough; but the whole content of the play has been symbolized for the beholder by the iconic quality of movement, spectacle, and language, as well as by the specific symbols of the Lamb of God and of Rachel and the Innocents as types of a larger experience than the immediate. By these formal means the play is given the psychical distance which is essential to art, and a richer meaning. The unknown author's particular combination of diverse elements in this Fleury play, supported by centuries of tradition and a whole culture, produces an individual work of art.

The performance presumably came at the end of Matins on Innocents' Day, December 28, but the text contains no trace of the buffooneries frequently associated with the season of the Feast of Fools. Karl Young inferred that the main action was probably represented in the space before the choir screen of the abbey church, between the nave and the choir, with some use also of nave and aisles. Several stations are required: one for Herod enthroned, with his soldiers about him; another for the manger, probably placed near a door of the church, as in another play from the same monastery; a place to represent Egypt for Joseph and Mary and the child to retire to; presumably aisles and ambulatory for the procession of the Innocents; and at the end, the choir, which stands for Paradise, into which the young martyrs are received.

The play begins and ends with joy, in utter assurance; and at the center is the traditional episode of cruelty and murder and grief. It opens with a formal procession of boys in white robes, representing the Innocents, at their head a lamb to which a cross is attached, which seems to lead them. As they pass through the church the boys sing a glad apocalyptic antiphon: "O how glorious is the kingdom in which all saints rejoice with Christ, clad in white robes. They follow the Lamb whithersoever it goeth," and another antiphon, of Advent, "Send the Lamb, O Lord, ruler of the earth." Meanwhile, at his station Herod's pomp is formally established when his armor-bearer offers him his scepter. An angel appears above the manger, warning Joseph to take the young child and his mother and flee into Egypt. As he departs, Joseph, not seeing Herod, sings a confident responsory: "Egypt, weep not, for thy ruler will come to thee, before whose sight the depths shall be moved, to free his people from the hand of the powerful. Behold the Lord God shall come with might." When a soldier announces to the king that he has been deceived by the Magi, who had departed another way, Herod, evilly enraged, seizes his sword and attempts to kill himself, but being prevented and pacified by his attendants, he turns his anger outward, speaking a Sallustian tag of the Magi plays: "I will quench my fire in ruin."

Before his angry eyes now comes the procession of the Innocents, singing verses of the offer of their purity to the sacred Lamb, and their trust that through him we shall be saved. A soldier suggests to Herod that he avenge his wrath by putting them to the sword, hoping that Christ will be killed among them. Herod gives the order, handing his sword to the soldier, and as the killers approach, the lamb is quietly withdrawn from the midst of the children, who sing "Hail, Lamb of God, hail, who takest away the sins of the world, alleluia." In vain the mothers beseech the soldiers to spare these young lives, while the children are struck down and lie prostrate. But this is no realistic death, for from above an angel sings to them in words suggested by Isaiah, "Ye who are in the dust, awake and cry aloud." From their prone position, the children sing the question: "Why, our Lord, dost thou not defend our blood?" to which the angel replies, "Endure yet a little while, until the number of your brethren is fulfilled."

Then Rachel is brought in, with two women who seek to comfort her. Standing over the children's bodies, and sometimes fainting, she sings in verse and prose laments of these tender limbs madly struck down, which neither piety nor youth could protect. She laments for the wretched mothers forced helplessly to see this sight. The consolers try to divert her grief to joy that the children are blessed in Paradise, but Rachel will not be comforted or cease to pour out floods of tears for the irrevocably dead children and for the joy of parents turned to sorrow. As the comforters urge her to dry her eyes, she passionately remembers her own loss. In anguish she probably lifts up inert small bodies, for we are told that the women lay the children back, questioning if anyone is to be wept for who will possess the heavenly kingdom. But Rachel falls upon the bodies, singing a Good Friday antiphon, "My spirit is anxious within me and my heart is troubled within me," until the women lead her away. After this human grief comes the turn, for from high above an angel speaks to the slain, with the divine words, "Suffer the little children to come unto Me, for of such is the kingdom of heaven," and the boys rise up and enter the choir, singing a glad song of the power of Christ.

The epilogue is brief and joyful. During the preceding movement Herod's death is symbolized in dumb show by his removal from his throne, which his son Archelaus assumes. At the angel's instruction Joseph returns from Egypt with Mary and the child, singing an antiphon of the Assumption, "Rejoice, rejoice, Mary, Virgin," and the play concludes triumphantly with the Te Deum.

The beauty of this play lies in the representation of the specific story through formalized symbolic suggestion, a unified presentment in act and word with deep associations. It touches universal human grief at the death of the young and innocent, and by traditional lyric language and symbol which look before and after, expresses the hope and confidence by which in Christian terms sorrow can be borne. It constitutes a complete dramatic experience.

E. Catherine Dunn

3. Voice Structure in the Liturgical Drama: Sepet Reconsidered

The works of Marius Sepet on the origin and development of medieval drama have undergone a curious fate in the century since his first publication. He has been the object of extravagant praise and of severe criticism, but strangest of all, his books have been misread as fundamentally by his admirers as by his enemies. The earliest review of *Les Prophètes du Christ* (Paris, 1878)[1] warmly praised its author for discovering the origins of modern theater in the dialogued reading of the Passion in Holy Week.[2] This astounding reduction of a complex theory to but one of its incidental supporting analogies foreshadowed the miscomprehension to which his total work has been subjected.[3]

1. Originally a series of articles published in the *Bibliothèque de l'École des Chartes* from 1867 to 1878. I cite both the articles and the book, although the former are more widely accessible in the United States. I have found no differences in text between the articles and the book.
2. *Bibliothèque de l'École des Chartes*, XXXIX (1878), 572; notice unsigned.
3. European scholars, from Paul Weber in 1894 to Glynne Wickham in 1959, have generally approved Sepet's thought while modifying and correcting phases of its basic thesis; E. K. Chambers regarded *Les Prophètes* as epoch-making, and Émile Mâle's history of medieval religious art was heavily indebted to it. American scholars have been much more reserved in their acceptance, Karl Young supporting the evolution of the Latin Prophet Play from a lection of Christmas Matins, but, like Hardin Craig and others, demurring at the broader theory, namely, that this Latin play underlies the Old Testament series in the vernacular cycles. For European scholars, see Paul Weber, *Geistliches Schauspiel und kirchliche Kunst in ihrem Verhältnis erläutert an einer Ikonographie der Kirche und Synagoge* (Stuttgart, 1894), pp. 42–48 (Weber's book is devoted largely to the theme of Ecclesia and Synagoga, but it would never have been written without the impetus of Sepet's work); E. K. Chambers, *The Medieval Stage* (Oxford, 1903), II, 52, n. 2; Émile Mâle, *Religious Art in France in the Thirteenth Century*, trans. from the 3d ed. by Dora Nussey (London and New York, 1913), pp. 131–75; Glynne Wickham, *Early English Stages*, I (London, 1959), 230. Wilhelm Meyer's caustic criticism was an isolated but serious instance ("Fragmenta Burana," *Festschrift zur Feier des Hundertfünfzigjährigen Bestehens der Königlichen Gesellschaft der Wissenschaften zu Göttingen* [Berlin, 1901], pp. 53–56); it is matched by a more recent but less scholarly attack in Benjamin Hunningher's *Origin of the Theater* (Amsterdam and The Hague, 1955; New York, 1961), pp. 6–7. For American scholars, see Karl Young, *The Drama of the Medieval Church* (Oxford, 1933), II, 170–71, 304–6; Hardin Craig, *English Religious Drama of the Middle Ages* (Oxford, 1955), pp. 73–74 and

Historians of the drama usually discuss only his first book, *Les Prophètes du Christ*, most of them showing no knowledge of the later one, *Origines catholiques du théâtre moderne* (Paris, 1904).[4] The most important contribution of the latter is a special kind of exploration into the origins of the religious drama. It probes the voice patterns in the liturgical chant of the Carolingian era for their dramatic potential and places emphasis on the structure of lesson and responsory in the office of Matins. This insight of Sepet's has never been appreciated for the contribution it can make to criticism of the liturgical plays,[5] a question separate from the controversial origins of the vernacular cycles. It is this theory of voice structure that I am considering in the present essay.[6]

It may be easier to understand this later achievement of Sepet in the area of liturgical drama if we consider the intellectual milieu in which he worked. He himself provided the clues to the background of his scholarly growth in the shared excitement and stimulation proffered by two great movements of nineteenth-century France. These were the liturgical study sponsored by Dom Prosper Guéranger at the restored abbey of Solesmes, and the literary history (particularly medieval) that flourished in Paris at specialized centers like the École des Chartes and the Bibliothèque Impériale (now Nationale). He pays tribute to the men associated with both of these interests, while taking his own place among them as a distinguished scholar.

The liturgical renewal sponsored by the Benedictine community at Solesmes was the starting point of all the modern liturgical movements in Europe and America.[7] After the young Guéranger succeeded in restoring the abbey in the 1830s from its suppression during the French Revolution, it became a focus of study of the Gregorian chant and the exemplar of its performance in a solemn and splendid manner. Dom Gué-

---

passim; Grace Frank, *The Medieval French Drama* (Oxford, 1954), p. 80; O. B. Hardison, Jr., *Christian Rite and Christian Drama in the Middle Ages* (Baltimore, 1965), pp. 258–59; V. A. Kolve, *The Play Called Corpus Christi* (Stanford, Calif., 1966), p. 86. A strange essay on Sepet occurs in a chapter of Oscar Cargill's *Drama and Liturgy* (New York, 1930), pp. 60–92, and is unfavorably reviewed by G. R. Coffman in *Speculum*, VI (1931), 610–17, and by N. C. Brooks in *Journal of English and Germanic Philology*, XXX (1931), 433–39.

4. Henceforth cited as *Origines*.

5. [See, however, E. Catherine Dunn's own work, cited below, n. 42.]

6. I wish to acknowledge a general indebtedness to the lectures and writings of my colleagues J. Craig LaDrière, now at Harvard, and G. Giovannini on the theoretical problems of "voice and address" in literature. See LaDrière, "Voice and Address" in *Dictionary of World Literature: Criticism, Forms, Technique*, ed. Joseph Shipley, 3d ed. (Paterson, N.J., 1960), p. 443; Giovannini, "Agnolo Segni and a Renaissance Definition of Poetry," *MLQ*, VI (1945), 167–73.

7. Louis Bouyer, C. O., *Liturgical Piety* (Notre Dame, Ind., 1955), pp. 53–58.

ranger's own historical research, best represented by *L'Année liturgique*, has suffered twentieth-century challenges to its methods and insights, and he is now revered more for the dynamism of his personality and his great zeal than for actual historical scholarship. His involvement in the religious controversies of nineteenth-century France left him little of the quiet leisure necessary for the research he had initiated, and it was to be his disciples like Dom Fernand Cabrol and Dom Henri Leclercq who would accomplish something of his desire in historical study.[8] As the century advanced, other students outside Solesmes produced works on the liturgy, among whom Sepet singled out for special mention Msgr. L. Duchesne[9] and Msgr. P. Batiffol[10] as influences on his own views of liturgical drama.

With the literary historians Sepet's relationship is less that of disciple than of colleague, and he became a leader among these men at a very young age. His pages are nevertheless marked by tributes to his associates, and no one is more frequently mentioned than Gaston Paris, to whose essays and personal correspondence he refers so enthusiastically. A close second is Léon Gautier, who was graduated from the École des Chartes a few years before Sepet and who soon became a faculty member there. His lifelong study of the medieval Latin trope kept pace with his friend's researches in the liturgical drama.[11] Besides these acknowledged ties of inspiration and rivalry, there is an obvious general indebtedness to the work of other prominent medievalists like Joseph Bédier, which is likely to suggest itself to a reader of his pages today. The small coteries of professional scholars in the France of his time provided the kind of intellectual calibre and scientific exactitude which were associated on a larger scale with the contemporary German universities and their achievements in Graeco-Roman classical studies. It was, indeed, the Académie des Inscriptions et Belles-Lettres[12] that immediately expressed warm praise for the young Sepet's first publication in book form

8. These two Benedictines edited the *Dictionnaire d'archéologie chrétienne et de liturgie* (henceforth cited as *DACL*), 15 vols. (Paris, 1907—). Dom Leclercq wrote an estimate of Guéranger for *The Catholic Encyclopedia* (New York, 1910), VII, 58–59. The article for *The New Catholic Encyclopedia* (New York, 1967), VI, 831–32, is by M. Ducey. See also "Solesmes, Abbey of," by L. Robert in the new edition of the encyclopedia, XIII, 418.

9. *Origines du culte chrétien* (Paris, 1893).

10. *Histoire du bréviaire romain* (Paris, 1893). I have used the English translation by Atwell Baylay (London, 1912).

11. Léon Gautier, *Histoire de la poésie liturgique au moyen âge: Les tropes* (Paris, 1886). Only vol. I was published.

12. *Origines*, p. v; the report of the Académie's reaction to his work was written by Gaston Paris and published in the *Bibliothèque de l'École des Chartes*, XL (1879), 77–80.

and encouraged him, on the judgment of its president (Édouard Laboulaye), to pursue further the implications of *Les Prophètes du Christ*.

Against such a background of interest and criticism, then, a theory about the origin and development of medieval drama could be given thorough consideration. Sepet was always fascinated by the relationship of mimetic and musical artistry in the liturgical plays, and he conceived of medieval drama fundamentally in terms of musical dialogue. He therefore interpreted its history more comprehensively than present scholars tend to do. We have come to take for granted today, at least until the recent appearance of Professor Hardison's book,[13] the notion of the drama as originating in the tropes associated with the Easter Introit, embellished and transformed into plays.[14] We readily forget that it was only in the last quarter of the nineteenth century that such an origin was propounded by Léon Gautier, Sepet's colleague mentioned above, who taught courses in medieval Latin poetry at the École des Chartes. It was not until 1886 that Gautier's volume on the tropes[15] appeared, thirty years after his exploratory doctoral thesis and after many years of lecturing at the École. Sepet was one of those who hailed the achievement of his friend,[16] but he had already established his own reputation in 1878 with the theory of the Prophet Play as a dramatized *lectio* of the Divine Office. Although he accepted Gautier's idea that the late Carolingian tropes were the first compositions to become actual *plays*, he retained his own conception of the fundamental dramatic origins in chanted lessons and responsories. This hypothesis is equal in importance to his theory of the Prophet Play, and actually underlies it.

I

The dramatic character of the church's official worship[17] had revealed itself long before the late Carolingian era in which the

13. Hardison, *Christian Rite and Christian Drama in the Middle Ages*, challenges much of the accepted theory. His book, which appeared after the completion of this essay, follows a different line of attack from mine, searching for the origin of medieval drama in the Mass itself and in the Easter Vigil service, rather than in Introit tropes or Matins *lectiones*.

14. Karl Young, *Drama of the Medieval Church*, gives the full account in vol. I, chap. VI, "Literary Embellishment of the Liturgy: Tropes," pp. 178–97; chap. VII, "Dramatic Tropes of the Mass of Easter," pp. 201–22; chap. VIII, "The Easter Introit Trope in Transition," pp. 223–38.

15. See above, n. 11. Carl Lange, in Germany, published his *Die lateinischen Osterfeiern* (Munich, 1887) with the same view of the tropes. Hunningher, *Origin of the Theater*, pp. 6–7, has used Gautier to refute Sepet in a brief, sweeping manner that does justice to neither Frenchman.

16. *Origines*, pp. 7–8.

17. I am at the moment using the term "dramatic" in its broadest sense, and

tropes began to flourish, displaying itself rather in the Divine Office than in the liturgy of the Mass, and especially in Matins. The Office reached a high degree of organization and beauty in the Western church during the time of Pope Gregory in the late sixth century and was enriched by the musical artistry of the chant which bears his name. The use of the Psalter as the substance of the canonical hours was, of course, centuries older than this chant and first flourished in the churches of the East. The well-known account of a pilgrimage to Jerusalem by the Spanish Etheria (or Egeria) in the fourth century indicates that a night vigil service of psalms and lections, and comparable services at certain day hours, were flourishing at the Church of the Anastasis and were typical of Eastern liturgical worship.[18] The records of gradual adoption in the West are sparse, but a fairly complete outline of the process can be pieced together from such documents as the Benedictine *Rule* and the surviving *ordines* of the Roman churches and basilicas.[19] As the Divine Office achieved precision and splendor in the papal city itself, and preeminently at Saint Peter's, the adoption of it in other areas began, first in Anglo-Saxon England (seventh century) and, more formally and methodically, in Frankish territory under Charlemagne (eighth century).[20] A priceless document recording the state of the Roman liturgy in the Carolingian period and the acceptance of it north of the Alps is the *De ordine antiphonarii*,[21] written by Amalarius of Metz about 830, after his study of the Roman practices.

The concept of musical dialogue as the basic constituent of the liturgical drama demands an exploration of these Roman offices in their formative period and therefore a search beyond the tropes and sequences

---

deliberately avoiding the noun "drama." The liturgy, as I see it, is not drama, but participates in some of its qualities. This question exercised Karl Young (I, 79–111), and he challenged Chambers's notion of dialogue as the essential constituent of drama (*Medieval Stage*, I, 81–82). Hardison's study (pp. 35–79), in proposing that the Mass is drama, challenges Young's insistence upon fictive impersonation as the generic factor. I consider "impersonation" in more detail below, pp. 56 ff.

18. Dom Jules Baudot, *The Roman Breviary: Its Sources and History*, trans. by a priest of the Westminster Diocese (London, 1909), pp. 49–55; Batiffol, pp. 15–18. See *The Pilgrimage of Etheria*, ed. M. L. McClure and C. L. Feltoe (London, 1919) and *Itinerarium Egeriae*, ed. E. Franceschini and R. Weber (Turnhout, Belgium, 1958).

19. Batiffol, pp. 30–66; for additional documentation of this history see the article "Leçons" in Cabrol-Leclercq, *DACL*.

20. Young, I, 178–81; H. F. Muller, "Pre-History of the Mediaeval Drama: The Antecedents of the Tropes and the Conditions of Their Appearance," *Zeitschrift für romanische Philologie*, XLIV (1924), 544–75; J. Handschin, "Trope, Sequence and Conductus," *New Oxford History of Music* (1954), II, 128–74.

21. *Amalarii episcopi opera liturgica omnia*, ed. J. H. Hanssens, 3 vols. (Vatican City, 1948–50), III, 9–109.

of the ninth century. Sepet was probing not merely the presence of question and response in tropes, but all the varied and complex types of choral chanting which the Roman liturgy had developed by the time that the Frankish clergy supplanted the "Gallican" form of services with this Roman chant. He isolated the impulse toward drama found in "all the kinds of antiphonal-chant, using that phrase in its broadest sense (choral alternation and interchange between the precentor, or leader, and the choir, or between two sides of the choir)."[22]

These two kinds of choir performance are usually referred to now as responsorial and antiphonal chant, respectively, the former being distinguished by the responsive and supportive interplay between a single or a few voices and those of the total choral group.[23] Antiphonal singing, on the other hand, is the normal method of rendering the psalms in the Office, the single verses being sung by each semi-chorus in turn. There is less approximation to genuine dialogue in this method, because it is simply the breaking up of a piece into arbitrary units without relationship to a real shift of "voice" or speaker in the alternate chanting. Responsorial singing constitutes a much closer approach to dialogue than the antiphonal because the division of parts often involves "address" to the whole choir by their precentor. This single cantor delivers the initial response to the reading which all have just heard from the lector. The precentor's response may be given, for example, in the words and thus, in effect, the voice of Isaiah, which he appears to assume as his own. Hearing the precentor intone these words (the basic text of the *responsum* or reply), the choir, breaking in to echo a portion of them, is in turn interrupted by the precentor, who adds yet another thought to his responsive address. Continuing in this fashion, precentor and choir, by cumulative extension and repetition of their collective thought, effect a dialogic response both to the reading and to each other in a kind of group meditation.

Although this method is not confined solely to the Matins Office, it is there used most extensively and dramatically in the lessons and responsories of the nocturns. The lesson *(lectio)* is the chanting, by an appointed member of the choir, of a passage ordinarily taken from the Holy Scripture or the church fathers. The selection has a special relationship to the liturgical season or to the particular feast being cele-

22. *Origines*, p. 14: "toutes les variétés du chant *antiphoné*, en prenant ce mot dans son sens le plus étendu (alternance et réciprocité chorale entre le préchantre et le choeur ou entre deux sections du choeur)."

23. Young, I, 25; Higini Anglès, "Gregorian Chant," *New Oxford History of Music*, II, 113–19. These two types do not, of course, exhaust the techniques available to a choir.

brated. At the conclusion of the lector's task the precentor and choir sing the responsory, which may be a restatement, a commentary, or a lyrical expression of the joy or grief implicit in the passage. In a very real sense the lector himself has been addressing the group of his fellow choristers through a quoted voice, and they reply in a manner and voice suitable to the particular occasion, led and, so to speak, encouraged, as we have seen, by their precentor. In the Carolingian period the responsory was more elaborate than in modern times, as Pierre Batiffol explains;[24] it contained several *versus* to be sung as refrains by the chorus. Moreover, the precentor chanted the whole text of the *responsum* (the opening passage) before its complete repetition by the chorus, instead of chanting merely the first word of it and leaving the rest of the sentence to be taken up by the group.[25]

Sepet, who knew Batiffol's historical account of the pre-Carolingian liturgy well, quoted at length his commentary on the dramatic potential of the Matins responsories as they were performed in the eighth century.[26] Both Frenchmen were struck by the close approach to drama in these nocturnal responsorial chants, but Sepet probed more deeply and developed the theoretical problems of literary form much more carefully, because he had already analyzed the role of the lesson and responsory in the Prophet Play many years earlier. The composite unit formed by the reading and the musical commentary was a *cadre* or framework for dramatic structure, as he demonstrated in the relationship of these two elements.

Because the lessons were taken from Scripture (with gradual admission of saints' lives) the content of the reading was, on the whole, narrative in reference. An organized distribution of the lections according to the liturgical season meant that virtually the entire Bible was thus read during the year,[27] along with homilies by the church fathers upon these biblical selections, the homilies originally forming part of the nocturns only in the Sunday office.[28] This predominantly narrative structure of Matins, in Sepet's view, constituted a framework for the dramatization of events when a theatrical performance was built into the recitation on certain great feast days. It was Matins rather than Vespers at which this kind of adaptation could occur, because Vespers is formed of psalms and hymnody and does not as readily support the weaving of an action, a narrative plot, into its design.[29]

24. Batiffol, pp. 88–89.
25. Young, I, 54–55.
26. Sepet, *Origines*, pp. 10–14.
27. Baudot, p. 78.
28. Batiffol, p. 79.
29. Sepet, *Bibliothèque*, XXIX (1868), 138–39; *Les Prophètes*, pp. 114–15.

The responsories which follow the lessons are of expository refer-ence, although they often include brief narrative statements. In their eighth- and ninth-century forms they were frequently of a lyrical character, constituting the meditative restatement of an event with wonder, gratitude, joy, or even lamentation. Sepet speaks of the respon-sory as "that little poetic and musical arrangement," one of the chief functions of which was "to set the tone of the celebration of joy or of sadness solemnized by the Church."[30] The striking of a theme and the playing of variations upon it were such marked features of the respon-sories that the entire office of the day was given form in this way. Batiffol observes, for example, that the whole office of the First Sunday in Ad-vent was named from the opening words of its first Matins responsory, "Aspiciens a longe."[31] A certain poetic freedom was ordinarily present in the diction itself, for the language of the responds in the early me-dieval period was not quoted from Scripture but was a mosaic of sen-tences and phrases drawn from the biblical text and rendered rather liberally and poetically.[32]

The "Aspiciens a longe" was one of the responsories loved by Ama-larius of Metz, and he discussed it in detail.[33] It was also much admired by Sepet and by Batiffol, both of whom quoted it appreciatively. It may be of value to present the text as an illustration of such compositional form:[34]

PRECENTOR [assuming the voice of Isaiah]. Gazing from afar, behold, I see the power of God coming and a cloud covering the whole earth. Go to meet Him and say: Tell us whether Thou art He Who is to reign among the people Israel.

30. Sepet, *Origines:* "cette petite composition poétique et musicale" (p. 14); "de caractériser le sens de l'anniversaire de joie ou de deuil célébré par l'Église" (p. 10).
31. Batiffol, p. 87.
32. Ibid., pp. 81, 87.
33. *Liber de ordine antiphonarii* (n. 21 above), chap. VIII, pp. 37–38.
34. Sepet, *Origines,* pp. 13–14, gives the Latin text:
LE PRÉCHANTRE. Aspiciens a longe ecce video Dei potentiam venientem, et nebulam totam terram tegentem. Ite obviam ei et dicite: Nuntia nobis si tu es ipse qui regnaturus es in populo Israel.
LE CHOEUR. Aspiciens . . . tegentem.
LE PRÉCHANTRE. v. Quique terrigenae et filii hominum, simul in unum, dives et pauper!
LE CHOEUR. Ite obviam ei et dicite:
LE PRÉCHANTRE. v. Qui regis Israël, intende. Qui deducis velut ovem Joseph! Qui sedes super Cherubim.
LE CHOEUR. Nuntia nobis si tu es ipse qui regnaturus es in populo Israël.
LE PRÉCHANTRE. v. Tollite portas, principes, vestras, et elevamini portae aeternales, et introïbit.
LE CHOEUR. Qui regnaturus es in populo Israël.
LE PRÉCHANTRE. Gloria Patri et Filio et Spiritui sancto.
LE CHOEUR. Aspiciens a longe. . . . Ite obviam ei . . . in populo Israël.

CHOIR. Gazing from afar, behold, I see the power of God coming and a cloud covering the whole earth.
PRECENTOR. All those born of the earth and all the sons of men, together as one, rich and poor!
CHOIR. Go to meet Him and say:
PRECENTOR. Thou Who rulest Israel, turn to us. Thou Who leadest Joseph like a sheep! Who sittest upon the Cherubim!
CHOIR. Tell us whether Thou art He Who is to reign among the people Israel.
PRECENTOR. Open your gates, O princes, and ye eternal portals, be lifted up, and He will enter,
CHOIR. Who is to reign among the people Israel.
PRECENTOR. Glory be to the Father, and to the Son, and to the Holy Spirit.
CHOIR. Gazing from afar, behold, I see the power of God coming and a cloud covering the whole earth. Go to meet Him and say: Tell us whether Thou art He Who is to reign among the people Israel.

Although there is no strict impersonation of roles here, since at one time the precentor speaks the words of the *filii hominum* and at another the chorus takes them up, there is nevertheless a dialogic situation in the "address" of the precentor and the choir, first to the children of men, and successively to the Messiah, to the *principes*, the *portae aeternales* and to the Holy Trinity. One can probably say even more than this, for the chorus is symbolically the *filii hominum*, or the faithful of Israel, and its entreaty "Nuntia nobis si tu es ipse qui regnaturus es in populo Israel" is more than an echo of the precentor's (Isaiah's) words; it is a plea uttered in its own choral right. The same kind of appropriation can be seen in the prayerful directive, "Qui regis Israel, intende," although it is the precentor who chants the line as a response to the choral command, "Ite obviam ei et dicite," expressed as a plural imperative to the *filii hominum*. However fascinating or perplexing the patterns of voice and address may become *within* the responsory itself, it is nevertheless important not to lose sight of the larger interrelation between *lectio* and *responsorium*, in which the latter is a single entity confronting the passage of Holy Scripture read by the lector, and thus a vocal reply to it.[35]

Even apart from the meaning structure of these two related elements, the very musical character of the *lectio* and *responsorium* created an artistic patterning. "The responsory," Sepet observed, "seems intended to inject variety into the performance of the liturgy, in causing the differentiated chant of the choir to follow upon the somewhat monotonous recitative of the lector."[36] This musical relationship can be ob-

35. Sepet, in one of his earliest articles, *Bibliothèque*, XXIX (1868), 127, remarked that the responsory was an adaptation of the two forms of chanting, responsorial and antiphonal (*Les Prophètes*, p. 103).
36. *Bibliothèque*, XXIX, pp. 127–28; *Les Prophètes*, pp. 103–4: "Ce répons semble

served also in the sung Mass even in modern times, in which the Gradual
serves as a chant of the responsorial type following upon the simple
recitative of the Epistle.[37]

The *Mystère d'Adam* is the play that most clearly realizes the potential for dramatic form of the combined lection and responsory. Sepet
called it "a dramatic lection imitated from the liturgical lection."[38] The
piece is, then, a lesson punctuated at certain crucial points by responsories. The story of Adam, Eve, Cain, and Abel has been transformed
from scriptural narrative into a drama by use of dialogue freed from
the lector's controlling voice. There is a prologue, however, giving the
antecedent action in the form of a strictly liturgical *lectio*, "In principio
creavit Deus"; and toward the end (l. 745) there is another such lesson,
the "Vos, inquam" introducing the procession of prophets (a *lectio*
which formed one of the Matins readings in the office of Christmas-
tide).[39] The responsories are introduced in each case by a rubric
"Chorus cantet,"[40] indicating that the liturgical choir even at this date
(twelfth century) was still replying in the long-established manner to
the events arranged in the narrative sequence of the *lectio*. There are in
the play five responsories from Matins of Septuagesima Sunday, beginning with the "Formavit igitur dominus" at line 20, and two from the
office of the Monday in Septuagesima week. In my estimation, Sepet's
analysis of the *Adam* into these precise liturgical counterparts was a
more important contribution to the history of medieval drama than was
his theory about the developing Prophet Play, for which his essay first
became known.

It was in this article also that Sepet discussed another term which has
special value for the understanding of voice structure in all medieval
religious drama. I refer to *la voix de l'Église*, his designation for the
"speaker" of the responsories, as distinguished from the mimetic voices
of the characters who take part in the scriptural story—Adam, Eve, the
Devil, Cain, Abel, God the Father. Their dialogue is in the vernacular
(Anglo-Norman), but the choral chants are in the liturgical Latin. This

---

destiné à jeter de la variété dans les exercices de la liturgie, en faisant succéder
le chant varié du choeur à la mélopée un peu monotone du lecteur."

37. Anglès, "Gregorian Chant," p. 119, classifies the Gradual as responsorial chant.

38. *Bibliothèque*, XXIX, p. 133; *Les Prophètes*, p. 109. [With this summary of
Sepet's view of the *Mystère*, cf. Hardison, pp. 259–60, esp. p. 260, n. 17, where nine,
not five, responsories from the Gregorian *Liber responsalis* are found relevant to
the *Mystère*.]

39. *Bibliothèque*, XXIX, 126; *Les Prophètes*, p. 102.

40. *Le Mystère d'Adam*, ed. Paul Studer (Manchester, 1918, repr. 1949). The
Latin lines, including stage directions, are numbered separately from the Anglo-
Norman text. The play is translated into English by Sarah E. Barrow and William
H. Hulme, "Antichrist and Adam," *Western Reserve University Bulletin*, vol.
XXVIII, no. 8 (1925).

distinction in linguistic medium is highly significant, not only of the stage which the drama had reached at this period, but also of the choral function in the total work. The familiar chanting of these Matins responsories marked the incursion, at crucial junctures, of an official interpretative voice commenting upon the dramatic conflict and bringing the incidents into perspective by clearly drawing the lines of God's providential plan as the background of the particular action.[41] As I have attempted to show in detail elsewhere,[42] this complex pattern of mimetic and interpretative voices accounts for much of the stylistic beauty and much of the meaning-structure in medieval plays even at the most advanced cyclic stages, like that of the Towneley plays.

Sepet suggested that this responsorial chanting gave to the *Adam* play something of the character associated with Greek tragic theater. It is evident throughout his scholarly work that he was haunted by a desire to write a major study of the relationships between ancient tragic drama and the medieval religious plays.[43] From his earliest article on the *Processus prophetarum* in 1867 until the publication of *Origines catholiques* in 1901 he scattered casual allusions to the Greek plays throughout his essays, and among the most important of the analogies which he drew was that between the choral responsories of the *Adam* and the choral odes of the ancient dramatic performances. The function of the two choral groups shows great similarity in the universalizing and deepening of the single incident or isolated conflict—in the Greek play through the natural wisdom of the community's elders, in the medieval drama through the supernatural vision of the church *(la voix de l'Église)* articulated by a choir of monks or cathedral canons. A careful reading of Sepet's observations gives the impression that his first thoughts favored a lineal descent of medieval religious drama from an ancient Hellenic tradition but that he gradually yielded this theory in favor of an independent phenomenon arising in the late Carolingian era in a manner strikingly similar to that of the pre-Christian culture. Not only did the *Mystère d'Adam* give occasion for such conjectures, but other plays, like the *Lazarus* drama of Hilarius and the *Lazarus* of the Fleury Playbook,

---

41. Sepet, *Bibliothèque*, XXIX, 135; *Les Prophètes*, p. 111.

42. See "Lyrical Form and the Prophetic Principle in the Towneley Plays," *Mediaeval Studies*, XXIII (1961), 80–90; "The Prophetic Principle in the Towneley *Prima pastorum*," in *Linguistic and Literary Studies in Honor of Helmut A. Hatzfeld* (Washington, 1964), pp. 117–27; and "The Literary Style of the Towneley Plays," *American Benedictine Review*, XX (1969), 481–504.

43. In the Preface to *Origines* (p. vii) he says that he was encouraged to undertake such a work as a young man by the eminent Hellenist Jules Girard, and that again in 1900 he was urged to the same enterprise by another classical scholar, Georges Perrot. Sepet still at this time expressed the hope of writing such a book, but he never did so.

elicited from him fine analogies, such as his application of the term *dithyrambique* to all of the semi-liturgical twelfth-century plays, a term appropriated from the early phases of Greek tragedy.[44]

II

We may say in recapitulation, then, that Sepet recognized the various forms of musical dialogue as fundamental to the origin of medieval drama in the sense, at least, that such chanted dialogue provided the context within which genuine drama arose. He recognized, too, the special role of the Matins lections and responsories in producing the mimetic patterns that passed from liturgical prayer into drama. Although Introit tropes of the *Quem quaeritis* type were the first chants to be transformed into actual plays (about the middle of the tenth century), these dialogued tropes were themselves only a phase of the long-continued experimentation with voice and impersonation for which lections and responsories were the "workshop." A further consideration of the *lectiones* themselves may now clarify the process by which the dialogue in a narrative could be freed from the control of a basic voice and thus emerge as mimesis or drama. This is one of the recurrent problems of literary technique in all periods of world drama, because many plays (including a goodly number of Shakespeare's) are technically a transformation of some narrative, like romance or novella, into a mimetic structure.

Sepet had a terminology which he applied rather casually to his analysis of the lections. Recognizing that the "Vos, inquam" sermon, which became the Prophet Play, occurred in the liturgy as a *lectio* of Christmas Matins and that its dialogue was subordinated to a basic voice, he posited a struggle between the enveloping monologue and a dialogue enchained within it.[45] The structure was like that of a novel: "Thus it is that a novel, dramatic as it is, is by no means a play. Dialogue can exist in a novel, but it is, if I may be permitted the expression, bound within the monologue."[46] This metaphorical way of phrasing the problem approximates the distinctions made more precisely by Plato and Aristotle in antiquity between *diegesis* and *mimesis* (with their variations), distinctions used by Craig LaDrière today in his theory of voice and address.[47]

44. Sepet, *Origines*, pp. 38 and 43–46.

45. *Bibliothèque*, XXVIII (1867), 9; *Les Prophètes*, p. 9.

46. P. 9; *Les Prophètes*, p. 9: "C'est ainsi qu'un roman, si dramatique qu'il soit, n'est point une pièce de théâtre. Le dialogue peut exister dans un roman, mais il est, qu'on me passe l'expression, comme enchaîné dans le monologue."

47. See n. 6, above.

The lector appointed for the Matins reading (there might be several in turn for the separate nocturns) had always delivered the selection in recitative, charged as he was with rendering all the roles. By the early ninth century there was an advance toward drama in the modulation of the lector's tones so as to distinguish one quoted speaker from another, and from his own narrative voice. The same period may also have seen the introduction of different lectors to represent the various speakers. This process of freeing the dialogue from its "envelope" was, after all, a gradual appropriation of personality. It was not simply the division of a narrative among individual voices; it was the assumption of roles by actors—in a word, impersonation. There are various degrees of this achievement throughout the Middle Ages, from the ninth to the fifteenth centuries. It is not a strictly chronological or evolutionary progress, and Sepet did little service to his great work by using metaphorical language borrowed from biological evolution. Conscious experimentation was involved, as he well knew, and some of the most advanced stages of the process occurred early (e.g., in the twelfth-century *Mystère d'Adam*) and some of the most awkward solutions of the problem were still visible in the late fourteenth century, as in the pedestrian Expositor of the Chester cycle. Evidence of these attempts to increase dramatic immediacy in the liturgical readings is now fragmentary and isolated, because so many texts of the medieval service books have perished. Moreover, as Father Richard Donovan has surmised, relatively few medieval lectionaries have actually been studied.[48] The evidence is heterogeneous and sometimes indirect, coming from a related and analogous type of religious service, like the chanting of the Passion in the Holy Week Masses, rather than from surviving manuscripts of the Matins office. The scope of the present essay does not permit a full consideration of the long process but only references to crucial texts which reveal types of experimentation underlying them.

The most valuable survivals of such recitative are the manuscripts of the Holy Week Passion readings, in which the Gospel accounts are marked in such a way as to show musical variation in the respective speeches of Christ, the crowd, the apostles, etc. Sepet regarded these as survivals of a method which was applied to other readings besides the special ones of Holy Week, for instance, to the Mass *lectiones* on great feasts and to the readings in the canonical hours. He conjectured, since he could not prove the point beyond question, that this custom of quasi-dramatic narrative chanting had begun about the middle of the ninth

48. Donovan, *The Liturgical Drama in Medieval Spain* (Toronto, 1958), p. 156.

century and had continued at least into the twelfth century.[49] The Passion readings, as they survive in the manuscripts, have rubrics consisting of letters or symbols inscribed near the words of the different speakers in the Gospel accounts, for example the letter *c* or the letter *a*. A number of historians, including Sepet, have taken these to be indications of the speaker's identity and of a separate "role" for a chanter.[50] Karl Young, however, showed clearly that these symbols are musical conventions indicating intensity, pitch, and velocity. He credited Notker Balbulus, the tenth-century monk of St. Gall, with an authoritative explanation of them in musical parlance.[51] (Ekkehard IV, chronicler of St. Gall, attributed the first use of the symbols to a certain "Romanus," a cantor who came to the monastery on a visit from Rome about 800 A.D.[52]) The letter *c* usually indicated acceleration of speed, and the letter *a* elevation of pitch. A codification of the symbols and their occurrence in the Passion texts led Young to infer that the words of the Lord were regularly chanted slowly and on a low pitch, those of the Jews rapidly (with high pitch), and the narrator's rapidly and on a pitch intermediate between that of Christ and the Jewish representatives.

This analysis of Young's gives support to Sepet's basic hypothesis that the Passion reading contained a measure of dramatic appropriation to particular roles, but only to the extent that a single narrator was charged with the task of modulating his voice to show the respective variations. Young was himself convinced that the use of different cantors to render the various speakers was a very late medieval practice (fifteenth century), and was not involved in the Carolingian or Cluniac customs. The point is a much debated one, and among those who have favored the early medieval use of it (*mélopée multiple*, as the French call it) have been E. Du Méril, K. Hase, l'Abbé Eugène Müller, and Gustave Cohen. The last-named historian stated positively in 1906 that the dialogued Passion readings date from the ninth century, and he did not retreat from this postion in the second and third editions of his book,[53] even though Young's work had intervened with the skeptical view about the early dating.[54]

49. Sepet, *Origines*, pp. 16–19.
50. *Bibliothèque*, XXVIII (1867), 10; *Les Prophètes*, p. 10.
51. Young, "Observations on the Origin of the Mediaeval Passion-Play," *PMLA*, XXV (1910), 325 ff.
52. Ibid., pp. 324–25.
53. *Histoire de la mise en scène dans le théâtre religieux français du moyen âge*, 3d ed. (Paris, 1951), p. 18.
54. In addition to the 1910 article, cited in nn. 51 and 52, see *The Drama of the Medieval Church*, I, 100–101, 550–51.

There can be no doubt, at any rate, that in the Carolingian age the chanting of the Passion was characterized by the quasi-dramatic modulation of the lector's voice as he assumed the different roles of the speakers, and it may well be true that distribution of the narrative among several cantors had also been attempted by this time. Sepet found in one of the earliest of surviving Passion plays a marked vestige of this narrative voice from the Holy Week readings, although the piece contains dialogue and impersonation of a truly theatrical nature. The text is a thirteenth-century one from the Benedictine monastery in Munich, contained in the manuscript of the so-called *Carmina Burana*,[55] and includes not only the trial and death of the Lord but also several events preceding the Last Supper, among them the raising of Lazarus. Throughout the play there are passages of narrative, usually based on responsories and antiphons (as Young has identified them). Clearly they are meant to be chanted by a lector (or sung by a chorus), for some of them are explicitly marked with the rubric "clerus cantet" (e.g., ll. 155, 158, 208); with "Pueri" (ll. 31 and 33); with "Et chorus cantet" (ll. 115 and 203). The most notable passage is the short scene of Lazarus' release from the tomb, which may be translated from the Latin as follows:[56]

> Then let Jesus go to raise Lazarus; let Mary Magdalene and
> Martha hasten there, weeping for Lazarus, and let Jesus chant:
>   "Lazarus, our friend, is sleeping; let us go and
>   rouse him from slumber."
> Then let Mary Magdalene and Martha, weeping, sing:
>   "Lord, if You had been here, our brother would not
>   have died."
> And thus, as they are silent, let the lector chant:
>   "The Lord, seeing the sisters of Lazarus weep, shed tears
>   at the tomb in the presence of the Jews and cried out."
> And let Jesus chant:
>   "Lazarus, come forth."
> And the lector is to chant:
>   "And, bound hands and feet, he came forth, who had been as
>   a dead man."

This Benedictbeuern play is an interesting but problematic text, comparable to some early French plays containing similar vestiges of a basic narrative voice.[57]

55. The entire play is printed in Young, I, 518–33.
56. Young's text, ll. 151–58.
57. Sepet suggested (*Origines*, esp. pp. 144, 159–61) that all of the surviving vernacular plays from the twelfth and thirteenth centuries show traces of this enveloping narrative device, viz., the Anglo-Norman *Resurrection*, the *Mystère d'Adam*, the *Jeu de Théophile*, and Jean Bodel's *Jeu de saint Nicolas*. He was cautious in his postulates, however, and aware that other explanations could here be

The *mélopée multiple* and the struggle of dialogue with its enveloping monologue can be studied most directly, however, not in the Passion chants or Passion plays, but in the famous *lectio* of Christmas Matins known as the "Vos, inquam." Here the complete progress from lection to drama is documented at every stage. This study was, of course, the one undertaken in Sepet's *Les Prophètes du Christe* and needs only a brief recapitulation here for students of the medieval drama. The original form of the piece was that of a sermon erroneously attributed to Saint Augustine, a homily on the Messias addressed primarily to Jewish auditors and marshaling the prophetic testimonies to Christ's identity and his mission as given in the Old Testament.[58] It was this homily that appeared in the High Middle Ages as a *lectio* of Matins in many dioceses and was variously assigned[59] to the Fourth Sunday in Advent, to Christmas Day, the ferias preceding it, or even to the Feast of the Circumcision on January 1. In its lectionary form[60] the basic speaker marshals the prophets in direct address ("Dic et Moyses"; "dic et tu, Abacuch"), but he himself quotes their prophecies, using the word *inquit* to introduce each one, thus enchaining the dialogue within his third-person reference or enveloping account. The freeing of the quoted speeches for a *mélopée multiple* by cantors is clearly shown in a text from Salerno, in which the summons to each prophet is assigned to "Lector" and the prophecies themselves to individual speakers, who engage even in little snatches of dialogue beyond their prophecies, as in the cases of David and the pagan king Nebuchadnezzar. Although the Salerno text was not known by Sepet, the existence of its type was one of his brilliant conjectures,[61] and it was verified only after his death. Young, in printing the text,

---

offered. The problem in each play would need separate and detailed consideration, and some of the questions have already been debated by scholars, with differing conclusions. Thus, Grace Frank regards the narrative passages in the Anglo-Norman *Resurrection* as an attempt to adapt a drama to a recitation (*Medieval French Drama*, in n. 3, p. 89); while M. K. Pope sees them as a commentary designed to preserve the sense of past time in the midst of dramatic representation (*La Seinte Resureccion, from the Paris and Canterbury MSS* [Oxford, 1943], Anglo-Norman Text Society, IV, cxxiv–cxxv). Miss Pope suggested this interpretation, which is virtually that of Sepet, in disagreement with her co-editor, Jean Wright, who favored the notion of a drama adapted for a reading audience (ibid., pp. cxxii–cxxiv). The editors cite previous controversy over these narrative lines on the part of F. Schumacher, G. Cohen, Petit de Julleville, E. Roy, and M. Faral (p. cxxiii, nn. 1 and 2).

58. The address to Jewish auditors forms only a part of the complete sermon, which is entitled *Contra Judaeos, Paganos, et Arianos sermo de symbolo*.

59. Young, II, 131.

60. Both Sepet and Young quote it as it appears in a twelfth-century lectionary from the diocese of Arles (B.N. MS lat. 1018).

61. Sepet, *Bibliothèque*, XXIX (1868), 120–21; *Les Prophètes*, pp. 96–97.

favored its interpretation as typical of other lost versions of this nearly dramatic type, a step between sermon and true drama.[62] A further advance of the lection can be seen in the eleventh-century version from St. Martial de Limoges, in which the cantor who represents the pseudo-Augustinian voice chants only a summons to each prophet, without any of the expository sermon which had still been present in the Salerno text. The prophecies themselves, chanted by other cantors in turn, are rhymed and set to musical notation.[63] Sepet regarded this text as the first Prophet *play*,[64] but Young, in line with his cautious insistence upon full impersonation as the test of genuine drama, hesitated to call it one. It has no rubrics indicating costume or action, and he therefore reserves the designation of the first Prophet Play to the thirteenth-century text from the cathedral of Laon, the earliest surviving Latin *Prophetae* with such rubrics.[65] Here, David is indicated as appearing in royal garments, Moses as carrying the tables of the Law, and Balaam as riding in on the ass destined to figure so much in later Prophet Plays.[66]

Beyond this point we need not pursue the history of the "Vos, inquam" *lectio*, the firmest evidence for Sepet's theory about the indebtedness of medieval drama to the Matins lection by the freeing of its dialogue. One final comment might be added, however, to show the relationship of the prophetic lection to the responsory in this liturgical office. A manuscript from Tours contains a set of directions for a Prophet Play of the same stage in dramatic development as that of Laon. The cantors who represent the prophets are to enter the choir processionally after the ninth *lectio* of Matins, and, when they have delivered their testimony each in turn and at the summons of two choir members, the *ordo* calls for the chanting of the ninth responsory in the pulpit, apparently led by the "duo clericuli" who have acted as summoners.[67] The text of the Tours play does not survive, but the description of the performance clearly indicates that even at this advanced stage of the drama we are dealing with a phenomenon still an integral part of the *lectio-responsorium* pattern. Young conjectured that the pseudo-Augustinian sermon may have supplied the material of several lections here and that the Prophet Play may have been an illustrative adjunct;

---

62. Young, II, 137–38. The Salerno text is a sixteenth-century printed one, but Young regards it as a survival of an earlier medieval tradition rather than a late imitation.

63. Young, II, 138 ff. and notes.

64. Sepet, *Bibliothèque*, XXVIII (1867), 24; *Les Prophètes*, p. 24.

65. The Anglo-Norman *Mystère d'Adam*, a version of the Prophet Play in the vernacular with detailed stage directions, is of the twelfth century.

66. Young, II, 145 ff.

67. Young, II, 153, quotes part of the text from Martène, *De antiquis Ecclesiae ritibus*, as evidence that the play belonged to the January 1 liturgy (Feast of the Circumcision).

this could be so, but in any case it supports the principle formulated by Sepet in connection with the *Mystère d'Adam*,[68] that the *lectio* itself received dramatic structure while retaining its function in the office and while still appearing in conjunction with its responsory in the age-old manner.

As a final problem in the relationship between musical dialogue and impersonation in the Matins office, we might consider Sepet's position on the *Quem quaeritis* tropes generally regarded since Gautier as the earliest religious dramas. The tropes were insertions into the liturgy at such places as the Kyrie, Introit, and Agnus Dei of the Mass, but it was the Easter Introit trope which became the basis of the first plays. There has been a surprising divergence of opinion among historians about the *Quem quaeritis* and its dramatic nature. As I indicated earlier,[69] Léon Gautier and Carl Lange thought of this trope as genuine drama when it was sung as part of the Introit. Sepet accepted this notion without challenge, including the presence of at least minimal impersonation in the roles of the angels and the three Marys. In more recent times, however, Karl Young took a firm stand against the Introit trope as drama, demonstrating that the surviving texts do not contain rubrics for costume, gesture, or action which would indicate full impersonation of the roles.[70] Only after the removal of the trope from the Introit to the office of Matins are such rubrics present in the manuscript. Grace Frank has supported this judgment of Young's,[71] but Hardin Craig seems to follow the earlier view of Gautier that even the most primitive *Quem quaeritis* trope (text from St. Gall) contains dialogue, action, and impersonation.[72]

The crux of the matter is, of course, the term "impersonation," which means the fictive assumption of an identity. Young regarded it as involving both speech and action in imitation of another.[73] I believe that Young is justified in his precision about this matter, but that the French historians were assuming impersonation as a natural consequence of dialogue, without demanding explicit evidence for it. When Sepet did advert to the nature of impersonation in dialogue he was vague about it, never using more exact terminology than such phrases as "appropriation more or less complete of the different voices to the words of the characters who appear in the liturgical narrative."[74] Although he did not contribute

68. See above, pp. 53–55.
69. See above, p. 47, and nn. 13–16.
70. Young, I, 220–22, 231.
71. Frank, p. 21.
72. Craig, *English Religious Drama of the Middle Ages*, p. 31.
73. Young, I, 80–81.
74. Sepet, *Origines*, pp. 16–17: "appropriation plus ou moins complète de ces voix diverses aux paroles des personnages qui figuraient dans la narration liturgique."

a sharp analysis of the phenomenon by this kind of language, he has nevertheless provided a support for Young's more careful discernment by his own emphasis upon the Matins lection and responsory as the matrix of drama.

To repeat, then, the *Quem quaeritis* trope was never a play in the Introit position but achieved its potential form only in the Matins locale to which it was transferred in the tenth century. In the fifty texts of the play printed by Young as genuine drama on the *Visitatio sepulchri*, thirty-seven designate the last responsory of Easter Matins as immediately preceding, while eight other texts refer to the "Te Deum laudamus" as immediately following.[75] These references clearly establish the context of the plays in the Divine Office. Young accounted for the transfer of the dialogue from the Introit to this place on various grounds,[76] for example, the appropriateness of the dawn as the moment for representing the Marys' visit to the tomb, and the custom of reading the Gospel of the day just before the Te Deum. It must be remembered that Easter Matins, in both the Roman and the usual monastic observance, contained only one nocturn,[77] and that normally the Gospel for this feast (Mark 16:1–7), narrating the visit to the tomb, formed the first *lectio* of the nocturn.[78] Moreover, the last responsory, following the third lesson, was itself a brief repetition of sentences from this Gospel, sometimes slightly altered or troped.[79]

Although Young does not cite Sepet's work on the Matins *cadre* in connection with the present question, Sepet's basic principle helps to illuminate the transfer of the *Quem quaeritis* to this place in the Office. The narrative character of the *lectio* and the lyrical responsory to it had served as a quasi-dramatic experience in the Office for centuries, and in the case of Easter Matins, they probably attracted the dialogue to this locale as the most fitting place in the day's observance for a truly dramatized, fully impersonated representation of the *Visitatio sepulchri*. In this way the Easter dialogue was subjected to the same kind of "control" and influence as the "Vos, inquam" sermon, and in this context the simple *Visitatio* not only became drama but was gradually elaborated into the great *Ludus Paschalis*, a play with three major scenes: the *Quem quaeritis*, the hastening of Peter and John to the tomb, and the appearance of Christ to Mary Magdalene as a gardener.[80] The addition of these two later scenes to the *Visitatio sepulchri* occurred at approximately the

75. Young, I, chaps. IX and X.
76. Ibid., I, 231–36.
77. Ibid., I, 64 and 547.
78. Ibid., I, 60, n. 1.
79. Ibid., I, 232–33.
80. Carl Lange (*Die lateinischen Osterfeiern*) was the first to separate the texts into these three incremental stages.

same period as did the full elaboration of the prophet plays, namely, in the late eleventh and twelfth centuries.[81]

The real origin of the drama, then, as Sepet grasped it, was the whole complex of dialogued lections and responsories in the Matins office, for which the chanted Passion readings of Holy Week simply serve as analogous testimony, as surviving witnesses to lost stages of a great experiment which finally produced at Matins genuine dialogue and impersonation. This theory penetrated more deeply into the genetic context of the drama than did the work of Léon Gautier and Carl Lange, both of whom confined their view to the area of the Introit tropes and thus erected a foreshortened history of the liturgical and mimetic conditions.

The many possibilities of musical variation and lyrical expression in the responsorial chanting made the chorus reply to the Matins *lectio* a thing of beauty comparable to the Greek tragic chorus. The narrative of the Scripture reading by the lector afforded a ground plan for dramatic dialogue and action, and when *lectio* was accompanied by *responsorium* the complex unit served to create a type of nearly operatic sacred performance which held the attention and devotion of the spectators in long and solemn services. Much of the vernacular spoken drama, even in the time of cycles and pageant wagons, is explicable in terms of this majestic recitative and elaborate choral commentary. There is an interplay of dramatic dialogue with expository comment throughout the length of the mystery cycles, in such a way that the interpretative voice (like that of the liturgical chorus) unifies the protracted and often variegated series of actions, and also provides lyrical reflection and meditative response to the unfolding of God's providential plan for man's salvation.[82] This basic role is often shared temporarily by an Expositor or chorus with dramatic characters themselves, so that the latter become "aspects" of the expository voice. This circumstance gives an opportunity for poetic speech or musical chant of great artistic beauty and a whole range of stylistic effects closely related to the musical nature of liturgical prayer in the Divine Office. Here rather than in modern realistic action and character portrayal one should seek the methods of stylistic analysis for medieval mystery cycles.[83]

81. The second and third scenes are found in manuscripts only from the twelfth century onwards. See Mrs. Frank's discussion of the chronology, pp. 24–25.

82. This is the type of analysis that I have applied to the Towneley cycle in the articles mentioned above in n. 42.

83. The efforts to evaluate medieval plays in terms of fidelity to "real life," whether in comic roles like Cain's servant or in serious ones like Abraham's, miss the whole technique of fictive characterization in which complex roles contain different "voices" dovetailed into a specious unity. One of the voices may be choral or interpretative in function and wholly alien to the real life identity or function of the *dramatis persona*.

William L. Smoldon

4. The Melodies of the Medieval Church Dramas and Their Significance

I

The late Karl Young, in the Preface to his monumental work, *The Drama of the Medieval Church* (Oxford, 1933), wrote the following:

> Another aspect of these plays which has been generally unexplored is their melodies. I do not feel called upon to apologize for having treated these pieces from an exclusively literary point of view, and were a defence required, one could cite eminent precedents. It is an obvious fact, however, that since the plays of the Church were actually sung, our knowledge of them cannot be complete until such of their music as exists has been published, elucidated and heard. . . . The adequate editing and exposition of the music associated with the dramatic texts . . . would assist a demonstration of relationships, and would probably disclose unsuspected traditionalisms or originalities through-out the body of plays. Its chief contribution, however, would consist, I think, in opening to us the full charm of these dramatic pieces. . . . (I, xiii–xiv)

With the music of most of these works "elucidated," and a number of them "published and heard" in their true and complete shapes, I propose to show in the course of this article that each of Karl Young's prophecies can be found to have been fulfilled. I would question, how-ever, whether the "*chief* contribution" would be "the opening to us of the full charm of these dramatic pieces." Equal in importance are the new facts, regarding the genesis and development of early music-drama and medieval music generally, which come to light when the melodies are studied in detail and depth.

It might have been better if the distinguished Karl Young *had* realized the necessity for apologizing for omitting serious consideration of the music. "Eminent precedents" do not excuse this neglect, which has continued past his time. What has been forgotten by the "literary" writers on the subject is that the works that they are considering are

[Reprinted with extensive changes from *Comparative Drama*, II (1968), 185–209, by permission of the author and the editors. Copyright 1968 by *Comparative Drama*.]

not just dramas (relying on text and *spoken* delivery alone to bring about their effects), but *music*-dramas, in which every word is sung, and where the effects of the dramatic texts are often enough considerably enhanced by the vocal melodies given to them. The techniques of this vocal music are far subtler than is commonly supposed.

Moreover, as I have indicated above, much general evidence of importance concerning every aspect of the development of these music-dramas can be gathered, once comparative studies based on the music are made. Certainly much knowledge can be, and has been, obtained from literary conclusions alone, but it is my experience that any dogmatic statement made concerning these works, based on evidence drawn from a text, must be tested by reference to the accompanying musical setting. The latter evidence may confirm the textual conclusions, but occasionally, sometimes importantly, it confutes them.

There was a much earlier protest than mine against this obsession with the texts of those works which disregards entirely their musical settings. Some years before 1860, when manuscripts of "liturgical drama" were beginning to attract attention, the great pioneer musicologist, C. E. H. de Coussemaker, had been making a special study of the examples available to him which happened to show their musical settings on stave-lines (twenty-two in all), and in that year he published transcriptions of them, under the title of *Drames liturgiques du moyen âge*. Gregorian paleography was in its infancy (it was Coussemaker who first realized the basic principles of neume notation);[1] the Benedictines of Solesmes had not begun to publish the results of their scholarly labors towards restoring the authentic melodies of the Roman liturgy; yet Coussemaker's book is a historical landmark, even though, denied the opportunity for comparisons such as access to a large number of manuscript versions would have afforded him, he made numerous errors of musical transcription.[2] But he was well aware of the real nature

1. Most of the earlier church music-drama melodies were written in unheighted or roughly heighted neumes, mere reminders to the singers of the rise and fall and note-groupings of the tunes that they already knew. In an age sparse of books, medieval memories were long and retentive of detail; thus, usually, an eventual "stave" version would turn up to cast quite a clear light on what was intended by the cryptic neumes. The situation was not always so difficult. Certain unique works, such as, for example, the group gathered in the so-called Fleury Playbook, and the single and extensive Beauvais music dramas, *Daniel* and *Peregrinus*, were presented in the manuscripts with their music written on four-line staves with clef markings, thus affording comparatively few problems.

2. His reading of the musical setting of "Quem quaeritis in sepulchro," the first sentence of the trope to the Introit of the Easter Mass, as it appears in neumes in a certain eleventh-century French manuscript, was borrowed by Sir E. K. Chambers,

of the material he was handling. Objecting to the "text only" treatises that were already current, he wrote in the Preface to his own work:

... mais leurs publications, qui reproduisent des pièces dramatiques, sont in-complètes; elles offrent une lacune regrettable. Les editeurs[3] les ont dé-pouillées de la musique qui les accompagne, et qui en est une partie substantielle et intégrante. . . . Que dirait-on d'un auteur qui, voulant nous initier aux opéras joués sous Louis XIV par exemple, se contenterait de reproduire les libretti de Quinault?

(In other words, as far as Quinault's libretti were concerned, it really would have been necessary to mention the slight contributions made by a composer of the name of Jean-Baptiste Lully.)

A more substantial part had been banished than perhaps even Cousse-maker realized. What he does make very clear is that what we have are in-deed *music*-dramas, and that the texts are in fact no more than libretti. . . .

II

Lest it be thought that I have been unkind to that great scholar, Karl Young, let me seek an occasion for defending him, and this with the weapon of musical evidence. Recently, a work has ap-peared (O. B. Hardison, Jr., *Christian Rite and Christian Drama in the Middle Ages: Essays in the Origin and Early History of Modern Drama* [Baltimore, 1965]) which seeks to prove certain novel theories regard-ing the origins of medieval church music-drama, by, oddly enough, textual evidence alone. The texts, it would seem, are almost all drawn from those presented in Young's own volumes, this no doubt being a matter of convenience for reference. I gather that one of Hardison's contentions is that the celebrated three exchanges of the *Quem quae-ritis* Easter Sepulchre trope dialogue and the Easter Sepulchre music-drama type containing that dialogue, had their origins, *not*, as set out by Young and generations of previous literary scholars, from "a sponta-neous new birth and growth" of dramatic form within the trope itself (Young, I, 1 and 178) but from already existent liturgical ceremonies of a dramatic nature. I have greatly admired the knowledge displayed by Hardison of medieval church rites and practices, and also the ingenuity

---

and printed in characters of gold on the cover of the latter's *The Mediaeval Stage,* vol. II. Unfortunately, both the pitch and the modality of the music as there given are incorrect. The first note should be considered as being D, and the B-flat clef sign should be cancelled.

3. He mentions, among others, such still-remembered names as du Méril, Danjou, Lusarches, Felix Clément, Didron, and Mone. There were many more such "textual" editors to come, right up to the present time.

of the author's arguments founded on them. But there is one grave flaw in the structure. When one is dealing with the *Quem quaeritis* trope, the Easter Sepulchre dramatic activities, and indeed the whole of the histrionic art of the medieval church, it is not just "Christian Drama" that is being handled, but "Christian *Music*-Drama," and the musical settings of these Latin texts will be found to be just as valuable evidence as are the "libretti"—and frequently more so. There is also to be considered the nature and history of tropes and their music. Therefore I have been surprised to find that this lengthy treatise, which sets out to establish a new basic theory on the subject, shows a total disregard of the music that certainly should be involved. . . .

To make clear that musical evidence supports Young's traditional view and runs counter to Hardison's hypothesis, I turn now to the most intriguing melody in the whole of the church music-drama movement, that which sets the three sections of the *Quem quaeritis* dialogue. I use the word "melody" in the singular, since, like innumerable similar situations to be found in the Roman liturgy itself, the setting given to the text is always recognizable, varying only in lesser note-details in whatever part of the Middle Ages it is encountered. The same of course may be said of the *Quem quaeritis* dialogue *text*, where, from center to center and country to country, small verbal rearrangements and substitutions can be found, some of them significant.[4] In my opinion, however, the musical differences to be distinguished are even more illuminating for the establishment (or otherwise) of "relationships," as I shall try to show in due course.[5]

4. As a result of my having isolated into the appropriate chart (with its music) each appearance of any antiphon, responsory, or other liturgical item, together with any pseudo-antiphons and any other non-liturgical compositions in common use among church music-drama versions, I believe that I could solve the identity of any such from an *incipit* of no more than a single word and its neume music.

I am in this article disregarding an alternative *Quem quaeritis* dialogue exchange, later in date, with a new text and a new musical setting. It was a purely German novelty, first on record in an eleventh- to twelfth-century "First Stage" Easter music-drama, Einsiedeln 366, a unique version. There is first the normal dialogue with its usual music, and then (the idea being, apparently, that one could take one's choice) a dialogue that begins with "Quem quaeritis, o tremulae mulieres, in hoc tumulo plorantes? . . ." The new setting is in the Phrygian-mode, rather dull as compared with the earlier, vital music. Perhaps the arranger of a fourteenth-century version from Engelberg (MS 314) thought just that, since his setting *begins* in the terms of the older one, and although he uses the new text, he allows himself one or two other musical reminiscences. About thirty examples of the new dialogue text and music survive, almost all in "Sepulchrum" versions of the "Zehnsilberspiel" type. The established dialogue version, with its music, continued elsewhere undisplaced.

5. To carry the point further: In *Quem quaeritis* trope versions and the briefer examples of the dramatized ones, the identity of the one or more additional items

The earliest known appearance of the *Quem quaeritis* dialogue is in a manuscript of extra-liturgical compositions (called a "troper") belonging to the monastery of St. Martial de Limoges.[6] In the volume are many other examples of free composition, known as *tropes* and *sequences*, which had crept, all unauthorized, into the services of the church. All the great centers in Christendom seem to have tolerated a degree of such unofficial composition and to have produced tropers, but nowhere else was there a hive of such activity in the tenth and eleventh centuries as at St. Martial. A recent and scholarly study by the eminent musicologist, Jacques Chailley, *L'École Musicale de St-Martial de Limoges jusqu'à la fin du XIe siècle*, reveals as never before the monastery's *avant-garde* position in the field of musical invention, being concerned not only with melody but with the first stirrings of polyphony. The manuscript in question, now in the Bibliothèque Nationale, Paris, is the troper now known as B.N. MS lat. 1240. The portion containing the *Quem quaeritis* trope dates from 933–936 A.D. There is a photographic reproduction of the relative page in *The Drama of the Medieval Church* (vol. I, facing p. 210). It shows Aquitaine musical notation in its early stages of development. The general setting-down is disgracefully careless, with other trope items scattered haphazard. The *Quem quaeritis* trope itself is troped, "fore and aft," by two familiar companion tropes. It is plain that the Introit that follows is suffering an "internal" troping; *incipits* of its inner sentences ("posuisti . . .", "mirabilis . . .", "scientia . . .") turn up all over the place together with the correct "Alleluias" for the Introit, as their music shows. Little heed need be paid to the fact that the standard first *incipit*, "Resurrexi," is not to be traced in the welter. Its presence can be taken for granted. . . .

From what I have already said concerning St. Martial de Limoges,

---

before and/or after the *Quem quaeritis* dialogue sentences serves as useful evidence when comparisons between versions are attempted. The selection of the added items seems at times to be a matter of regional choice, but at other times it is hard to account for. Whatever conclusions are drawn, however, it is necessary also to look at the musical situation, for a textual similarity may be deceptive. Let us take an item that Professor Hardison has mentioned more than once, "Surrexit Dominus de sepulchro qui pro nobis pependit in ligno." This text appears widely among church music-dramas, and was indeed used for a liturgical antiphon, one included in Hartker's tenth-century *Antiphonale*. In the majority of cases where it appears after the *Quem quaeritis* dialogue it will be found to be using the antiphon music, but quite a number of dramatic versions have a different setting, apparently non-liturgical. Another composition mentioned by Hardison—"(Alleluia): Resurrexit Dominus hodie . . ." (surely not an antiphon but a trope)—has different settings, characteristic respectively of French and Italian versions.

6. [See Paul Evans, *The Early Trope Repertory of Saint Martial de Limoges* (Princeton: Princeton University Press, 1970), published after the appearance of Smoldon's article.]

it will be apparent that I incline to the opinion that the genesis of the Easter *Quem quaeritis* trope took place there. An attractive, neatly balanced dialogue was framed, and set to a vital, well-constructed tune of the "new style" that was a feature of this "new art" of trope and sequence composition. Clearly, it caught on, as did certain other tropes and sequences, with the result that it quickly swept through Christendom. Regions chose to edit text and melody, together with prefacing and rounding-off items, each in its own way, but, as I have maintained, and as a full-scale examination of the settings will show, without altering basic structures. Whether or no B.N. 1240 (with its dialogue already troped) represents the abbey's first *Quem quaeritis* attempt, or whether we must seek for it (probably in vain) some decades further back in time, I am encouraged by the fact that Chailley looks in the same direction. Indeed, my tentative opinion is not firm enough for him. He states categorically: "Sainte-Martial de Limoges a sans doute inventé le trope *Quem queritis*" (p. 373). Anything that Chailley says concerning St. Martial is deserving of respect.

III

Let us now seek the basic structure of the trope dialogue music to which I have referred, by examining the setting as given in B.N. 1240. If I had no more than these ill-written, carelessly heighted Aquitaine neumes to work from, little progress would have been possible. Fortunately, however, from the last decade of the tenth century and the beginning of the next there has survived a very useful group of St. Martial tropers with examples of the Easter trope dialogue. Their Aquitaine neumes are still without any guiding horizontal line, but they are better written and more accurately heighted, and in some cases have end-of-line "directs." All this is sixty and more years after B.N. 1240 (and how much must have perished in between!), yet here we have manifestly the same "house" version with the few small musical differences that the passage of time could be expected to bring.[7] Also, the later group has come to prefer different rounding-off items before the Introit *incipit* "Resurrexi. . . ." Instead of "Alleluia, resurrexit Dominus. . . ." they have "Alleluia, ad sepulcrum residens angelus . . ." and "En ecce completum est. . . ." But in regard to the

---

7. B.N. 1240 is unique in preferring, in the second sentence, "ipse dixit" instead of the "predixerat" of the other St. Martial versions. But the music is the same. I must call attention to one small musical difference between B.N. 1240 and the later St. Martial tropers; not one of the actual notes, but a rhythmic one, concerned with the syllables of "coe-*li-co*-lae." I will refer later to its significance.

dialogue music itself, I feel that with the aid of the neumes of the later
St. Martial tropers I can read the pitches of the B.N. 1240 notes with full
assurance, except for some parts of the music of the third section, where
there seem to be differences of opinion among the group as to the
heighting of some of the neumes (or perhaps merely differences in standards of carefulness). The most painstakingly written appears to be
B.N. MS lat. (nouv. acq.) 1871, and when in doubt I have relied on its
pitches.[8]

A general statement is possible regarding this melody wherever it
appears. It is in the Dorian or "re" mode, or, more specifically, in Mode
II, starting and ending on D, and with its melodic line ranging both
above and below that pitch. At times during the centuries it will be
found transposed to the perfect fourth above, with the use of B-flat. In
example 1 I give a transcription of a portion of the B.N. 1240 version,
rendering the music on five lines in the modern black-note substitute for
plainchant notation, the syllable groupings of the notes indicated by
slurs, the whole transposed up a perfect fourth for convenience in fitting
into the normal G-clef stave.

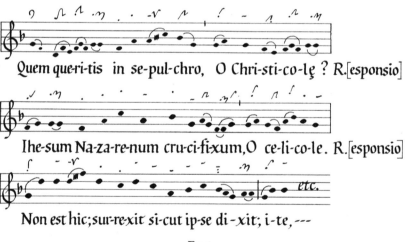

Ex. 1

What then are the outstanding features of the melody which make
its identity clear, for all the editings of time and distance? In order
to economise space, I am writing the numerous short examples that I
need in sol-fa rather than in staff notation. After all, sol-fa is as ancient

8. There is no proof that this manuscript was actually written at St. Martial, but
Chailley (p. 117) considers it closely associated.

as the ancient Greeks, and is frequently employed by the Benedictines of Solesmes in their writings. If we assume the normal diatonic major scale (in any key) to be:

do   re   mi   fa   sol   la   si[ti]   do[1]

we may, for convenience, abbreviate the terms to:

d   r   m   f   s   l   t   d[1]

I hope to make my points clear by using this "shorthand" method. It will be seen that in the case of the leading tone, I am substituting for "si" the more modern "ti." Where a syllable is given two or more notes, I "slur" these by placing them in italics.

Now for the tune. There is almost always an opening dip, from r to l_1 ("Quem quae-").[9] Mostly, we find d as an intermediate light note— a "liquescent"—as in our example. The purpose of this "liquescent" was to enable the singer to join neatly any awkward consonants that happened to be in contact (in this case, the letters "m" and "q"). Sometimes the d liquescent is not written in, sometimes the leap from r to l_1 (liquescent) is taken with the first syllable. With "quaeritis" the tune returns to r, usually via two *torculus* forms *(l_1dt_1, drd)*, but these sometimes simplify to *dt_1, dr*. The next three notes again represent a characteristic, the upward triadic stride, d m s, sometimes with the second or third note decorated, e.g., d m *mfs*[10] or d *ms* s. The "vocative" part, "o Christicolae," I shall pass over for the time being. The setting of the reply, "Jesum Nazarenum," is clearly founded on the opening music, the essential d and r followed once again by the upward-moving triad.

The setting of "Non est hic" can also be termed a "characteristic" one. Almost all surviving examples, whether French, German, Italian, or Spanish, and including the Limoges group and the St. Gall versions, give the words the dramatic, ringing uplift, *rl* l *ltd*[1]. A few French versions, more modest as to pitch, write d r *rl*. Small note-variants are to be found for each version.

A few words must be spared on the matter of the music of the two balancing vocatives, "Christicolae" and "coelicolae." This involves a consideration of the earliest trope dialogue version surviving at St. Gall, MS 484, of later date than the St. Martial one, and belonging to about the

9. [The superscript after the note indicates that the note falls in the octave above; the subscript, in the octave below.]

10. Where, as in this instance, the notes of a syllable cover an upward-moving third, the middle unit is sometimes written as a *quilisma*, shaped in broken fashion as indicated in the example, and treated more lightly than the adjacent notes. There is reason to believe that the gap of an upward-moving third may have often been filled in in performance even without the written *quilisma*.

middle of the century. The St. Martial setting of "Christicolae" is r dt_1 drd r—, obviously derived from the opening music. The "coelicolae" setting, however, is different: rd mf m r.[11] On the other hand, the St. Gall 484 music, which otherwise differs only in small details from that of St. Martial and shows the "characteristics" already spoken of, presents a new feature: the verbal rhyme of the vocative phrases is matched by a *musical* rhyme; both "Christicolae" and "coelicolae" are set by the notes rd ms r r—. Stave versions that make certainties of the St. Gall neumes are late and comparatively scarce, but it can be definitely said that any dialogue version belonging to the St. Gall group will have this musical rhyme as a "thumb-print," either as already given, or (two variants) rd ms m r—, or as rd ms mr r—. This may seem to be a small matter to mention, but this trick of having a musical as well as a verbal rhyme at the vocative phrases is seen also in some French dialogue versions. The short musical motives are individual, and seem to link together several versions, calling attention at the same time to other common features. A group that includes the early trope version Paris, Arsenal 1169 (c. 996–1024), B.N. 9449 (eleventh century) and B.N. (n.a.) 1235 (twelfth century) makes use of the rhyme rd m fm r. Another, that includes Cambrai 75 (eleventh century), Reims 265 (twelfth or thirteenth century), and Paris, St. Géneviève 117 (thirteenth century), has mr d mfm r. All the above-mentioned French manuscripts make use of the exceptional "non est hic" music mentioned previously (d r rl), its first-known appearance being in the Arsenal 1169 version. I have found that such small musical clues have at times certainly revealed a few of the "unexpected relationships" prophesied by Karl Young; however, remembering the limits of this article, I am not able here to give full treatment to this. . . .

IV

Let us once again examine the *Quem quaeritis* Easter dialogue with closer attention to its possible origin. As I have already shown, manuscript evidence makes it clear that its musical setting was one that was common to all Christendom. Karl Young, concerned only with its text, is content to trace it to a trope form. O. B. Hardison, who operates within the same limits, thinks that the dramatic element was so strongly present within the services of the medieval Church as to make it probable that the three-stage question, reply, and further reply, which we find in both trope and dramatic forms, arose from a liturgical ceremony. He summarizes his theory as follows:

11. This is as in B.N. 1240. The later St. Martial tropers have a slight rhythmic variation: rd m fm r.

"An analysis of *Quem quaeritis* manuscripts in these terms consistently leads to the conclusion that the dialogue originated not as an Easter trope but as a ceremony associated with the vigil Mass" (p. 219). Unfortunately, "these terms" did not include any sort of consideration of the music. As he can produce no manuscript evidence of the existence of such a ceremony, he can do no more than visualize a textual reconstruction (pp. 215ff.) which, he admits, can be only "theoretical" and "extremely tentative." He favors certain manuscript texts of late date, including the well-known Tours exchange,[12] the forms of which he believes support his theory. I can offer no musical criticism here, since these texts with their *incipits*—"Quem quaeritis," "Jesum Nazarenum," "Non est hic"—happen all of them to be "ordinariums," a type of service book which, because of its very purpose, is stripped of its music.[13] Nevertheless, I fully expect that had the music been written in, even in just the *incipit* form, I should have found it to be the familiar setting.

Both Young (I, 203) and Hardison (pp. 165, 171–72, 174) are at pains to marshal a number of liturgical items in the forms of Easter antiphons, and responsories with their verses, pointing out very reasonably (Young on behalf of his trope, Hardison for his liturgical ceremony) that here was the raw material to suggest the text of the three-item dialogue. All these items, *and* their musical settings, are thoroughly well known to me. They are all to be found in Hartker's tenth-century *Antiphonale*, together with their neume settings. I have rendered the music of all of them into modern notation (with, let me hasten to acknowledge, occasional help from the good Fathers of Solesmes in cases of obsolete or more obscure antiphons). I can give only brief examples from the long list, and have chosen the most familiar phrases. Here are the beginnings of three antiphons, the music rendered in sol-fa:

$$\text{s} \quad \text{s} \quad \textit{sl} \quad \text{s} \quad \text{s} \quad \text{f} \quad \text{l} \quad d^1 \quad \textit{td}^1\textit{ls} \quad \textit{ld}^1$$
(a) Je-sum, quem quae-ri-tis, non est hic, sed
$$\textit{ld}^1 \quad \text{s} \quad \text{s}$$
sur-re-xit. . . .

$$\text{s} \quad \textit{sd}^1\text{l} \quad \textit{ls} \quad \text{f} \quad \textit{sl} \quad \text{l} \quad \text{s} \quad \text{s} \quad \text{s} \quad \text{t} \quad d^1 \quad \textit{r}^1\textit{m}^1 \quad r^1$$
(b) No-li-te ex-pa-ve-sce-re Je-sum Na-za-re-num
$$r^1 \quad \textit{d}^1\textit{t} \quad \textit{ls} \quad d^1 \quad \textit{d}^1\textit{r}^1\textit{d}^1\, d^1 \quad \textit{d}^1\textit{l} \quad \text{s} \quad \textit{ld}^1 \quad d^1$$
quae-ri-tis cru-ci-fi-xum; non est hic. . . .

$$\text{s} \quad \text{s} \quad \text{s} \quad \text{s} \quad \text{s} \quad \textit{sf}\,\text{s} \quad \text{l} \quad d^1 \quad d^1 \quad \textit{ts} \quad \textit{td}^1\textit{ls} \quad \textit{ls} \quad \text{f}$$
(c) Je-sum, qui cru-ci-fi-xum est quae-ri-tis, al-le-lu-ia,
$$\textit{sf} \quad \textit{sl} \quad d^1 \quad d^1 \quad r^1 \quad \text{t} \quad \textit{d}^1\textit{l} \quad \textit{ls}\,\text{f} \quad \text{s} \quad \text{l} \quad d^1 \quad \text{t}$$
non est hic, sur-re-xit e-nim si-cut di-xit vo-bis. . . .

12. See Young, I, 224–25.
13. See Young, I, 20, for a definition of an "ordinarium" ("ordinary"). Note that it was the usual state of affairs for the "libretto" texts to be given as *incipits*.

All of the music of all of the items quoted by the two writers is straightforward, normal Gregorian chant, the responsories (as is usual) a little more melismatic than the antiphons. But nowhere, *nowhere* in that music is there a phrase of melody that suggests the patterned, balanced phrases of the *Quem quaeritis* dialogue music as I have already given it.[14] One cannot imagine how phrases from a ceremony concerned with a vigil Mass could turn into a trope composition, music and all, such as that found as the dialogue in B.N. 1240. I cannot remember such a derivation ever having been proposed concerning any other famous trope. Tropes had a far different origin, as we shall see.

Karl Young wrote a very interesting chapter on tropes and sequences, those unofficial additions that were made to various parts of the Roman liturgy. It was a practice that began in the ninth century, or even before, and was tolerated right up to the time of the Council of Trent. Young dealt with the subject comparatively briefly, concerned of course only with the texts, but I am inclined to wonder whether the sheer *bulk* of the movement is generally realised. It was one of "free composition," which had no hesitation in invading the age-old liturgy with *invented* material—texts and music. It was to be found at work all over Christendom, but nowhere more industriously than at St. Martial de Limoges during the tenth and eleventh centuries.

Since I believe that insufficient attention has been paid to the nature of the music of the tropes, which represented a comparatively late intrusion into the realm of Gregorian chant, I should like here to quote some extracts from the writings of the well-known musicologist Jacques Handschin, who is recognized as being an authority on the origins and history of tropes and sequences:

. . . the music which was the foundation of this new art was already finding its way into the liturgy in the time of Amaldar [early ninth century]. Since music was highly valued at this period we must suppose that this type of music was in accordance with the taste of the times. . . . The new melodies are more vivid, less ornamental and sometimes remarkably impressive. . . . Agobard, speaking of the danger that such music would swamp the liturgy, quotes passages from St. Jerome directed against 'theatrical art.' We must therefore conclude that the influx came largely from the secular music of the period, which would otherwise have left no traces—or perhaps it would be more correct to say that the Church musicians worked on the same lines as their secular colleagues. (*New Oxford History of Music*, II, 148)

14. Some of the material quoted, with its official music, reappeared in various Easter dialogue versions, both trope and dramatic, but only as "extra" items, outside the dialogue (e.g., "Venite et videte . . . ," "Cito euntes . . .").

In another article, the same writer comments, "Every trope is in principle intended to combine with a given Gregorian song, as an introduction to it, or as an interpolation."[15]

Let us consider the categories of tropes in more detail. There appear to be three divisions: (1) the purely musical type, taking the form of a vocal flourish, a *melisma* added to the normal item; (2) the purely textual type: the addition, alone, of a new text, fitted to the notes of an already existing *melisma* (e.g., Kyrie II—the *Fons bonitas* troping by Tuotilo); (3) the musical-textual type, with which we are mostly concerned. Here we have both new text and new music. This type was most frequently employed for troping Introits and the simpler chants of the Ordinary of the Mass (Gloria, Sanctus and Agnus Dei). They were inventions, but their music usually conformed to the neumatic style of the item they were troping, and *(nota bene)* occasionally even borrowed a short motive from it. The Introits were favored targets for such tropings, none more frequently chosen, as Apel has pointed out (p. 438), than "Puer natus est nobis . . ." from the third Mass of Christmas Day. The troping could be *intercalatory* (phrases inserted between the original liturgical phrases), or *introductory*, the trope coming first and leading in some relevant and linking fashion into the beginning of the Introit.

Let us consider now the relationship of the Easter *Quem quaeritis* (introductory) setting with that of the Introit which it precedes. When (after all doors and windows have been closed and the household has been warned in advance) I sing through the B.N. 1240 or the St. Gall 484 trope versions and then pass straight on to "Resurrexi . . ." and the whole of the Easter Introit setting, I feel confirmed in my belief that here are definite melodic affinities, two items of music that blend in style. What may perhaps most catch the ear would be a "motive" similarity such as I have previously referred to. The first phrase of the trope music should be compared with what I give in example 2—two successive, interspersed "Alleluia" settings, taken from the Introit. There is no doubt in my mind that the *Quem quaeritis* dialogue, whenever and wherever invented, took its first form as a *trope;* one that was *intended* to belong (as it clearly does) to the Introit of the *Easter* Mass. The whole nature and history of tropes makes it impossible that it could have been generated from a previous liturgical ceremony which, indeed, seems to have nothing more than a "theoretical" existence.

15. "The Two Winchester Tropers," *Journal of Theological Studies*, XXXVII (1936), 35, as quoted in Gustave Reese, *Music in the Middle Ages* (New York, 1940), p. 186.

(a) al - le -lu -ia: po-su - etc.

(b) al -le -lu - ia : mi-ra —— etc.

Ex. 2

Both Young and Hardison call attention to tropes of the Introits of Masses of other feast days which are of the same dialogued pattern as the Easter Introit trope, and which might therefore represent imitations. I would have my reservations regarding that famous composition *Hodie cantandus,* a trope of the Christmas Introit, "Puer natus est. . . ." There seems little reason to doubt the tradition, supported by that informative monk of Einsiedeln, Anselm Schubiger,[16] that the composer was the famous Tuotilo (d. 915), who produced many tropes. He probably had no need of patterns, and no form of the Easter trope may have been known to him. Certainly we have no evidence that he invented it. Anyway, the music of the question and answer in *Hodie cantandus* (beginning "Quis est iste puer . . .") bears no relation to that of the Easter trope.

The affinities between the *texts* of the Easter trope and the Shepherds' Christmas trope, "Quem quaeritis in praesepe . . ." are quite apparent. But, as I have already pointed out, there is no link between their melodies except for the few brief and hardly significant moments already referred to.[17] The earliest surviving manuscript show-

16. *Die Sängerschule St. Gallens* (Einsiedeln, 1858). He transcribes "Hodie cantandus" as No. 41 of his *Exempla.*

17. I must not omit mention of the instances when it would appear that the Christmas dialogue was unable wholly to forget the Easter music. In the *Officium Pastorum* from Rouen (B.N. MS lat. 904 [thirteenth century]) and also in the Magi-Herod music-drama from the so-called Fleury Playbook (twelfth century) the question put to the Shepherds at the Manger ("Quem quaeritis in praesepe?") is set to the *Easter* music, almost as if the spell of the earlier melody could not be shaken off for a while. Unless it happens that the unheighted neumes of the Christmas trope as given in Oxford, Bodleian Douce 222 represent the same trick, then the two French works are unique in sharing it. But there are further similarities between them. They both borrow from Saint Luke the passages beginning "Nolite timere . . ." and "Transeamus usque Bethleem . . ." and are unique among Christian music-dramas in doing so (the verses are not used in the liturgy as antiphons). Furthermore, when the respective settings are compared, they will be found to differ by not more than a few notes. All this is more than coincidence. There is no

ing the trope of the Christmas Mass Introit is the (St. Martial de Limoges) B.N. 1118 of the late tenth century. Other dialogued Introit tropes often cited (e.g., the Ascension trope, "Quem creditis super astra . . ." and the "Quem creditis natum in orbe . . ." of the Nativity of St. John the Baptist) show by their vocative phrases obvious imitations of the *text* of the Easter trope. But there is no taking-over of the music. I have investigated the settings of all of them. Each is independent, since each belonged to its own particular Introit. . . .

I turn now to the matter of the earliest surviving example (or rather, examples) of a truly *dramatic* version of the Easter Sepulchre dialogue, that represented by the well-known Winchester documents. Regarding St. Ethelwold's *Regularis Concordia*, I can add nothing to the enormous amount already written concerning it, since the brief text belonging to it is without its music. I bear in mind, however, the manuscript's admission that the monastic customs of Fleury and of Ghent had been drawn upon. However, there is no specific mention of the Easter Sepulchre drama as having belonged to either.

Hardison, in discussing the *Regularis* dramatic text and rubrics, makes what to me is a most extraordinary statement:

. . . Its dialogue is in what will henceforth be called the "abbreviated form." Instead of the familiar *Quem quaeritis in sepulchro, o Christicolae*, the rubrics give only *Quem quaeritis*, and the Marys reply only *Ihesum Nazarenum*. Editors have assumed that the dialogue is given as a series of *incipits*, but the frequent recurrence of the abbreviated form in later manuscripts suggests that versions using it should be considered a distinct type. Since they have other features in common, they raise the possibility, first suggested by Klapper, that the dialogue was originally an extremely brief exchange of Biblical phrases supplemented by antiphons. (Hardison, p. 197)

In support of his claim Hardison directs us, in a footnote, to eleven separate texts, printed in Karl Young's first volume. To me, the simplest explanation of the "abbreviated forms" that he quotes, is that they come mostly from ordinariums and breviaries,[18] which because of their nature are not as a rule interested in the musical settings of the liturgy, but make a habit of textual *incipits*.[19] None of the examples quoted

---

doubt that *Officium Pastorum* belonged to the diocese of Rouen. Thus, for the reasons already given (and a few others) I am inclined to believe that the Magi-Herod music-drama written out in the Fleury Playbook began its career at the ancient capital of Normandy. If I am correct, then this will be another example of music having revealed an "unsuspected relationship."

18. One example is from a missal, and a few are quoted from "unidentified manuscripts."

19. Karl Young, speaking of the ordinarium, says: "Usually this service book contained no complete part of the liturgical text itself, but merely the *incipit*" (I, 20).

shows any music. One can of course weave all kinds of theories around such truncated texts, provided that there is no musical evidence to trip one up. This I hope to provide.

Glancing at the manuscripts that Hardison quotes, I note that they all tend to treat the antiphons that precede and follow the "abbreviated" *Quem quaeritis* dialogue in a similar *incipit* fashion. On this showing, he should perhaps have written that the dialogue probably "was originally an extremely brief exchange of Biblical phrases supplemented by *abbreviated* antiphons." Yet surely no choir ever sang, for example, the two words "Ardens est," and then cut the rest of the antiphon? I turn to my photos in search of an ordinarium which *does* take some heed of music-settings. Certainly some of them do. In a number of cases one finds neumes above a *Quem quaeritis* trope or dramatic text (probably as being less familiar) while most of the surrounding liturgical items are left bare. Such a version is revealed on a couple of pages from a thirteenth-century ordinarium from Zurich, Rhenau MS 59, mentioned by Karl Young (I, 596). In it liturgical antiphons and responsories are cut down to *incipits* everywhere, but occasionally they get a few "reminding" neumes above (e.g., "Et valde mane." and "Venite et videte locum."). A brief *Visitatio* version appears as: "Quem quaeritis."; "Jesum Nazarenum."; "Non est hic." But above all three of these *incipits* appear the right and proper neumes of the standard setting.

The case, I think, is proved. The "abbreviated form" as a "distinct type" is a myth, and the *incipits* that we meet with are—just *incipits*. . . .

Continuing to speak of Winchester, Hardison also says, "It is impossible to think of the *Regularis Quem quaeritis* as the product of more or less haphazard embellishment and improvement on a St. Gall original composed about 910" (p. 194). I quite agree, especially since there is no real evidence as to the existence of a St. Gall original composed around 910.[20] But with the hint concerning Fleury and Ghent borne in mind, one's thoughts are turned in another direction. No one can doubt that the links between the *Regularis* version of the dialogue and that of the Winchester Troper must have been close. I am well acquainted with the beautifully written, approximately heighted, Anglo-Saxon neumes of the Winchester Troper version. Put in their place on my charts of the settings of the three dialogue items, they reveal with-

20. Another point: if the Winchester documents had had anything to do with St. Gall, they wouldn't have employed the item, "Alleluia, resurrexit Dominus hodie, leo fortis . . . ," which is set in the Winchester Troper as a distinctly French composition. St. Gall 484, with its balanced musical rhymes, appears to me to represent a more sophisticated version of the dialogue setting than B.N. 1240.

out fear of contradiction that here we have the music of the St. Martial tropers and the few other versions that lean to Limoges. Winchester even has that same rhythmic peculiarity at the inner syllables of "cae-*li-co*-lae" as B.N. 1240, which is otherwise unique. Why all this should be I don't know. Perhaps the music came via Fleury. Unfortunately the latter shows nothing to connect it at that date with dramatic activities. A tenth- or eleventh-century *Quem quaeritis* from Apt in southern France (Apt 4) is also very close to Winchester in its musical setting, and shares its peculiarity (not found at St. Martial) of adding "di-centes."[21] The Winchester Troper dialogue music has a *quilisma* between the first two units of the first *torculus* ("quae-"). I have already mentioned, in footnote 10, that where the upward interval of a third was concerned, the gap seems, in performance, to have been filled lightly, whether or no a *quilisma* was written in. A more serious question might be that in the Winchester text (unlike that of St. Martial) there is no "o" before "Christicolae." But . . . the Winchester Troper has for the last syllable of "sepul*chro*," neumes which can be represented by *frrm;* B.N. 1240 has *fr* for "-chro" and *rm* for the vocative "o."[22] It seems then that even in the case of the earliest surviving dramatized *Quem quaeritis* version we find ourselves back to St. Martial de Limoges!

It seems apparent to me that on the musical evidence, the *Quem quaeritis* dialogue with its setting, in both trope and dramatic uses, arose from a no more remote source than the trope form itself.[23] We have

21. I once constructed a chart of the music of all the dialogue versions from all over Christendom that used the "dicentes" ending, but found that it seemed to indicate no special links or have any practical significance. The *Regularis* version (without music) has instead "a mortuis," which is unique, as far as I know, except in a late sixteenth-century printed Italian version, much distorted musically.

22. It is of course noticeable that in the text of the Easter dialogue as written in St. Gall 484, "Christicolae" appears without its vocative "o," even though everywhere we meet with "o coelicolae." This is paralleled in quite a number of other versions, including most of the Italian examples of the eleventh and twelfth centuries (but *not*, be it noted, in the cases of the Limoges tropers, including B.N. 1240, and the vast majority of the French versions). The fact has led to speculation in some quarters that in the original dialogue "Christicolae" actually did stand alone, and that only later was the "o" added, in order to balance the two vocative phrases.

My theory is that the "o" of "Christicolae" has been there from the beginning—in sound, if not always in script. The syllable before "o Christicolae" is the last syllable of "sepulchro"; thus the immediate repetition of the same vowel sound could in performance bring about a running-together—a more or less continuous "o" sound. In an age when memory and not the written sign was the chief reliance of the singers in the services, it could easily be that when a writing-down was called for we should at this point find a single "o" recorded, that of "sepulchro." [For author's detailed evidence, see original article.]

23. I recall that there are three instances (within my knowledge) of *Visitatio*

many, many manuscripts showing the *Quem quaeritis* three-item dialogue, set always, through the centuries, to a standard music, but never a manuscript giving the alleged ceremony from which the composition is claimed to have been derived. In any case, to a student of the origin and history of tropes the very idea of the *Quem quaeritis* composition, with its "new style" of vigorous patterned music, being "derived" from a previous piece of Gregorian ceremonial chant seems fantastic. Tropes were just tropes, new, "free" compositions, intended for a specific purpose. Let us recall Handschin's words: ". . . in principle intended to combine with a given Gregorian song."

We do not know when or where the dramatic presentation of the Sepulchre scene was actually first attempted, any more than we know definitely where the first version of the Eastern introit trope was composed (even though St. Martial remains to me a hot favorite). What is needed is the discovery of more and earlier manuscripts, with *music*. On this subject, only theories, not proofs, can be spun with words.

Certainly many other problems connected with church music-drama remain to be solved, and many of Karl Young's theories (and techniques) are to be questioned, as must the findings and opinions expressed in any great treatise after the passage of years and the continuation of research. But such research as we are considering must not continue under the handicap from which it has too often suffered heretofore. The warning voice of Édouard de Coussemaker must continue to reach our ears across the span of a century, and those who write on the subject of church music-drama will neglect at their peril the music which accompanies every syllable of the libretti as an equal and illuminating partner. . . .

---

versions replacing the expected *Quem quaeritis* exchange by a composition (common to all three) founded on some of the antiphon material referred to on p. 73, above. The manuscripts are Klosterneuburg 574 (thirteenth century), Melk 1094 (fifteenth century) and St. Florian XI, 434 (fifteenth century). The item commences, "Nolite expavescere . . . ," and has the same florid musical setting in all three versions. The music, however, is not that of the antiphons.

Howard Mayer Brown

5. Musicians in the *Mystères* and *Miracles*

Unlike the earlier liturgical dramas in which actors sang large portions, and unlike the sixteenth-century Passion plays of Lucerne,[1] which employed hundreds of *Spielleute,* mystères and miracles required neither frequent and elaborate musical numbers nor a large performing force. Music had no leading part in the dramas, but served merely as an adjunct to the often brilliant spectacle. As one more decorative element, music certainly had an important place in these mélanges of realistic illusion, dazzling display, and pedantic edification; but the underlying didactic intention of the plays would not have been altered by interpolating either a greater or a lesser amount of pageantry and ornamentation. Motets, chansons, plainsong, and instrumental pieces simply helped to make the dramas more impressive. Without music—and probably many of the poorer provincial productions had very little indeed—the mystères and miracles would not have been much different, only a little less spectacular. These were not musical plays; they were plays with incidental music. And there were comparatively few kinds of scenes in which such interruptions were traditionally demanded.

The platform representing heaven was the principal place from which the music sounded. Most of the vocal pieces were sung by a choir of angels stationed in this mansion. The instrumentalists, too, normally sat there to play their *siletes* and their *pauses.*[2] One manuscript, which preserves miniatures by Hubert Cailleau and Jacques des Moëlles depicting the stage for the 1547 production of the *Passion* at Valenciennes,

[Reprinted from Howard Mayer Brown, *Music in the French Secular Theater, 1400–1550* (Cambridge, Mass.: Harvard University Press, 1963), pp. 42–57, by permission of the author and the publisher. Copyright 1963 by the President and Fellows of Harvard College.]

1. Described in Marshall Blakemore Evans, *The Passion Play of Lucerne: A Historical and Critical Introduction,* MLA Monograph Series, vol. 14 (New York, 1943).

2. [A *silete* is a piece of music used to quiet the spectators, whereas a *pause* is any musical interlude. See Brown, *Music in the French Secular Theater,* pp. 140–68.]

even labels this raised platform "Lieu pour jouer silete."[3] And time and time again the rubrics in the play texts read, "Adoncques se doit resonner une melodye en Paradis," or "Lors soit fait en Paradis grande joye et melodie," or some other similar phrase.

Apparently the chorus could on occasion move from heaven to another mansion for a single number. Thus in the 1501 Mons *Passion* there is a reminder to the *meneur du jeu* to tell the singers to go temporarily to limbo: "Cy doivent estre advertis ceulx qui chantent les motez en Paradis, de descendre de Paradis et eulx en aller au Limbe, pour chanter ung motet, quand on leur dira."[4] Perhaps they leave heaven also during the entry into Jerusalem, although the directions are not so specific: "Ici soit chantét ung motet en Jherusalem." All of the actors on stage may have sung monophonically in this place; Jean Michel's revision of this play seems to call for such a solution: "Ycy se arrestent tous ung peu loing de la porte de Hierusalan et chantent touz: 'Gloria laus.' "[5]

When the stage directions call for the angels to sing a specific piece of music, the text is apt to be either in Latin or in French. The Latin pieces may come from any part of the sacred service, including the Ordinary of the Mass. Both a Kyrie and a Gloria appear in the Greban *Passion*.[6] But hymns predominate. In the *Martyre de Saint Denis* the angels sing "Gloria tibi, Domine," while the decapitated martyr takes his head quite literally in his hands. The heavenly choir performs "Aurora lucis" near the beginning of the *Resurrection de Jesus-Christ* by Eloy Du Mont,[7] and in the same play Gabriel sings "Regina coeli," one of the antiphons BVM that resemble hymns, while the Virgin Mary appears to Christ on earth.[8] Both "Vexilla regis" and "Veni creator spiritus" are among the hymns most often specified for performance by angels as they descend from heaven to earth. And the hymn of thanksgiving, "Te Deum laudamus," sung either on stage or in church immediately following the final speech, almost invariably ends a mystère.

3. Reproduced among other places in Gustave Cohen, *Le Livre de conduite du régisseur et le compte des dépenses pour le Mystère de la Passion joué à Mons en 1501* (Paris, 1925), facing p. lxxxvi; in Émile Picot, *Catalogue des livres composant la bibliothèque de feu M. le baron James de Rothschild* (Paris, 1884–1920), IV, 336; and in Nicole Decugis and Suzanne Reymond, *Le Décor de théâtre en France du moyen âge à 1925* (Paris, 1953), pp. 20–21.

4. Cohen, *Le Livre de conduite*, p. 340.

5. Ibid., p. 270.

6. Gaston Paris and Gaston Raynaud, eds., *Le Mystère de la Passion d'Arnoul Greban* (Paris, 1878), pp. 66, 317. Since Louis Petit de Julleville, *Les Mystères* (Paris, 1880), vol. II, contains a catalogue of mystères complete with bibliographical references, none will be given here for individual plays discussed, except where passages are quoted directly.

7. Paris, Bibliothèque Nationale, MS fonds fr. 2238, fol. 72.

8. Ibid., fol. 72[v].

Most of the French texts sung by the heavenly choir are religious, although in the Greban *Passion* God requests chansons as well as motets to celebrate the entrance of Christ into heaven. In view of the vagueness of musical terminology in these plays, however, the angels may well have performed the sort of *chanson spirituelle* that appears several times in other passages of the same play. On the first day, for example, they sing a rondeau, "Quand humanité sera mise en vertu primeraine,"[9] and a *Chançon aux angles tous ensamble* beginning "La festivité vient que le seigneur."[10] Pirro's summary of music in the fifteenth- and sixteenth-century theater, abundantly rich in examples, cites many other passages where specific pieces, both sacred and secular, are requested.[11]

The printed edition of the Rouen *L'Incarnation et la nativité de Notre Sauveur et Rédempteur Jésus-Christ* (n.p. n.d.) leaves room for polyphonic music, both French and Latin, to be written in by hand.[12] And a four-part motet composed for the theater survives in two manuscripts which preserve a play not strictly within the dramatic tradition under discussion but related to it, a Flemish miracle on the life of Saint Trudon. Written at the Monastery of Saint-Trond near Liége in 1565 and 1566, both manuscripts contain the Flemish play and a Latin translation of it, for which the local choirmaster, Jean Vrancken, supplied the motet "In fata dum concesserit."[13] . . . It differs in no fundamental way from any other sixteenth-century motet in the style of pervading imitation. We can assume, therefore, that polyphonic music written expressly for a sacred play is not likely to have any special stylistic traits. If the local choirmaster were neither ambitious nor talented enough, motets need not have been composed newly for the occasion. Appropriate music already at hand could easily have been interpolated at the necessary places.

Angels sang polyphony in other plays as well. Both Greban and Jean Michel in their *Passions* require God's speeches to be sung by three voices, "ung hault dessus, une haute contre et une basse contre, bien accordées."[14] Reese suggests that the hymns may have been sung in

9. Paris and Raynaud, eds., p. 43.
10. Ibid., p. 63.
11. André Pirro, *Histoire de la musique de la fin du XIVe siècle à la fin du XVIe* (Paris, 1940), pp. 124–34.
12. The music is discussed in Jacques Handschin, "Das Weihnachts-Mysterium von Rouen als musikgeschichtlicher Quelle," *Acta musicologica*, VII (1935), 98–110. There is a modern edition of this play by Le Verdier.
13. The complete piece is printed, with a description of the manuscripts and other commentary, in Roger Bragard, "Une Composition musicale de 1565 provenant de l'abbaye de Saint-Trond," *Bulletin de l'Institut Archéologique Liégois,* LV (1931), 184–204.
14. Cohen, *Le Livre de conduite,* p. 180.

fauxbourdon,[15] and he gives other examples of passages that unambiguously call for polyphonic interpretation. But plainsong was also used. Just as the Rouen *Incarnation* leaves space for part music, a single four-line staff without musical notation occurs a number of times in *La Création, la Passion, la Résurrection*.[16] In one or two places this has been filled in with what appears to be white mensural notation mostly in ligatures. . . . And the Eloy Du Mont *Resurrection* includes notated chant for almost all of the sung passages in that play. Probably the final Te Deums were among the other numbers sung monophonically by the angels in heaven and possibly by the other actors and the audience as well.

The way such a heavenly choir must have looked can be seen in the well-known miniature by Jean Fouquet, now in the library at Chantilly, illustrating the *Mystère de Sainte Apolline* for a book of hours.[17] This mid-fifteenth-century example corresponds so closely to the descriptions in archives, and to the requirements of the play texts, that it may be considered a typical musical stage arrangement, generally valid for any of the mystères performed during the entire period. On the left, a raised platform represents heaven. A comparatively small chorus of angels is grouped around God; an organist and several other musicians stand and sit in the front row of the neighboring scaffold. The *ménétriers* are playing various wind instruments, three slide trumpets, two cornetts (?), and a bagpipe (see pl. 1). Occasionally the instrumentalists were hidden behind the scenes, and angels held instruments in their hands, pretending to play them, but this was by no means customary.[18]

Outside of heaven, music is to be found in the mystères and miracles most frequently in the pastoral scenes. The image of the happy shepherd spending his carefree days singing, dancing, and playing on one of a variety of rustic wind instruments seems to have captured the imagination of the time. A shepherd almost never appears on any kind of fifteenth- or sixteenth-century stage without at least talking about

15. Gustave Reese, *Music in the Renaissance* (New York, 1954), pp. 150–51.
16. Paris, Bibliothèque Nationale, MS fonds fr. 904.
17. Reproduced frequently, among other places, in Cohen, *Le Livre de conduite*, facing p. xlviii; in Decugis and Reymond, *Le Décor*, p. 18; in Edmund Bowles, "The Role of Musical Instruments in Medieval Sacred Drama," *Musical Quarterly*, XLV (1959), facing p. 76; and in Richard Southern, *The Medieval Theatre in the Round* (London, 1957), facing p. 94. The latter book, a brilliant and convincing defense of the thesis that medieval plays were often staged not on a straight platform set with many mansions but within an enclosed circular area, discusses the Fouquet miniatures at some length (pp. 91–107).
18. Such an arrangement is found in the 1474 Rouen *Incarnation* (fol. 57), but Bowles, pp. 74–75, is mistaken in implying that this was the usual arrangement. One of the examples he cites (p. 80) is not a mystère at all, but a mystère *mimé*.

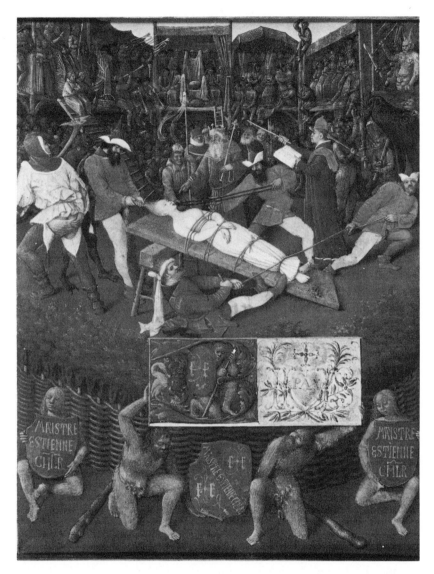

1. Jean Fouquet. The Martyrdom of Saint Apollonia. From *Le Livre d'heures d'Etienne Chevalier*. Courtesy of the Musée Condé, Chantilly. (Photo: Giraudon, Paris.)

music. In the 1474 Rouen *Incarnation* the talk is involved enough to include paraphrases from Jean de Muris,[19] at the end of which the two

19. Discussed in Henry Lavoix, "La Musique au siècle de Saint Louis," in Gaston Raynaud, *Recueil de motets français des XIIe et XIIIe siècles* (Paris, 1883), II, 224–31.

shepherds sing a duet for tenor and *dessus*, "Io son garenlo." This play, which gives more detailed instructions for performance than any other, allots a larger proportion of the vocal numbers than usual to the shepherds. Among other things they sing a five-part "Requiescant in pace," an elaborately conceived ensemble with alternating speech and song, and a closing number which, exceptionally, is not a Te Deum but a three-part chanson of seven stanzas beginning "Nature humaine en ses suppos." Sometimes in a more traditional play the shepherds will dance and sing, as in the 1501 Mons *Passion,* and in the nativity plays one of them almost always leaves a recorder as one of the humble gifts to the Christ child. But just as often the *bergiers* and *bergières* will merely talk. In the Greban *Passion,* for example, the pastoral scenes are distinguished by the number of dialogued rondeaux which they contain, but no rubric states categorically that the shepherds actually play, or sing, or dance.

Music of a sort can sometimes be found in hell. In the 1509 *Mystère des trois doms,* for example, Proserpine and three devils sing a litany with the refrain "Lucifer, exaudi me."[20] And other passages besides those cited in Reese[21] make clear that Lucifer and his cohorts were called upon to perform. But more often than not scenes in hell required sound effects instead of music. The noises that emanated from the underworld were sometimes made by organ pipes, by *tambours,* or by other musical instruments, and sometimes "fait par engiens," evidently metal pipes, barrels filled with stones, and gunfire.[22]

Instruments, however, had more to do than merely to imitate devilish sounds. Before a play ever began, the ménétriers would have been at work, playing in the processions which often conducted the actors from their homes, or from the church where a preliminary Mass had been sung, to the place where the performances were to be given.

During the play itself, instrumentalists might have been expected to perform several kinds of roles. In the first place, trumpet fanfares not only mark entrances and exits of royal personages but also precede royal decrees and other public announcements. Thus in the 1509 *Mystère des trois doms* the character called "La Trompette" has to read aloud several laws promulgated by his employer, the governor of Vienne. Each time he begins with a threefold fanfare, probably the same kind that would have preceded any proclamation in the fifteenth

20. Paul-Émile Giraud and Ulysse Chevalier, eds., *Le Mystère des trois doms, joué à Romans en MDIX* (Lyons, 1887), p. 377.

21. Pp. 150-51.

22. More examples of sound effects from hell may be found in Bowles, pp. 78-79. The reader should, however, be warned that this article contains misinformation, incorrect bibliographical references, and other inaccuracies, so that serious doubt may be cast on its conclusions.

and sixteenth centuries. The several *siletes de trompettes* in the same play occur when important people come on or leave the stage, and these were undoubtedly also fanfares. By extension, many of the places in other religious plays marked simply "pause" or "silete" may well have involved stereotyped fanfare figures.

"Pause" and "silete" are the words that most frequently indicate the presence of music in the mystères and miracles. Unfortunately, the exact nature of these instrumental interludes is nowhere clearly stated. Fanfares would be appropriate only for some of them. More elaborate music must have been performed on occasion. Since the possibilities of theatrical instrumental music will be more thoroughly discussed in dealing with secular plays, suffice it to say here that such interludes frequently interrupt the action in religious theater. They may indicate that a scene has ended, fulfilling the same function as a curtain. They may accompany some pantomimed stage action, as when Noah's Ark is built near the beginning of the 1501 Mons *Passion*.[23] And they may be used to fill in pauses while the actors move from one part of the stage to another, as happens frequently in the same play. In any case no more specific examples need be given here, since virtually every mystère contains at least one or two.

These few traditional kinds of scenes: celestial, pastoral, demonic, and regal, together with the transitional *pauses*, account for most of the music in the great religious spectacles. Occasionally a musical number will appear outside of these fairly rigidly defined limits. On the third day of the Mons *Passion* for example, Florence, the daughter of Herodias, dances a *morisque* to the sound of pipe and tabor. And on the morning of the same day, Mary Magdalene and her companions sing a chanson. More than once a playwright used secular music to symbolize Mary's profligacy.[24] Pagans sing in a queer invented language in both the 1474 Rouen *Incarnation* and the 1509 Romans *Mystère des trois doms*, among other plays. And Jews are also given gibberish to sing. Music figures as well in diverse places throughout the sacred theatrical repertoire, but never often enough in any one kind of scene to allow generalizations.

The sources are remarkably consistent about what musical forces were necessary to perform a mystère or miracle with suitable pomp and pageantry. The mainstay of any of these municipal undertakings would have been the choir of angels, capable of singing plainsong but with enough soloists for part music. An organist would have been

23. Cohen, *Le Livre de conduite*, p. 23.
24. See Gustave Cohen, *Études d'histoire du théâtre en France* (Paris, 1956), pp. 212, 220–21.

associated with the chorus. A few trumpets and drums, a pipe and tabor, and one or two miscellaneous *haut* wind instruments complete the normal and customary performing ensemble. The Fouquet miniature shows a group composed of these elements, and almost all of the other information which survives about stage practices in the *mystères* corroborates this general arrangement.

For the *Mystère des trois doms* at Romans, for example, four trumpeters were brought from Vaucluse to play for the *monstre* (procession) and also during the performances. Four *tambourin* players were also paid. No other payments to musicians appear in the accounts.[25] The presence of the chapter choir may be inferred from the fact that the chapter was one of the sponsors of the performance, and also from the mention of "chantres" in the play text. That the choir brought along their organist is clear from the rubrics, which specify from time to time a "silete d'orgues," or a "silete d'orgues et de chantres en paradis."

Almost the same arrangements were made for the Mons *Passion* in 1501. Only one trumpet player appears to have been hired, Godeffroy le Roy, who had "sonné la trompette par 8 journées . . . pour assembler chacun jour les jeuweres."[26] The only other musicians mentioned in the expense accounts were the "vicaires et orghanistres de l'Eglise Saint Nicolay en la rue de Havrech et qui avoient esté empeschiés tous les jours dudit Mistère sur lidit Hourt, tant en avoir deschantét et jeuwét des orghes."[27] Two of the stage directions in the play text, however, seem to imply that more instruments were used. Early in the play, when Noah leaves the Ark, he prays; after his prayer "on chante en Paradis ung silete, ou on jue des menestreux ou de quelques instrument, ou poze d'orgues."[28] The rubric could suggest that a large musical ensemble allowed for many alternative possibilities in arranging musical interludes. Yet the direction is quite vague, and leaves great latitude to the performers. The fact that Herodias's daughter dances the morisque to the sound of a tambourin, or pipe and tabor, has already been mentioned. Possibly Godeffroy le Roy could play more than one instrument. Although trumpet players generally are listed apart from ménétriers, at least some of them could perform on other instruments as well. In 1554 in Béthune, for example, Jehan Danezin was paid for having "plusieurs fois sonné la trompette et fiffre,"[29] almost the same combina-

25. Printed in the modern edition by Giraud and Chevalier.
26. Cohen, *Le Livre de conduite*, pp. lxviii, 541.
27. Ibid., pp. xcviii, 575.
28. Ibid., p. 29.
29. Alexandre de la Fons, baron de Mélicocq, "Drame du XVIᵉ siècle," *Annales archéologiques*, VIII (1848), 271.

tion that would have been required here. All the other rubrics designating music in the Mons manuscript could easily have been executed by the forces known to be there, a chorus, an organ, and one trumpet.

Notices from less well documented performances tell the same story. When Montferrand performed the *Mystère de la Passion* in 1477,[30] the neighboring town of Riom sent over its trumpeters and an organist, and Clermont furnished ménétriers to reinforce the local trumpeters and tambourin players. Although neither the exact size of the musical ensemble nor a precise listing of the kinds of instruments played by the ménétriers survives, one of the items on the expense account[31] may record the amount of money spent for food for all of the musicians on the third Sunday of the performance. Present on that day were "messire Symon Gendre, prebstre organiste, Jehan le Musnier, aussi organiste, Guillaume le Barbier, barabarat taborin, Jean Alasseur, tronpete, Jehan Roselet, Jehan trompete, Arnault de la Voloye, Loys de Gerzat, Jehan Sabatier, tronpete, Jacques Cipierre, plates tronpetes de Riom, Pierre le Barbier, Loys Nodal, Guillaume et Anne Meniers de Montferrand." If all of these people were musicians, if all of the trumpeters are listed together, and unless some of the performers were absent that day, this would make a total performing ensemble of two organists, seven trumpeters, and four unspecified ménétriers, to which should be added two more "tronpetes de la tour" who are mentioned in an additional listing of expenses. Although this group is slightly larger than the ones for either Mons or Romans, its composition shows the same kind of standardization noted before.

An organ was used in the *Jeu St. Georges* presented at the court of René II, Duke of Lorraine, in 1487; he paid Pellegrin, an organ maker, for his services. Louis Paris mentions a performance by the town of Rheims of the Jean Michel version of Greban's *Passion* in 1490, in which the choirboys took part;[32] divine services had to be rearranged to permit them to sing. The only musicians paid by the town council of Montbéliard in 1488 for a *Jeux de Mgr. Saint Maintbeuf* were tambourin players, "la tronpette de Mgr. de Nuefchaistel," and "Messire Lorans organiste." When Montbéliard gave the *Jeu de Monseigneur Sainct Sebastien* in 1503, the community again sent away for musicians; there were tambourin players from Porrentruy, Souchan, and Granvilliers, and trumpeters from Neufchâtel and Altkirch. Besançon did the same in

30. See André Bossuat, "Une représentation du Mystère de la Passion à Montferrand en 1477," *Bibliothèque d'humanisme et renaissance*, V (1943), 327–45.

31. Ibid., pp. 338–39.

32. *Le Théâtre à Reims depuis les Romains jusqu'à nos jours* (Rheims, 1885), pp. 33–38.

1508 for their performance of the same play, and again trumpets and drums are the only instruments mentioned: four trumpeters from Basel, and a tambourineur from Berne. Athis-sur-Orge performed two mystères and a morality in eight days in 1542, and the only payment recorded for music was a sum to the painter Christofle Loyson, and to his servant, who both played *tambourins de Suisse* during the monstre. Only one instrument was necessary for the performances themselves.[33]

The *procès-verbal* concerning the *Passion* played at Vienne in 1510 mentions musicians in the following terms: "touchant les joueurs, ils firent si très bien et sans fault la plus belle silence à force trompectes en nombre de neufz et instrumens de toutes sortes orgues chanteries."[34] But if this notice seems to contradict all of the preceding ones, the reason may be only that the critic is using literary hyperbole in describing this ensemble of "instrumens de toutes sortes," a phrase which is by no means uncommon in a variety of fifteenth- and sixteenth-century documents. Local pride may have overcome his strict regard for the facts, and he has left for posterity the most extravagant report possible of this provincial spectacle. Perhaps he names specifically only trumpets and organs because no other instruments actually played. The only archival notice that is more explicit in linking a greater variety of instruments with productions of mystères and miracles is the description of the procession to the 1496 production of the *Mystère de Saint Martin* at Seurre in Burgundy.[35] The reporter writes that the actors marched to the sound of "trompetes, clerons, bussines, orgues, harpes, tabourins et aultres bas et haulx instrumens," an improbable combination in any case. This may be another example of exaggerated zeal; or Seurre may have been unusually well equipped musically.

Most of the other documents imply that the group of chorus, organ, trumpets, drum, pipe, and several other *haut* instruments was a usual one for religious plays. This specific combination should probably be considered an abstract concept, capable of variation, and slightly altered to fit the demands of each individual occasion. Expediency, preference, and local custom may have created more divergence from

33. On Lorraine, see Albert Jacquot, *La Musique en Lorraine*, 3d ed. (Paris, 1886), pp. 19–20; on Montbéliard, see A. Tuetey, *Étude sur le droit municipal du XIIIe et du XIVe siècles en Franche-Comté et en particulier à Montbéliard* (Montbéliard, 1864), pp. 284–92; on Besançon, see Ulysse Robert, *Les Origines du théâtre à Besançon* (n.p., 1900), p. 68; and on Athis-sur-Orge, see S. W. Deierkauf-Holsboer, "Les Représentations à Athis-sur-Orge en 1542," *Mélanges . . . offerts à Gustave Cohen* (Paris, 1950), pp. 202–3.

34. Giraud and Chevalier, eds., *Mystère de trois doms*, pp. 891–92.

35. Édouard Fournier, ed., *Le Théâtre français avant la renaissance* (Paris, n.d.), pp. 172–74.

this norm than the fragmentary records suggest, but the over-all organization of the musical forces from play to play and from locality to locality would have been roughly the same. *Bas* instruments, for example, would not have appeared very often, because they would not have been appropriate for the grand outdoor stages on which these extravaganzas were performed.

Occasionally, more and different instruments could have participated. Rubrics and other sources sometimes make this clear. The painted canvases at Rheims,[36] for example, which may have been used as backdrops for a performance of the *Mystère de la vengeance de Jhesus-Christ* around 1530, include one scene with a slightly raised stage for musicians. They are playing rebec, slide trumpet, pipe and tabor, and one other unspecified wind instrument, to accompany a round dance, probably a *branle*, going on in the middle of the canvas. And Pirro cites several plays which specify both haut and bas instruments.[37]

These unusually diverse groups of instruments need never have been mentioned in the expense accounts. If one of the actors playing a shepherd could perform on the recorder, he would not have been paid more money for his talent and no report would indicate this added refinement. If Mary Magdalene were an accomplished amateur lutenist, she might well have accompanied herself while singing a chanson. An exceptional community might have had at its disposal an extraordinarily large number of musicians, or an unusual assortment of instruments. A town council, or a single playwright or director, could have been extremely interested in the effects possible with a variety of musical alternatives. But in the absence of clear direct proof of such practices, and in the presence of such definite indications of a customary usage, any strong statement that a wide variety of musical instruments participated often in the religious theater must remain pure speculation.

The chorus of angels, the most important part of the musical ensemble and the one almost invariably present in the religious plays, would have been assembled from the local church choir led by the *maître de chapelle*, and would have been accompanied by the church organist. In spite of the fact that a number of the archival notices cited above omit mention of payments to singers altogether, the normal arrangement seems fairly certain, since the rubrics specify "chantres" and since the local church was often one of the sponsors of a production.

---

36. Reproduced in Decugis and Reymond, *Le Décor*, pp. 30–31. One of them is also reproduced in Geneviève Thibault, "Le Concert instrumental dans l'art flamand au XVᵉ et au début du XVIᵉ," *La Renaissance dans les provinces du Nord* (Paris, 1956), facing p. 203.

37. *Histoire de la musique*, pp. 128–29.

Only occasionally, however, do notices clearly state that the choirboys participated. Thus in 1476, when the Confrérie de Saint-Romain in Rouen wanted to give a performance of a mystère within the church itself, very special permission had to be granted. In this case, the chapter was more than willing to comply. They not only helped with expenses, lent the necessary things for the construction of the platforms, and allowed their chaplains and "deux enfants de choeur . . . chargés du rôle d'anges" to perform, but they even changed Office hours and stopped the church bells in order not to disturb the audience.[38] Because the churches often helped to subsidize the productions, salaries would have been paid to the singers only exceptionally, at Valenciennes, for example, in 1547, when the choirboys, "les petits enfants lesquels estoient angelz et ne avoient point de parchon," each got a small token sum.[39] Provincial archives reveal that choirboys were in fact in the habit of singing for various local events outside of regular liturgical services. Cardevacque includes a list of four or five annual events of importance to the town,[40] aside from extraordinary functions such as royal entries, in which the choir participated.

At least one volume survives which contains mystères written expressly for children, and presumably for choirboys. Among the noëls of 1512 by François Briand, "maistre des escolles de Sainct Benoist" in Le Mans, are "quatre histoires par personnaiges sur quatre évangilles de l'advent a jouer par les petis enfans les quatre dimenches dudict advent." Music figures in each of these four short plays in the form of noëls, some of which are notated in two parts. Perhaps the Mystère de la nativité by Barthélemy Aneau, printed in 1539, was also meant to be performed by choirboys, for it consists almost entirely of sung portions. Like the Briand, it is included in a volume of noëls.[41]

The fact that church choirs almost always sang in mystères and miracles can be indirectly shown by citing the number of various musicians who, in their capacities as maîtres de chapelle, can be connected with the religious theater. In fact, the man who was perhaps the most famous playwright of the period, Arnoul Greban, was also a

38. E. Gosselin, Recherches sur les origines et l'histoire du théâtre à Rouen avant Pierre Corneille (Rouen, 1868), pp. 23–24.

39. Maurice Hénault, Représentation d'un Mystère de la Passion à Valenciennes au XVIᵉ siècle (Valenciennes, 1890), p. 19.

40. Adolphe de Cardevacque, La Musique à Arras depuis les temps les plus reculés jusqu'à nos jours (Arras, 1885), pp. 31–32.

41. The Briand plays and noëls have been reprinted in Nouelz nouvaulx and Quatre histoires, ed. Chardon. Most of the Aneau mystère is included in Henri Lemeignen, ed., Vieux noëls composés en l'honneur de la naissance de Notre-Seigneur Jésus-Christ (Nantes, 1876), II, 70–81.

choirmaster and organist, serving at Notre-Dame in Paris for a period
of at least five or six years around the middle of the fifteenth century,
exactly the time when he was writing his *Mystère de la Passion*.[42] Jean
Daniel, *dit* Maître Mithou, an organist at Angers during the 1520s and
1530s also wrote plays, some of them apparently mystères. But since the
only ones extant which can even be tentatively ascribed to him are secular, his work will be discussed later. Perhaps the anonymous author of the
1474 Rouen *Incarnation* was also a choirmaster, in view of the many
explicit and detailed musical directions and the breadth of musical
knowledge demonstrated in that play. Aside from these few playwrights, other musicians are named in records as having been responsible
for preparing productions. In 1525, for example, Pierre de Manchicourt,
"maistre de la grand escolle" at Béthune, directed the plays presented
"devant la halle," presumably as a part of his duties. And Jean Mouton
is cited as a play director in Amiens while he was there as maître de
chapelle.[43]

Not all of the musicians who directed plays were famous composers
as well. Jean Gillier, the choirmaster at Romans in 1509, was one of
the entrepreneurs for the *Mystère des trois doms*.[44] And in Mouton's
town of Amiens, in 1499, Jehan Menchen, "maistre des enfans," was
one of seven people who petitioned the municipal government for permission to produce a Passion; it was denied them, since the council decided to sponsor the play itself.[45] Even more precise information is given
by Pansier[46] about the role in a mystère assigned to Jean de Castre,
maître des enfants de choeur at the Église Saint-Symphorien in Avignon
in 1470. Since in the play he had to invoke the devil and give several
anathemas, he swore before a notary that the devil had no claim on his
soul, for he did those things solely because his part demanded them!
Examples of masters of the choirboys participating in municipal theater
could be multiplied, but these few are enough to show clearly that the
heavenly choir came from the local church, and that choirmasters and
organists were familiar with dramatic technique through practical
experience.

42. See Henri Stein, "Arnoul Greban, poète et musicien," *Bibliothèque de
l'École des Chartes*, LXXIX (1918), 142–46.
43. On Manchicourt, see Alexandre de la Fons, baron de Mélicocq, "De l'art
dramatique au moyen âge," *Annales archéologiques*, VIII (1848), 161; on Mouton,
see le baron A. de Calonne, *Histoire de la ville d'Amiens* (Amiens, 1899), I, 348.
44. Giraud and Chevalier, eds., p. xxix.
45. Hyacinthe Dusevel, "Documents relatifs aux mystères et jeux de personnages
représentés à Amiens pendant le XVe siècle," *Archives de Picardie*, I (1841), 218–19.
46. P. Pansier, "Les Débuts du théâtre à Avignon a la fin du XVe siècle," *Annales
d'Avignon et du comtat Venaissin*, VI (1919), 13–14.

The entrepreneurs of mystères and miracles used the church choir to furnish vocal pieces because it was the nearest and most convenient, perhaps the only, established musical group in the community capable of doing the job. Similarly, they may often have employed the town band of ménétriers to supply instrumental music. Very little direct evidence supports this conjecture. Only occasionally do expense accounts make clear who the instrumentalists were. In 1477, for example, at Montferrand, two of them are described as "tronpetes de la tour,"[47] that is, town waits, whose duties included standing guard in a tower or belfry. As with the church choirs, the dearth of notices specifically mentioning these men may be due to the fact that their employer, the town council, partly sponsored such events, and hence they may have been required to play as a regular part of their job.

Lefebvre prints a notice which, although it dates from the very end of the sixteenth century or perhaps later, explains precisely the duties of such a municipal ménétrier:

De toutte ancienneté la ville a eu cincq joueurs d'instruments musicaux qui sont sermentez. Leur fonction est de jouer du hautbois au beffroy tous les samedis de l'année, la veille des festes solennelles, d'aller aux processions solennelles, en manteau rouge avec un plastron d'argent portant l'escusson de la ville, aller de nuit la veille de l'an à la porte de chaque magistrat jouer des hautbois, et en faire de même le jour de la Toussaint à l'hôtel de ville après la création de la Loy.[48]

In other words, they had to play for every civic occasion which required music. Although the notice does not mention theater, the participation of the town waits in a mystère or miracle, or in a royal entry or some other spectacle staged by the community, seems entirely appropriate. On the other hand, some of the payments to ménétriers may have been in recompense for having stayed in the tower to see that no harm came to the town while everyone else was attending the play. Pansier gives an especially large number of notices referring to the guard duties of the waits.[49]

The description of the Lille arrangement is inaccurate in at least one way. Lefebvre shows that the city did not always hire five players, but sometimes only four.[50] In 1423 they are listed as "Abreham Maillet, trompette, Grart Bresot, Lotard Cambier et Lotard Eighelin, menestrels." This distribution of forces may have been a common one, perhaps the

47. In Bossuat, "Une représentation," p. 330.
48. Léon Lefebvre, *Notes pour servir à l'histoire de la musique à Lille* (Lille, 1906), p. 6.
49. "Les Débuts du théâtre," pp. 5–7.
50. *Notes pour servir*, p. 5.

most usual one, in the fifteenth century. The town of Troyes, for example, regularly employed one trumpet player and three ménétriers, "joueurs de hautbois."[51] And a contract of 1501 between the town of Arras and four musicians gives evidence of exactly the same grouping:

Retenue de quatre joueurs de hault-vent y compris le trompette.

Ledit jour Messieurs les Eschevins en nombre par l'advis comme dessus at esté retenus aux gaiges de ladite ville quatre joueurs de hault-vent, assavoir une trompette et trois joueurs de hault-vent, lesquels ont promis et seront tenus de jouer chacun jour au beffroi d'icelle ville au mattin à l'eure de la porte ouvrir et au soir à l'eure de la porte clore et incontinent apprès que le clocque des portes clore et ouvrir aura cessiet le sonnerie . . . lesquels joueurs ont promis et serent tenus de clore et reffermer tous les huis dudit beffroy et de non partir de la ville sans avoir congié de Messieurs.

Et ont promis de venir résider en ceste dite ville au jour Saint Remy prochain venant.[52]

These descriptions all cite the trumpet player apart from his colleagues; perhaps his duties were more exclusively involved with musical signals, fanfares, public announcements, and the like, while the "joueurs de hault-vent" played more elaborate pieces. The three minstrels may normally have used two shawms ("hautbois") and a slide trumpet, the combination mentioned by Tinctoris as a favorite one for dances, and one pictured innumerable times in fifteenth- and sixteenth-century documents. And this instrumentarium possibly became a usual one in the religious plays.

None of these hypotheses can be stated very positively, since documentation is too vague and our present state of knowledge too limited. When an expense account lists musicians, they could as easily be men living in the town but hired by no civic corporation. Many places had no official ménétriers. The unhappy sequel to the contract of 1501 in Arras, for example, is another council ruling dated February 1506, five years later,[53] releasing the minstrels from their duties. "Considerant les grans affaires et charges de la ville," Arras could no longer keep up the luxury of town waits. Even in a city as large as Lille, life was often not easy for a performing musician.[54] In 1491, the ménétriers petitioned the town council for help because they could not make a living. Because of the wars no one was getting married, and the annual town festival, the Fête de l'Épinette, had been suspended indefinitely. In 1578, the town

51. Théophile Boutiot, "Recherches sur le théâtre à Troyes au XVe siècle," *Mémoires de la Société d'Agriculture, des Sciences, Arts et Belles-Lettres du départment de l'Aube,* 2d ser., V (1854), 427–28.
52. Printed in Cardevacque, *La Musique à Arras,* pp. 63–64.
53. Ibid.
54. Lefebvre, *Notes pour servir,* pp. 30–32.

minstrels were taken off the payroll because of economies made necessary by the plague. And in 1600 the musicians were again disbanded, because the belfry from which they usually played had been demolished.

This lack of a municipal instrumental ensemble may partly explain the number of archival notices cited above which mention payments to instrumentalists coming from other towns. Or it may be that civic pride and love of ostentation account for some of them as well. In order to make the spectacle as impressive and as luxurious as possible, a town would have wanted to expand the group of four players to include as many more as would come, or as they could afford. The remark of the Vienne critic that there were nine trumpets for the *Passion* there in 1510 can be better appreciated in this new context. To townspeople used to hearing one lone trumpeter signaling that all was well at the end of the day, nine trumpets sounding all together must have seemed a wonder indeed.

At least one contract exists between musicians and producers which, although it involves neither a municipality nor town waits, explains very well how many such theatrical organizations must have worked. In 1540 in Paris, three private persons, Pierre Veau, François Huette, and Pierre Charpentier, decided to perform "le mistaire et vie de Sainct Christofle" in the Hôtel d'Orléans. In order to further their schemes they made formal agreements with a carpenter and with three musicians: Nicolas de Louvières of the rue Mouffetard and Jean La Volle, both *joueurs de tambourins de Suisse*, and Étienne Boullard, *joueur de fiffre*. The musicians promised

de jouer desd. instrumens de tabourins et fiffres pour les dessusd. oud. jeu et mistaire Sainct Christofle, et aussi par chascun jour de feste et demenche qu'ilz jouront led. mistaire et vie parmy les rues et carrefours de Paris et le jour de la monstre desd. jeux et aussi de batre par l'ung d'eulx des sonnettes, si mestier est, et ce songneusement bien et devement, comme il appartiendra selon le jeu, et tant à l'entrée que à l'issue dudict jeu et jusques à ce qu'il soit fyny, moiennant . . . (x s. vi d.) pour chascune journée d'eulx tous ensemble qu'ilz jouront . . . ; et pour ce faire seront tenus lesd. de Louvieres et ses autres consors de eulx trouver à heure de dix heures du matin pour le plus tard; aussi lesd. Veau & ses consors les seront tenuz nourrir lors et les paier . . . au soir de la journée qu'ilz auront joué . . . ; et seront tenuz eulx trouver à lad. monstre de samedi prochain en huict jours pour faire lad. monstre, et le dimenche ensuivant et les autres jours dud. jeu aussi eulx y trouver sans faulte.[55]

Unless Pierre Veau and his company performed a play which no longer

55. Ernest de Coyecque, *Recueil d'actes notariés relatifs à l'histoire de Paris et de ses environs au XVIe siècle* (Paris, 1915), I, arts. 1513 and 1514.

survives, this notice probably concerns the earlier and shorter of the two extant mystères based on the life of Saint Christopher. The longer of the two, by Claude Chevalet (Grenoble: Anemond Amalberti, 1530), was written especially for the city of Grenoble, takes four days to perform, and requires 120 actors, plus more mansions than could possibly have been squeezed onto the small stage ordered by the three Parisians from their carpenter. Their specifications include only a heaven large enough to accommodate an angel on either side, and a hell. According to the stage directions in the shorter mystère (Paris: veuve Jehan Trepperel and Jehan Jehannot, n.d.), the music was supplied chiefly by three angels, Saint Michael, Gabriel, and Raphael, only two of whom sing at any one time. Productions of this sort which the entrepreneurs had organized solely for their own profit would obviously have been less elaborate than one prepared by a whole community. The number of instrumentalists, two drummers and a fife player, corresponds with the dimensions of the play. And these ménétriers, probably hired from the Guild of Saint Julian, had to perform a number of different tasks. They not only played for the performances—so the contract says, even though no rubrics indicating instrumental music are to be found in the play text—but they also had to advertise them in the streets of Paris each morning of the play's run, march in the monstre, and ring bells at the beginning and end of each day. Theater musicians had to be adaptable.

Even though this 1540 performance deviates in certain respects from most others, it nevertheless may be used to illustrate once more the norm. For here again the standardized musical ensemble reappears, albeit in miniature. The chorus has been reduced to two angels, and the organ omitted. One pipe and two drums replace the full complement of trumpets, drums, pipes, and "joueurs de hault-vent." But the differences are more of degree than of kind, and similarities with all of the other mystères and miracles are recognizable in spite of the variations.[56]

56. [For a companion volume to the book from which this essay was taken, see Howard Mayer Brown, *Theatrical Chansons of the Fifteenth and Early Sixteenth Centuries* (Cambridge, Mass.: Harvard University Press, 1963), which contains music and lyrics for sixty French *chansons* used in the production of plays.]

Laura Hibbard Loomis

6. Secular Dramatics in the Royal Palace, Paris, 1378, 1389, and Chaucer's "Tregetoures"

> For I am siker than ther be sciences   1139
> By whiche men make diverse apparences,
> Swiche as these subtile tregetoures pleye.
> For ofte at feestes have I wel herd seye
> That tregetours, withinne an halle large,
> Have made come in a water and a barge,
> And in the halle rowen up and doun.   1145
> Somtyme hath semed com a grym leoun;
> And somtyme floures sprynge as in a mede;
> Somtyme a vyne, and grapes white and rede;
> Somtyme a castel, al of lym and stoon;
> And whan hem lyked, voyded it anon.   1150
> Thus semed it to every mannes sighte.

These lines from Chaucer's *Franklin's Tale*[1] report what a sometime clerk of Orleans has heard concerning scenic marvels which "subtile tregetoures" had made appear in a large hall. Later on, in ll. 1185–1214, we are told that this same clerk and his sick brother, Aurelius, both now in Orleans and both sitting comfortably for an hour or so in the book-lined study of another Orleans clerk, are shown by him hunters killing deer, falconers with their hawks, knights jousting, dances in which Aurelius himself appears with his lady. These moving pictures are frankly attributed to the "magyk" of this master clerk who, when he wished to end his entertainment, simply clapped his hands and it disappeared. Though to us today it may seem even more "magical" that Chaucer's imagination should thus cosily, by over five centuries, have anticipated motion pictures in the home, even as, in the *House of Fame*,

[Reprinted from *Speculum*, XXXIII (1958), 242–55, by permission of the publisher. Copyright 1958 by the Mediaeval Academy of America.]
1. F. N. Robinson, ed., *The Works of Geoffrey Chaucer*, 2d ed. (Boston: Houghton Mifflin, 1957). For close parallels, among those cited by Robinson, p. 724, l. 1141, to the passage quoted and to ll. 1190–98, see Mandeville's account of wonders seen at the Great Khan's court (ed. Hamelius, EETS O.S. 153 [1919], I, 143, 156). On Chaucer's use of Mandeville, see also Josephine W. Bennett, *The Rediscovery of Sir John Mandeville* (New York, 1954), pp. 224–26; *MLN*, LXVIII (1953), 531–34.

ll. 1070–83, where words turn into images, he seems to anticipate television, there can be no doubt that, like his own contemporaries, the poet did accept magic as part of his world. Despite one strong expression of skepticism in the *Franklin's Tale*, l. 1131, "swiche folye is nat worthe a flye," and perhaps a hint of it in the "Thus *semed* it" of l. 1151, magic does play an important part in the plot, and its various "apparences" have usually been accepted as "magical visions."[2] Chaucer's "tregetours" have always been glossed as jugglers or magicians.[3] But jugglers obviously could never have produced at a feast in a hall such weighty effects as a movable boat and a castle, both made to appear and disappear. Nor, as we shall see from the records which follow, did magicians have anything to do with them either. Similar effects had in actual fact been seen by hundreds of people in the royal palace in Paris in 1378 and 1389. Of the first production there we have, incredible as it may seem, both an official eyewitness account and an official contemporary picture.

Our photographic reproduction of that picture comes, by permission of the Bibliothèque Nationale in Paris, from the almost full-page illumination in one of its treasured manuscripts, Fr. 2813, f. 473v (pl. 2). That splendid volume, made between 1375 and 1379, contains the *Chronique de Charles V*, for which this and many other contemporary illustrations were made. It has been monumentally edited and studied by R. Delachenal.[4] Our picture illustrates that great occasion on Wednesday, 6 January 1378, when the French king sumptuously entertained at dinner

2. J. S. P. Tatlock, "Astrology and Magic in the *Franklin's Tale*," *Kittredge Anniversary Papers* (Boston, 1913), p. 341.

3. W. W. Skeat, ed., *Complete Works of Chaucer*, III (1894), 271, 273, notes to *House of Fame*, Bk. III, ll. 1260, 1277, listed earlier forms of *tregetour*: OF. *tregiteor;* Ital. *traggettatore;* Prov. *trasjitar*, all having to do with the idea of juggling. The Prov. form "would answer to a Low Latin *trans-iectare* . . . to throw across . . . cause to pass. Thus, the original sense of *trejetour* was one who causes rapid changes, by help of some mechanical contrivance." Skeat here followed Thomas Tyrwhitt, *The Canterbury Tales* (London, 1830; reprinted from 1775–78 edition), IV, 268, who, in a long note on *tregetour*, defined the word as meaning ". . . a juggler who, by sleight of hand and machines, produced such illusions . . . as are supposed to be effected by enchantment. . . . That a great deal of machinery was requisite to produce the *apparances*, or illusions, enumerated in the *Franklin's Tale*, is certain." Neither editor produced any evidence for the machines or for their actual use. See below, n. 7. For *Colle Tregetour*, see Robinson's note, *House of Fame*, p. 785, l. 1277.

4. *Les Grandes Chroniques de France, Chroniques des Regnes de Jean II et Charles V*, ed. R. Delachenal, 4 vols. (Paris, 1910–20), II, 232–44; *Histoire de Charles V*, 5 vols. (Paris, 1909–31), V, 95–99. These two works will be referred to respectively as *Chronique* and *Histoire*. The *Histoire*, V, chap. 2, gives a historical-literary estimate of the *Chronique*'s account of the emperor's visit to Paris, which Delachenal (V, 78) felt surpassed even Froissart in reportorial completeness. The account was supervised, if not written, by the chancellor, Pierre d'Orgemont (*Chronique*, IV, 1; *Histoire*, I, xviii; Index, V, 503).

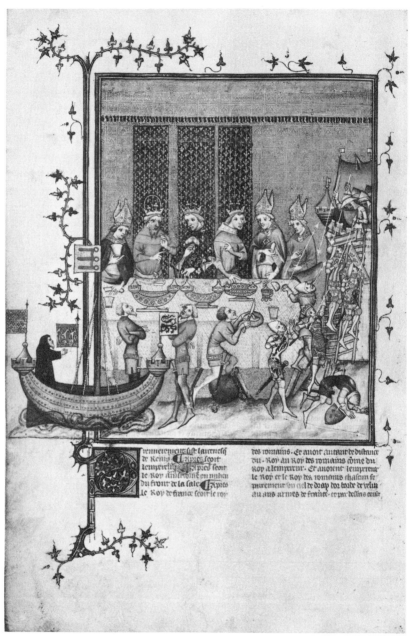

2. The First Crusade as enacted 6 January 1378 in the Royal Palace, Paris. From *Chronique de Charles V*, MS Fr. 2813, f. 473v. Courtesy of the Bibliothèque Nationale, Paris.

his learned, imperial uncle, Emperor Charles IV.[5] The *Chronique* is especially precise and detailed in telling of what happened at that feast in the royal palace, the Palais de la Cité.[6] In commenting on the feast and the dramatic entertainment offered, the *Chronique* (II, 236) even speaks of their representation in this very picture, "ci après pourtraite et ymaginée." Text and picture alike amply confirm the report of Chaucer's Orleans clerk that at a feast in a great hall there had in truth appeared "a water and a barge," also a castle too! The chronicler speaks admiringly not only of the handsome, realistic fashioning of these necessarily large objects, but of how skilfully they were moved about, "tres legierement" (II, 244), by men concealed within. At the end, "les diz entremets furent remenez en leurs places premiers," (II, 242), or, in Chaucer's words, were "voyded." The "tregetoures" who enacted roles in this royal *entremés, mystère mimé sans parolles,* interlude, pantomime, whatever one chooses to call it, who made or who moved its large stage properties about, were certainly not magicians, not jugglers. They were the unknown men, actors, craftsmen, *artisans mécaniques,* who, in effective unison, produced spectacular results.[7] That such an exceptional palace performance—in no wise an idle *mommerie . . . pour resjoir les dames*—would be long talked of, that the fame of it would go abroad, is certain. In informal talk, after 26 January 1378, courtly French negotiators might have spoken of it to the English negotiators sent to arrange a marriage between Richard II and the little French princess who died so un-

5. On the learning and piety of Emperor Charles IV see S. H. Thomson, *Speculum,* XXV (1950), 1–20: *Cambridge Mediaeval History* (Cambridge, England, 1932), VII, chap. VI (by K. Krofta).

6. Some writers on the Louvre wrongly state that the great feast was given there. Cf. L. Hautecoeur, *Histoire du Louvre, 1200–1928* (Paris, 1928), p. 11; A. Blum, *Le Louvre du palais au Musée* (Paris, 1946), p. 28. The official *Chronique* (II, 222) tells of the emperor's arrival at the Palais, and of his departure from it (II, 244), on the morning after the great feast, to go on a visit to the Louvre. Delachenal (*Histoire,* II, 269) discusses the king's use of the Palais de la Cité for great occasions. Cf. *Histoire,* V, Index, "Louvre" and "Palais." Accounts of the Palais dating from 1323, 1400, and 1440, may be found in Le Roux de Lincy, *Paris et ses historiens aux XIVe et XVe siècles* (Paris, 1867), Index, "Palais"; B. Sauvan and J. Schmidt, *Histoire du Palais de Justice, de la Conciergerie et de la Sainte Chapelle* (Paris, 1825), pp. 19–24. The Palais was given over to the exclusive use of Parlement in 1431. Largely destroyed by fires in the seventeenth and eighteenth centuries, it was rebuilt as the Palais de Justice. Cf. H. Haynie, *Paris, Past and Present* (New York, 1902), pp. 47–52.

7. For many instances of the skill of medieval mechanics in producing animated automata and other magic-seeming contrivances see Merriam Sherwood, "Magic and Mechanics in Medieval Fiction," *Studies in Philology,* XLIV (1947), 567–92, and Gerard Brett, "The Automata in the Byzantine 'Throne of Solomon,'" *Speculum,* XXIX (1954), 477–87. The castle of Hesdin in Artois was, in the fourteenth century, full of "engiens d'esbattement" (Sherwood, p. 587). See below, n. 23.

expectedly on 23 February. Chaucer, though unnamed, may have been among them, as he certainly had been in 1377, but records show that his lively, Gascon-born friend, Sir Guichard d'Angle, was commissioned on 16 January and went abroad with the other English negotiators.[8] Or again, at any time after December 1381, when Anne of Bohemia, the emperor's daughter, came to England to become its queen, some courtly Bohemian in her service, might, from his own memory of the emperor's visit to Paris, have recalled for the English poet, that night of splendor and of spectacle. But rumor's ways of conveying information are as innumerable as they are unpredictable.

Before taking up the account itself in MS fr. 2813, something of its curious history must be noted. Though the *Chronique* was printed from other manuscripts by Paulin Paris in 1838,[9] his two brief footnotes calling attention to the illumination and to the dramatic entertainment both pictured and described in the royal manuscript, went almost unnoticed. As an art treasure, MS fr. 2813 has long received from art critics due recognition as a good example of typically Parisian, late fourteenth-century style; special comment on f. 473v has not been lacking.[10] Historians have, of course, long valued the *Chronique de Charles V* as an outstanding historical document. In 1952 the *Shorter Cambridge Medieval History* (II, fig. 181) even reproduced f. 473v for its documentary value in picturing the meeting of two great rulers. Delachenal, after editing the text, made in his *Histoire* (V, 92–98) a careful study of the events of 6 January 1378, but naturally had no interest in the dramatic performance as such. Surprisingly, historians of medieval French drama[11]

8. For documents touching on the controversial issue as to whether Chaucer was in France in the early months of 1378, see Haldeen Braddy, *Review of English Studies*, XIV (1938), 3–5; *Three Chaucer Studies*, Part II, *"Parlement of Fowles* and Its Relation to Contemporary Events"* (New York, 1932), pp. 18–26. Cf. *Life Records of Chaucer*, Chaucer Society, 1900, pp. 203–4. Cf. Robinson, p. xxii; M. Chute, *Geoffrey Chaucer of England* (New York, 1946), pp. 118–24.

9. *Les Grandes Chroniques de France*, ed. Paulin Paris (Paris, 1838), VI, 384, n. 1; p. 386, n. 1: "Voilà bien le premier sens de ce mot (*entremés*), divertissement donné pendant l'intervalle des services. Nous allons voir une mise-en-scène du XIVe siècle, telle qu'on la chercherait ailleurs, car le seul MS de Charles V contient ce qui suit." For a more accurate account of the MSS, see Delachenal, *Chronique*, II, 238, n. 3.

10. A. Michel, *Histoire de l'Art* (Paris, 1907), III, 131 f.; C. Couderc, *Album de portraits d'après les collections du département des manuscrits* (Paris, 1910), p. xi; Delachenal, *Chronique*, IV (*Miniatures du MS de Charles V*), 1–12, 35–36, pl. XLI: "Le grand entremets." Bibliothèque Nationale, *Manuscrits à peintures du XIIIe au XVIe siècle* (Paris, 1955), p. 60, No. 123. See also n. 31, below (Martin).

11. Émile Roy, *Études sur le théâtre français du XIVe et du XVe siècle: La Comédie sans titre* (Paris, 1902), pp. cxxxii–cxxxvi, spoke briefly of the royal dramatic spectacles of 1378 and 1389; so, likewise, for the 1378 spectacle, did Gustave

have done little more than mention occasionally the fact that a dramatic spectacle was given on this occasion. Misled, perhaps, by the omission or great abbreviation of the account in some manuscripts of the *Chronique*, or by the very short notice of the evening's entertainment in Christine de Pisan's book about Charles V,[12] they have failed to realize that the royal manuscript gives a meticulously detailed, eyewitness account. Though sometimes noting the subject matter, they have not, to the present writer's knowledge, commented on its exceptional nature in 1378. For these reasons the text of this official account with its details about stagecraft in the palace and this official illustration are presented together here. They are of vital interest for their own sake and also for their possible relation to a later theatrical enterprise in the same place. But it was, apparently, in 1378 that in France a first memorable effort was made, and this under royal auspices, to stage a notable *event* in human history.

After a careful account of how in the morning the king and the emperor had devoutly visited the Sainte Chapelle, the *Chronique* (II, 235–56) tells how they and their retinue proceeded "par la Grant Sale du Palais, jusques au hault de la table de marbre," how they sat at that table, King Charles with the emperor at his right, the archbishop of Rheims at the emperor's right, at the king's left, the son of the emperor, Wencelas of Luxembourg, King of the Romans (since his election in 1376), and at his left three bishops, of Brusseberc (Braunsberg), of Paris, and of Beauvais; the illumination shows but two. Behind the three royal figures were resplendent hangings. On five raised platforms were five large tables for the noblest guests, and these were protected by barriers from the throng of more than eight hundred knights who likewise, in the great hall, shared in the banquet of three elaborate courses, each of ten dishes. Before this great audience the *entremés* was given, as the official chronicler modestly reported, "mieulx et plus proprement . . . que en escript ne se puet mectre."

Cohen, *Histoire de la mise en scène dans le théatre religieux français du moyen âge* (Paris, 1951), p. 64 (reprinted from 1906, 1921). He called attention (n. 2) to the probable influence of the *mystères mimés* on the *mystères parlés*, a subject still awaiting full investigation.

12. Christine de Pisan, *Le Livre des fais et bonnes moeurs du sage roy, Charles V*, ed. S. Solente (Paris, 1936–40), II, 112–14. According to this edition (II, xxxix) Christine wrote in 1404 and used for her source for the emperor's visit Vat. lat. 4791. She thought the entertainment of 6 January "pertinent pur exemples donner à telx princes," but gave a brief confused account of two "entremez . . . la cité grande et belle . . . et puis la nef où Goudeffroy de Billon estoit."

CHRONIQUE DE CHARLES V
(ed. Delachenal, II, 238–42)

L'ystoire et l'ordenance fu comment Godefroy de Buillon conquist la sainte cité de Jherusalem. Et fist le Roy faire à propos ceste hystoire, que il li sembloit que devant plus grans en la Chrestienté ne povoit on ramentevoir, ne donner exemple, de plus notable fait, ne à gens qui mieulx peussent, deussent et fussent tenus tele chose faire et entreprendre, ou service de Dieu. Et, pour mieulx figurer la besoigne et plus plainement la cognoistre, fu fait ce qui s'ensuit. Ou bout de la sale du Palais, qui estoit entreclos telement que on n'en povoit riens veoir par dehors, avoit une nef bien façonnée, à forme d'une nave de mer garnie de voille et de mast, chastel devant et derriere, et de tous autres abillemens et ordenances, qui appartiennent à nef pour aler sur mer, et estoit si joliement painte et abilliée, et tres richement et plaisanment. Et dedenz estoit garnie de genz par semblance armez bien joliement, et estoient leurs cotes d'armes, leurs escuz et banieres des armes de Jherusalem, que Godefroy de Buillon portoit; et jusques à douze estoient, come dit est, armez des armes des notables chevetaines, qui furent à la dite conqueste de Jherusalem, avecques le dit Godefroy. Et estoit au devant, sur de bout de la dite nef, Pierre l'Ermite, en l'ordenance et maniere et au plus près qu'il se povoit faire, selon ce que l'ystoire raconte. Et fu la dite nef mise hors à gens qui couvertement estoient dedenz, et fu menée tres legieremet par le costé senestre du dit Palais, et si legierement tournée, que il sembloit que ce fust une nef flotant sur l'eaue, et ainsi fu amenée jusques au grant dayz, ou dit costé de l'autre part, qui fu le destre costé de la dite sale. Et après ce, fu mis, hors de la place d'encosté où la dite nef estoit partie, un entremés fait à la façon et semblance de la cité de Jherusalem, et y estoit le temple bien contrefait selon l'espace, et là avoit une tour haulte, assise delez le temple, ainsi comme les Sarrazins ont de coustume, où ilz crient leur loy. Là avoit un vestu en habit de Sarrazin tres proprement, et qui, en langue arrabique, crioit la loy, en la maniere que font les Sarrazins. Et estoit la dite tour si haulte que celui qui estoit dessus joignoit bien près des trefs de la dite salè. Et le bas, tout entour de la dite cité, où il avoit forme de creneaux et de murs et de tours, estoit (p. 242) garny de Sarrazins, armez à leur maniere, et banieres et panons, et ordenez à combatre pour deffendre la cité. Ainsi fu amené à force de gens, qui estoient dedenz si couvers que on ne les povoit veoir, jusques devant le dit grant dayz, à la destre partie. Et lors se mistrent les deux entremés l'un contre l'autre et descendirent ceuls de la nef, et par belle et bonne ordenance vindrent donner assault à la cité et longuement l'assaillirent, et y ot bon esbatement de ceuls qui montoient à l'assault à eschielles, qui en estoient ravalez et abatuz à terre. Et finablement monterent dessus ceuls de la nef et conquistent la dite cité, et getoient hors ceuls qui estoient en habit de Sarrazins, en mectant sus les banieres de Godefroy et des autres. Et mieulx et plus proprement fu fait et veu que en escript ne se puet mectre. Et, quant l'esbatement fu parfait, les diz entremés furent remenez tous entiers en leurs places premieres.

Après ce, fu le disner finé. . . .

In this detailed record of the actual performance, as also in its pictorial representation, there are some most unexpected elements. Who would have supposed that in 1378 the instinct for realism would have gone so far as to represent a Saracen in the act of calling *in Arabic* other Saracens to prayer? Who would have thought that the heroic exploit of conquering Jerusalem in 1099 would be shown with enjoyable moments of comic relief, as when knights fell sprawling from their ladders? The illumination shows a careful use of costume and accessories to differentiate the personages of the *entremés*. The Saracens have dark faces and a turban-like twist of cloth around their helmets. The arms of the Crusaders are anachronistic, but Christian heraldry does significantly differentiate the Crusaders from their foes. From the boat float the banners bearing the arms of Jerusalem (stern), of Auvergne (masthead), of England (center spearhead), of Flanders (prow), and these arms appear again on the Crusaders attacking Jerusalem.[13] The text speaks of twelve men in the boat besides Peter the Hermit, and the unseen men who, from within, moved it about. In representing only the solitary figure of Peter the Hermit in the boat, as well as in showing only two (instead of three) bishops at the right end of the royal table and only one tower to represent Jerusalem, the artist was practicing a wise artistic economy that left his picture clearer and more forceful. He was, even so, attempting a far more complicated composition than was common at the time, and he was uncommonly realistic in his presentation of the royal hangings, the *table d'honneur*, the boat, tower, and ladders. There is even some attempt at portraiture of the king and the emperor.

The importance of this *entremés* on the First Crusade, its subject matter ostensibly chosen by King Charles himself, has not been recognized. To be sure, the memorable subject was known through chronicles and such poems of the *Cycle de la Croisade*[14] as the *Chanson d'Antioche*, the *Chanson de Jérusalem* and others. In the royal library of the Louvre the catalogue of 1373 (G) listed no fewer than thirteeen manuscripts with the name of Godfrey de Bouillon appearing in the title of each one; all of these were in prose. One very large volume (No. 1025; G, 32), described as "tres bien historié," may conceivably have been used to provide pictorial suggestions for the royal *entremés*.

There is good reason to suppose that King Charles, between 1373 and

---

13. Delachenal, *Chronique*, IV, 36 n. 4, thus identified the four ship banners. His earlier identification (II, 240, n. 4) of the center banner as bearing arms of Normandy, he here changed to those of England. Cf. Fox-Davies, *Art of Heraldry* (London, 1904), p. 121, quoted Glovers' Roll, about 1250, "le Roy d'angleterre porte Geules trois lupards d'or," the heraldic leopard being a certain position of lion. See below, the *Pas Saladin*.

14. R. Bossuat, *Manuel bibliographique de la littérature française du moyen âge* (Melun, 1951), pp. 84–88, *Supplément* (1955), p. 34; E. Roy, "Les Poèmes français relatifs à la première croisade," *Romania*, LV (1929), 411–68. For *Godfrey de Bouillon* text in the royal library, see L. Delisle, *Recherches sur la librairie de Charles V* (Paris, 1907), pp. 207 f. and Index.

1378, was led from reluctance to consider a new Crusade to some sympathy with the idea of following the great example of Godfrey of Bouillon. Constantly at the king's side, as his close personal friend and one of his official counsellors, was that notable French diplomat, traveler, and religious enthusiast, Philippe de Mézières,[15] of whose special interest in drama more will be said. From Mézières's youthful days as an ardent Crusader, from his pilgrimage to the Holy Land, from 1359–69, when he served as chancellor to the king of Cyprus, from his return to Paris in 1373 until his death there in 1405, he seems never to have deviated from the supreme purpose of his life, the liberation of the Holy Land.[16] In 1367–68 he wrote the first *Regula militaris Passionis Jhesu Christi*, the new order of chivalry by which he hoped to aid in that ultimate liberation; forty years later he was still at work on its later revision. The Louvre library of Charles V contained Mézières's own *lamentation de Jérusalem sur la neglience des chrétiens*. But it must have been by talk, rather than by his writings, most of them of later date, that Mézières brought Charles V somewhat to share in his own great aim. The second sentence quoted above from the *Chronique* attributes definite intention to the king.

There was widespread interest in the fourteenth century in the idea of a new crusade. In 1365 a brief success was achieved in the temporary capture of Alexandria, but the movement ended in the Crusaders' dreadful defeat at Nicopolis in 1396. Among all who had worked for the Crusade, Philippe de Mézières has been called "the greatest of all the propagandists."[17] When his king was to entertain the emperor in 1378 this courtier-diplomat,[18] already experienced in dramatic representation, was just the man to perceive the advantage of giving the good "exemple"

15. A fundamental study is N. Jorga's *Philippe de Mézières (1327–1405) et la croisade au XIVᵉ siècle* (Paris, 1896). For more recent studies of his literary, especially of his dramatic work, see below, nn. 16, 19, 37.

16. Dora M. Bell, *Étude sur* Le Songe du Vieil Pelerin *de Philippe de Mézières* (Geneva, 1955), pp. 142, 181. In her valuable study of this still unpublished allegory, she thus summarizes (p. 142) the advice it gives to young Charles VI: "au lieu de lire les histoires du roi Arthur . . . il vaudrait mieux s'inspirer de l'exemple de Godfroy de Bouillon et s'aguiser l'esprit en écoutant les conseils d'Ardant Désir qui prêchait la paix entre les princes chrétiens en faveur d'une croisade générale pour la reconquête de la Terre Sainte."

17. A. S. Atiya, *The Crusade of Nicopolis* (London, 1934), pp. 26, 124. The first chapter surveys crusading efforts in the fourteenth century, a subject greatly expanded in his *Crusade in the Later Middle Ages* (London, 1938); cf. Index, for Philippe de Mézières. For the latter's own exhortations to a crusade see Jorga, pp. 342, 347, 352, 482, 489, 492.

18. Jorga, p. 428, for presence of Mézières in Paris in 1377–78. In *Le Songe du Vieil Pèlerin* he referred to the feast given by Charles V for the emperor in 1378 (Bell, p. 158).

of the First Crusade before two great rulers; he was also just the man to see to it that it had handsome settings and enough "esbatement" to please such a courtly audience. Such an excursion into secular history, divorced from all religious legend, was a bold innovation, but its subject was of supreme concern to the one man at the French court who had already had the extraordinary experience of presenting in Venice (about 1370) a celebration "cum representatione," and then in Avignon, on 21 November 1372, a liturgical play staged with great splendor. For this we have Mézières's own text and stage directions.[19] It would be strange if, a few years later, his practical experience were not used for the successful production of this palace *entremés*, from which inspiration for a new Crusade might come, his own most passionate hope. The single performance, given before a king, an emperor and his son, before their great vassals, had an audience of European significance and prestige.

Secular elements had, of course, long since invaded French religious drama,[20] comic themes and roles were developing separately into farces, impersonation of legendary or vaguely historical personages in processions and fetes had long been known. "Chivalric and Dramatic Imitations of Arthurian Romance"[21] were familiar in the thirteenth century; by 1330 even the burghers of Tournai had a Round Table society and were inviting other towns to attend jousts imitative of Arthur's. But these semidramatic imitations of Arthurian romance were revels making no distinction between actors and audience, and they did not reach the status of drama much before 1400. Where, indeed, in records of French dramatic performances before 1378 can we find any use of secular history to compare with the royal *entremés* of that year? For it every device of drama except dialogue was used, but it had at least one speaking part. It was enacted in a restricted area where large stage properties were moved about by men who must have had considerable training to ac-

19. The liturgical play concerned the presentation of the Blessed Virgin Mary in the temple. It was discovered by Karl Young (*PMLA*, XXVI [1911], 181–250). See K. Young, *The Drama of the Medieval Church* (Oxford, 1933), II, 225–45, for complete text of play and stage directions; Hardin Craig, *English Religious Drama of the Middle Ages* (Oxford, 1955), pp. 78–79; Grace Frank, *Medieval French Drama* (Oxford, 1954), pp. 64–65, 70–73, 157, and Index for Mézières.

20. For a recent, compact, and authoritative survey of religious and secular elements in early French drama, see Mrs. Frank's book, especially chaps. X ("Beginnings of the Miracle Play"), XII ("Les Miracles de Notre Dame"), XVI ("The Fifteenth Century, Survivals, Staging"), XIX ("Serious Non-Religious Plays: The Beginnings of Comedy"), Bibliography, pp. 272–88. See below, nn. 32–38.

21. R. S. Loomis in *Medieval Studies in Memory of A. Kingsley Porter* (Cambridge, Mass.), pp. 79–97. For a secular play, Arthurian only in the hero's name, and dating from the late fourteenth century, see R. Guiette, "De *Lanseloet van Denemerken* et des *Abele Spelen*," in *Mélanges d'histoire du théâtre du moyen âge . . . offerts à Gustave Cohen* (Paris, 1950), pp. 229–39.

complish the smoothness of motion so praised in the *Chronique*. Historic personages were distinguished by costume and gesture, and the mimetic, continuing action in which they appeared had a distinct beginning and end. The performance, given as interludes were, till a much later time than this, between the courses of a banquet,[22] was for the entertainment of an audience, whatever its moral and inspirational meaning too. Splendidly staged, for a splendid occasion, it would seem to have been the first time in France that a historical *event*, unrelated to biblical or saintly legend, was used for dramatic representation, and this under royal auspices. Can it have been forgotten when, eleven years later, for another great occasion, in the same royal palace, another subject was chosen, again from human history, from nonreligious story, a subject that likewise required a ship and a towered "cité"?

For this *entremés* of 1389 we have again what seems to be an eyewitness account. In Froissart's particularly vivid description of the entry into Paris in that year of the queen, Isabelle of Bavaria, he remarked with satisfaction that he was present when she passed along the street of St-Denis and saw the staged representation of the *Pas Saladin*, of which more presently. That he was also present the next day, Monday, 21 June, when Charles VI gave a great dinner in the Palais de la Cité, is probable, for Froissart's details, as will be seen from the passage quoted below, were amazingly precise. They tell us how the great marble table was extended, of those who sat there, of the barriers erected to control the host of guests, more than five hundred ladies, and great numbers of servitors, ushers, and minstrels. The account is reminiscent of that given for the great dinner of 1378, an occasion strangely unmentioned by Froissart. For present purposes the outstanding part of his narrative comes when he says he will not record the many notable dishes that were served at the dinner of 1389, but instead will speak of the "entremets; qui y furent, qui furent si bien ordonnes que on ne povoit mieulx."

CHRONIQUES DE FROISSART
(ed. Kervyn de Lettenhove, XIV [1872], 15)

Au milieu du palais avoit ung chastelet ouvré et charpenté en quarrure de quarante pies de hault et de vingt piés de long et de vingt piés de large et, avoit quatre tours sur les quatre quartiers, et une tour plus haulte assés ou milieu du chastel, et estoit figuré le chastel pour la cité de Troye la Grant, et la tour du mylieu pour le palais de Ylion, et là estoient en pennons les armes des Troiens, telles que du roy Priant, du preu Hector son fils et de ses enffans, et aussi des roys et des princes qui furent enclos dedens Troye avoec euls. Et aloit ce chastel sur quatre roes qui tournoient par dedens moult

22. L. Wright, "Notes on *Fulgens and Lucrece*, New Light on the Interlude," *MLN*, XLI (1926), 97–100. This English interlude (about 1500) reveals the continued traditional method of presentation.

soubtillement, et vindrent ce chastel requerre et assaillir autres gens d'un lés qui estoient en ung pavillon lequel pareillement aloit sur roes couvertement et soubtillement; car on ne veoit riens du mouvement, et là estoient les armoieries des roys de Grèce et d'ailleurs, qui mirent jadis le siége devant Troye. Ancoires y avoit, sicomme en leur ayde, une nef trés-proprement faitte où bien povoient (estre) cent hommes d'armes, et tout par l'art et engin des roes se mouvoient ces trois choses, le chastel, la nef et le pavillon. Et eut de ceulx de la nef et du pavillon grant assault d'un lés a ceulx du chastel, et de ceulx du chastel aux dessusdis grant deffense. Mais l'esbatement ne peult longuement durer pour la cause de la grant presse de gens. . . .

Froissart goes on to tell how this performance was brought, by royal command, to an abrupt end; a large table collapsed and, from the consequent crowding and the heat, ladies began to faint. Short as is the account, however, it leaves no doubt that the Fall of Troy was to have been set forth, and that for it large stage properties had been constructed— or reconstructed. The very measurements are given for the Troy set, and in view of the statement in 1378 that a man in the high tower of Jerusalem nearly touched the ceiling of the palace hall, it is interesting to know that the central Troy tower was higher than the four lesser towers around it. Both "cities" were strongly built, for both had to endure assault. From the point of view of theatrical mechanics it is important to note Froissart's specific statement that it was "par l'art et engin des roes," by the device of hidden wheels, that in 1389 the stage city, ship, and *pavillon* were moved about. Though Froissart's emphasis on wheels seems to imply something new, it is probable that they had also been used in the 1378 production, where a boat with thirteen men visibly in it, and a castle with its defenders, had to be moved about.[23] The Troy ship must have been large indeed to justify Froissart's guess that it might hold "cent hommes d'armes;" like the Crusaders' ship, it must have been handsomely made and painted. Perhaps, in the recesses of the "Grand Palais" of Saint Louis, grandly enlarged in 1313 by Philippe le Bel, there was storage room where such important, costly stage properties could be kept indefinitely. But whether the Troy properties were the same or newly built, the likeness between the two sets is unmistakable. Medieval heraldic conventions were observed for ancient Troy as for the

---

23. A movable castle was no new thing: "ung grant chasteau . . . allant par engien moult richement," was recorded in Valenciennes, 1330. Cf. R. Withington, *English Pageantry* (Cambridge, Mass., 1918), pp. 85–94. Roy, *Théatre français*, p. cxxxii, noted Froissart's reference to wheels. Roy also noted, from an account of 14 January 1408, the still unpaid expenses of a painter, Colart de Laon, incurred for royal celebrations, including that of 1389. In regard to stage ships in the later fourteenth century, D. Penn, *The Staging of the "Miracles de Nostre Dame par personnages"* (New York, 1933), marked (p. 39) the use of ships in five of these plays, and (p. 19) the mimic sea, a masonry basin built for them in the stage floor. Her account (p. 39) of the dramatic performances of 1378 and 1389 is confused.

Jerusalem of 1099, and for each set the glow of heraldic banners must have added splendor to the scene. Both productions were given in the course of a royal banquet, and Froissart's use of the same terms, *entremés* for a performance between courses, and *esbatement* for entertainment, is to be noted. Despite the fiasco in which, through no fault of its own, the Troy *entremés* ended, the rumor of its splendid "apparences" may well have gone abroad to whet anew men's wonder that a ship and a castle could thus suddenly appear in a great hall. In that case the rumor might have reached Chaucer at a time when he was fully embarked on his *Canterbury Tales* and when, at last, there was a three-year truce (1389–92) between England and France.

Without further discussion of these two indoor performances, we may turn to Froissart's account of the outdoor performance of the *Pas Saladin*. To this almost every commentator on the emerging secular drama of France has referred, so we need only note that it was enacted on a raised stage (*l'eschafault*) with a castle upon it, that the warriors bore heraldic arms, that the Christians assaulted the Saracens with great vigor. Speaking parts were given to King Richard of England, who asked and received permission from the French king to make this assault, an indication of how easily these *mystères mimés* could pass from pantomime to speech. Its subject matter is of special interest; its historic kernel seems to have been the relief of Jaffa in 1192 by Richard and his knights.[24] By 1300 the *Pas Saladin*,[25] an extant French poem, gave vogue to a new, supposedly historical story of how Richard and twelve companions had held an imaginary pass against Saladin, of how a Saracen spy, recognizing the Christian heroes, reported their famous names and Saladin retreated. The poem was designed to please descendants of those Christian heroes, and representations of them and their arms henceforth were frequently depicted in castle wall paintings, in carvings on wooden chests or ivory caskets, in tapestries such as the Black Prince gave his son in 1376, or on a golden seal possessed by Charles V of France in 1379.[26] Some such familiar representation of the *Pas Saladin* perhaps influenced the illuminator of MS fr. 2813, for there, on f. 473v, among the leaders of the First Crusade is not Duke Robert of Normandy, but Richard Coeur de Lion of the Third Crusade. He wears his crown and

24. R. S. Loomis, "The *Pas Saladin* in Art and Heraldry," *Studies in Art and Literature for Belle da Costa Greene* (Princeton, N.J.), pp. 83–91, origin, p. 90.

25. The *Pas Saladin* was discussed by Gaston Paris, *Journal des Savants*, 1893, pp. 486–98, and was published by F. Lodeman, *MLN*, XII (1897), cols. 21–34, 84–96. Richard I of England, as duke of Normandy, was considered a vassal of the French crown.

26. Loomis, "The *Pas Saladin*," p. 85.

his blazon of the three gold leopards of England.[27] But a mistake like this did not matter much; what did matter was the pride and inspiration which men were coming to feel in human history and its heroic records. Even in the early thirteenth century, the compiler of the *Historia Regum Francorum* (to 1214) had thus expressed his purpose: "ad ostendendum quo deveniat humana sublimitas, ad exemplar vitae hoc opusculum attemptavi. . . . Historia est vitae speculum."[28] His prologue was taken up and expanded in 1276 by Primat in his French translation, *Les Grandes Chroniques de Saint-Denis.*[29] In commenting on these and other acts connected with the development of historiography in France, Professor Walpole (p. 358) has observed: "By 1276 educated Frenchmen of all sorts and conditions were reading in their own tongue official histories of their kings, identifying themselves with the national history as the inheritors of its past, the makers of its present and the example for those to whom its future would belong, finding entertainment in its action and moral profit in its teaching—a mirror of life indeed."

There could hardly be a better commentary on the mood and purpose which, coupled with the hope for a new Crusade, had led, in 1378, to the selection of *Godfrey of Bouillon* as a subject for the royal *entremés*. In 1389 municipal, as well as royal, authorities may have participated in choosing the *Pas Saladin* for a street performance.[30] But it would not have been chosen had it not been a popular, familiar subject which "history," as then understood, had made famous. At the same time and presumably for the same reasons, the Troy *entremés* was planned for lavish presentation before the young Charles VI. Medieval Frenchmen, like medieval Britons, liked to believe their race descended from the mighty Trojans of antiquity and in particular from that son of Hector, Francio, from whose name the French often derived their own. Even a late fourteenth-century manuscript such as MS fr. 2713, f. 4, has the conventional beginning of the ancient chronicles: "Le premier chapitre

27. See above, n. 13.

28. Quoted by R. N. Walpole, "Philip Mouskés and the Pseudo-Turpin Chronicle," *University of California Publications in Modern Philology,* XXVI (1947), 356, from the complete prologue as printed in N. de Wailly's "Memoires, Chroniques de Saint Denis," *Académie des Inscriptions,* XVII, Pt. 1 (1848), 403–5, Appendix.

29. Walpole, p. 417, n. 36, 42; also p. 359: "Between 1200 and 1276 . . . we see the separation of history from the poets and its establishment as a new literary genre."

30. P. Sadron, "Notes sur l'organisation des représentations théatrales en France au Moyen Age," *Mélanges . . . offerts à Gustave Cohen,* pp. 205–18, observes (p. 209) the regularized use of the same places in Paris streets for the giving of outdoor performances.

parle comment francois descendirent des Trojens. Quatre cens et quatre ans avant que rome fu fondee regnoit Priant en Troie la Grant . . ."[31]

In the mid-fifteenth century, in connection with a huge Troy drama, we shall find this same sense of the historicity of the Troy story and its special significance for the French, a powerful, avowed inspiration. But it is of more immediate interest to note that by 1395 the transition had been made from the earlier dumbshows to secular drama, and a complete play exemplified that trend away from religious themes to those of "history" which we have noticed in the pantomimic *Godfrey of Bouillon*, the *Troy*, and the *Pas Saladin*.

Again we meet with the purposeful hand of Philippe de Mézières, who, having already translated into French Petrarch's Latin version of Boccaccio's story of Griselda, proceeded to dramatize his own French prose version, and to versify from it over seven hundred lines.[32] This dramatized *l'Estoire de Griseldis* is known in a single, illustrated manuscript (B.N. MS fr. 2203), possibly the one said to have been given Charles VI when he attended its performance.[33] The Prologue affirms that the story is

> D'une dame la vraye histoire   42
> Qui tant est digne de memoire
>
> Et fu ceste hystoire averie   47
> Au vray effect en Lombardie.

This emphasis on the truth of the story calls to mind the same author's earlier exhortations to the young Charles VI, whose tutor he had been,

31. The illumination on this same page, f. 4, shows the siege of Troy and Francio at Sicambre (cf. H. Martin, *La Miniature française du XIII⁴ au XV⁴ siècle* [Paris, 1923], pp. 48, 95, fig. 80; B. N., *Manuscrits à peintures*, p. 60). For a richly documented study of the Trojan descent and the Francus (Francio) legend, unknown before the seventh century, see Maria Klippel, *Die Darstellung der frankischen Trojanersage in Geschichtsschreibung und Dichtung vom Mittelalter bis zur Renaissance in Frankreich* (Marburg, 1936). This should be supplemented by Jacques Poujol, "Etymologies légendaires des mots *France* et *Gaule* pendant la Renaissance," *PMLA*, LXXII (1957), 900–914, which continues the study of the Francus and Trojan legend into the age of disbelief. The legend was still widely read in the fourteenth century in the version in *Les Grandes Chroniques de France*, ed. J. Viard, Société de l'Histoire de France, vol. CXX (Paris, 1920–37), I, 9, 11 ("Francions fu fiuz d'Hector"). Jorga, *Mézières*, p. 30, notes his reference to the legend.

32. *L'Estoire de Griseldis*, ed. Barbara Craig (Lawrence, Kans., 1954), pp. 3–10, Bibliography, pp. 69–70. The historic existence of Griseldis was not doubted by her supposed descendants. Cf. N. Jorga, *Thomas III, marquis de Saluces: Étude historique et littéraire* (St-Denis, 1893), pp. 82–85; E. Golenistcheff-Koutouzoff, *L'Histoire de Griseldis en France au XIV⁴ et au XV⁴ siècle* (Paris, 1933), pp. 133 f. See below, n. 36.

33. [See Roger Sherman Loomis, *A Mirror of Chaucer's World* (Princeton: Princeton University Press, 1965), figs. 151–60, for photographs and commentary.]

to read "es hystoires authentique des IX preuz [the Nine Worthies], de la bataille de Troye[s], d'Alixandre et des Romains."[34] In a still extant letter, written in May-July 1395 to young King Richard II of England, Mézières urged him to read "le cronique autentique du dessus dit marquis de Saluce et de Grisildis, escripte par le solempnel docteur et souverain poète, maistre Francois Petrac."[35] It was still the ardent hope of the inveterate propagandist that, through the marriage of Richard to the little Isabelle, daughter of Charles VI, peace might be made between the two realms and so lead to their union in fighting the infidel. The letter has the same arguments that are offered in the play to its hero urging him to take a wife, and it was a Grisildis that Mézières wished for a wife for Richard. In Mrs. Frank's recent and authoritative book on French drama in the Middle Ages, she, who had already done so much to establish the authorship of *Grisildis*, acclaims it "as our first example of a French play that is serious but non-religious."[36] She observes that an added character in the play, the aged "quint chevalier," is a kind of self-portrait of Mézières himself. Certainly the author was using developed drama here as purposefully, and for the same purpose, but for a different king, as, seventeen years before, he had (in all probability) instigated and directed the *Godfrey of Bouillon entremés*. In each case it was by a past example (which he believed to be true) from human history that he wished to influence his present time; as the personal friend of Charles V and Charles VI he had unusual opportunity to present his ideas before the court.

Among the plays subsequent to the *Grisildis* of 1395 but having likewise secular and historical themes, Mrs. Frank[37] lists the *Siège d'Orleans* (about 1470) in which for the first time Joan of Arc entered the stage world, the *Mystère* (or *Vie*) *de S.Louis*, written before 1472 and played in Paris, the *Mystère de Jules César* at Amboise in 1500, and *l'Istoire de la Destruction de Troye la grant*,[38] which Jacques Milet of Orleans wrote between 1450 and 1452. The first three have palpably historical subjects whatever unhistorical elements intrude into them, but to savor the sense of historicity which Milet wished to give his Troy drama, we must turn to his own words. He was basing it on Guido delle Colonne's *Historia destructionis Trojae*, the thirteenth-century Latin prose version which more or less superseded, as being more authoritative, the earlier and finer

34. Jorga, *Mézières*, p. 26, n. 3, quoting from *Le Songe du Vieil Pelerin*.
35. Ibid., p. 482; Craig, ed., *Griseldis*, p. 5.
36. Frank, *Medieval French Drama*, chap. XV (*Griseldis*); also *MLN*, LI (1936), 217–22. Cf. Craig, p. 5.
37. *Medieval French Drama*, pp. 209–10.
38. Ibid., pp. 206–9. The first edition of Milet's play was reproduced by E. Stengel (Marburg-Leipzig, 1883).

Roman de Troie of Benoît de Sainte-More.[39] Milet was writing as a typically medieval lover of the ancient story, as a typically medieval dramatist using the familiar *mise-en-scène* of a many-mansioned stage which included ship, towers, and many blazoned banners. Eighteen of the Trojan princes had such banners and they may have been introduced, as Thomas Oliver[40] has suggested, in honor of the noble families of France. Milet was young and ambitious when he wrote his play with its compliments to French princes (Prologue, vss. 80–105) bearing the name Charles, and his glorification of his own sovereign, King Charles VII (1422–61), whose name in the play Priam sees rising to the top of the Wheel of Fortune (vss. 25064–25112).[41] Milet may have known, through reading Froissart, that the Troy story had been chosen for the royal entertainment in 1389, but he probably did not know of the *Jeu du Siège de Troie* performed at Avignon in April 1400.[42] The Troy story had attained new life in the fourteenth century, but it was as something ancient, memorable, and true that Milet turned the story into a play of 27,984 verses intended for a four-day presentation. There is no evidence of its actual performance, but twelve manuscripts and as many early editions show that it had success in book form.[43] In his Prologue (vs. 272) and again in vs. 25076 he asserted that five thousand years had passed since Troy fell. He pictures himself, most unhistorically to be sure, as wandering in a flowery meadow, and finding there a beautiful tree with fair shields hanging upon it which represent *le lineage de France* (vs. 290). Digging down into the roots of the tree, he finds ancient Trojan weapons. For him, as for his French ancestors from the eighth century, the real root of the matter was their belief in the descent of the French from the Trojans. It was this thought, still one to conjure with, which inspired Milet to write his huge play, to pay homage as best he could to the enduring thought of *Troye la grant:*

39. T. E. Oliver, *Jacques Milet's Drama, "La Destruction de Troye la Grant": Its Principal Source; Its Dramatic Structure* (Heidelberg, 1899), sections 8–11 ff. He established Guido delle Colonne's *Historia Destructionis Troiae* as Milet's primary source.
40. Oliver, No. 244. The suggestion still invites investigation.
41. Oliver, Nos. 2–4, on Milet's reference to "Charles septiesme" (vs. 25064 ff.). See Petit de Julleville, *Les Mystères*, II, 572, for identification of the three princes named Charles in the Prologue.
42. Gustave Cohen, *Études d'histoire du théâtre en France au moyen âge et à la Renaissance* (Paris, 1956), pp. 164–66, cites an Italian letter, written in Avignon on 14 June 1400, which refers to the *Jeu du Siège de Troie*, as recently played there and as similar to that at which the Duc d'Anjou had been present in (so Cohen conjectures) 1382.
43. Frank, *Medieval French Drama*, p. 206.

Trouuay les armes des troyans,[44]   270
Donc lost de France est descendu
Passé apres de cinq mille ans.
Lors ie me prins a pourpenser
De faire listoire de troye,
Et a mon pouoyr composer
Tout au mieulx que ie pourroye.
Et pour ce que bien ie sauoye
Que aultreffois a esté escripte
En latin et en prose laye,
Si ay voulu euiter reddicte,   280
Et ay proposé de la faire
Par parsonnages seullement,
Pour monstrer le vray exemplaire
A lueil tout euidamment,
Comme il appert tout clerement
A ceulx qui la lisent ou voient,
En lonneur et exaulcement
Des escussons qui y paroient,
Et semblablement a lonneur
De tout le lignaige de France.   290

44. Stengel's ed., Prologue, pp. 4–5.

Alan H. Nelson

7. Some Configurations of Staging in Medieval English Drama

Although most medieval dramatic texts have been lost to us, many survive, including liturgical plays, Corpus Christi plays, moralities, saints' plays, and interludes. But the texts preserve mainly dialogue, and rather few directions for staging and spectacle. Evidently playwrights assumed that actors would understand and simulate the appropriate conventions without elaborate instructions. We may glean some hints concerning production from stage directions and even occasional diagrams in play manuscripts. But we must also depend heavily on other kinds of evidence: civic records, pictorial analogues,[1] and contemporary allusions or descriptions. With these in mind we can attempt a reconstruction of the drama through a careful reading of the dialogue, inferring what lines of action the dialogue requires, or assumes, and tempering our inferences with a common-sense awareness of what may have been effective and possible.

Medieval staging conventions were largely established in the tenth-century liturgical dramas which developed within the divine services of the church.[2] Perhaps the most definitive convention was the practical

1. Important investigations in this area include Emile Mâle, *L'Art religieux du XIIe siècle en France* (Paris, 1922), pp. 122–50; Gustave Cohen, *Histoire de la mise en scène dans le théâtre religieux français du moyen âge*, 2d ed. (Paris, 1926); W. L. Hildburgh, "English Alabaster Carvings as Records of the Medieval Religious Drama," *Archaeologia*, 93 (1949), 52–102; Otto Pächt, "Pictorial Representation and Liturgical Drama," in *The Rise of Pictorial Narrative in Twelfth-Century England* (Oxford, 1962), pp. 33–59; and M. D. Anderson, *Drama and Imagery in English Medieval Churches* (Cambridge, 1963). Many other studies are mentioned in the notes to these works.

2. Major essays on medieval staging from this century include E. K. Chambers, *The Medieval Stage* (Oxford, 1903), II, 1–105; Matthew Lyle Spencer, *Corpus Christi Pageants in England* (New York, 1911); Gustave Cohen, *Le Théâtre en France au moyen âge*, 2 vols. (Paris, 1928); Allardyce Nicoll, *Masks, Mimes and Miracles* (London, 1931), pp. 194–209 (hereafter cited as Nicoll, *MMM*); Grace Frank, *The Medieval French Drama* (Oxford, 1954), pp. 65–73, 161–75; Hardin Craig, *English Religious Drama* (Oxford, 1955), pp. 115–50 (hereafter cited as Craig, *ERD*); Richard Southern, *The Medieval Theatre in the Round* (London, 1957) (hereafter cited as Southern, *MTR*); and Glynne Wickham, *Early English Stages*, Vols. I and II, pt. 1 (London, 1959 and 1963) (hereafter cited as Wickham,

distinction between localized and unlocalized playing areas.[3] This distinction derived from the fact that certain architectural features or scenic devices in the church building were designated and viewed as fixed, named localities, while the rest of the playing area was regarded as undifferentiated space. In the *Regularis concordia* (c. 970), the three monks who play the Marys at Easter Matins are directed to advance "to the place of the sepulcher with hesitating steps, as though searching for something."[4] Only the sepulcher itself has a local identity. The area in which the Marys conduct their search before arriving at the tomb is not a garden, a cemetery, or an open field. At most it represents merely the space between one locality and another, say between Calvary and the sepulcher. But in this instance it is immaterial where the Marys come from, so we cannot say even that the area lies between two specified places. It is simply unlocalized space, and to define it more precisely results in error and confusion at worst, irrelevance at best.[5]

The localized area, called a *domus, locus,* or *sedes* in Latin, and a "mansion," "room," "hall," "house," or "place" in English, was normally delineated by some more or less distinctive piece of scenery: a throne, an altar, a curtain, or perhaps an elaborate architectural frame. The unlocalized area, on the other hand, might be any other space lying within the total acting area. It was called the *platea* in Latin. In English it was called the "place." Since the English term, "place," remains ambiguous, it is safer to designate the two kinds of theatrical space by the Latin terms *locus* and *platea*.[6]

The distinction between *locus* and *platea* was not absolute: the *platea*

EES). See also Richard Hosley, "Three Kinds of Outdoor Theatre before Shakespeare," *Theatre Survey*, 12 (1971), 1–33; and Bamber Gascoigne, "Fouquet's 'Rape of the Sabine Women,'" *Theatre Survey*, 12 (1971), 155. Other studies are given in footnotes above and below.

3. This is a well-established classification, accepted by all the authors in n. 2. For more particular discussions, see Southern, *MTR*, pp. 219–36; Robert Weimann, "*Platea* und *Locus* im Misterienspiel: Zu einem Grundprinzip vorshakespearesches Dramaturgie," *Anglia*, 84 (1966), 330–52; and O. B. Hardison, Jr., *Christian Rite and Christian Drama in the Middle Ages* (Baltimore, 1965), pp. 262–74.

4. Aethelwold, *The Monastic Agreement*, ed. and trans. Thomas Symons (London, 1953), pp. 50–51. Translation here is mine.

5. Southern, *MTR*, p. 236, objects to the term "unlocalized." He insists that the *platea* was thought of as theatrical playing space only, never as geographically significant. This goes too far, for the *platea* can represent a real though ill-defined location which bears some relationship to a well-defined *locus*. See the example of the road to Damascus in my discussion of the *Conversion of St. Paul* below.

6. See Nicoll, *MMM*, p. 195, for a more complete set of terms. I am following Chambers's (inconsistent) practice of using *locus* as the singular, *loca* as the plural form of this term, a practice which, despite its peculiarity, has the warrant of scholarly tradition.

might on occasion become localized by an appropriate reference in the dialogue, and a throne could be Herod's hall for one play and Pilate's for another. But while a visibly marked *locus* might be disregarded in an action for which it was irrelevant, it could not be used for a purpose unsuited to its architectural character.

The *platea* could be a circumscribed and delimited central area in a relatively permanent theatrical enclosure, or simply "the green," or "the street," as in the famous stage direction from the Coventry cycle: "Here Erode ragis in the pagond and in the strete also."[7] The *locus*, on the other hand, was frequently a raised platform, either a stationary scaffold stage, or even a wagon. This type of stage was called a "pageant." It is conceivable, in turn, that a single pageant might have been large enough to contain both several *loca* and an area for unlocalized action.[8]

Our conception of the medieval wheeled stage, or pageant wagon, is generally based on the account by David Rogers, an early seventeenth-century antiquarian from Chester: ". . . these pagiantes or cariage was a highe place made like ahowse wth ij rowmes beinge open on ye tope the lower rowme they apparrelled & dressed them selues, and in the higher roume they played, and they stoode vpon 6 wheeles."[9] But a six-wheeled wagon is a rare and mechanically imperfect vehicle.[10] More-over, it is difficult to imagine that multistoried wagons were often used, even for special events such as plays. The Norwich Grocers' cart is surely a more reliable model: "A Pageant, yt is to saye, a Howse of Waynskott paynted and buylded on a Carte wt fowre whelys. . . . A square topp to sett over ye sayde Howse."[11]

Doubtless most wagons had four wheels, and when they were used for plays, the producers would have used the natural bed of the wagon

7. *Two Coventry Corpus Christi Plays*, ed. Hardin Craig, 2d ed., EETS e.s. 87 (London, 1957), p. 27.

8. See Craig, *ERD*, pp. 122–23; and M. James Young, "The York Pageant Wagon," *Speech Monographs*, 34 (1967), 1–20. Young in particular, who attempts to discover the size of the York wagons through an analysis of the cycle text, begs the question of whether the dramatic plays were performed on the wagons.

9. W. W. Greg, ed., *The Trial and Flagellation with Other Studies in the Chester Cycle* (London: Malone Society, 1935), pp. 146–47. A variant version, pp. 165–66, attributes four wheels to the carriages.

10. For proper steering, a six-wheeled wagon must be provided with two pivoted axles, rather than the single pivoted axle required for a four-wheeled wagon. The management of the second pivoted axle presents a difficult problem in mechanics and steering geometry which was not satisfactorily resolved even in the nineteenth century. The funeral car of the duke of Wellington has pivoted front and rear axles, joined by cross-chains. But the chains tend to slacken during a tight turn, allowing the rear axle to pivot out of control. On multistoried wagons, see Craig, *ERD*, pp. 125–26.

11. Ibid., p. 124.

3. Louvain pageant wagon. The Annunciation. From Edward van Even, *L'Omgang de Louvain* (Brussels and Louvain, 1863). Courtesy of Harvard University Library.

4. Louvain pageant wagon. The Nativity. From van Even, *L'Omgang de Louvain*. Courtesy of Harvard University Library.

as the major playing area. An architectural structure, like the Norwich Grocers' "Howse," might be mounted on the wagon, providing cover and scenery. Action could perhaps be mounted on the roof of this "Howse," though such scenes were probably limited to heaven: God in his throne, angels in choir, or perhaps Christ at the Ascension. The area beneath the wagon may have been used also, as a hiding place, a hell, or conceivably even as a tiring room, though the wheels and other parts of the undercarriage would have presented an obstacle to easy movement.

The most suggestive evidence of the appearance of pageant wagons comes from two pictorial analogues showing processions in Louvain in 1594 (see pls. 3 and 4) and in Brussels in 1615 (see pls. 5 and 6).[12]

12. George R. Kernodle, "The Medieval Pageant Wagons of Louvain," *Theatre Annual*, 1 (1943), 58–62; and Leo van Puyvelde, *L'Ommegang de 1615 à Bruxelles* (Brussels, 1960). See also Sheila Williams and Jean Jacquot, "Ommegangs Anversois du temps de Breugel et de van Heemskerk," in *Les Fêtes de la renaissance* (Paris, 1956, 1960), II, 359–88 and pls. XXXI–XXXVII.

5. Brussels pageant wagon. The Annunciation. From Leo van Puyvelde, *L'Omme-gang de 1615 à Bruxelles* (Brussels, 1960). Courtesy of the Victoria and Albert Museum, London. Crown copyright.

Both processions are late, and neither is English or even dramatic: yet an inspection will show that the wagons might be quite serviceable for acting. Each wagon shown constitutes a single *locus*, providing scarcely any area for unlocalized action. We must imagine, then, that where wagons were used for plays, either the *locus* was confined to a smaller portion of the wagon, or additional areas were used for the *platea*, either the ground around the wagon, or an auxiliary platform.

Glynne Wickham has argued that the playing area of wagons was sometimes extended by the use of a second wagon, free of scenery and placed adjacent to the first.[13] Several records from Coventry seem to confirm this, for they point to special scaffolds which had two regular wheels and at least one "trendyll," or caster wheel, something like a pushcart.[14] These could not have gone easily in a procession fully loaded,

13. Wickham, *EES*, I, 170–74. Cf. Young, "York Pageant Wagons," pp. 10–12.
14. See *Two Coventry Corpus Christi Plays*, ed. Craig, p. 109, for the years 1570 and 1572.

6. Brussels pageant wagon. The Nativity. From van Puyvelde, *L'Ommegang de 1615 à Bruxelles*. Courtesy of the Victoria and Albert Museum. Crown copyright.

but might have been drawn into position at a station for use at need. However, we have little evidence that this technique was widespread; we must imagine that the ordinary *platea* was the humble earth.

When wagons were used, they were not moved during the course of an individual play. For most theatrical purposes, therefore, stationary scaffolds would have been just as suitable as wagons.[15] However, scaffold pageants would have had to be dismantled at the end of each season, while wagons could be drawn undercover into a "pageant house" to be stored for use next year. Moreover, a wagon could be used both for a procession and for a play, and some may have seen such double service.

Most medieval plays or cycles of plays called for more than one *locus*. These *loca*, whether scaffolds or wagons, were deployed in a variety of ways. They could be distributed some distance from one another, so that it would have been necessary for the audience to move from one stage (or station) to another between plays. Usually, however, the *loca* were so situated that the audience could view the whole dramatic action without changing position. In this case the *loca* could be strung out in a line, or set in a circle, as was more frequently the case, especially in England. The famous Valenciennes theater apparently preserves linear characteristics (see pl. 7).[16] The miniature of the martyrdom of Saint Apollonia, by Jean Fouquet, on the other hand, preserves circular characteristics (see pl. 1). All surviving diagrams of English and Cornish medieval stages indicate a circular deployment of the *loca* about a central *platea*.[17] This arrangement, which has been the center of much recent debate,[18] is now known as "theater-in-the-round." In *The Castle of Perseverance*, best known of theater-in-the-round

15. On the practical distinction between wagons and scaffolds, see Anne Cooper Gay, "The 'Stage' and the Staging of the N-Town Plays," *Research Opportunities in Renaissance Drama*, 10 (1967), 135–36.

16. For a recent study of the Valenciennes theater, see Elie Konigson, *La Représentation d'un mystère de la Passion à Valenciennes en 1547*, Collection "Le Choeur des Muses" (Paris, 1968). For a discussion of the Fouquet miniature, see Southern, *MTR*, pp. 91–120.

17. For a discussion of these sketches and their implications, see F. E. Halliday, ed., *The Legend of the Rood* (London, 1955), pp. 18–43; and Wickham, *EES*, II, pt. 1, 59–72.

18. See below, Schmitt, pp. 292–315. See also Merle Fifield, *The Castle in the Circle*, Ball State Monographs, 6 (Muncie, Ind., 1967), and "The Arena Theatres in Vienna Codices 2535 and 2536," *Comparative Drama*, 2 (1968), 259–82; Wickham, *EES*, II, pt. 1, 158–72; Alan H. Nelson, "Early Pictorial Analogues of Medieval Theatre-in-the-Round," *Research Opportunities in Renaissance Drama*, 12 (1969), 93–103; and K. M. Dodd, "Another Elizabethan Theater in the Round," *Shakespeare Quarterly*, 21 (1970), 125–56.

plays, one additional *locus,* the castle, was situated in the middle of the *platea* (see pl. 8).[19]

I have so far avoided mention of the method which most students of the drama have assumed was normal for the production of Corpus Christi plays in England. Testimony concerning this method, as for the six-wheeled cart, comes from the seventeenth-century antiquarian David Rogers, who describes what we may technically call a "true-processional" production. A long cycle consisting of many short episodes is presented to audiences gathered at stations situated along a prescribed route. The individual plays are mounted on wagons which are drawn from station to station. All the plays are pesented to all the audiences in order, from first to last.[20]

It has only recently become apparent that this method of staging plays is inconvenient and in some instances impossibly time-consuming for actors and audiences alike. It may be doubted whether the true-processional technique was ever extensively employed.[21] Nevertheless, from York and other cities come records which point to something very much like true-processional productions. These records point to

19. Southern, *MTR,* provides an elaborate discussion of the staging of *Castle of Perseverance,* including an analysis of the problems entailed in positioning a *locus* in the center of the *platea.*

20. Rogers's testimony has been printed many times, but for a definitive text see Greg, ed., *Trial,* pp. 146–47 and 165–66.

21. See Martial Rose, *The Wakefield Mystery Plays* (London, 1961), pp. 17–26; and Alan H. Nelson, "Principles of Processional Staging: York Cycle," *Modern Philology,* 67 (1970), 303–20. Cf. A. M. Kinghorn, *Medieval Drama* (London, 1968), pp. 69–72.

7. Valenciennes theater. From Valenciennes Passion, MS Fr. 12536, f. lv–2–2 bis. Courtesy of the Bibliothèque Nationale, Paris.

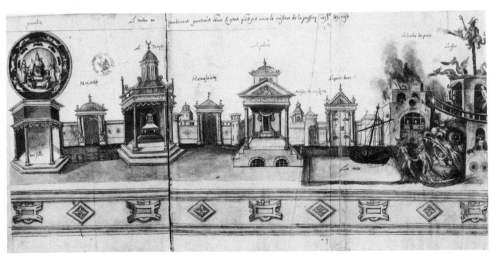

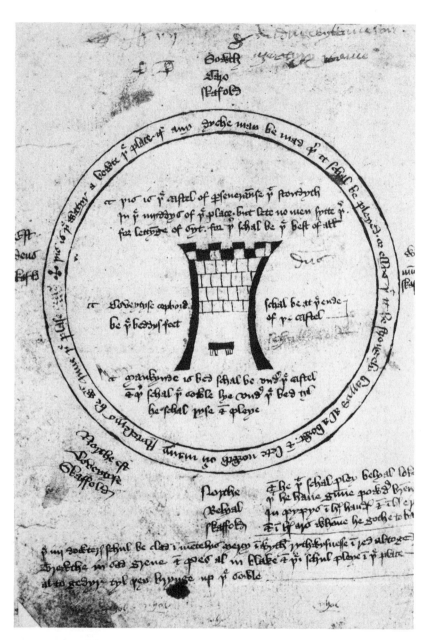

8. Sketch for *The Castle of Perseverance*. From Macro Manuscripts, c. 1400–1475, MS V.A. 354. Courtesy of the Folger Shakespeare Library, Washington, D.C.

the existence of multiple pageant wagons, episodes, and stations (though rarely of multiple audiences or multiple performances by single casts). A full analysis of all pertinent evidence in light of recent discoveries has yet to be accomplished, so that whatever is said here must be somewhat tentative and hypothetical, intended more to stimulate thought than to provide final answers. Still, we may permit ourselves to search for possible alternatives which could account for the processional characteristics of certain extant plays, particularly the Corpus Christi plays.[22]

Pageants decked out with scenes from the Bible were not unique to Corpus Christi plays, and in fact were found frequently in elaborate nondramatic processions. The two chief methods of displaying these pageants were exemplified by civic or ecclesiastical processions on the one hand, and by royal entries on the other. In the procession, pageants moved through the streets past stationary audiences. In the royal entry, the audience, that is the king and his entourage, moved past stationary pageants.

The royal entry is a well-documented phenomenon, dating from at least 1313, when Philip IV welcomed Edward II of England into Paris. The Life of Christ, from Nativity to Resurrection, was presented at different stations, with scenes such as the Last Judgment intermixed with secular scenes such as Reynard the Fox.[23] At each station the king would pause to observe the stationary pageant. Sometimes such pageants would include action, dialogue, or a formal speech. But many were mute. In 1424, when the duke of Bedford entered Paris, he saw "a very beautiful mystery of the Old Testament and the New ... and this was done without speaking or singing, just as if [the actors] were images upon a wall."[24]

The phrase "sans parler" is found in descriptions of many French pageants, though in the royal entry short speeches would not significantly hinder the progress of the procession. This is because the pag-

22. The question of processional staging and alternative techniques is discussed for German drama by Neil C. Brooks, "Processional Drama and Dramatic Procession in Germany in the Late Middle Ages," *Journal of English and German Philology*, 32 (1933), 141–71, esp. 142–44. See also Wolfgang F. Michael, *Die geistlichen Prozessionsspiele in Deutschland*, Hesperia, 22 (Baltimore, 1947), esp. pp. 6–7, and *Frühformen der deutschen Bühne*, Schriften der Gesellschaft für Theatergeschichte, Bd. 62 (Berlin, 1963).

23. Louis Petit de Julleville, *Histoire du théâtre en France: Les mystères* (Paris, 1880), II, 186–88. On the general subject see Bernard Guenée and Françoise Lehoux, *Les Entrées françaises de 1328 à 1515* (Paris, 1968). See also Robert Withington, "The Early 'Royal Entry,'" *PMLA*, 32 (1917), 616–23, and *English Pageantry* (Cambridge, Mass., 1918, 1920), I, 124–97; and Wickham, *EES*, I, 51–111.

24. Petit de Julleville, *Histoire*, I, 192 and II, 190. Translation mine.

eants have only one important audience. It is quite otherwise with a procession of pageants which moves past multiple stationary audiences, whether the spectators line the streets or assemble at designated viewing stands or stations. Brief speeches can be given in such a procession, but only if they are begun and ended within the hearing of any given spectator as the procession makes its way through the city. Extended actions which require a pageant to stop before an audience are as vexing to a procession as a stalled car is to traffic on a one-lane road. The procession in effect comes to a standstill, and can make progress only by fits and starts. Each pageant hinders the movement of the pageants which follow it. Stopping must in fact be forbidden in a procession. A famous directive from Draguignan in France, issued in 1558, specifically warns participants in the "play" not to stop while the procession is under way, lest they waste too much time and add to the confusion of the day. Extended dialogue was forbidden: speeches were required to be numerous but short. It seems most likely that this "jeu" was not a dramatic play at all, but merely a procession of wagons, each introduced to the spectators along the way by a brief speech.[25]

A true-processional dramatic production is distinguished from such a pageant procession by the requirement that each play stop for an extended time before each of the many gathered audiences. The impracticality of extensive true-processional playing stems from the accumulation of these time periods throughout the production, a phenomenon which is greatly aggravated if the individual episodes are of varying length.[26]

A simple but effective alternative to true-processional playing is to restrict each play or group of plays to a single performance at a single station, while presenting different parts of the cycle successively at different stations. In this case the audience would have to move from station to station, very much as in the conduct of a royal entry: the single audience would go to the first station to see the first play or group of plays, then to the second for the next group, and finally to the last station for the last set of plays. Of course the audience would contain all those who have come to see the production, and might be very large. The movement of the audience from station to station could be a source of confusion. But the problems of such a production would be relatively minor compared to those entailed by true-processional staging. Moreover, this "station-to-station" technique, involving the movement of the audience, has an important advantage: in a cycle which used pageants from a procession, a huge number of wheeled *loca* might have to be crowded or

25. Ibid., II, 209.
26. See Nelson, "Principles of Processional Staging," pp. 304–5 et passim.

maneuvered into the theater area. Far better to park smaller groups of wagons at several stations, and let the audience move from station to station.

The relatively unknown English *Conversion of St. Paul* preserves the station-to-station method of production, though probably it did not make use of wheeled pageant wagons.[27] The play opens at Jerusalem. Near the end of the first part occurs the stage direction, "Her Sale rydyth forth with hys seruantes a-bowt the place, [and] owt of the p[lace]." A dance follows Saul's exit, and then a spokesman named Poeta tells the audience:

> ffynally of this stacon thus we mak a conclusyon
> besechyng thys audyens to folow and succede
> with all your delygens this generall processyon.

A Latin note indicates that this station is finished and that the next follows.

Evidently the spectators move in procession from this station to the next. When they have assembled at the second station, Poeta announces, "Here shalbe brefly shewyd with all our besynes / At thys pagent saynt poullys conuercyon." Saul and his entourage have apparently remained at some distance while the audience has gathered, for now occurs the stage direction, "Here commyth saule rydyng in with hys seruantes." In his opening speech Saul names his destination: "My purpose to Damask fully I intende." Thus this station represents the road to Damascus. While still on the *platea*, Saul is struck blind by a flame, and tumbles from his horse. Shortly appears the direction: "Here the knyghtes lede forth sale in-to a place, and cryst apperyth to annanie . . ." By "place" we must here understand a *locus*, called in the text a "house," and also a "goodly mansyon." Evidently this *locus* is provided with an architectural structure, for Annanias asks, "who ys with-in?" and Saul answers, "I am here, saule. cum in, on goddes benyson." Furthermore, as Saul kneels in contemplation, the Holy Spirit appears above him and descends to him. Having accepted baptism from Annanias, Saul tells him, "Go forth yowur way: I wyll succede / In-to what place ye wyll me lede."

After this the general procession begins again: Poeta announces the conclusion of the station, and a stage direction notes that the third station shall follow. J. Q. Adams identifies the third station as Jerusalem, but in

27. Quotations in my text are from *The Digby Mysteries*, ed. F. J. Furnivall, EETS e.s. 70 (London, 1882), pp. 25–52. Also printed in Joseph Quincy Adams, *Chief Pre-Shakespearean Dramas* (Cambridge, Mass., 1924), pp. 212–24. Mary del Villar, "The Staging of *The Conversion of Saint Paul*," *Theatre Notebook*, 25 (1970), 64–68, asserts (incorrectly, I think) that the play was given stationary performance.

fact the station does not stand for any geographical locality. It simply contains the *locus* of Annas and Caiaphas and another *locus* for a devil, marked by a "chayre." The devils bemoan Saul's conversion, and Saul, now become Paul, is brought before the high priests. The play then alludes to Paul's escape over the city walls in a basket but ends rather abruptly with an apology from Poeta. It is not impossible that originally the play went on to enact more episodes at more stations.

The Conversion of St. Paul is not perhaps the best that medieval drama has to offer, but it is the only extant English text which contains full internal evidence of processional staging. Yet it does not exemplify true-processional techniques but rather the simpler station-to-station, audience processional technique, the only satisfactory alternative which at the same time possesses full processional characteristics. The production is referred to within the text as a "processyon."

It is not possible to leap to the conclusion that this method was used in the production of other English plays with processional characteristics. In fact, the Coventry Corpus Christi play (which must be distinguished from the N-Town or Hegge cycle, misnamed *Ludus Coventriae*) is a clear example of a cycle given in the true-processional manner. Coventry had more than one station, for when Queen Margaret came to see the plays in 1457, she sat at the station where the plays were first presented. Other records point to the use of a second station, and to activities of the actors "between the plays."[28] Coventry did not have ten stations, however, as Hardin Craig once suggested. It probably had only two, or at most three.[29]

Both surviving Coventry plays are "bunched"; that is, several episodes are brought together into a longer play. The longest of these is 1,200 lines, requiring about an hour and a quarter at the least for performance. This amount, and more for the journey between stations, would have to be added to the length of the production for each additional station.[30] Hence the wisdom of Craig's later assertion that "for the playing of these long plays all in one day ten stations seem too many."[31]

Civic records from Wakefield are late and ambiguous, but the cycle text may contain some clues to the manner in which the plays were staged.[32] An allusion in the play of Cain and Abel has suggested to some

28. See expenses recorded by Cappers in *Two Coventry Corpus Christi Plays*, ed. Craig, pp. 94–95.

29. See ibid., pp. xiii–xiv: the three worlds for burning seem to set a maximum limit of three presentations.

30. See Nelson, "Principles," pp. 307, 318–19, and 315, n. 2.

31. Craig, *ERD*, p. 294.

32. Quotations in my text are from *The Towneley Plays*, ed. George England and Alfred W. Pollard, EETS e.s. 71 (London, 1897).

historians that the cycle was originally performed in or near the Goodybower quarry.[33] However, another bit of dialogue suggests even more
strongly that the plays, or at least the Conspiracy and Crucifixion, were
performed in front of a church. After Christ's body is taken down from
the cross, Joseph says, "Now bear we his body into the kyrk." This is
nonsense as narrative, but might represent a concession to staging practice. Other events, particularly the Purification, support this argument.
Simeon goes to the "kyrk," which he otherwise calls the temple, and
there cries, "Oure bellys ryng by thare oone." This miracle is realized
in the stage direction, *"Tunc pulsabunt."* The logical way to comply
with this direction would be to ring the real church bells. If these plays
were performed in front of a church, the entire cycle must have been
performed in a stationary manner, either in a single location, or at several
stations. It is remotely possible, though, I think, doubtful, that the station
for the early plays was Goodybower quarry.

Another argument against true-processional production for Wakefield
is the repeated appearance of certain large scenic devices in different
plays. Many plays make use of a hill and a hall, often gratuitously. If the
production were true-processional, either numerous pageant wagons
would have had to be outfitted with a hill and a hall, or each station
would have had to provide a hill and a hall as stationary props. In either
case stage construction would be highly redundant. Gratuitous redundancy of *loca* or large props is generally incompatible with the requirements of sensible true-processional staging.

Wakefield records and texts make only ambiguous references to
pageants in relation to plays.[34] It seems probable that wagons were used
chiefly for a nondramatic procession. Movement in the dramatic plays
is frequently on horseback, and clearly a good deal of the action takes
place on the street or in a large central *platea*. Examination and comparison of the Mactatio Abel, Noah, and the Magi plays suggests that the
playing space was characterized by multiple scaffolds surrounding a
platea, and that while localized action took place at specific locations,
among them a hill and a hall, the movement and much of the action was
conducted on the ground between scaffolds. This would provide for
Cain's team of horses and plow, as well as for the hill on which Garcio
sits to taunt him; for Noah's mobile ship, as well as for the hill on which

33. See Martin Stevens, "The Staging of the Wakefield Plays," *Research Opportunities in Renaissance Drama*, 11 (1968), 116.

34. Records printed in A. C. Cawley, ed., *The Wakefield Pageants in the
Towneley Cycle* (Manchester, 1958), pp. 124–25. The Wakefield records were discussed at the 1969 MLA Convention medieval drama seminar. A report on this
discussion is to be published in *Research Opportunities in Renaissance Drama*, 13
(forthcoming).

his wife sits to do her spinning; and for the three Magi who enter on horseback, as well as for the raised hall where Herod so kindly receives them. In the Scourging, the torturers bring Christ away from a *locus*, Pilate's hall, into the *platea*. There they exclaim, "we ar worthy greatte lose / that thus has broght a kyng / ffrom sir pilate and other fose / thus into oure ryng." This sounds like nothing so much as theater-in-the-round.

The Late Banns of the Chester cycle end with the admonition, "And if any disdaine then open is yᵉ doore / That lett him in to heare . . ."[35] Scholars have been quick to dismiss the implication that the Chester cycle was performed indoors. If we may trust the account by David Rogers, the plays were presented in a true-processional fashion along the four principal streets of the city. Since the cycle was given over three days, *a priori* arguments against true-processional production do not seem to apply, as they do for York. But it is always a mistake to take David Rogers too easily at his word. His account is late and garbled, and is demonstrably false on several counts.[36] Possibly he has confused a dramatic production with a nondramatic procession of pageants presented with speeches at stations along the processional route. Perhaps more telling than any statement by Rogers is the legal record of a dispute in 1568 between two Chester residents over the use of a piece of property in Bridgestreet:

Mem. That whereas varyaunce presently dependeth betwene John Whitmore, Esquier, upon thon partie and Anne Webster, widow, tenaunt to George Ireland, Esquier, upon thother partie for and concerning the claime righte and title of a mansion, Rowme, or Place for the Whydson plaies in the Brudg gate strete . . . it is now ordered that forasmuche as the said Mistres Webster and other the tenants of the said Mr. Ireland have had their place and mansyon in the said place now in varyaunce in quiet sort for ii tymes past whan the said plaies were plaied. That the said Anne Webster in quiet sort for this presente tyme of whydsontide during all the tyme of the said plaies shall enjoy and have her mansyon, place, and the said place and Rome now in varyaunce. Provided alwaies that the having of the possession of the said Rowme, place, or mansyon shall not be hurtfull nor prejudice to nether of the said parties in whom the right of the said premisses is or hereafter shalbe found or proved to be. . . .[37]

In play manuscripts the words "mansion," "Rowme," and "Place," signify a stage *locus*, but in legal parlance they traditionally signify a building, more particularly a house or a hall. We know from other documents

35. Greg, ed., *Trial*, pp. 159–60.
36. See F. M. Salter, *Medieval Drama in Chester* (Toronto, 1955), pp. 54–58.
37. Rupert Morris, *Chester in the Plantagenet and Tudor Reigns* (Chester [1895]), p. 302, n. 2. Cf. Leonard Powlick, "The Staging of the Chester Cycle: An Alternate Theory," *Theatre Survey*, 12 (1971), 119–50.

that John Whitmore claimed property in Bridgestreet,[38] and evidently in this case he was disputing the right of George Ireland and his tenants, particularly Anne Webster, to use the Bridgestreet property for the Whitsun plays. It seems unlikely that John Whitmore, who belonged to a prominent Chester family, was primarily interested in the revenue derived from the plays. It is true that the document concludes with a conditional financial settlement, but the year of the dispute, 1568, suggests that the real issue was whether the plays should be permitted in this place at all. For us the crucial point is that the Chester Whitsun plays may have been performed, at least in later years, in the hall of some private home or public house in Bridgestreet. This does not entirely preclude the possibility that the dramatic plays were produced elsewhere as well, perhaps even on the pageant carriages as they made their way through the city. Still, the idea of indoor performances before limited audiences contradicts the received notion that the plays were written primarily for popular consumption. These documents may therefore force us to alter traditional theories concerning the staging and even the human significance of the plays.

The N-Town cycle seems recently to have attracted more attention than any of its English counterparts.[39] Although the cycle has no obvious geographical home, such an elaborate text must originally have been written for a particular city. Hardin Craig, and more recently Stanley Kahrl and Kenneth Cameron, have urged Lincoln as the true home of the orphan.[40] It may be doubted, however, whether Lincoln ever had an extensive Corpus Christi cycle. Moreover, the N-Town text has more dialectal affinities with East Anglia than with Lincolnshire.[41] The provenance of the play is best regarded as still in question.

This doubt calls into question Cameron and Kahrl's use of Lincoln records to fill in gaps in our knowledge of the N-Town cycle. It may be that Lincoln records are quite irrelevant. Cameron and Kahrl also entertain the hypothesis that although much of the present text is suitable

38. Ibid., pp. 236–37.

39. For an important early study, see Esther L. Swenson, "An Inquiry into the Compositon and Structure of Ludus Coventriae," *University of Minnesota Studies in Language and Literature*, 1 (Minneapolis, 1914). See also Timothy Fry, "The Unity of the *Ludus Coventriae*," *Studies in Philology*, 48 (1951), 527–70; Robert Weimann, "Platea und Locus"; Anne Gay, "The 'Stage' and the Staging of the N-Town Plays"; and Kenneth Cameron and Stanley J. Kahrl, "Staging the N-Town Cycle," *Theatre Notebook*, 21 (1967), 122–38, 152–65. Quotations in my text are from *Ludus Coventriae*, ed. K. S. Block, EETS e.s. 120 (London, 1922).

40. Craig, *ERD*, pp. 239–80; Kenneth Cameron and Stanley J. Kahrl, "The N-Town Plays at Lincoln," *Theatre Notebook*, 20 (1965–66), 61–69.

41. See Mark Eccles, "*Ludus Coventriae*: Lincoln or Norfolk?" *Medium Aevum*, 40 (1971), 135–41.

only for a stationary production, at an early date the cycle was in some manner processional.[42] It is generally agreed that the Banns represent a fairly reliable picture of the cycle as it was performed at an earlier time. However, the Banns cannot be interpreted as announcing a true-processional cycle. A single starting time, "vj of þe bell," is announced, whereas a true-processional production has as many starting times as stations. That the cycle announced by the Banns was produced at a single place, is implied in the speech of the second *vexillator*: "we purpose to shewe in oure pleyn place / in þe xxxj[ti] pagent . . ." This "pleyn place" suggests something on the order of theater-in-the-round.

Another argument against true-processional production is found in the gratuitous redundancy of the stage *loca*. According to the Banns, in pageant XXX, after the Crucifixion:

> Seynt johan Evyn þer as I ȝow plyth
> doth chere oure lady with al his myth
> And to þe temple anon forth ryth
> he ledyth here in þat stownde.

After the Resurrection, which occurs in play XXXIII: "Than doth cryst jhesu on to his modyr sew / and comfortyth all here care in temple þer she lyse." If this were a true-processional play, the Crucifixion would require, in addition to Calvary, a temple, whose only function would be as a place for the Virgin to retire at the conclusion. It is gratuitous in the sense that a temple is not a necessary part of the action but rather only a convenience which could easily be dispensed with if it were not in fact convenient. Another temple would be necessary for the thirty-third pageant. This pageant absolutely requires a hell, a paradise, and a sepulcher, already a large order for a wagon. Once more, the temple is the one dispensable item. In fact, the temple is not mentioned at all in the text of play XXXIII.

With these bits of evidence to support the more general argument against true-processional production, we may infer that the N-Town cycle with all its dependent or independent parts was always given a stationary production. Evidence for any use of pageant wagons is essentially nil. The distinguishable parts of the cycle do not therefore reflect radically different methods of stage production. Nor is it likely, as Cameron and Kahrl surmise, that different parts of the extant text were presented in radically different ways on successive days or years.[43] The

42. Cameron and Kahrl, "Staging," p. 135. The authors admit the difficulty of true-processional staging at Lincoln and suggest that one or at most two places might have served for stations.
43. Ibid., p. 164.

distinction is merely in the number of *loca* and the complexity of stage movement.

The extant text of the cycle has clearly been subject to many changes which are not reflected in the Banns. The two most distinctive modifications are in the Marian group and in the two-part Passion play. The "original" parts are the plays of the Old Testament, the earlier life of Christ, and the post-Resurrection episodes. Simplicity of stage practice is best reflected in the Old Testament plays, which together require only a heaven, a hell, a paradise, a bush, and a hill.[44] A heaven is needed for the first four plays. Noah, the fourth play, introduces a convention found frequently throughout the cycle, both in the old parts and the new. God sends his angel as a messenger to earth rather than confronting his subjects in person. God is therefore presumably located on a high scaffold, at some remove from the *platea*. In the narrow space of a pageant wagon, the intermediary would scarcely have been necessary.

Heaven as a *locus* is required in sixteen distinct parts of the cycle, including the Old Testament, the Marian group, the Passion, and the post-Ascension group. In eight more plays an angel appears without any specific indication that he has descended from heaven. Therefore, in sixteen certain and in eight possible plays out of thirty-four distinguishable episodes, a heaven is required. It seems likely that a single heaven served a single stage area during each step of the cycle's development.

Heaven in the N-Town text is called "hevyn halle," and is large enough to accommodate not only God and his throne, but a messenger angel, an angel choir, and an organ. It is clearly elevated, since it is also called "hevyn hille," "hevyn toure," and "hyȝ hall," and is situated "above sunne and mone," and "aboue cherubyn halle." Movement between heaven and earth is accomplished by ascending and descending. Heaven is provided with gates.

Hell is called a "sty," a "pyt," a "celle," and a "donjoon." It is lower than heaven, probably at ground level, since Satan falls and "slydes" down at his expulsion. Like heaven, it is provided with "gatys," also called a "derke dore." Hell may be located at a lateral remove from heaven, since after Lucifer has changed from an angel to "a devyl ful derke," he exclaims: "Now to helle þe wey I take."

Paradise, described as a "gardeyn," and provided with ample vegetation and a "tre þat is of Cunnyng," is distinct from but probably near heaven. When God has created Adam, he says, "Now come fforth Adam to paradys." Thus Adam is created outside paradise and subse-

---

44. With regard to the following discussion of *loca* and *platea*, cf. ibid., pp. 152–65.

quently led in. After giving his commandment to Adam, God leaves paradise: "Adam go forth and be prynce in place / ffor to hefne I sped my way." Satan, cursed by God, bemoans the fact that "man xulde leve above þe sky / where as sum tyme dwellyd I / and now I am cast to helle sty / streyte out at hevyn gate." Unless this is entirely rhetorical, it seems that paradise is at an elevation approximating heaven's. At any rate it is located substantially above ground level, as can be inferred from Satan's parting speech: "At þi byddyng ffowle I falle / I krepe hom to my stynkyng stalle." Adam and Eve are also driven "extra paradisum," though they leave with greater dignity. After they are gone, "þe ʒatys be schet with godys keye." Then they "walke forth in to þe londe," probably into the *platea*.

The only other *locus* required for the Old Testament plays is a hill, "ʒon hey hylle" of the Abraham and Isaac story. This hill is later named the "hill of godys vesytacion." It is possible that the hill is located near the heaven scaffold, for God's angel gives Abraham the initial directive concerning Isaac, and later intervenes in haste to prevent the sacrifice. A New Testament play, the Temptation, also requires an actual hill, the "hyʒ hyl" indicated by Satan. The substantial nature of this hill is attested by a stage direction requiring that Christ "transit cum diabolo super montem." The Temptation completed, singing angels minister to Jesus.

Neither of these instances constitutes proof, but other plays in the cycle provide good evidence that a theatrical hill was situated directly below the heaven scaffold. This hill is Mount Olivet, which first appears in the Agony in the Garden: "here jhesus and his discipulys go toward þe mount of olyvet and whan he comyth a lytyl þer be-syde in a place lych to A park he byddyt his dyscipulys A-byde hym þer . . ." As in the Temptation, a ministering angel descends to Christ: "here An Aungel descendyth to jhesus and bryngyth to hym A chalys with An host þer in." Since the angel *descends* to Jesus, the hill must be located directly beneath heaven.

This is confirmed by the use of Olivet in the Ascension. Christ first shares food with his disciples, and then exhorts them: "therfore rysyth up and ffolwyth me / On-to þe mownte of Olyvete." Having arrived, Christ says: "now I stey streyte ffrom ʒow to hevyn." Then, "hic Ascendit ab oculis eorum et in celo cantent etcetera." The line of dialogue implies a direct, vertical ascent into heaven. The precise manner may be inferred from the angel's next speech: "In a clowde As ʒe hym seyn / Steyng vp so xal comyn A-geyn / Of Al mankynde þis is serteyn / jugement xal he make." But if Christ is conveyed from Olivet to heaven by a hoist disguised as a cloud, his return at the Last Judgment does not apparently occur quite as anticipated here. In this ultimate episode Christ calls out, "Come hedyr to me to myn hyჳ hall," and "Welcome ჳe be in hevyn to sitt." He therefore remains in heaven rather than descending to earth. Nevertheless, the location of the Last Judgment was traditionally imagined as being immediately above Olivet.[45] This tradition would be satisfied visually if the relation of the heaven scaffold to the hill was as I have suggested.

At the Last Judgment the gate by which Satan originally departed once again becomes the object of attention: "Peter to hevyn ჳatys þou wende and goo / þe lokkys þou losyn and hem vndo." Peter answers: "The ჳatys of hevyn I opyn þis tyde / Now welcome dere bretheryn to hevyn i-wys / Com on and sytt on goddys ryght syde . . ." Our original impression of the capaciousness of heaven seems confirmed. It is also possible that the good souls, as foretold in the play of the Prophets, find their way, along with the patriarchs liberated at the Harrowing of Hell, into Adam's paradise. Perhaps paradise is thus located to the right of God as he sits in heaven.

Another *locus* which bears some proximity to heaven is the temple. This structure, located in Jerusalem, has a prominent altar. The most appropriate location for this temple, as for heaven, is the east. Moreover, there are indications that good characters approaching the temple follow the Virgin's pious example: Maria "genuflectet ad deum."[46] This could be accomplished best if heaven were located more or less behind and above the altar and church. Messengers from heaven seem to have had easy access to the temple: first "þe Aungel bryngyth manna in A cowpe of gold lyke to confeccions · þe hefne syngynge"; then "here xal comyn Allwey An Aungel with dyvers presentys goynge and comyng, and in þe tyme þei xal synge in hefne þis hympne . . ."

The altar stands in the middle of the temple, and has free space around it, since in the Trial, Joseph and Mary proceed seven times each around it. Moreover, three seats are situated at some distance behind (and probably on a level slightly above) the altar: Abiჳachar the Bishop sits "inter duos legis doctores." Later, when the twelve-year-old Jesus comes to the temple, the two doctors, having recognized his superior wisdom, seat him in a higher chair, taking inferior chairs themselves: "hic adducunt ihesum inter ipsos et in scanno altiori ipsum sedere faciunt ipsis in inferioribus scannis sedentibus . . ." The temple itself is situated on a raised platform, for persons approaching are urged to "come up."

45. See below, Leigh, p. 276.
46. Cf. *Ludus Coventriae*, ed. Block, p. 73, rubric following l. 40.

In fact, the temple is approached by the fifteen steps or "grees" which the Virgin climbs as she recites the penitential psalms.

Since the temple is located in Jerusalem, the "gyldyn gate" where Anne and Joachim meet to exchange their fruitful kiss is probably located adjacent to it. This may be used again for Christ's entry into Jerusalem. The stage directions require that Jesus first "rydyth out of þe place," and then come again into the place "at þe gate."

Another *locus* which seems to be part of the heaven complex is the house of Joseph, who first announces at the temple that he and the Virgin have "non hous of oure owne," but then makes arrangements for a modest residence which is called a "lytyl praty hous," a "pore place," and a "sympyl habitation." The house is probably imagined to be in Nazareth. That this is a theatrical *locus* seems implied in the words of the bishop, who tells the Virgin that "iij damysellys xul dwell with ȝow in stage." It is also called a "halle," a word with similar theatrical connotations. When Joseph returns from his nine-month absence, he asks the Virgin to "vn-do youre dore," a detail which appears again in the Assumption when the disciples appear "ante portam marie," and "before youre yate." In the latter episode, the Virgin has returned to her home in anticipation of her death. John explains that "by a whyte clowde I was rapt to these hyllys," and Peter later explains that the several disciples were conveyed in "Diverse clowdys . . . before youre yate." At his Ascension, Christ went up into heaven from the top of a hill by means of a cloud. At the Death of the Virgin, Christ evidently descends to earth in a similar fashion. He proclaims: "I am dyssend on to here of whom I dede sede." The descent seems to be direct rather than requiring lateral movement. Christ then takes the "anima marie" from the Virgin's body into his breast, saying, "Wyth this swete soule now from you I assende."

After the Death of the Virgin, the disciples carry the body to a sepulcher, an action which distinctly requires lateral movement. After the burial those princes who had attempted to desecrate the body and who would not be converted, are dragged off to hell. Then appears the stage direction concerning Christ: "hic descendit et venit ad apostolos." The phrase indicating lateral movement, "et venit," had not occurred at the Death of the Virgin. Having walked to the sepulcher, Christ replaces the soul into the body, and Maria arises, saying "Lo me redy with you for to wend." The Assumption follows, probably after a walk to the base of heaven hill.

The theory of medieval theater-in-the-round as propounded by Richard Southern does not fully recognize the existence of scenic clusters such as the N-Town heaven complex. Clusters of *loca* are well known in Continental dramas. The plan of the Lucerne Easter play, for example, shows a Mount Olivet, with a park at its base, located below and to the right of heaven. A ladder is provided for easy communication between the adjacent *loca* (see pl. 9).[47] The relationship of Olivet to heaven approximates the requirements of the N-Town cycle. The Valenciennes "theater" also deserves notice (see pl. 7). Allardyce Nicoll feels that the famous pictorial representation "does not illustrate more than eight of the mansions actually used," but Elie Konigson argues convincingly that the stage structures shown in the "theater" did multiple service for all the buildings shown in the long series of detailed pictures which belong to the same manuscript.[48] This stage resembles the heaven-cluster of the N-Town cycle, since it includes heaven, the temple, Nazareth (the house of the Virgin?), and the Golden Gate. Also included in the group are hell, limbo, and the house of the bishops.

Stage clusters are of practical service in scenes which require immediate communication between two or more *loca*, for example, between heaven and Olivet. In the scheme imagined by Southern, and appropriate to *Castle of Perseverance*, each *locus* is situated at a different compass point around the *platea* and movement from one to another always requires a "crossing." Stage clusters also serve as visual representations of geographical relationships: the Last Judgment takes place immediately above Olivet; the Golden Gate and the temple are both located in Jerusalem. This provides for some efficiency of signification and design.

The heaven-cluster is not the only group of *loca* in the N-Town cycle. In the Cherry Tree episode, which occurs on the way to Bethlehem, Maria asks Joseph: "What tre is ʒon standynge vpon ʒone hylle?" The hill in question is immediately adjacent to the Nativity scene. This may be seen by examining the relationships of *loca* in several related plays. When Joseph speaks to the shepherds who have come to pay their respects to the Child, he addresses them as "Herdys on hylle." Similarly, when the Magi leave the Nativity scene they immediately succumb to sleep: "Downe I ley me vpon this banke / Vnder this bryght sterre i-wys." When they fall asleep the angel addresses them precisely as Joseph had addressed the shepherds: "ʒe kynggys on this hill." The fact that the star shines above the hill is final proof of the proximity of the hill to the Bethlehem stall. It is the star which the first shepherd calls the

47. For a full study of this play, see Marshall Blakemore Evans, *The Passion Play of Lucerne: A Historical and Critical Introduction*, MLA Monograph Series, 14 (New York, 1943).

48. Nicoll, *MMM*, p. 195; Konigson, *La Représentation*, esp. pp. 37–51.

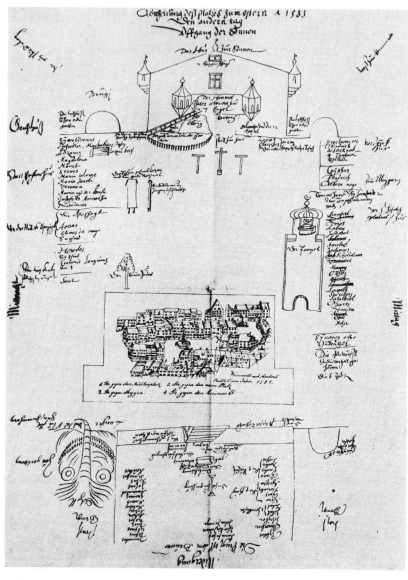

9. Sketch for the Lucerne Passion. Reproduced from Allardyce Nicoll, *Masks, Mimes, and Miracles* (London: George G. Harrap & Co., 1931; New York: Cooper Square Publishers, 1964), fig. 136, p. 199.

"grett lyght with shene shyne . . . Evyn above bedleem / I saw it brenne thryes." There is no indication that the star is not stationary.[49]

That this hill is surmounted by a tree may be argued from the fact that as the Magi follow the star after entering the *platea* on horseback, Herod's "seneschallys" addresses them, "Kyngys iij / vndyr þis tre." The mention of the tree is entirely gratuitous from a narrative stand-point, but we know that the Magi had followed "the glemynge of ʒon gay sterre," and we may surmise that the star was on a hill, along with a tree which served for the Cherry Tree episode.

The stable of the Nativity is "desolat with-owty Any wall," a "pore logge," no doubt containing a manger and an ox and an ass. Joseph leaves the house to fetch the midwives, and says to them, "streyte to my spowse walke we þe way." They probably approach the *locus* from the *platea*. This cluster of *loca* therefore includes a stable upon a scaffold, and a hill with a tree and a star.

Even more efficient in a practical sense than a stage cluster is the use of a single *locus* to represent several different locales successively. Three sepulchers are required for the cycle, but one stage *locus* might serve for all. The first appears in the Death of Lazarus. It is somewhat un-clear whether this is a cave hewn in the rocks, a hole dug in the ground, or a sarcophagus resting above the ground. It is called a "cave" on the one hand, and a "cley pitt" and a "deep pit" on the other. Similar am-biguity is found with respect to the sepulcher of Christ. Peter goes into the sepulcher ("intrat monumentum"), suggesting a cave; but on the other hand, Pilate says, "On every corner now is sett my seale," dis-tinctly suggesting a rectangular sarcophagus.

Perhaps the stage *locus* in both cases was a sarcophagus within a cave, a solution found in many pictorial accounts of the episode. One promi-nent instance of this is found among the illuminations of the Valenciennes Passion (see pl. 10).[50] The same arrangement might be used in the Death of the Virgin. If this method were adopted, the sepulcher could not be seen from all sides, but only from the front. The stage direction describ-ing the knights' journey to Christ's tomb confirms that it lay outside the perimeter of the *platea*: "here þe knytys gon out of þe place."

A cave outside the *platea* would facilitate the action from the Cruci-

---

49. Cf. Cameron and Kahrl, "Staging," pp. 130–31. It is true that the shepherds and Magi follow the star. Cameron and Kahrl point to the stage direction, "stella celi extirpauit." But this could be accomplished by a star which disappears and reappears at the same spot, above Bethlehem. The authors' use of the Lincoln Cordwainers' records, which include an inventory of three stars with a cord, seems to me unwarranted, as does their imaginative picture of three separate stars on ropes pulled over the heads of the players.

50. Cf. ibid., p. 162.

10. The Entombment. Detail from Valenciennes Passion, MS Fr. 12536, f. 239v–240. Courtesy of the Bibliothèque Nationale, Paris.

fixion to the Resurrection. While the body of Christ hangs on the cross, his soul, the "anima christi," appears, and then exits into hell. After this occurs the Deposition: the body is taken from the cross and placed in the sepulcher. Thereupon "anima christi" departs from hell, sending the patriarchs to paradise, and goes to where the body has been lying. The problem is that the "anima christi" must now disappear, while the body of Christ, arisen from the dead, plays once more. This could not be accomplished easily if the sepulcher were in the *platea*, for then the actor playing "anima christi" would either have to hide indefinitely in the sepulcher, or walk off, making two "living" Christs appear simultaneously. The disappearance of the second actor could be managed easily if the sepulcher were located on the edge of the playing area. A stage cave would provide a perfect hiding place, and the actor's exit could be made out the back.

Another *locus* which may have served several functions is a castle.

Herod of the Adoration of the Magi first enters the *platea* on horseback and then goes to his "ryal paleys": "Wyghtly fro my stede I skyppe down in hast / to myn heyȝ hallys I haste me in my way / ȝe mynstrell of myrth blowe up a good blast / Whyll I go to chawmere and chaunge myn array." It is obvious that the castle is quite elaborate. Minstrels are located on or near the stage. Part or all of the platform is a functional "chawmer" or enclosure where Herod disappears to change his garments. He then sends his "seneschallus" to invite the Magi "On to his dwellynge." When the Magi agree to go "to þe kyngys halle," they are commanded: "Ffolwith in stownde / vpon þis grownde / to þe castle rownde." This last item may constitute evidence of the castle's shape. Herod sits "in trone," and is addressed by the first of the Magi as "kynge in kage ful hye." "Kage," like "halle," may be a bit of stage jargon used to denote a scaffold.[51] Ample acting space must have been available, since in ignorance of his impending doom Herod calls upon his servants to "sett a tabyll" where he feasts while the minstrels "blowe up."

This elaborate *locus* might possibly serve also for Emmaus, which is called "ȝone castell," and which was typically portrayed in art as a castle rather than merely a "village," as the Vulgate "castellum" more properly implies. Moreover, the Emmaus scene also requires a table at which Christ "Dede sitte" while he breaks bread with the disciples. The curtain provided by Herod's "chawmere" would have been useful in effecting Christ's disappearance.

In the Entry into Jerusalem, Christ tells his disciples, "Go to ȝon castel þat standyth ȝow Ageyn," to fetch the ass with foal which he rides first out of the *platea* and then into Jerusalem, through the gate of the city. If this is the *locus* used as Herod's castle in the Nativity plays, it would be sufficiently elaborate also for Simon's house, the location of the Last Supper. It is true that Simon refers to it as "my poer hous," but it is also called a "place" and a "hall," and contains the "ordenawns" for the Last Supper, that is, a large table prepared for the Paschal Feast, ample enough to accommodate thirteen men. This *locus* opens and closes as the action is focused on Christ or on the conspirators. The curtain which concealed Herod's costume change may serve for this purpose also.

Simon Leper's hall, while spoken of as a "house," has few obvious details to suggest a domestic structure. The house of Lazarus, on the other hand, is probably more homelike. The third consolator says to Mary Magdalene, "hom to ȝour place we xal ȝow wysse," and Martha

---

51. See *Ludus Coventriae*, ed. Block, glossary, "kage."

says to her, "Sustyr magdalen com out of halle." "Place" and "hall" may here be technical terms. Martha here calls her sister in response to Jesus' injunction in which "place" may be taken as the equivalent of *platea:* "go calle þi systyr in to þis plas." This interpretation seems to be justified by an earlier speech of Martha's in which she says to Mary Magdalene while standing in her hall, "I xal go forth in þe strete / to mete with jhesu if þat I may." One necessary prop in this scene is a bed, on which Lazarus lies down to die. Conceivably this *locus* could have been used for other purposes in the play, the "hous" of Zachary or the "hous" or "chawmere" of the woman taken in adultery. The latter has a "dore" which is broken down as the authorities enter, and also, in all probability, a bed.

The *loca* I have described so far have been primarily inferred from the dialogue, though in some cases, for example Simon Leper's house, additional information has been supplied from stage directions. But the revised Passion Play requires several additional *loca* which must be described primarily from stage directions. Passion I begins with the rubric, "Here xal annas shewyn hym-self in his stage . . ." He sends a messenger to Caiaphas. The reception of this messenger is anticipated by the rubric, "in þe mene tyme cayphas shewyth him-self in his skafhald." Mrs. Anne Gay distinguishes the stage from the scaffold but then admits that the two terms are synonymous,[52] and in fact the two high priests probably have nearly identical halls. In returning from Caiaphas' *locus* to Annas', the messenger encounters "Leyon" and "rewfyn," who meanwhile "shewyn hem in þe place." The two scaffolds are not in the same cluster, since communication between them must be effected by a crossing. Practically all that can be said for certain about the two scaffolds is that they both have thrones and are raised: "Annas goth down to mete with cayphas."

The place of this meeting is the most interesting and enigmatic of all the *loca* in the N-Town cycle. It is described in the next following stage direction: "here þe buschopys with here clerkys and þe Pharaseus mett and [at? in?] þe myd place and þer xal be a lytil oratory with stolys and cusshonys clenly be-seyn lych as it were a cownsel hous . . ." Perhaps the best models for this arrangement are the trial scenes from a twelfth-century psalter leaf in the Victoria and Albert Museum (see pl. 11).[53] This manuscript shows two circular configurations of high priests and commoners. Christ is led into the center of the circle in the first scene, and is tormented with the crown of thorns in the second. The N-Town

52. "The 'Stage' and the Staging of the N-Town Plays," pp. 136–37.
53. For a full discussion of these miniatures, see Nelson, "Early Pictorial Analogues," pp. 93–101.

11. Details of the Passion. From twelfth-century psalter leaf miniatures, MS 661. Courtesy of the Victoria and Albert Museum. Crown copyright.

council house, however, is enclosed. When Christ enters Simon Leper's house for the Last Supper, "in þe mene tyme the cownsel hous beforn seyd xal sodeynly onclose schewyng þe buschopys prestys and jewgys syttyng in here Astat lych as it were A convocacyone . . ." In alternating scenes, the council house and Simon Leper's house open and close as the action is concentrated now at one place and now at the other.

The conclusion of this alternating sequence is signaled by the following elaborate rubric: "Here The Buschopys partyn in þe pLace And eche of hem takyn here leve by contenawns resortyng eche man to his place with here meny to make redy to take cryst and þan xal þe place þer chryst is in xal [*sic*] sodeynly un-close rownd Abowtyn shewyng cryst syttyng at þe table and his dyscypulys eche in ere degre . . ." Mrs. Gay takes the words "un-close rownd Abowtyn" as proof that Simon Leper's house, like the council house, was located in the *platea*. Why otherwise would it open on all sides?[54] But the words do not necessarily mean "on all four sides," and could as easily mean "on three sides." It seems unlikely that two *loca*, each blocking the view of the other, would have been permitted in the middle of the *platea*.

Passion II probably employs the same major scaffolds as Passion I,

54. "The 'Stage' and the Staging of the N-Town Plays," pp. 137–38.

but uses them differently. In Passion I, Annas and Caiaphas have separate scaffolds and Herod and Pilate do not appear. In Passion II, as the procession enters the *platea*, "þe herowdys takyn his schaffalde . and pylat and annas and cayphas here scaffaldys . . ." Annas and Caiaphas take the same scaffold, as the messenger indicates by his speech:

> All heyle my lordys · princys of prestys
> Sere cayphas and sere Annas lordys of þe lawe
> tydyngys I brynge ʒou · reseyve þem in ʒour brestys
> Jhesus of nazareth is take · þer-of ʒe may be fawe
> he xal be browth hedyr to ʒou anon.

This is confirmed by a stage direction: "here bryng þei jhesus be-forn Annas and C."

Pilate has a separate scaffold, as Caiaphas indicates: "Massanger to pylat · in hast þou xalt gon." A rubric confirms this: "here pylat syttyth in his skaffald." Just as Annas sends a messenger to Caiaphas in Passion I, so in Passion II Caiaphas sends a messenger to Pilate inviting him to a meeting "At þe mothalle." When the two high priests are in the "mothalle" with Pilate, three Jews "ledyn jhesu A-bowt þe place · tyl þei come to þe halle." They question him, but getting no satisfaction, soon "þei take jhesu and lede hymn in gret hast to þe herowde · And þe herowdys scafald xal vn-close shewyng herowdys in astat all þe jewys knelyng except Annas and Cayphas þei xal stondyn . . ."

Herod's scaffold is a large, curtained enclosure. As the first stage direction in Passion II indicates, Herod takes to his scaffold before the play begins. As soon as Contemplacio finishes his prologue, there appears the rubric, "here þe herowdys xal shewe hymself and speke." He boasts and threatens, consulting his soldiers about Jesus. His speech, as Robert Weimann points out,[55] ends with a stated intention to withdraw: "Thanne of þese materys serys take hede / Ffor A whyle I wele me rest / Appetyde requyryth me so in dede / and ffesyk tellyth me it is þe best." Offering this gratuitous motivation, Herod disappears within his *locus*, only to reappear as the messengers approach.

This disappearance is strongly reminiscent of the first Herod's behavior in the Magi plays and suggests an original connection between the two episodes in spite of any late revision of the Passion sequence. As for the two parts of the Passion, it seems likely that the separate scaffolds for Annas and Caiaphas in the first are also used in the second, although now Annas and Caiaphas share one and Pilate takes the other. Similarly, the spacious house of Simon Leper, used for the Last Supper in the first, may become Herod's scaffold in the second.

A separate, small scaffold is probably used for Pilate's wife. Satan, who enters "in to þe place in þe most orryble wyse," explains his concern over the prospective death of Jesus and is admonished by a demon yet in hell not to let him die. Then, "here xal þe devyl gon to pylatys wyf . þe corteyn drawyn as she lyth in bedde and he xal no dene make but she xal sone After þat he is come in . makyn a rewly noyse comyng and rennyng of þe schaffald and [in?] here shert . and here kyrtyl in here hand . and sche xal come beforn pylat leke A mad woman . . ." Pilate's wife is thus found on a raised scaffold, and, like Herod, is "discovered" at the appropriate moment. Her scaffold is separate from Pilate's, since she has to go "of þe schaffald" in order to come to him. Pilate by this time is sitting on his own scaffold. Thanking his wife for the warning, he tells her, "now to ȝour chawmer ȝe do sewe." In sum, her scaffold is separate, curtained, and contains a bed. Perhaps it is the same *locus* used for the woman taken in adultery and for Lazarus.

After the devil's warning, the Jews bring Jesus "in to þe cowncel hous" for a private interview. This finished, "pylat letyth jhesus A-lone [in the council house] and goth in to þe jewys [Annas' and Caiaphas' scaffold]." Having washed his hands, "þan pylat goth A-ȝen to jhesu and bryngith hym" into the presence of the Jews. Pilate then announces that all shall be brought to the bar: "here þei xal brynge barbaras to þe barre and jhesu and ij þewys in her shertys bare leggyd and jhesus standyng at þe barre be-twyx them . and annas and cayphas xal gon in to þe cowncelle hous qwan pylat syttyth." The bar of justice is thus located within the council house. When Pilate has finished the necessary judicial formalities, he "xal rysyn and gon to his schaffalde, and þe busshopys with hym . . ." Christ is left in the hands of the mob, who beat him and crown him with thorns, finally dragging him away "with ropys." This all occurs "in þe place," where they meet Simon, whom they urge to take the cross and "bere it with vs to kalvarye."

A single allusion is made to "þe mownte of Calvary," but this reference to a mountain cannot be taken as an absolute requirement of staging. The Crucifixion probably occurs at the east edge of the *platea*. Pilate and the high priests watch the Crucifixion from Pilate's scaffold, for after the Virgin has made her lament at the foot of the cross, "here xal pylat come down from his shaffald with Cayphas and Annas and all here mene and xul come and lokyn on Cryst . . ." Pilate writes out the scroll: "so forth all þei xal gon Aȝen to þe skaffalde . . ." From this vantage point, the three, with their entourage, witness the conclusion of the action. The frequent coming and going of characters suggests that the place of the cross was easily accessible, and thus not a platform or a hill.

The *platea* was surely large enough to contain some such major action as the Crucifixion. As in the Wakefield plays, Noah and his family find refuge in a practicable, wheeled ship which moves in and out of the "locum interludij." Between Joseph's Trouble and the Visitation occurs the marginal notation, "et sic transient circa placeam." Similarly, the Summoner Den, in contemplating his proclamation, says, "And I xal gon in þis place them for to somowne." As with the use of heaven and the descending messenger angel, the persistent references to an open *platea* in the original and in the two revised parts of the cycle suggest that all parts of the extant cycle always used roughly the same staging techniques. The parts are not radically disparate.

The most reasonable hypothesis concerning the development of the N-Town cycle is that two major parts of the early cycle announced by the Banns were at some later time produced independently, and that in these independent performances the several parts suffered certain changes. These changes were not so much in dialogue as in elaboration of incident, movement, and stage requirements. The Passion sequence in particular essentially expanded the number of *loca* without eliminating any important *locus* which had been required by the early cycle. Thus, if a theater is elaborate enough for the Passion sequence, it will nearly accommodate the entire cycle. Cameron and Kahrl are, I think, mistaken when they suggest that the extant text could not have been produced *in toto* as it now stands.[56] All parts are compatible with theater-in-the-round, or with any other arrangement which permits a substantial number of *loca* to be situated near a large *platea*. It is true that the two parts of the Passion Play were once produced in two successive years.[57] But this is an observation based on a local stage direction and cannot preclude the possibility that the extant manuscript was assembled to expedite an unbroken performance, or a performance which spanned several successive days.[58] This is certainly the import of the Banns, which, even if written for a somewhat different play, are still retained in the text.

There is no evidence that the cycle was ever true-processional. On the contrary, the redundancy of stage *loca*, much of which is gratuitous, militates against this. But if every named locale were represented by a distinct theatrical *locus*, there would scarcely be room around the *platea* to contain them all. The cluster-technique serves to consolidate a number of loca around the all-important heaven scaffold. The multiple use of a generalized *locus*, like the castle, further reduces the number

56. Cameron and Kahrl, "Staging," p. 123 et passim.
57. See *Ludus Coventriae*, ed. Block, p. 271, ll. 5–20.
58. See ibid., p. 327, stage direction: "finem 1ª die Nota."

of scaffolds to a manageable quantity. The seams and joints between the various parts of the N-Town cycle are still visible. But the special techniques of clustering and multiple-use bring to theater-in-the-round an economy of means and a cold practicality which could never be matched by the true-processional technique. Processional characteristics in medieval plays are probably for the most part a vestige of the mute processions in which the Corpus Christi cycles most likely had their origin. In the N-Town Passion we have the most determined effort in all the cycles to move away from the episodic style which is their inheritance from the predramatic procession of pageants.

Jerome Taylor

8. The Dramatic Structure of the Middle English Corpus Christi, or Cycle, Plays

The view that the Middle English Corpus Christi, or cycle, plays are loosely strung together and that such dramatic effectiveness as they may incidentally possess was achieved through a sort of creeping invasion of the drama by coarse scenes from everyday life, wholly out of keeping with any original religious content and purpose, is notorious. And while there have been attempts, notably by Eleanor Prosser, E. C. Dunn, Timothy Fry, and Waldo McNeir,[1] to argue that the plays possess an effective dramatic unity rooted precisely in doctrine, the older view still persists.

It is the purpose of this paper to suggest that the promulgating documents and liturgical texts of the Feast of Corpus Christi provide the key to seeing that the cycle plays—each cycle in its totality—do indeed possess a structural or dramatic unity and effectiveness rooted in doctrine, though in a doctrine more subsumptive and less formalized and particular than the doctrine of penitence proposed by Miss Prosser or the abuse-of-power theory of the redemption proposed by Dom Timothy Fry. I wish to speak first of the Feast of Corpus Christi and of the doctrine, or rather the theology of human history and society, which that Feast implies; second, of certain concepts central to that theology of history and society as these receive academic elaboration in medieval political theory; and finally, of the overall structure of the cycle plays themselves.

In assessing the relationship between the Feast of Corpus Christi and

[Reprinted from Bernice Slote, ed., *Literature and Society* (Lincoln: University of Nebraska Press, 1964), pp. 175–86, by permission of the author and the publisher. Copyright 1964 by the University of Nebraska Press.]
1. Eleanor Prosser, *Drama and Religion in the English Mystery Plays* (Stanford, 1961); E. Catherine Dunn, "The Medieval 'Cycle' as History Play: An Approach to the Wakefield Plays," *Studies in the Renaissance*, VII (1960), 76–89; Timothy Fry, O.S.B., "The Unity of the *Ludus Coventriae*," *Studies in Philology*, XLVIII (1951), 527–70; Waldo McNeir, "The Corpus Christi Passion Plays as Dramatic Art," *Studies in Philology*, XLVIII (1951), 601–28. [Having appeared in 1964, the present article could not acknowledge V. A. Kolve's *The Play Called Corpus Christi* (Stanford, 1966) or utilize his many insights.]

the Corpus Christi play, scholars have been distracted by a twofold historical problem which really belongs to the external history of the stage.
First, as F. M. Salter and Glynne Wickham have convincingly shown,[2]
the appearance of the cycle play in English, so far as we know, belongs
to the last quarter of the fourteenth century rather than to the first, and
there is, thus, a gap of some sixty years between the general observance
of Corpus Christi throughout England in 1318 and our earliest documentary evidence that Corpus Christi plays were performed at Beverley
and York in 1377 and 1378. Second, there is nothing in the documents
establishing the Feast or in the liturgical texts themselves to suggest that
the celebration should feature, in Hardin Craig's words, a specifically
dramatic "ocular and corporeal representation of the whole story of
man's fall and redemption."[3] The easy generalization of our literary histories, which tell us that the cycle plays arose out of the Corpus Christi
procession, has been rejected by many: "It is possibly an ineradicable
heresy," protests Craig;[4] "we should surely question how plays ever
became attached to a procession, a form of celebration so antipathetic to
their performance," cautions Wickham.[5]

   In considering the relevance of the Feast of Corpus Christi to the
cyclic drama, I wish to prescind from the question of *how* the Feast and
its procession came to attract drama as such. The fact is that they did,
and that separate, preexisting plays associated with the Nativity and with
Easter were grouped into a single cycle of cosmic scope. I wish to ask
what there is about the intention of the Feast which sheds light upon the
internal thematic structure of the cyclic drama, whenever and for whatever external reasons that drama became an established part of the Corpus Christi celebration; a question whose relevance is suggested by Wickham's observation that "it is useless to go on arguing about the likely
impact of the institution of the Feast of Corpus Christi on the drama if
we have failed even to enquire why the Feast itself was instituted."[6]

2. F. M. Salter, *Medieval Drama in Chester* (Toronto, 1955), pp. 29–80, 115–28;
Glynne Wickham, *Early English Stages, 1300 to 1660* (New York, 1959), I, 133–49,
esp. 142–43.

   3. Hardin Craig, *English Religious Drama of the Middle Ages* (Oxford, 1955),
p. 128. Craig does, however, assert a *thematic* connection between Feast and plays
(pp. 133–34).

   4. Craig, p. 134. Craig traces the origin of the "heresy" to Charles Davidson,
Studies in the English Mystery Plays (New Haven, 1892). Karl Young also protests
against the view that the plays arose from the procession: *The Drama of the Medieval Church* (Oxford, 1933), II, 425.

   5. Wickham (see n. 2, above), p. 122. But see above, Alan H. Nelson, "Some
Configurations of Staging in Medieval English Drama," and the observation (p. 147)
that "Processional characteristics in medieval plays are probably . . . a vestige of the
mute processions in which Corpus Christi cycles most likely had their origin."

   6. Wickham, p. 9.

The Feast of Corpus Christi was first instituted for local celebration within the diocese of Liége by Bishop Robert of Thourette in the year 1246. In the letter promulgating its celebration, a document seldom reproduced or cited, Bishop Robert builds his explanation of the Feast around Psalm 110:4–5: "The merciful and gracious Lord has made a remembrance of his wonderful works: he has given food to those who fear him. . . . he will declare the power of his works to his people." These verses the bishop uses to explain that the Lord established the Eucharist, the "food" of the psalm, as a memorial of wonders he has performed because of his testament, or oath, to save erring man. The Feast, says the letter, is consistent with the divine purpose in establishing the Eucharist, for the new and special celebration will bring before the mind of the faithful those wonders which the Eucharist was intended to commemorate.[7]

Psalm 110 as a whole appears early in first vespers on the vigil of the Feast, and verse four is paraphrased as an antiphon in such a way as to bring out the commemorative function of the Eucharist forcefully: "The merciful Lord has given this food to those who fear him as a memorial of his wonders." Thomas Aquinas, who had the final hand in arranging the texts for the Feast, remarks in a sermon excerpted for Matins of the Feast-day itself: "It is suitable to the devotion of the faithful that they should bring to mind the institution of so salvific and so wonderful a mystery . . . in order that in this one sacrament they may praise the power of God, which works so many marvels." Sermons by Augustine, John Chrysostom, Cyprian, Ambrose, Cyril of Alexandria, and Hilary form the lessons for Matins during the octave of the Feast and provide a conspectus of God's works through numerous allusions which relate these works to the Eucharist. Ambrose's treatment of the Creation affords a good example of the method. "How is it that what is

7. The relevant passage in the letter may be translated as follows: "Although the Lord, mindful of his testament forever, was also mindful of the wonders he would perform for man even before he performed them; and although, after fixing a memorial of those wonders in this most holy work [of the Eucharist], he emphasized his intention, saying, 'As often as ye do this thing, do it in memory of me'; still, it should not be thought blameworthy if, in addition to the remembrance we daily make upon the altar, weak in memory as men are, we decree that once each year, in more special and solemn fashion than our daily observance allows, . . . this precious and awesome and unspeakable mystery be recalled to the faithful" (in Anton Joseph Binterim, *Die vorzüglichsten Denkwürdigkeiten der Christ-Katholischen Kirche* [Mainz, 1829], p. 277). Pope Urban IV, who first extended the Feast to the whole church in 1264, was an archdeacon of Liége under Bishop Robert and a principal consultant in the establishment of the Feast. For his bull, "Transiturus," see *Magnum bullarium Romanum*, III (1858), 705–8. For the full story of the Feast's establishment, see *Acta sanctorum*, X: *Aprilis tomus primus* (Paris, 1866), 457–64.

bread, is the body of Christ?" asks Ambrose. He answers: by the word of Christ, by the word of him of whom it is written, "The Lord commanded, and the heaven was made; the Lord commanded, and the earth was made; . . . the Lord commanded, and every creature was brought forth. . . . 'He spoke, and they were made; he commanded, and they were created.' And so I say to you, before consecration this was not the body of Christ; but after consecration it is the body of Christ. For he spoke and it became so; he himself commanded, and it was created so." As with the Creation, so with subsequent wonders and works of sacred history. All are variously brought before the mind's eye in the context of the Eucharist: the offering of bread and wine by Melchisedech; the obedient faith of Abraham; the escape from Pharaoh through the Red Sea; the Aaronic priesthood and the bloody sacrifices of the Temple; the incarnation; the miracles of healing and forgiveness wrought by Christ; the Passion; the Resurrection and Ascension; Pentecost and the ongoing spiritual combat of the faithful; the promised future glory. All the wonders, in other words, that find their place in the pageants of the Corpus Christi play.

But if the texts of the Feast stress the comprehensive commemoration of all God's wonders in the Eucharist, they stress also the kingship, the royal rule, of God and his Christ and the unification of mankind into one society under the divine rule. The Old Testament readings that comprise the lessons of the first nocturn of Matins from Trinity Sunday through the octave of Corpus Christi are taken from I Kings 1–8 and deal with the last days of the decadent Judges and with God's institution of the kingship in Israel. Though God sees the people's demand for a king as a rejection of his reign over them (I Kings 8:7–8), he responds by providing Israel with a human king who he intends shall be his servant. Saul, David, Solomon—though each proves imperfect— nonetheless prefigure the perfect kingship of Christ, eminently obedient to the divine Law, which he not only lives and preaches as man, but *is* as God. The invitatory for Matins of the Feast, combining the ideas of kingship and Eucharist, repeats as its refrain: "Let us adore Christ the King, ruler over the nations; he has given richness of spirit to those who consume him." The prayer for the Sunday within the octave asks that the faithful be given that fear and love which will secure them forever under the divine rule. The first psalm for the vigil of the Feast is Psalm 109, in which, according to Christian exegesis, the kingship of Christ is foretold: "The Lord said to my Lord: Sit thou at my right hand while I set thine enemies as a footstool under thy feet. The sceptre of thy power will the Lord send forth from Zion; thou shalt rule in the midst of thine enemies. Thine shall be the princehood in the day of thy power in the splendors of thy saints. . . . The Lord is at thy right hand; he shall destroy kings in the day of his wrath; he shall judge among the nations and fulfill their ruin." The connection between this psalm and the final judgment, dramatized in the concluding pageant of each cycle play, is obvious.

Mankind, over whom the divine King will rule when he comes in judgment, comprise one society, "that very society of saints in which there will be peace and full and perfect unity," says Augustine in one of the Matins lessons. The many grains and many grapes reduced to unity in the bread and wine manifest this unity, he tells us. "By this sacrament our Shepherd feeds us; in it we are made one body of Christ, one flesh," says Chrysostom in another lesson. Hilary speaks of that unity which is natural to men as being a perfect unity in this sacrament. "Men come to recognize the body of Christ, the Corpus Christi," declares Augustine, "if they do not disregard their *being* the body of Christ." Cyril of Alexandria, in yet another lesson, carries the theme of solidarity and integrity from the social to the individual level. As men are united in one society, so are the individual's powers of mind and body harmonized and integrated by this sacrament: "While Christ remains in us, the raging law of our members is quieted, piety is strengthened, perturbations of the mind are removed, diseases are cured; men, shattered, are made whole."

That medieval speculation on the social order, on the kingship by which society was governed, and on the law by which it was ordered was rooted in theological principles is given elaborate documentation in the studies of medieval political theory by Sir R. W. Carlyle and A. J. Carlyle, and Otto von Gierke.[8] The consensus of medieval thinking on the divine kingship over a unified mankind Gierke expresses as follows: "The Middle Age regards the Universe itself as a single Realm and God as its Monarch. God therefore is the true Monarch, the one Head and motive principle of that ecclesiastical and political society which comprises all Mankind. All earthly Lordship is a limited representation of the divine Lordship of the World."[9] And again:

. . . in all centuries of the Middle Age[,] Christendom, which in destiny is identical with Mankind, is set before us as a single, universal Community, founded and governed by God Himself. Mankind is one "mystical body"; it is one single and internally connected "people" or "folk"; it is an all embracing corporation (*universitas*), which constitutes that Universal Realm, spiritual and temporal, which may be called the Universal Church (*ecclesia*

8. Sir R. W. Carlyle and A. J. Carlyle, *A History of Mediaeval Political Theory in the West*, vols. I–VI (Edinburgh, 1930–36); Otto [Friedrich von] Gierke, *Political Theories of the Middle Age*, trans. F. W. Maitland (Boston, 1958).
9. Gierke, p. 30.

universalis), or, with equal propriety, the Commonwealth of the Human Race (*respublica generis humani*). Therefore that it may attain its one purpose, it needs One Law (*lex*) and One Government (*unicus principatus*).[10]

The Middle Ages held the ultimate Law by which creation is governed to be that divine Wisdom, Logos, or Word which was with God in the beginning, which *is* God, and which became incarnate in Jesus to save the creatures that had been made to its eternal pattern. This divine Wisdom, Word, or Eternal Law is the radical source and ultimate end or fulfillment, the Alpha and Omega, of each thing's nature. Particularly is it the radical source and law of human nature, and hence of the moral law extending to individual conduct and to the familial and political societies of men. Stretching from end to end mightily, and sweetly ordering all things (Wisd. of Sol. 8:1), it requires that human society and law promote the final end of man, that kings be subject to the law, subjects obedient to kings, wives to husbands, children to parents, servants to masters, the passions to reason, reason to faith, and mankind to God in Christ. Human insubordination to the divine Law is not only *lèse-majesté* against the Divine King; it is violation of one's nature, hence absurd, hence literally ridiculous or laughable. The insubordinate king is monstrous as a man, and he is a diabolical tyrant, not a king.[11]

The extended treatment given these points in medieval political theory discloses their centrality for all medieval speculation on the nature and destiny of society and of man. We can hardly be surprised that they dominate the Office of Corpus Christi, which brings the universal history of man before our view, or that they govern the structure, as I shall now contend, of the Corpus Christi play, which provides a dramatic imitation of that history.

I propose that the medieval view of the significance of the Eucharist, and the themes of the Feast instituted to remind men of that significance, as we have now seen them, are reflected in the object imitated by the Corpus Christi cycles in the totality of their pageants. This object I take to be the history of God's wonders, that is, of his responses, specifically, to man's defections from the divine Monarchy and Law and to man's consequent social, familial, and personal disintegrity.[12]

10. Gierke, p. 10.
11. Cf. Carlyle and Carlyle, V, 461: "The authority of the king, says Bracton, is the authority of law (or right) not of wrong; the king is the vicar of God the eternal king when he does justice, but he is the servant of the devil when he does wrong, and, therefore, the king is under the law as well as under God; there is no king where there is no law [citing Bracton *De legibus* iii. 90–92; i. 8, 5]."
12. Fry remarks, somewhat dryly, that scholars have rested content with the "generally safe assumption" that "the cycle plays in general are based upon the

This history presents a unified development from clearly defined beginning, through complication and crisis, to clearly defined end, so that the total dramatic projection of this history has a unity borrowed from the object it imitates. The imitation itself is deployed in episodes which, far from being loosely strung together, are bound into one design in one or more of the following three ways: (*a*) as *causally related* in a sequential action which knits together a whole series of men's responses to God's saving initiatives (e.g., without Noah's faith, there would have been no mankind surviving the flood; without the faith of Abraham, who was descended from Noah, there would have been no people of God; without the faith of Mary, who sprang from that people, there would have been no Redeemer; etc.); (*b*) as *exemplary* of one or another kind of faith or obedience, or license and disobedience, with the repetition of exempla suggesting a movement in the direction of what Elder Olson has called "the pattern play";[13] (*c*) as *figural* in Erich Auerbach's sense,[14] that is, with an early episode finding its complete significance in a later one which it foreshadows and adumbrates. Structurally considered, therefore, the cycle play is both unified and polymorphic, with at least three kinds of relevance operating singly or together to account for the inclusion and the ordering of particular episodes in one overall design.

If we pursue the line of sequential action, we find that in all of the cycles it follows in generalized form the classic stages of "plot." After the purely factorial or expository presentation of God as divine King and Wisdom, Alpha and Omega, and the prototypical disobedience of the angels, comes the initial equilibrium situation: man in paradise and at peace with God, the beginning of the action proper. Man's first disobedience, which involves the inordinate rule of desire over reason and of woman over man, is the exciting force of the conflict which follows. The complication presents, first, the division of mankind into basically two strains—the seed of Cain, prolonged in the wicked rulers of men (Pharaoh, Herod, Caesar, Pilate, Caiaphas, and their minions), and the friends and instruments of God, represented by Abel, Noah, Abraham, the prophets, the Magi, Mary, and climactically Christ. The

---

theme of the Redemption of man" ("The Unity of the *Ludus Coventriae*," p. 528). This paper attempts to be more precise by going beyond the notion of "theme" (since a theme can appear sporadically) to the object imitated by the action as a whole; and by defining the specific aspect under which "the Redemption of man" is viewed.

13. Elder Olson, *Tragedy and the Theory of Drama* (Detroit, 1961), pp. 46–47.

14. Erich Auerbach, "Figura," in *Scenes from the Drama of European Literature* (New York, 1959), pp. 11–76.

conflict between these two groups provides the substance of the complication. In Christ's defeat of evil through love, God asserts and finally
vindicates his rule. The crisis centers in the plays concerning Christ,
building from episodes of his public life to the core-group detailing the
crucifixion, the acme of obedience to the will and law of God, undergone *as* and *for* man by the God-King. The crisis, however, is suspended
or prolonged as the faithful are invited to live and to preach the consequences of Christ's redemptive death, continued in the Eucharist, which
the Feast and its plays were instituted to honor. That redemptive death
is not vindicated as a triumph for Christ and the body of his faithful
until the Judgment scene, and there is a secondary building up of tension
and conflict in the Anti-Christ action which immediately precedes the
final resolution. In that resolution God's wonders are recapitulated and
his double title to Majesty as Creator and Savior reasserted. The action
is perhaps, as has been claimed, a divine comedy in the special and restricted medieval sense of "comedy." But it is above all a serious action:
a melodramatic tragedy in the confirmation of disaster for the wicked
who are deservedly damned, and a tragedy of narrowly averted disaster
for the rest of mankind, even for the saints, since God's interventions,
while expected, given his promise, are beyond all men's expectations and
deserts.

If we pursue the figural and exemplary lines, those coarse comic
scenes, allegedly disruptive of doctrinal-dramatic unity, likewise take
on a significance, for the comic characters uniformly derogate from
the established position of God as King or as the sweetly ordering Law
that penetrates all departments of the social fabric. The ranting bombast
and horrific strut, and even the physical disease and death, of the tyran-
nical rulers are repeated dramatic and external projections of the violent
disorder entailed upon all insubordinateness, literally ridiculous, to the
natural or Eternal Law. Lucifer's folly as he lays claim to the majesty
and throne of God in the opening scenes of the cycles is the figure
and prototype of all subsequent earthly tyranny, and all such tyranny,
in turn, is not only the anti-type of the divine kingship but exemplary
of the condition of rebellious man magnified to extremity. Similarly,
the ludicrous recalcitrance of Noah's wife, prefigured in Eve's conduct
toward Adam, extended in the relationship of a Towneley Mak and
Gyll, and contradicted in the docility of Mary toward Joseph, exemplifies the absurdity of disorder in the domestic sphere, as does the strife
between Cain and his servant. As for the contemporary realism of the
comic scenes, allegedly at odds with the religious spirit of the plays,
Auerbach, in his study of the *Mystère d'Adam*, has so thoroughly vindicated such mixture of sublime and low styles and such interpenetration

of past and present by reference to the medieval theology of history that it suffices to refer to his treatment and to recall his summation of the matter: "In principle, this great drama contains everything that occurs in world history . . . and hence there is no basis for a separation of the sublime from the low and everyday. . . . Nor is there any basis for concern with the unities of time, place, or action, for there is but one place—the world; and but one action—man's fall and redemption. . . . The everyday and real is thus an essential element of medieval Christian art and especially of the Christian drama."[15]

The proposal that the Middle English cycle plays are unified seems inconsistent with their multiple authorship and the continuous revision they underwent. Yet, we must be prepared to admit, as Hardin Craig, for example, does with respect to the Hegge cycle, the marvel of "a theological intelligence motivated by structural imagination that lasted from age to age in the development of a great cycle of mystery plays."[16] What this paper has defended is not so much a thesis as an interpretive hypothesis. Having reviewed the correspondences between the Feast of Corpus Christi and the drama that bears its name—correspondences rooted in a common intention to commemorate the wonders by which the divine King reintegrates the creaturely kingdom disobedient to his law; and having seen how the history of these wonders can be considered as the unifying action of the Middle English cycle plays, we are perhaps entitled to urge that this hypothesis deserves testing in future detailed analyses of the separate plays. If fully established, this view of the doctrinal-dramatic unity of the cycles will require that we revise the notion that this drama "was not striving to be dramatic but to be religious";[17] or that it succeeds as drama only where it fails to be religious; or that while it is religious, no distinctive theological ideas underlie its structure; or that, religious or not, it is in any case structurally disunified and dramatically ineffective; or that since it is untragic it cannot have influenced the development of Renaissance tragedy;[18] or that we must not approach it with structural expectations arising from the study of drama in general.[19] At stake are current and altogether fundamental judgments concerning the Middle English Corpus Christi, or cycle, plays.

15. Erich Auerbach, *Mimesis* (New York, 1957), p. 138.
16. Craig, *English Religious Drama*, p. 265.
17. Ibid., p. 5.
18. Cf. Willard Farnham, *The Medieval Heritage of Elizabethan Tragedy* (New York, 1956), pp. 173 ff.
19. Craig, pp. 5–6.

John R. Elliott, Jr.

9. The Sacrifice of Isaac as Comedy and Tragedy

I

Nearly forty years ago George R. Coffman published an eloquent appeal for "The Study of the Corpus Christi Plays as Drama."[1] Since that time Coffman's plea has been more than answered. Performances of the medieval biblical cycles in York, Chester, Grantham, London, and elsewhere have proven their immense theatrical vitality, revealing to modern audiences the power and subtlety of dramatic techniques once considered crude and artless. Critical studies have confirmed the evidence of the theater by showing the careful artistry that went into the medieval dramatizations of subjects once thought to be artistically intractable and devoid of literary interest. As a result, these plays have ceased to be mere historical curiosities and have become for us works of art, as impressive in their scope and intensity as the greatest products of medieval literature.

In one respect, however, the critical revaluation of medieval drama is currently taking a quite different course from that proposed by Coffman. In order to determine the dramatic merits of these plays he assumed that critics would necessarily proceed by assessing "their independence and originality," measuring the degree to which they overcame "the limitations of their subject matter," and deciding "whether dramatic effectiveness or interest in the religious theme" was the guiding principle of their authors. The more we have studied the medieval biblical cycles the clearer it has become that they achieved their dramatic qualities not in spite of their religious content but because of it. The writings of Gardiner, Craig, Salter, Prosser, Wickham, Hardison, and Kolve have made it clear that medieval drama remained at all times a religious drama, and that it derived its characteristic dra-

[Reprinted from *Studies in Philology*, LXVI (1969), 36–59, by permission of the author and the publisher. Copyright 1969 by the University of North Carolina Press.]
1. George R. Coffman, "A Plea for the Study of the Corpus Christi Plays as Drama," *SP*, XXVI (1929), 411–24.

matic techniques directly from the forms and purposes of Christian
worship.[2] As Kolve has emphatically declared, "What we find in this
drama is not in fact an opposition of interests—the religious and the
secular, the devotional and the profane—but rather a single coherent
dramatic intent." If medieval playwrights created a drama of lasting
appeal, they did so out of methods and materials that were peculiarly
medieval and peculiarly Christian. To assess the "effectiveness" of this
drama solely by the light of modern critical principles is to run a serious
risk of misinterpreting the actual effects it was intended to have.

Nowhere is this more apparent than in the explanations that have
been offered by modern critics of the function of comedy in the
Corpus Christi play. They have dealt almost exclusively with what
they commonly refer to as "comic elements"—that is, with a few individual episodes, excerpted from the whole, such as the story of Noah or
the Wakefield Second Shepherds' Play, which contain broadly farcical
or satiric effects. Drawing their definitions of comedy from such sources
as Bergson and Meredith (comedy as social criticism), or Freud and
Bentley (comedy as the release of repressed impulses), the critics, while
applauding the spirit of these episodes, have invariably dismissed them
as irrelevant, if not antithetical, to religious worship. They have concluded, in the words of one recent writer, that "comedy in the mystery
cycles arose as a kind of inchoate mass protest against the disciplines of
religion."[3] A medieval critic, however, would have seen the matter very
differently. To begin with, he would not have talked about comic
"elements" in the biblical cycles at all, for to him the entire cycle would

2. Harold Gardiner, *Mysteries' End* (New Haven, 1946); Hardin Craig, *English
Religious Drama of the Middle Ages* (Oxford, 1955); F. M. Salter, *Medieval
Drama in Chester* (Toronto, 1955); Eleanor Prosser, *Drama and Religion in
the English Mystery Plays: A Re-evaluation* (Stanford, 1961); Glynne Wickham,
Early English Stages, 1300–1660 (London, 1959–63); O. B. Hardison, Jr., *Christian
Rite and Christian Drama in the Middle Ages: Essays on the Origin and Early
History of Modern Drama* (Baltimore, 1965); V. A. Kolve, *The Play Called Corpus
Christi* (Stanford, 1966).
3. William G. McCollom, "From Dissonance to Harmony: The Evolution of
Early English Comedy," *Theater Annual*, XXI (1964), 69–96. Similar views have
been expressed by Charles Mills Gayley, "An Historical View of the Beginnings of
English Comedy," in *Representative English Comedies, from the Beginnings to
Shakespeare* (New York, 1903), I, xx; Irena Janicka, *The Comic Elements in
the English Mystery Plays against the Cultural Background (Particularly Art)*
(Poznan, 1962), p. 24; Juanita Jones, "The Theory of Comic Drama in England
before 1625," University of Iowa dissertation, 1942, p. 138; A. P. Rossiter, *English
Drama from Early Times to the Elizabethans: Its Background, Origins and Developments* (London, 1950), pp. 38–41; Frederick T. Wood, "The Comic Elements
in the English Mystery Plays," *Neophilologus*, XXV (1939–40), pt. I, 39–48,
pt. II, 194–206; Ola Elisabeth Winslow, *Low Comedy as a Structural Element in
English Drama from the Beginnings to 1642* (Chicago, 1926), pp. 17–18.

have been a *Commèdia*, a "comedy." In the Middle Ages the term
"comedy" referred primarily to the *structure* of a narrative or a drama:
Comedy begins in adversity and ends in joy; Tragedy begins in prosperity and ends in misery. By this definition, the form of Christian history, and hence of any drama imitating it, was clearly comic rather than
tragic. Moreover, in spite of the distinctions usually drawn between
the genres in theory, in practice they were by no means mutually
exclusive. Comedy was the larger and more inclusive of the two forms
and might contain tragedy within it—a phenomenon noted, for instance, by many of the commentators on Dante. Dante conceived of
his poem as a "Comedy" even though it included, as his medieval commentators pointed out, much material that might separately be labeled
"tragic" or even "satiric."[4] Although there is no "Letter to Can Grande"
and no contemporary commentary explaining the aesthetics of the
Corpus Christi play, the case is plainly similar. Where the modern critic
sees a "serious" tragic drama into which a few shrewish wives and
thieving shepherds have blasphemously intruded, the medieval critic
would have seen a divine comedy that embraced and transcended the
tragedies of the Fall of Man and the Sacrifice of Christ. As Hardison
has written of the Christian ritual that gave birth to medieval drama,
"the ritual structure characteristic of the Mass and the Church year . . .
is comic, not tragic. The mythic event celebrated is rebirth, not death,
although it is a rebirth that requires death as its prelude. The experience of the participants is transition from guilt to innocence, from
separation to communion."[5] The drama that derived from this ritual
was comic in structure at the same time that it was "serious" in purpose,
and it was the structure of the whole that gave shape and meaning to

4. See, for instance, the Commentary of Benvenuto da Imola, written c. 1375,
at the time when the English biblical cycles were being formed:
   . . . Only this is to be carefully noted, that this book [the *Divine Comedy*],
just as it is said to contain every branch of philosophy, so it contains every
branch of poetry. That is, if one looks closely, tragedy, satire, and comedy.
It contains tragedy, because it describes the deeds of Popes, princes, kings,
barons, and other rulers and nobles, as appears throughout the whole book.
It contains satire, that is, denunciation, because it denounces marvelously and
boldly every type of evil doer, sparing no one on account of his position,
power, or birth. Therefore, it might be more fitting to call the book a satire
than a comedy or a tragedy. Nevertheless, one might well call it a comedy,
for according to Isidore Comedy begins in sadness and ends in joy. Even so,
this book begins with a sad theme, that is, Hell, and ends in joy, that is
Paradise, or the essence of the divine.
(Quoted in A. Philip McMahon, "Seven Questions on Aristotelian Definitions of
Tragedy and Comedy," *Harvard Studies in Classical Philology*, XL (1929), 97–198,
which contains a thorough discussion of medieval definitions of comedy and
tragedy, with the relevant texts.)
5. Hardison, *Christian Rite*, p. 284.

the individual episodes. That this structure produced scenes of feasting, mirth, and invective is not to be wondered at. Its real significance is to be measured by the imprint it left on even its most potentially tragic episodes.

One of the clearest examples of the influence of the cycle's ritual-comic structure on the dramatic character of an individual episode is the story of the Sacrifice of Isaac. Not only did this story contain many potential elements of tragedy, but it remained popular as a dramatic subject well into the sixteenth century, when it was in fact interpreted as a tragedy. By comparing these later versions, particularly the *Abraham Sacrifiant* of Théodore de Bèze (1550), with the treatment of the story in the English Corpus Christi play we may see some of the means by which medieval dramatists were able to subsume tragedy under comedy, as well as the changes that were necessary in the relation of drama to religious ritual before Renaissance playwrights could transform the subject into a tragic one.

II

To most modern critics both the Old Testament story and the medieval dramatizations of the Sacrifice of Isaac have seemed to belong to the literature of tragedy. A. P. Rossiter feels that Abraham's "tragic strength" is one of the dramatic high points of all the cycles. The Brome Manuscript version has been especially praised as a fulfillment of the story's tragic potentiality. John Speirs feels that the element of tragedy inherent in the Old Testament story—"the tragedy of a father under an overriding obligation or doom to slay his own son"—is "realized in the play," and J. B. Moore has claimed that it is "an excellent example of realistic tragedy, though it chances to have a happy ending." One recent students' edition of the Brome play even contains an analysis of Abraham's *hubris* and compares him with Othello.[6] To the medieval audience, however, the Sacrifice of Isaac was more likely to have appeared as a story of triumphant joy than as a story of tragic suffering. The typological meaning with which it had been imbued since the time of Saint Augustine makes this clear. According to Augustine, the sacrifice of the son by the father was a foreshadowing of God's willingness to sacrifice his son for the redemption of mankind. An elaborate set of figural correspondences followed from

6. Rossiter, *English Drama*, p. 72; John Speirs, *Medieval English Poetry: The Non-Chaucerian Tradition* (London, 1957), p. 325; J. B. Moore, *The Comic and Realistic in English Drama* (Chicago, 1925), p. 43; Vincent F. Hopper and Gerald B. Lahey, *Medieval Mystery Plays* (Great Neck, N.Y., 1962), p. 31.

this central identification. Because Abraham prefigured God, and Isaac, Christ, the wood carried by Isaac to the sacrificial hill foreshadowed the cross of Calvary (much is made of this detail in all the cycle plays) and the ram caught by his horns in the briers (Gen. 22:13) signified the Christ of the vicarious atonement crowned with thorns.[7] (The Cornish drama carries the typological symbolism even further by naming Gabriel as the angel who stays Abraham's sword.)[8] All the medieval dramatic versions of the Sacrifice of Isaac derive their characterizations from this figural interpretation. Abraham, as a type of God, necessarily offers his sacrifice willingly, out of faith and love. Isaac, as a type of Christ, voluntarily endures his suffering out of faith and obedience. The reprieve from God, when it comes, is thus a reward for steadfastness, not a fortuitous happy ending.

If the dramatists had followed typological symbolism exclusively, of course, as some narrative treatments of the story did, the result might well have been scarcely recognizable as human drama. The *Cursor Mundi* reports of Abraham simply that

> To oure lorde he was so trewe
> That myghte no pite make him rewe
> But he had levere his childe spille
> Then do ageyn his lordis wille.[9]

Similarly, the *Metrical Paraphrase* of the Old Testament gives a remarkably unfeeling dialogue between Abraham and his son:

> And to hys sun thus sayd he ryght,
>   "Sun, I sall make offerand of the."
> Ysaac sayd with semland lyght,
>   "ffader, os god wyll, behoveyse yt to be.
> what hest to hym that ye hath heght
> leffe yt noght for luf of me."[10]

In the commentaries of the Fathers, however, there was ample precedent for the dramatists' interest in detailed human motivation. While modern critics tend to find such an interest at odds with the ostensible theological significance of the story, medieval writers saw no incompatibility between the specific human causes of biblical events and the divine purposes they served. As Erich Auerbach has pointed out,

7. Augustine, *The City of God*, xvi, 32, trans. Demetrius B. Zema and Gerald G. Walsh (Washington, D.C., 1950–54). For a survey of the typological interpretation of the story, see Rosemary Woolf, "The Effect of Typology on the English Medieval Plays of Abraham and Isaac," *Speculum*, XXXII (1957), 805–25.
8. *The Ancient Cornish Drama*, ed. Edwin Norris (Oxford, 1854), I, 103–5.
9. *Cursor Mundi*, ed. Richard Morris, EETS 57 (London, 1874), ll. 3133–36.
10. *A Middle English Paraphrase of the Old Testament*, ed. Herbert Kalen (Göteborg, 1923), ll. 711–16.

figural interpretation differs from classical *allegoresis* in its emphasis on the reality and importance of the literal level of meaning.[11] The literal sense of biblical narrative was an objective historical truth, which yielded its deeper spiritual meanings only when its concrete reality had been perceived and understood. In writing of Abraham, Augustine insisted that "Abraham our father was a faithful man who lived in those far-off days. He trusted in God and was justified by his faith. His wife Sara bore him a son. . . . Whatever Scripture says about Abraham is both literal fact and prophecy."[12] Accordingly, in addition to explaining the typological significance of these events, Augustine also sought to convey their impact upon the real human beings to whom they happened. He dealt directly, for instance, with the issue that most interests modern critics, the seeming arbitrariness and immorality of God's command to Abraham to slay his son. Augustine was well aware that God's purposes might appear arbitrary and immoral to men, and his ultimate faith in their rationality did not diminish any of their mystery for him. In the *Confessions* he wrote, with Abraham in mind, that "many actions which appear worthy of men's disapproval are approved by Thy testimony, and many praised by men are condemned before Thee. . . . When Thou suddenly commandest something which is unusual and unforeseen, even a thing which Thou hast formerly forbidden, and although Thou hidest for the time the reason for Thy command, who will doubt that it should be done, even though it be opposed to the social conventions of some men?"[13] God's will is rational, but men may be unable to perceive its rationality. This faith and the ability to act upon it without question are what chiefly distinguish the medieval characterizations of Abraham from those of the Renaissance. In *The City of God* Augustine declared that "Not for a moment . . . could Abraham believe that God took delight in human sacrifices, although he knew that, once God's command rang out, it was his not to reason why, but to obey."[14] He adds that Abraham's virtue consisted chiefly in maintaining his faith that God would keep his promise to multiply his seed, even though the command to slay Isaac would seem logically to negate such a promise. Medieval writers were fully aware, then, of the human anguish involved in the story of Abraham and Isaac, but even so their emphasis is not on tragic tension and paradox, but on reconciliation, reward, and renewal.

11. Erich Auerbach, " 'Figura,' " in *Scenes from the Drama of European Literature*, trans. Ralph Manheim (New York, 1959), pp. 11–76.

12. Augustine, *Sermo* II. 6.

13. Augustine, *Confessions*, iii. 9, trans. Vernon J. Bourke (New York, 1953).

14. Augustine, *City of God*, xvi. 32.

Of even closer relevance than patristic commentary to the dramatic versions of the Sacrifice of Isaac is the position occupied by the story in the liturgy of the medieval church. In the series of biblical readings for the masses and offices of Lent the events of Christian history were given a literary form that was essentially dramatic. Beginning with Septuagesima Sunday, these readings recapitulated the entire history of the world. Their arrangement followed the conventional medieval division of history into seven ages (Adam to Noah, Noah to Abraham, Abraham to Moses, Moses to David, David to the return from captivity, the return from captivity to Christ, Christ to the Last Judgment). The rhythm thus created of periodic renewal and release from bondage gave to the Lenten liturgy the same dramatic structure that informed the ritual plot of the Mass. The story of Abraham's sacrifice was alluded to in a responsory for Quinquagesima Sunday. The dominant themes of the readings for that day are faith and redemption by grace. The Gospel selection contains references to the resurrection of Christ and to the miraculous salvation of the blind man of faith (Luke 18:31–43). These two themes continued to be yoked together in Quinquagesima services up to the time of the cycle plays, and furnished the background against which medieval audiences were instructed in the significance of the Abraham and Isaac story. In Mirk's *Festial*, for example, a collection of homilies intended as models for parish priests, the sermon for Quinquagesima concerns the repentance proper to Lent. It illustrates the relation of spiritual suffering to salvation by linking Quinquagesima with Easter Sunday though the numerological symbol of "the nowmbur of fyfty," the number which "bytokenyth remission and ioye." The homily explains this symbolism:

For yn the old lawe, ych fyfty wynter, all men and woymen that wern sette wyth service and bondage, thay wern made fre in gret ioy and murth to hom. Wherfor thys nowmbur bygynnyth thys day, and endyth yn Estyrday, schewyng that yche godys-servand that ys oppressyd wyth tribulacyon, and takyth hit mekely yn his hert, he schall be made fre yn his resurrecyon: that ys yn the day of dome, and be made the ayre of the kyngdome of Heven.[15]

The meekness of heart that endures suffering in order to receive salvation is then illustrated from divine history by the reading of the story of Abraham and Isaac. Just as Quinquagesima is a promise of Easter, so the sacrifice of Isaac is a promise of God's sacrifice of his own Son to redeem mankind. Mirk's sermon on penance can therefore end on a note of joyful expectation:

15. John Mirk, *Mirk's Festial: A Collection of Homilies*, ed. Theodor Erbe, EETS e.s. 96 (London, 1905), p. 74.

Thus may Crist well be called Isaac that ys to undyrstond laghtur for mony a soule. He broght out of helle laghyng that yode thedyr, ful sor wepyng . . . thus was fygur of Chrystys passyon longe or he wer borne.[16]

Isaac brought laughter into the world, and his suffering was only a prelude to the redemption which would transmute all suffering into eternal joy. For this reason the story was also read during the Easter vigil service.[17]

Two points of major importance for our understanding of the dramatic versions of Abraham and Isaac emerge from this sketch of the exegetical and liturgical uses of the story in the period leading up to the establishment of vernacular biblical drama. First, the typological tendency of medieval biblical exegesis meant that the Abraham and Isaac story derived its meaning not only from its intrinsic characteristics but from its context in the rest of human and divine history. The story was not self-contained but looked before and after: its significance came from its fulfillment of previous events and its foreshadowing of later ones. Second, through the function of the story in the liturgy its dramatic versions inevitably took on the ritual-comic structure characteristic of the liturgy and Mass, for it was the historical divisions recorded in the Lenten readings that furnished the rationale for the selection of Old Testament episodes in the Corpus Christi play.[18]

III

All six of the extant medieval English dramatizations of the Sacrifice of Isaac, though they differ widely in minor details, exhibit

16. Ibid., p. 78. The name "Isaac" means literally "laughter" in Hebrew. The name was given to Isaac because when God told the 99-year-old Abraham that Sara would bear him a son, "Abraham fell upon his face and laughed" (Gen. 17:17); and when the Angel told Sara the same, "she laughed behind the door of the tent" (Gen. 18:10). Much was made of this etymology by medieval commentators, who also made a special effort to convert the sexual sarcasm implied in the biblical account into something more nearly resembling religious joy. Augustine wrote: "The laughter of Abraham is an exultation after triumph, not the derision of one who fears to fall. . . . At the same time, the Angel first reproached her for a laughter of joy that was lacking in faith, but later confirmed her faith. . . . Once he was born and given that name, Sara proved how little there was in her laughter of scorn and derision and how much of gratitude and joy" (City of God, xvi. 26, 31). St. Ambrose called Isaac the symbol of joy achieved by enduring tribulation with patience (Letters, trans. Beyenka [New York, 1954], p. 463).

17. There is evidence that the sixteenth-century Cretan play of The Sacrifice of Abraham was intended for performance on Easter Sunday. See F. H. Marshall, Three Cretan Plays (London, 1929), p. 9.

18. See Hardin Craig, "The Origin of the Old Testament Plays," MP, X (1913), 473–87; Adeline M. Jenney, "A Further Word as to the Origin of the Old Testament Plays," MP, XIII (1915), 59–64; Hardison, Christian Rite, pp. 88–89; and Kolve, The Play Called Corpus Christi, pp. 33–56.

an identical dramatic form. This form has six parts. First, a Prologue, usually spoken by Abraham, recapitulating his life and, in some texts, reviewing the whole of human history since the Creation; second, the Angel's Command to Abraham to sacrifice his son, and Abraham's assent; third, the Journey to "the land of Vision," during which Isaac bears the wood for the fire and Abraham laments his task; fourth, the Preparations for Sacrifice, during which Abraham announces his intention to Isaac, who expresses both fear and obedience; fifth, the Staying of the Sword and the appearance of the ram in the briers; sixth, the Release of Isaac from his bonds, God's Promise to bless Abraham's seed, and the Journey homeward with rejoicing. (The Chester and Brome plays add a seventh part, an Epilogue spoken by an Expositor explaining the typological and moral significance of the play.)

The ritual basis of this plot is clear. It is derived not from the biblical narrative, but from the Mass and the Easter liturgy. As Hardison has observed, "The Mass is comic in structure, having a descending action, a crisis, a reversal-recognition, and a joyful resolution. In terms of emotion this represents a movement from *tristia* to *gaudium*. In terms of allegory it is a presentation of the central events of Christian history. . . . The Easter liturgy has the same structure, emotional pattern, and historical associations."[19]

As long as the drama remained distinctively medieval, the authors of the Abraham and Isaac plays fitted their dramatic techniques to this ritual plot. Characterization, movement, gesture, theme, and tone are all consistent with comic structure. This in no way prevented the best of the plays from attaining that intensity and "seriousness" which led J. Q. Adams to call the Brome *Sacrifice of Isaac* "the best example of pathos in the early drama."[20] Nevertheless, the pathos is always subordinate to the central purpose of the plays—the celebration of the power of man's faith and the magnitude of God's mercy. Pathos is only a single note in the tonality of the whole.

The principal function of the Prologue in each of the plays is to place the experience of Abraham in the larger context of Christian providential history, and thus to show that the ultimate control of human destiny lies beyond man himself. The Wakefield Prologue recapitulates not only the events of Abraham's life but the whole of human history from the Fall of Man to the present. Against the bitter consequences of the Fall, it places the "marvels" which have occurred periodically since that time as pledges of God's mercy, such as the preservation of Noah from the Flood and the escape of Lot from Sodom

19. Hardison, *Christian Rite*, p. 83.
20. J. Q. Adams, *Chief Pre-Shakespearean Dramas* (Cambridge, Mass., 1924), p. 117.

(ll. 25–30).[21] Other texts carry the recapitulation of history beyond the Fall to the Creation. "At my bidding," declares God in the Dublin Prologue, "was wrought bothe good man & synnere, / All in joy to have dwellid, tyl adam to syn fell" (ll. 3–4). By beginning with an evocation of the paradise from which man has fallen and concluding with God's promise to restore him to it, these plays epitomize the joy-to-sorrow-to-joy movement of the Cycle as a whole. The Dublin Prologue announces that God has ordained a special role in history for Abraham—to affirm what Adam denied, to please where Adam displeased (ll. 9–13). The life of Abraham is established as a microcosm of the life of mankind. Like Adam, he will be tested, but like the New Adam, he will not be found wanting. In this résumé of Abraham's life the drama depends less on biblical fact than on the function of the Prologue in a ritual plot. Whereas the Bible records the repeated favors God had showered upon Abraham, the drama dwells instead on his "mourning," his "sorrow," and his "travail," looking only to the future for "succour" and "oil of mercy" (Wakefield, ll. 4–21).

The framework of divine purpose established by the Prologue makes more understandable the readiness with which Abraham assents to God's seemingly arbitrary command to sacrifice his son. Never in the medieval versions does Abraham challenge the justness of the command. In the Wakefield play, for example, Abraham replies unhesitatingly:

> A, lovyd be thou, lord in throne!
>   hold over me, lord, thy holy hand,
> ffor certis thi bidyng shall be done. (ll. 74–76)

A stage direction in one of the Chester manuscripts prescribes that "here Abraham answereth very meekly to god" (l. 215n.), after which he tells Isaac to "make thee ready, my Derling, / for we must doe a lyttle thing" (ll. 229–30). At the same time, Abraham is fully human: while he is quick to acknowledge his duty and obedience to God, he is equally quick to confess the anguish that it costs him. "But yitt the fadyr to scle the sone / grett care it causyth in my thought," he admits in the "Coventry" version (ll. 9–12). "Alas for ruthe," he complains, "it is pite" (l. 100). So great, in fact, is the pathos of the scene that the modern reader is likely to feel a tension which he can only call tragic. To us,

---

21. References to the English versions of *Abraham and Isaac* are drawn from the following texts: Wakefield: *The Towneley Plays*, ed. George England and Alfred W. Pollard, EETS e.s. 71 (London, 1897); York: *York Plays*, ed. Lucy Toulmin Smith (Oxford, 1885); Chester: *The Chester Plays*, pt. I, ed. Hermann Deimling, EETS e.s. 62 (London, 1893); "Coventry": *Ludus Coventriae*, ed. K. S. Block, EETS e.s. 120 (London, 1922); Brome and Dublin: *The Non-Cycle Mystery Plays*, ed. Osborn Waterhouse, EETS e.s. 104 (London, 1909).

Abraham cannot become divine on such terms as these without ceasing to be human. He must, we feel, choose one or the other. This conflict between the human and the divine was indeed to become the tragic core of Bèze's *Abraham Sacrifiant* in the sixteenth century. In the medieval versions, however, the conflict is described in this way only once, in a marginal interpolation in the York manuscript attributed by Miss Toulmin Smith to a "late hand." There Abraham declares that "Nowe have I chose whether I had lever / My nowne swete son to slo or greve my God for ever" (*York Plays*, p. 64, n. 1). Nowhere else in this play, or in any of the others, does Abraham admit that there is any real choice to be made. For the medieval Abraham it is not a matter of absolute choice between two incompatible alternatives, but only a matter of establishing priority between them. He is called upon, not to show that he despises the world and loves only God, but simply to show that he loves God more than the world or its dearest object. Such an interpretation goes back at least to Saint Basil, who wrote that "the heart of Abraham was searched to see if he loved God with his whole soul and his whole heart, when he was commanded to offer Isaac as a holocaust, in order that he might show that he did not love his son above God."[22]

The doctrine of priority is especially clear in the Brome play. There Abraham first clearly defines the terms of his conflict:

> Wolle-com to me be my Lordes sond, (*sond:* messenger)
> And hys hest I wyll not with-stond.
> Yit Ysaac, my yowng sonne in lond,
> A full dere chyld to me have byn. (ll. 68–71)

He then makes equally clear the basis of his decision:

> I love my chyld as my lyffe;
> But yit I love my God myche more . . .
> Thow I love my sonne never so wyll,
> Yit smythe of hys hed sone I schall. (ll. 81–82, 86–87)

(There is a similar speech in the Wakefield play, ll. 122–28.) As a human being Abraham is not expected to overcome his emotional reluctance to carry out the command. But neither is the nature of the command presented as one that makes obedience incompatible with humanity. "In thy hart be no-thyng dysmayd," counsels the Angel, and Abraham agrees:

> Nay, nay, for-soth, I hold me wyll a-payd
> To please my God to the best that I have. (ll. 93–95)

22. St. Basil, *Exegetic Homilies*, trans. Agnes Clare Way (Washington, D.C., 1963), pp. 175–76.

As the time for the sacrifice draws nearer, Abraham expresses his paternal anguish fully and intensely:

> A! Lord, my hart reysyth ther-ageyn . . .
> I may not fynd yt in my hart hym to kill . . .
> Now, hart, wy wolddyst not thow breke on thre? . . .
> O! Fader of hevyn, what schall I do? (ll. 299, 304, 305, 311)

Yet when he has proved his willingess to carry out the deed, the Angel, staying his hand, compliments him on the obedience not only of his "wyll" but also of his "harte" (l. 320). There is nothing evil in Abraham's emotional reluctance, because it forms no real obstacle to a resolved will. Still less, in the context of the medieval versions of the story, is there anything noble about it, since it is by nature antagonistic to the benign purpose of God. In the York play Abraham apologizes to God "gyffe [if] my flessche groche or greve oght, / Or [before] sertis my saule assentte ther-till" (ll. 177–78). Of pathos there is much in Abraham's plight; of tragedy very little.

A similar issue arises, in the following episode of the Preparation for Sacrifice, around the suffering of Isaac. To fulfill his typological role Isaac must be a willing victim, and his anguish is never as intense as Abraham's. His association with the sacrificial lamb (the Chester play actually substitutes a lamb for the biblical ram in the briers) led most of the medieval dramatists to portray him as a mere child, rather than as the young man he is in the Bible, in order to emphasize his meekness and innocence. In the Dublin version, Isaac asks Abraham to bind his hands so that he may not interfere with the execution of the sacrifice, and to remove his clothes so that he will not soil them. In the "Coventry" and Chester plays he urges his father not to let his pity prevent him from fulfilling his vow to God. In the Brome, he protests against the sacrifice only until he is told the reason for it, whereupon he immediately acquiesces:

> Is.   And ys yt Goddes wyll that I schuld be slayn?
> Ab.   Ya, truly, Ysaac, my son soo good;
>   And ther-for my handes I wryng.
> Is.   Now, fader, agens my Lordes wyll
>   I wyll never groche, lowd nor styll. (ll. 187–91)

At the same time, though, Isaac is much more than a mere exemplary figure. He is horrified at his fate, and his submission to it does not come easily. While the "Coventry" and York plays largely fail to develop the pathos of Isaac's situation, the others all include such details as his fear of the bright blade of the sword, his cries to his mother, and his appeals to Abraham for mercy. In the Chester and Brome plays, he asks to be blindfolded and implores Abraham to use as few strokes as possible in cutting off his head. In the Wakefield play, Isaac asks Abraham to forgive him for his sins, and the effect is so moving that Abraham must lower his sword for an instant to wipe away his tears. In the Dublin, Isaac even goes so far as to protest against the irrationality and cruelty of God's command:

> Here I shal be dede & wot never wherefore,
> Save that god most have his wille. (ll. 218–19)

The poignancy of such a moment is very great, but it is not allowed to develop into tragedy. Even the most vehement and pitiful of Isaac's protests subside as soon as he is told the reason for his father's action. Only his fear remains, a fear which is natural and involuntary, not to be confused with uncertainty over the rightness of God's command and the duty of obeying it. The difference is an important one, reflecting the medieval distinction between natural fear and sinful fear. Natural fear is that which all men should expect to feel, and which even Christ felt in his humanity. Sinful fear, on the other hand, is a fear which is allowed to overwhelm the reason and to induce contempt for God.[23] In the Chester play, when Isaac is told that he must be killed, he cries out in fear of the sword, reminds Abraham that he is only a child, and asks what sin he has committed. When, however, Abraham explains that it is by God's command that he is to be slain, he vows to be obedient and urges his father to keep his own vow of obedience to God. After this, Isaac neither blames God nor questions the justice of the command, though he continues to be frightened of the sword, requests a blindfold, and implores his father to strike quickly and cleanly. Isaac's fear, then, far from undermining the play's moral lesson, is fully consonant with his typological role, for it is the same fear that Christ is to experience on the cross, in spite of his voluntary acceptance of his sacrifice. In the Wakefield *Crucifixion* Christ too asks what sin he has committed ("My folk, what have I done to the, / That thou all thus shall tormente me? / . . . what have I grevyd the?" (ll. 244–47), and, in his final agony, begs his father to save him ("My god, my god, wherfore and why has thou forsakyn me?" (ll. 579–80).

The peripeteia of the drama, therefore, does not come unexpectedly,

23. This point is discussed by Woolf, "Effect of Typology," with illustrations from Ludolphus Carthusiensis and St. Bonaventure.

Isaac's fear belongs to what the Schoolmen termed *propassio*, an involuntary perturbation of the feelings that may lead to sin but is not in itself culpable. *Propassio* is felt by animals and men alike. Among men, only Adam had the power to restrain "first motions" (*primi motus*) themselves, for he had been created with a perfect nature. Since the Fall, such control is beyond the power of men, including Christ. *Propassio* therefore becomes sinful only when it is consented to by the reason. (See Dom Odon Lottin, *Psychologie et morale aux XIIe et XIIIe siècles* (Gembloux, Belgium, 1948), II, 496–97; V, 303–4.

though in the most skillful of the versions, such as the Wakefield and the Brome, it comes with shattering effect. We know that even if Isaac is actually to die, it will be a triumphant, saintly death, not a tragic defeat. Abraham, however, has already expressed his faith that God will enable all to end happily. In some versions this faith is a very general one. Exactly how God will preserve them from harm he does not know, but he is trusting nonetheless:

> Son, care not therfore on never a side,
> But let god alone therwith this tyde,
> & for oure wey he shal purvyde
> & defend us from fere. (Dublin, ll. 152–55)

In the Chester and Brome plays, Abraham specifically announces his faith that God will provide "summ manner a best" as a substitute (Chester, ll. 269–72; Brome, ll. 143–46). In the Wakefield he is so confident of God's mercy that he anticipates the mood of joyful release in the last scene of the drama:

> We shal come home with grete lovyng:
> Both to & fro I shal us lede . . .
> We shall make myrth & grete solace,
> By this thyng be broght to end. (ll. 142–43)

We are thus prepared for the appearance of the Angel and the Staying of the Sword. The Angel's speech emphasizes reward and mercy. Because of Abraham's willingness to carry out the Command, he is told that "God wyll aqwhyte the well thi mede" ("Coventry," l. 192). In the Wakefield play the key words in the Angel's speech are "release" (l. 272) and "grace" (l. 275). The ram in the briers appears to Abraham as a "comfort aftyr grett trybulacion" ("Coventry," l. 208) and, since it is a symbol of Christ's vicarious atonement, as a pledge of the eventual redemption from death of all mankind. This redemption will flow from Abraham historically as well as symbolically, for God now promises a perpetual blessing on Abraham's seed:

> as thik as gravel in the see dothe ly,
> As thik thy sede shal multiply,
> & oon shal be borne of thi progeny
> that to all shal cause salvacioun. (Dublin, ll. 298–301)

The final scene of rejoicing follows, and it is both doctrinally and aesthetically appropriate. After such anguish, the Lord's reward comes with joyful relief to all the participants. In the Brome play, the Angel is "blythe" (l. 316), Isaac "full glad" (l. 343), Abraham "rygth myry" (l. 372). The brief reversion to pathos in the Brome play, when Isaac suddenly asks as he bends over the fire "ye wyll not kyll me with yowr sword, I trowe?" (l. 378), only serves by contrast to intensify the sense of relief. Most light-hearted of all the rejoicing scenes is the Dublin, which is expanded into seventy lines, during which Abraham and Isaac leap on their horses and hurry home to tell Sara of their good fortune. The York play concludes with the arrangements for the marriage of Isaac and Rebecca, that his seed may "springe and be spredde" (l. 361). The Chester version alone omits this scene of rejoicing, substituting for it a speech by an Expositor explaining the typological significance of the story.

The rhetoric of the medieval Abraham and Isaac plays is consonant, then, with their ritual-comic structure. Pathos is abundantly present but never for its own sake; rather it serves to heighten the peripeteia from sorrow to joy. Realistic characterization is delicately balanced with typological significance. Moral conflict is fully developed but never into tragic tension. This was so, however, only as long as dramatists retained medieval habits of mind. In the sixteenth century the Abraham and Isaac story came to be seen in a radically different light, a phenomenon which we can trace with considerable exactness not in England, where the Reformation brought a virtual end to the dramatization of biblical subjects, but in France. In addition to its appearance in the chief French biblical cycle, the *Mistère du Viel Testament*, the story was separately dramatized by an anonymous author in 1539 and again by Théodore de Bèze in his *Abraham Sacrifiant* of 1550.[24] Since all of these plays have the Bible as their primary source, the central elements in their plots—the pathos, peripeteia, and anagnorisis—are naturally the same. Yet in spite of this, very different effects are achieved in the two later versions. The changes occur principally in the rhetorical components of the plays —characterization, theme, tone—but also, and more significantly, in the structure itself. While they retain some separate elements of the ritual-comic plot, the shape of the whole is drastically altered in each. The effect of all of these changes, whether rhetorical or structural, is to turn the drama away from comedy toward tragedy.

IV

The revisions made in the medieval *Mistère* for the 1539 performance of *Le Sacrifice de Abraham* anticipate the direction in

24. The text of *Le Mistère du Viel Testament* dates from 1500. I use the edition of James de Rothschild, Societé des Anciens Textes Francais, 6 vols. (Paris, 1878– 91). The 1539 play was based on the *Mistère* text and printed in two slightly differing editions, each entitled *Le Sacrifice de Abraham à huit personages*. Both texts are included in Rothschild.

which Bèze was later to take the Abraham and Isaac drama. The Prologue of the older version had realized even more fully the themes contained in the English texts. In it God announces his desire for Scripture to show a prophecy that Jesus will redeem fallen mankind by demonstrating obedience to His Father. To prefigure this event, God will command a human father to deliver his son to death. A debate follows between Mercy and Justice over the wisdom of His decision, which God settles by declaring it necessary to show men the extent of his love in sacrificing his own Son for their redemption. The 1539 text omits this entire scene and replaces it with a speech in which God explains his command solely as a test of Abraham's obedience and as an opportunity for his spiritual perfection (*Mistère*, ll. 9610–93; *1539*, ll. 195–221). The whole framework of God's historical design and man's relation to it is thrown out, leaving only the human moral issue as the center of interest. To compensate for this omission, the 1539 text greatly expands the central section of the plot dealing with the reactions of Abraham and Isaac to the command. This structural alteration was noted by Rothschild, who thought it a fault on aesthetic grounds, since it obscured motivation and substituted lengthy verbal disquisitions for significant action.[25] It is, nevertheless, perfectly consonant with the author's interpretation of the moral significance of the story. In the medieval *Mistère* Abraham had accepted God's command without question, although he acknowledged the resistance to it of both "l'amour paternel" (l. 9892) and "nature si fort" (l. 9912). As we should expect from our study of the English plays, there was no question of these being evil emotions, nor of there being any fundamental incompatibility between the human and divine elements in man. In the 1539 version, on the other hand, Abraham immediately complains that God has given him a task above human capability ("Transcendant quant a son effect / Puissance d'humaine nature" [ll. 342–43]). In a long speech filled with biblical and patristic quotations, Abraham attempts to discover the possible reasons for God's command—something that had never occurred to any of the medieval Abrahams—finding comfort only in the conclusion that God's ways are inscrutable to men. He ends by apologizing for his "affections" and "naturelles passions," which he begs God to remove from him (ll. 481–87). Soon after, he is given another long speech, an imaginary dialogue in which he analyzes the conflict between Reason and Nature that he knows would take place in his wife Sara were she to learn of the command. He distinguishes completely between the two, advising her to subdue Nature in favor of Reason:

25. Rothschild, *Mistère*, II, iv.

> Veulx tu par ung regret humain
> Perdre l'amour du souverain?
> Yras tu a dampnation
> Par une humaine affection? (ll. 801–4)

Exclusive concentration on the moral issue in this play thus leads to its being carried to logical extremes unknown in the medieval drama. The idea of priority, of a gradual hierarchy of human faculties composed of various degrees of frailty and virtue, now yields to the notion of an absolute choice between human degeneracy and divine perfection. To be human is to be evil, and to obey the divine command requires the subjugation of all human impulses. The Abraham of the 1539 play is indeed scarcely human once he has accepted the command, for unlike the *Mistère* Abraham, whose heart breaks as he lifts the sword, this Abraham delivers over the waiting body of his son a dispassionate speech composed chiefly of scholastic abstractions commending the virtue of obedience (ll. 1227–44).

Bèze's *Abraham Sacrifiant* is a more skillful realization of the tragic implications of the 1539 text. In the Preface to the printed edition of the play Bèze confesses that he is uncertain whether the story he is dealing with is basically comic or tragic, but declares that he has chosen to treat it as a tragedy:

The matter that I have in hand . . . is partly tragical and partly comical . . . and because it holdeth more of the one then of the other: I thought best to name it a tragedie. (p. [7])[26]

The play is also called a tragedy on the title page of Arthur Golding's English translation of 1577. It is, in fact, one of the earliest Renaissance attempts to fuse the form of classical tragedy with Christian subject matter.

As we might expect from a Protestant writing in exile, Bèze's treatment of the Abraham and Isaac story is much closer in spirit to the Old Testament than are the medieval dramas. Bèze presents God's command to Abraham as a simple, irrational test of obedience, crushing in its effect upon an anguished human being. The historical significance of the incident as a pledge of man's redemption and as a prelude to the spreading of the chosen race through Abraham's seed is barely implied in Bèze's play. The Prologue that had established this significance in the medieval plays is omitted entirely: there is only a character named "Prologue" who invites the audience to be attentive. Bèze also omits the

---

26. For convenience I quote from the translation of *Abraham Sacrificant* by Arthur Golding, *A Tragedie of Abrahams Sacrifice* (London, 1577), ed. Malcolm W. Wallace (Toronto, 1906).

character of God from his play and replaces it with Satan, who tempts Abraham to indulge his human weaknesses. As a result, Abraham's significance as a type of the Father sacrificing his Son is greatly diminished. Instead, he is seen as an individual human being, without typological or allegorical overtones, who is confronted with an extreme moral conflict. The introduction of Satan has the effect of polarizing this conflict into a battle between spirit and flesh. As the Prologue announces:

> The flesh, the world, his owne affections
> Not onely shall be shewed in lively hew,
> But, (which more is) his faith shal them subdue.
>
> (Prol., ll. 40–43)

Even before the Angel appears to announce the command, Abraham prays to God lamenting his "wicked nature" and promising to remain "unweerie" in his obedience (ll. 239, 245).

If Abraham's conflict is definable in simple terms, it is by no means easily resolved. The tragic tone of Bèze's play stems from the acuteness with which Abraham feels the claims of the "flesh" as well as those of the spirit. "Flesh" is here both more evil and more powerful than it was in the cycle dramas. The medieval Abraham never ceased to be human while he aspired to be divine; Bèze's Abraham feels that he must choose one or the other. The difference may be seen at once in Abraham's reaction to the Angel's command. In the Brome play, it had been instant comprehension and consent: "Wolle-com to me be my Lordes sond" (l. 68). In Bèze, it is outraged disbelief: "What! burne him! burne him!" (l. 256). He asks for an explanation, and when he does not receive it, assumes that the Lord must be angry with him. He cannot decide what to do, and even wonders, like Hamlet, whether the apparition has not deceived him (l. 669). Bèze's Abraham is a rationalist who discovers that God's will is rationally incomprehensible and who is unable to accept his discovery. As late as the Sacrifice scene itself he has still not decided what to do and is still attempting to rationalize the command:

> So cruell offrings please not God perdye.
> He cursed Cayne for killing of his brother:
> And shall I kill myne Isaac and none other?
> No. no. Never doe soe. (ll. 686–89)

Such reasoning only leads him more clearly to the conclusion that God's will is irrational, and he wonders if men will ever be able to pray to him again (ll. 721–45).

Bèze uses the role of Isaac to heighten Abraham's anguish. He emphasizes Isaac's extreme youth, for example, not to bring out typological associations with the innocence of Christ, but solely to produce pathos.

Isaac asks to go with the shepherds to the fields (both this and the 1539 play devote whole scenes to pastoral songs and games), but is told that he is too young. When Abraham comes for him, Sara, who in the *Mistère* had urged Isaac to go with her husband to sacrifice, has a fearful premonition and begs him not to go, although Isaac assures her that he will return "in better plyght, / Than now I am in syght" (ll. 435–36). Further pathetic irony emerges from the shepherds' ignorance of why Abraham leaves them behind at the sacrifice scene and why he seems so sad. Most obvious of all is the pathos produced by Bèze's structural device of dividing the Sacrifice into two scenes and inserting between them a soliloquy by the grieving Sara. All these details serve to emphasize the isolation of Abraham and the magnitude of his decision. The audience is enabled to feel the difficulty with which Abraham arrives at his final realization that his resistance to the command is merely the work of "flesh," "fond affections," and "humane passions," and that God's will must take precedence over his reason (ll. 778–81). In spite of the acknowledged power of "humane passions," there is no allowance made for them in the Calvinist moral scheme of Bèze's play. It is Satan who stands by Abraham during his lamentations for his son. Abraham's love and fear are not natural emotions which can be harmoniously accommodated to the divine, but sinful ones which must be thoroughly uprooted. Bèze has no interest in depicting an Abraham who exhibits, like the medieval Abrahams, both pity and obedience at the same time. At the moment of sacrifice Abraham again opposes "obeysance" to "all that humane wit / Can say or think, to make me now to flit" (ll. 892–93). He has reached at last the moral state possessed by the cherubic Isaac all along, whose innocence protects him from "humane passions" and whom Satan grudgingly compliments for being "so stedie" (l. 841).[27]

Some of the features of Bèze's play are to be accounted for by personal and historical factors. The play was written shortly after the author's conversion to Protestantism, while he was living in exile in Switzerland. Bèze felt keenly the parallel between his life and that of the exiled Abraham, who received the favor of God. There are also some

27. Unlike the trembling child of the medieval drama, Isaac is frequently depicted in Renaissance literature as a paragon of piety and wisdom. Cf. DuBartas, *The Sacrifice of Isaac:*

> . . . his inclination
> Excels his birth and careful education.
> His faith, his knowledge, wit, and judgment sage
> (preventing times) anticipate his age.
> Being but a babe, he feares the living Lord,
> And (wise) depends upon his fathers word.
> —trans. Joshua Silvester (London, 1592), sig. A1.

topical anti-Catholic references. Bèze refers frequently to the Philistines' worship of idols, and his Satan wears the disguise of a monk throughout the play. Nevertheless, the main features of the work are only expansions of implications already present in the 1539 play, which was a Catholic production. The changes both dramas made in the medieval versions of the Abraham and Isaac story reflect a general cultural change and point forward to the classically oriented humanist drama that was to dominate the European stage during the next two centuries. Of this drama Curtius has written:

> This classical form of the drama, born of the Renaissance and Humanism, is anthropocentric. It separates man from the cosmos and from the forces of religion; it shuts him into the lofty solitude of the realm of ethics. The tragic figures of Racine and Goethe are placed before decisions. The reality with which they have to deal is the play of man's psychological powers.[28]

Between the medieval and Renaissance dramatizations of the Sacrifice of Isaac, then, it is the differences rather than the similarities that stand out. In no sense does the medieval drama in this instance merely pave the way for the emergence of more artistic and sophisticated forms in the sixteenth century. Rather, the Renaissance versions of the story are quite different in kind and reflect new ways of representing the relation between man and God. However meritorious in their own right, the Renaissance Abraham and Isaac plays retain only the bare outline of a dramatic form which, while it flourished, gave vital and lasting artistic expression to the deepest beliefs of its society.

28. Ernst Robert Curtius, *European Literature and the Latin Middle Ages*, trans. Williard R. Trask, Bollingen Series, vol. XXXVI (New York, 1953), p. 142.

Lawrence J. Ross

10. Symbol and Structure in the *Secunda Pastorum*

It might appear rather late in the day for a study of the unity of the Towneley *Second Shepherds' Pageant*. The Wakefield playwright's widely anthologized masterpiece, generally regarded as the finest single achievement of the English cycle drama, surely has been the most frequently and intensively studied play of its kind. However, its high repute still depends, to a very considerable extent, on appreciation of the brilliant farcical action, realistic characterization, and pungent social protest of its "secular" part rather than on judgments of the play as a whole. Such partial critical views, often prejudicially tinged with teleological assumptions about the development of secular drama, may be forcefully represented by A. C. Baugh's still influential opinion in *A Literary History of England:* "The length of the Mak episode is hopelessly out of proportion to the proper matter of the play. The *Second Shepherds' Play*, as a shepherds' play, is an artistic absurdity; as a farce of Mak the sheepstealer, it is the masterpiece of English religious drama."[1] Not many contemporary students can feel such a position entirely comfortable, or sufficient. The difficulty is, neither do they have the critical evidence really to substantiate the unsupported assertion of A. C. Cawley, the Wakefield Pageants' editor, that "the comedy is subservient to the sacred theme it so closely parallels," that in this, as in the Wakefield Master's other work, "The essential meaning of all these diverse elements, pagan, secular, and divine, is to be found in their author's fusion of them into a Christian pattern."[2] It is symptomatic of the state of criticism that a recent study begins by admitting that the play yet "raises a recurrent interpretive question" of the most fundamental kind: does it "function as a unified religious statement in a traditional craft cycle, or . . . primarily as a secular farce with a Nativity scene added?"[3]

[Reprinted from *Comparative Drama*, I (1967–68), 122–43, by permission of the author and the editor. Copyright 1967 by *Comparative Drama*.]
1. (New York, 1948), p. 273.
2. *The Wakefield Pageants in the Towneley Cycle* (Manchester, 1958), p. xxiv.
3. William M. Manly, "Shepherds and Prophets: Religious Unity in the Towneley *Secunda Pastorum*," *PMLA*, 78 (1963), 151.

Of course, such a question (however we may choose to formulate it) can be acute as well as recurrent only because the "secular" and "religious" parts of the play, so far from being flatly discrepant or simply disjunctive, are recognized to have been elaborately conjoined. Since Homer A. Watt's study of the play's unity a quarter-century ago, students have become increasingly aware of the detailed connections, the systematic parallels, in structure, theme, action, and language, binding the two contrasting plots, both of which center on a "nativity."[4] The problem now is whether the ligatures and parallels do anything more than mechanically span the gulf between what is taken to be disproportionately emphasized farce and the seemingly "displaced" Adoration scene. Merely the range of terms which have been used to describe the parallelism—"foreshadowing," "false imitation," "parody," "burlesque," "satire," "travesty"—shows how very far critics are from agreement about its nature and significance. Paradoxically, studies of the connections between its parts have exposed much of the intensely managed artistry of the play without convincing us of the essential integrity of its design, a design which really comprehends the satire and prophecy, the farce and mystery, the folk comedy and the Christian piety.

Two recent studies dealing with the *Secunda Pastorum* illustrate the need of further study to come to grips with this critical dilemma even as they extend our understanding of the play. William M. Manly questions whether the "parallels alone . . . do unify the play as felt religious drama" because he supposes that these, "being structurally implicit, require a sophisticated perception of pattern in the whole." Would not "a rural audience . . . tend to lose itself in the seven hundred and fifty-four lines of secular farce and . . . recover a sense of the play's religious purpose only in the final explicit Nativity scene?" He therefore emphasizes the "overt prophetic suggestion" in the farce scenes—"the forward linking undercurrent of Christian expletive in the shepherds' speech, the hints of a dramatically integrated [*Processus prophetarum*] in . . . their complaints, and the echoes of Antichrist in Mak"—in order to show that these "explicitly operate in the midst of the secular scenes to control the play as religious drama and to focus the immediate action on the final scene of Christ's birth."[5] The obvious and crucial disability of such an argument is that it ignores the dramatic action and substance of five-sixths of the play; it may be doubted that "the immediate action" can be shown to be meaningfully "focussed" on the sequent Adoration scene

4. "The Dramatic Unity of the *Secunda Pastorum*," in *Essays and Studies in Honor of Carleton Brown* (New York, 1940). Cf. Francis J. Thompson, "Unity in *The Second Shepherds' Tale* [*sic*]," *MLN*, 64 (1949), 302–6.
5. Manly, pp. 151, 152, 155.

without showing that the farce *as such* bears a significant relation to what follows. The other recent study, an article on double-plot in the English shepherds' plays by Margery M. Morgan, perceives this difficulty: "If their laughter at the farce did not prepare the onlookers to be the more deeply affected by the sacred climax, the dramatist has failed in his task despite all his ingenuity."[6] And she bears us forward toward a possible solution by arguing the thesis that the lay audience was prepared to see the play as a unity because they were already familiar with the plot formula on which the *Secunda Pastorum* is based. Her case for the conventionality, in other shepherds' plays, of the parallel plot structure used by the Wakefield Master is persuasive. Unfortunately, she assumes for his *Second Shepherds' Pageant* a general critical agreement which simply does not exist that "the whole play is more impressive than its secular part" because we now recognize its parts to be governed, in something more than a superficial sense, by "the single theme." In point of fact, in the case of the *Secunda Pastorum*, she merely asserts the existence of "a system of analogies, uniting the secular and sacred elements" without any detailed argument in substantiation sufficient, for example, to oppose so very different a view of the play's inclusiveness as that of A. P. Rossiter. And Rossiter's viewpoint demands consideration because, with the same parallel structure in mind, he found the play's characteristically "Gothic" significance to reside in a radical, and ultimately ironic, "ambivalence" posited on the lack of precisely the sort of unity Morgan would claim for it.

The wide implications of the problem of this play's unity are exposed by Rossiter's interest in it as an instance of "the strangely comprehensive two-ways-facingness [which] brings together," in medieval (and later) English drama, and in art as well, the remote, transcendental, and noble with the vulgar, brutal, gross, and base. Such complexities of matter and tone may invite our misconstruction. In the *Secunda Pastorum* Rossiter supposed "A travesty is effected by nearly exact parallelism. . . . Clowning and adoration are laid together, like the mystery and the boorishness in Breughel's *Adoration of the Magi*, or mystery and surrounding nescience in others of his pictures." He therefore concluded that the play leaves us "to wrestle with the uncombinable antinomies of the medieval mind: for these immiscible juxtapositions constantly imply two contradictory schemes of values"—an ambivalence whose "evaluated effect . . . reaches out towards a searching irony."[7] But there are clear critical

6. " 'High Fraud': Paradox and Double-Plot in the English Shepherds' Plays," *Speculum*, 39 (1964), 676–89.
7. *English Drama from Early Times to the Elizabethans* (London, 1950), pp. 53, 72.

dangers here: on the one hand, in projecting sixteenth-century ambivalence or modern skeptical irony on medieval dualities of tone, and, on the other, in ignoring characteristic medieval modes of resolving or comprehending such dualities. Certainly, we had best try to wrestle with the antinomies by medieval rules before deciding, always in a particular case, just how uncombinable they are. What this means in the present case is that our unreflective use of such disjunctive terms as "secular" and "religious" may depend on premises which are critically disabling. It is to say that our problem in grasping the unity achievable by the Wakefield Master's kind of double plot may rest upon the inadequacy of our literalistic assumptions about the modes of representation available to him, and demonstrably used by him. I suggest that these must control the way the analogies work in the play, and what they signify. And I propose first that we obtain a clue to these modes of representation by examining a passage revelatory of the ways in which the Wakefield playwright discovers significance in the literal.

I

For this initial purpose, we might turn to the less frequently studied part of the play. The two elements of the liturgical *Pastores* which in the *Secunda Pastorum* have undergone their most sophisticated development in English drama are the scene in the fields and the scene in which the Christ Child is adored by the shepherds. The Wakefield Master's elaboration of the former scene has claimed the lion's share of modern attention; the Adoration scene has been relatively ignored. The consequence is that criticism has missed the fact that it represents a development quite as extraordinary as the sheep-stealing farce and one equally indicative of the playwright's skillful stagecraft and intellectual sophistication.

It has been remarked that in all of the shepherds' plays, "including the liturgical *Pastores*, the secular characters are essentially a chorus grouped about the icon of the Nativity."[8] The function of the cycle play is to mediate by dramatic action between the audience, its life and experience, and the religious mystery. The total function of the "secular characters," basically the shepherds, is to serve as intermediary between the audience and the significance of the icon. This of course is the role prescribed by the scriptural text itself. The "country shepherds," traditionally the representatively humble men, are those vouchsafed the Lord's "good tidings of great joy"; they "go even unto Bethlehem to see this thing which is

8. Morgan, p. 689.

come to pass"; "And when they had seen it, they made known abroad the saying which was told them concerning this child" (Luke 2:8–17). The scene of Adoration, which dramatically presents the icon of the Nativity and the manner in which the shepherds relate to it, is the *direct* enactment of this mediation. It is one way in which the dramatic art of the Wakefield Master enables them really to fulfill the command "Tell furth as ye go" (l. 744).

The playwright's device to accomplish this purpose is brilliant in its dramatic economy. He uses the dramatized "Hail Lyrics"[9] spoken by the shepherds as, kneeling in turn, they greet and adore the Child, in combination with the very gifts they offer to him, to create "the icon of the Nativity" directly before the audience's eyes. This long climactic passage, ending with the Virgin's speech on the Conception (ll. 710–41),[10] is remarkable for the exquisite balance sustained between attestation of the divinity and majesty of Christ—Creator, Overcomer of Satan, Sovereign Savior full of Godhead—and apprehension of his tender, vulnerable, and implicitly sacrificial humanity. The latter burden is carried, at an immediate and literal level, through the shepherds' homely, warm, and humorous responses to the Divine Infant as a "yong child" called with loving possessiveness "my swetyng," "my barne": "a lytyll tyne mop" who "merys" and puts forth his "dall"; through the sympathy for his poverty and "poore wede"; and through the wry comic stroke of providing the Lord with a ball so the deprived Child can participate in the fashionable lordly game of tennis. The deeper significance of this theme of Christ's humanity is emphasized from the start with the phrase "I weyne" in the First Shepherd's speech; for a characteristic compression of time operates here, as elsewhere in the play: the Incarnation implies the Expiation by which "The fals gyler of teyn" will fully be "begylde." (It is like the misericord of the Annunciation at Tong where the traditional lily, centrally placed between the angel and the Virgin, strikingly blossoms into the Cross.)[11] We can glimpse the whole method of the passage in small in the calculated juxtapositions of the three rhymed lines of Gyb's speech ending with the reference to the Eucharist:

> Hayll lytyll tyne mop!
> Of oure crede thou art crop;
> I wold drynk on thy cop . . .

The gifts which the shepherds present to the Child—"a bob of cherys,"

9. See G. C. Taylor, "The Relation of the English Corpus Christi Play to the Middle English Religious Lyric," *MP*, 5 (1907), 18.

10. The reader will want the text before him. My references to Wakefield Pageants are to the Cawley edition.

11. Reproduced in M. D. Anderson, *Misericords* (Penguin Books, 1954), pl. 14.

"a bird," and "a ball"—serve to adumbrate the multiple significance developed by the "Hail Lyric" speeches. For, obviously, these offerings become attributes of the Christ Child in the visual stage tableau cumulatively developed through the passage. It may seem strange that the symbolic import of the shepherds' gifts should not have received much critical emphasis until now. The appearance at the start of the series of the unseasonable cherries, a fertile promise of further joy and plenty alluding traditionally to the miraculous burgeoning of nature at the Nativity, might have forewarned us of their further significance.[12] But, in the first place, these gifts do represent a break with English dramatic, and even, in one sense, artistic tradition. In medieval art in the English churches, where the Adoration of the shepherds is the main subject, the artists usually "visualized it in contemporary realism."[13] And in the shepherds' plays themselves, from the Shrewsbury Fragment on, the gifts are homely, rustic, even humorous.[14] The Wakefield Master could have got the idea for realistically homely gifts which at the same time bear symbolic value as attributes from the Continental tradition where, in a number of instances, one shepherd offers the finest lamb of his flock, another his shepherd's crook, and the third his pipe; the symbolism of these has been cited by Louis Réau: "L'agneau aux pattes liées signifie le sacrifice de Jésus; la houlette indique qu'il sera pasteur d'âmes et le chalumeau que ses disciples le suivront comme un nouvel Orphée."[15] However, the Wakefield gifts plainly were not selected with such an idealized pastoral symbolism in mind. A more likely source for the basic

12. Cawley, p. 113, cites *Sir Cleges*, ll. 224–26, where cherries are "tokenyng / Off more godnes that is comyng; / We shall haue more plenté"; also the cherry tree bearing fruit just before Christ's birth in the *Ludus Coventriae* pageant of the Birth of Christ, ll. 31–42 (ed. K. S. Block, EETS e.s. 120 [1922]. But see also notes 39, 40, below.

13. See M. D. Anderson, *The Imagery of British Churches* (London, 1955), p. 106.

14. Shrewsbury Fragment, in *The Non-Cycle Mystery Plays*, ed. Osborn Waterhouse, EETS e.s. 104 (1909): a horn spoon; in *The Chester Plays*, ed. Hermann Deimling, EETS e.s. 62 (1892): a "flackett" and a spoon, a cap, and "a paier of my wyues olde hose"; the masters' boys offer a bottle, hood, pipe, and a nuthook; in *The York Plays*, ed. Lucy Toulmin Smith (Oxford, 1885): brooch with bell, two cob nuts on a band, and a horn spoon; *Ludus Coventriae*: no offerings; in *Two Coventry Corpus Christi Plays*, ed. Hardin Craig, EETS e.s. 87 (1957): pipe, hat, and mittens; Towneley *Prima Pastorum*: spruce coffer, ball, and a bottle. In the Second Shepherd's "ball / That thou wold resaue" (ll. 471–72), we may perhaps see the seed from which the Wakefield Master's idea for the consistently symbolic gifts of the *Secunda Pastorum* grew.

15. *Iconographie de l'art chrétien* (Paris, 1957), II, 234–35. The lamb occurs as an offering in a panel depicting the Shepherds' Adoration in a window at East Harling, Norfolk; it is reproduced in M. D. Anderson, *Drama and Imagery in Medieval English Churches* (Cambridge, 1963), pl. 22a.

idea of symbolic offerings is, of course, the gifts of the Magi (evidently to parallel whom the shepherds originally were made three in number); for the widely broadcast traditional significance of the Wise Men's gifts, explicitly noted in plays on the subject in other English cycles, bears a direct relation to the burden of the popular "Hail Lyrics" underlying the Wakefield shepherds' speeches. But the inspiration for the specific gifts, at once simple and significant, must, it would seem, have come from medieval art, in which we find that all three of the Wakefield shepherds' gifts are among the most commonplace attributes of the Christ Child.[16] To the Wakefield Master's learning in music (already acknowledged in modern studies)[17] we must add his awareness of iconographic conventions pertinent to his subject matter.

Although the order of their presentation has, as we shall see, a significance of its own, it will make for more convenient reference to the iconographical traditions on which the Wakefield Master has drawn if we deal with the gifts, and their symbolic meaning, in the inverse pattern of their offering.

First, then, the "ball," which, in the hands of the Child is seen as the symbolic orb, and in the simple spherical form most frequently used, in the religious art of the period, for this ubiquitous motif. The "ball" was, in fact, another name for the symbolic orb, and the word yet appears with this meaning in Shakespeare.[18] As a motif it may be found, in every medium attempted during the period, in innumerable representations of such subjects as God the Father, Christ in Majesty or at the Judgment, the so-called Coronation of the Virgin, and the Virgin and Child. Especially pertinent are its appearances in Nativity scenes. In one English

16. Two of them are probably the most familiar objects held by the Child in the English alabaster carvings, in many of whose other details close iconographic relationships with the cycle dramas can be detected. See, on the latter point, W. L. Hildburgh, "English Alabaster Carvings as Records of Medieval Religious Drama," *Archaeologia*, 93 (1949), 51–101.
17. See N. C. Carpenter, "Music in the *Secunda Pastorum*," below, pp. 212–17.
18. See *Henry V*, IV.i.277; *Macbeth*, IV.i.121; and *OED*. In the morality *Wisdom* (*The Digby Plays*, ed. F. J. Furnivall, EETS e.s. 70 [1896], p. 139), the character "Wysdom of Christ" bears "In his left hand a ball of gold with a cross ther-vpon" (i.e., such an orb as in our pl. 14).
A few other English examples of the Child with the orb in its simple spherical form may be cited: embroidered chasuble, late thirteenth century, Acqu. T-673-1864, and alabaster statue, fifteenth century, Acqu. A140-1946 (Victoria and Albert Museum); cf. with the latter, Our Lady of Westminster Cathedral and the later figure (c. 1510) in the British Museum, Acqu. 1956, 7-1, 1. See also the Virgin and Child, mid-fifteenth century, in the Antel Chapel, Lower Lights, of All Souls College (in F. E. Hutchinson, *Medieval Glass at All Souls College* [London, 1949], frontispiece), and the sculptures reproduced by W. L. Hildburgh, "Medieval English Alabaster Figures of the Virgin and Child—II: Our Lady Seated," *Burlington Magazine*, 88 (1946), pls. IB, IIA and C.

12. Detail from the Nativity, with Saint Joseph and Donor. English alabaster table, fifteenth century. Courtesy of the Victoria and Albert Museum. Crown copyright.

alabaster "table" of the early "battlemented" type (between 1380 and 1420, Paderborn Cathedral), the orb held by the Child is almost super-erogatory since the transcendent power it signifies is implicit in the traditional gifts offered by the kneeling Magi to the King of Kings. In another, and later, alabaster carving (Victoria and Albert Museum) the dishlike mandorla with what appears to be a doll-image of the Divine Infant, orb in left hand, affixed to it, is so unnecessarily and curiously crude that it has justly been supposed due to direct influence on the carver of a cycle drama, where it is unlikely that an actual infant was used to represent the Child.[19] The use of the orb in a third Nativity table (pl. 12) may represent what may be called a "domestication" of the motif since the symbol of Christ's sovereignty now appears as the Child's toy ball.

19. See Hildburgh, "English Alabaster Carvings as Records," and Anderson, *Drama and Imagery*, p. 134, with reference to the stained glass of the Adoration of the Shepherds at East Harling cited above, n. 15. For reproductions of these two alabasters, see Hildburgh, pl. XIa, and Philip Nelson, "Some Fifteenth-Century English Alabaster Tables," *Archaeological Journal*, 76 (1919), pl. IV, 2.

Evidences of such a "domestication," which has its origin on the Continent in much earlier humanistic transformations of previous hieratic representation, are to be found in English art influenced by foreign artists a century before the Wakefield Master flourished. But even early instances of such influence can raise problems of interpretation. For example, Lawrence Stone finds evidence of the insular character of the Salting Diptych (c. 1305–15; Victoria and Albert Museum) in the rigid handling of the derived iconography of the Virgin and Child, which "follows the Parisian ivory carver's romantic innovations by which both Mother and Child are humanized, the former smiling tenderly and the latter playing with his toys, a flower and a little ball." Here, he remarks, "the Virgin's smile is frozen on her face and the Child's handling of his toys is more symbolic than real."[20] But it is symbolic indeed, as comparison with a stone corbel in Exeter Cathedral (pl. 13) carved perhaps fifteen or twenty years later (c. 1330–40) helps to show. The Virgin and Child in the lower part of the corbel are here emphatically represented as the Flowering of the Tree of Jesse, but the design of the group obviously imitates, if more crudely, the same pattern as was followed in the ivory diptych. The shape of the corbel itself naturally leads the eye from this group to the parallel figures of the enthroned Virgin and Christ in the Coronation of the Virgin of the upper part. And a notable aspect of the parallelism is that the little toy ball of the lower group pairs itself with the unmistakable orb, symbolizing Christ's universal power and sovereignty, in the higher one.

The bird as an attribute of the Christ Child is quite as commonplace as the orb, but evidently is a symbol of much more various and complicated usage. The number of separate categories which can be distinguished in its abundant and widespread appearances is so large as to appear almost bewildering. William H. Forsyth, who found the bird held by the Child too general a theme to render it useful in regional classification of fourteenth-century French sculptures of the Virgin and Child, remarks that he "has never seen a completely convincing clarification of this theme" although some of the associations which must be involved in its significances are, as he points out, well enough known.[21] Dorothy C. Shorr, who yields an entire subdivided section to "The Child's Preoccupation

20. *Sculpture in Britain: The Middle Ages* (Penguin Books, 1955), p. 149, and for reproduction of the diptych, his pl. 104.
21. "The Virgin and Child in French Fourteenth Century Sculpture," *Art Bulletin*, 39 (1957), 177, n. 29. Cf. Louise Lefrançois-Pillion, "Les Statues de la Vierge à l'Enfant dans la sculpture françoise au XIVe siècle," *Gazette des Beaux-arts*, 14 (1935), 129–49, 204–26, and Claude Schaefer, *La Sculpture en ronde-bosse au XIVe siècle dans le duché de Bourgogne* (Paris, 1954), p. 49.

13. Coronation of the Virgin; Virgin and Child. Detail from stone corbel, c. 1330–40. Nave, Exeter Cathedral, Devon, England. From Lawrence Stone, *Sculpture in Britain: The Middle Ages* (Penguin Books, 1955), pl. 129.

with a Bird" in her study *The Christ Child in Devotional Images in Italy during the XIVth Century*, admits that "The precise symbolism of the bird is not known" but states that "In a general way, it refers to the Soul and more specifically, includes the theme of the Passion, Death, and Resurrection."[22] The complexity of the iconographic problem, even where the species of bird represented is identifiable, is suggested by the publication of a whole monograph devoted to study of the symbolic goldfinch alone.[23]

22. (New York, 1954), p. 172.
23. Herbert Friedman, *The Symbolic Goldfinch* (New York, 1946). See especially his discussion of general significances of the bird in relation to the Child, pp. 7 ff. As he remarks, the extant examples of the Divine Infant with the bird from the fourteenth century alone are virtually countless.

The Wakefield Master's omission of the species of the Second Shepherd's bird suggests that a general significance, suitable to and controlled by his context, was intended. However, reference to significances which can be exposed by study of a few kinds of birds very commonly associated with Christ can be useful as background. The first is the dove. This type of spiritual purity and innocence, interpreted as an allegoric symbol of Christ in Jeremiah 25:38,[24] immediately suggests the Gospel episodes linking this bird with Jesus: in the Presentation of Our Lord in the Temple (Luke 2:24), in the Scourging from the Temple of the sellers of doves as merchandise (John 2:16), and in the descent of the Holy Ghost "like a dove" at the Baptism (Matt. 3:16 etc.). The association of the dove with the Holy Spirit is very powerful, and if Edward Hodnett was right in identifying the bird in the woodcut as a dove,[25] what may be the earliest instance in English printed illustration of the Divine Infant with both the orb and the bird (pl. 14) may in fact have been intended to symbolize the Trinity, since the orb often was used as an attribute of God the Father. Professor Cawley in fact has noted that the bird and ball of the *Secunda Pastorum* possibly may have such a significance.[26] The em-

24. See *Allegoriae in sacram scripturam,* s.v. Rabanus Maurus, in *PL* CXII, col. 898.

25. *English Woodcuts, 1480–1535* (Oxford, 1935), p. 169 (no. 410); cf. the similar design, no. 411.

26. P. 113.

14. "De nomine Jesu." Woodcut from [*Horae ad usum Sarum*], Wynkyn de Worde, 1513. From Edward Hodnett, *English Woodcuts, 1480–1535* (Oxford, 1935), fig. 57. First published in *Every man & woman ought to fast on ye wednesday* (1500).

phasis on triplex groupings in the play suggests this might be one justifiable mode of interpreting the symbols; however, it then appears surprising that the bird was not designated a dove and of course it has yet to be shown that the "cherys" are appropriate to such a symbolic scheme.

Quite as important is the fact that the dove, associated with Christ's spiritual primacy and with the Holy Spirit and its gifts, also is a symbol of simplicity, innocence, and contempt of the world. (Gen. 8:9, Ps. 54:7, and Matt. 10:16).[27] This specific symbolism (among others) no doubt colored the very widespread medieval use of a variety of birds—especially the small quick-flying ones—as symbols of "the spiritual man."[28] The bird as a symbol of the spiritual as opposed to the material, and of the "winged human soul," has of course very ancient Egyptian and Hellenic, as well as Judeo-Christian roots. What grows from these is the image of the Christian soul enabled to escape from spiritual capture, or bondage: "Anima nostra sicut passer erepta est de laqueo venantium" (Ps. 123:7):

> They shall come trembling as a bird out of Egypt,
> And as a dove out of the land of Assyria;
> And I will make them to dwell in their houses,
> Saith the Lord. (Hos. 11:11ff.)

And ultimately deriving from this symbolism is a general significance of *avis* itself which may represent (says Bersuire in his important *repertorium morale*) that "homo perfectus" whose heaven-seeking "pure and aerial life" Christians are to imitate.[29]

Illuminated by such exegesis are those works of art where a small bird is used to represent the Infant Jesus as spiritual exemplar who is to be the Savior. Among these might be placed the representations in which the bird (sometimes held by the Virgin) is blessed by the Child with an extended hand over it. Conceivably too, the many "domesticated" examples, especially the earlier ones, where the bird is a pet which the Child holds tethered on a string or to which he extends his finger, may be supposed symbolizations of Christ's "captivity" of the elect soul. That *per aves* may be symbolized *viri spirituales* is a firm tradition.[30]

---

27. *Allegoriae*, cols. 898–99: "quilibet simplex" (Ps. 54:7), "quilibet contemptor mundi" (Gen. 8:9), and "dona Spiriti Sancti" (John 2:16).

28. See Horst W. Janson, *Apes and Ape-Lore in the Middle Ages and the Renaissance*, Studies of the Warburg Institute, vol. 20 (London, 1952), p. 178.

29. *Dictionarium . . . moralis . . .* (Venetiis, 1583), I, Pars Prima, p. 231.

30. *Allegoriae*, col. 871; see also, s.v. *alae*, col. 857 and s.v. *volucres*, col. 1083. The *passer* of Ps. 123:7 is interpreted here (col. 1022), as elsewhere, as "quilibet a peccato conversus"; those in Ps. 101:8 and Ps. 83:4 are glossed as Christ and as "vir sanctus" respectively.

An early fifteenth-century bird on a string with the Child is to be seen in the

A similar double tradition *in bono* may be seen in symbolic use of the eagle. This bird, which already in ancient times served as a resurrection symbol, was taken to signify not only Christ (Deut. 32:11), but the human soul (Job 39:30) and especially the souls of the elect (Matt. 24:28).[31] "John" (writes Durandus) "hath the figure of the eagle," but "This also representeth Christ 'Whose youth is renewed like the eagle's' [Ps. 103:5] because, rising from the dead, He ascendeth into heaven."[32] To my knowledge, the eagle is very rarely used as an attribute in depictions of the Virgin and Child. But our plate 15, a fifteenth-century English alabaster table of the Tree of Jesse, may provide us with example. Here the Child, as the Fruit of this Tree, holds as attributes (as sometimes in earlier French sculpture [pl. 16], where he is rarely without one or the other)[33] both the bird and the ball. The bird in this piece appears to be an eagle, and it probably is meant to signify not only Christ's spiritual primacy but his role as resurrected Redeemer as well.

There is reason to suppose that the symbolic bird need not be an eagle to carry much the same burden of significance. As Saint Gregory says, "rightly is our Redeemer called a bird, whose body ascended freely into heaven."[34] Of course it is but a step from the image of Christ himself as

---

Fogg Art Museum's Acqu. 1947.24. A later but invaluable commentary on the pet bird as symbol of the *servus Christi* is to be found in Dürer's famous engraving, "Virgin and Child with the Monkey" (reproduced in Erwin Panofsky, *Albrecht Dürer* [Princeton, 1945], II, fig. 102), where the bound simian's involuntary servitude, a symbol of Christian control of irrational appetite, is contrasted with the voluntary "service" of the bird.

The earliest (presumably) English representation known to me in which the Divine Infant has his hand outstretched over a bird is a whalebone relief, twelfth century, in the Louvre, Paris; it is reproduced in Margaret H. Longhurst, *English Ivories* (London, 1926), pl. 25. The motif is later commonplace in ivory statuettes, e.g., the French, late fourteenth-century Virgin and Child in the Walters Art Gallery (Acqu. 71.241).

Very full illustration of the Child with his finger to the bird's beak, at least for fourteenth-century Italian representation, can be seen in Shorr, types 29 and 30. A good example in this country is the Amiens altarpiece, c. 1480, in the Chicago Art Institute, Acqu. 33.1060. There are a number of variations on the theme: in a panel by Taddeo di Bartolo (early fifteenth century) in the Fogg (Acqu. 1905.9) the Child crams his right forefinger into the mouth of the finch in his left hand; in a painting by Spinello Aretino (Monte Oliveto Altarpiece) in the same collection (before 1410; Acqu. 1917.3) the Child (as often later) offers his finger as a perch; etc.

31. *Allegoriae*, col. 862. For a basic study of the symbolism of the eagle, see Rudolph Wittkower, "Eagle and Serpent: A Study in the Transmigration of Symbols," *Journal of the Warburg Institute*, 2 (1938–39), 293–325.

32. William Durandus, *Rationale divinorum officiorum*, I.iii.9 in *The Symbolism of Churches and Church Ornaments*, trans. Rev. John Mason Neale and Rev. Benjamin Webb, 3d ed. (London, 1906), p. 46.

33. See Forsyth, p. 180.

34. In *PL* LXXVI, col. 1218.

15. Detail from Tree of Jesse. English alabaster table, fifteenth century. Courtesy of the Victoria and Albert Museum. Crown copyright.

the ascending "bird" to the Crucifixion where "the briddes lymes were brode spradde."[35] And this no doubt helps to explain "the somewhat fearful expression with which [the Child] contemplates" the bird in certain Italian representations, and the appearance of the bird with wings outspread in numerous northern ones (e.g., pl. 16):[36] the Crucifixion is implied. A resurrection theme, implicit in the eagle, readily recalls, more-

35. From the stanza of "The Festivals of the Church" quoted, from the version in Royal MS, 18 A x, below at n. 50.

36. See Shorr, pp. 172–73; a striking later example is Michelangelo's *Madonna Taddei* (c. 1505, Royal Academy, London). According to Forsyth, p. 173, n. 9, most of the numerous fourteenth-century French statues "in which the wings are spread out seem to come from Eastern France." For a clear fifteenth-century English example, see the alabaster carving, Acqu. A141-1946, in the Victoria and Albert Museum.

16. Virgin and Child. Detail from stone statue, fourteenth century. Church in Ville-Dommange (Marne), France. (Bildarchiv Foto Marburg.)

over, the popular apocryphal stories in which the Divine Child, Creator and Redeemer, shapes birds of clay (sparrows) and brings them to life.[37] Representations in which the Child blesses the bird or holds it by one wing may have been intended to evoke these stories; and we can certainly assume them and their symbolic burden alluded to in cases where the bird appears to be dead.[38] The choice of the motif of the Child and

37. See *Gospel of Thomas*, 4:2, in *The Apocryphal New Testament . . .* , trans. Montague Rhodes James (Oxford, 1955), pp. 59–60; cf. *Gospel of Pseudo-Matthew*, 27 (p. 76).

38. Of course in many works where we are tempted to detect presence of the "dead bird" motif, crudities in conception or execution, or damages, forbid assured identification. Three clear English instances of the motif in depictions of the Virgin and Child are the stone boss (162, between 1310 and 1320) in St. John the Baptist's Chapel, Exeter Cathedral (in C. P. J. Cave, *Medieval Carvings in Exeter Cathedral*

the bird for an English alabaster panel (Victoria and Albert Museum, Acqu. A52-1932) intended for the side of a tomb was, we may be sure, entirely appropriate.

A similar kind of multiple significance can be shown to be borne out by the "bob of cherys" offered by the First Shepherd. There are long and deep associations of the cherry with the Incarnation. Several saints' legends "involving a cherry tree in full blossom on Christmas day" are an established part of the "lore about the marvellous transformation of Nature on the night of Christ's birth."[39] And the practice, in various parts of Europe, of forcing cherry branches into bloom by Christmas— a limb of the genealogy of the Christmas tree—can be traced to the early sixteenth century and no doubt goes back very much earlier.[40] The use of the cherry in art comprises a confluent tradition equally rich and relevant.

The earliest extant use of the cherry as an attribute of the Christ Child seems to occur in a triptych by Lorenzetti (pl. 17). Here the image already is "domesticated"; the Virgin offers the fruit to the Child, who holds three cherries near his mouth. At the end of the fifteenth century, in Gerard David's "La Vierge à la Soupe au Lait" (Van Pannwitz Coll., Hartekamp), where "a bob of cherys" has been shown to have been painted by the Master over the wooden spoon he had originally placed in the Child's hand, it is perhaps understandable that a student of the painting has balked at the idea that the fruit has any more symbolic significance than the spoon.[41] In the Lorenzetti, however, in spite of the realis-

[London, 1953], pl. 40), the fifteenth-century misericord in the choir of Norwich Cathedral, and the embroidery on a cope hood from the second half of the same century in the Victoria and Albert, Acqu. T-46-1914.

39. See Clement A. Miles, *Christmas in Ritual and Tradition, Christian and Pagan* (London and Leipzig, n.d.), p. 268; Alexander Tille, *Yule and Christmas: Their Place in the Germanic Year* (London, 1899), pp. 170–71, 175, and citations.

40. See Tille, p. 174; Miles, p. 268.

41. R. Langton Douglas, "*La Vierge à la Soupe au Lait* of Gerard David," *Burlington Magazine*, 88 (1946), 289–92; he notes that the spoon, rather than the cherries, is found in the similar de Forest Madonna and Child and all copies of it. Douglas does not consider the possibility that the repainting of the spoon may have resulted from the demand for a detail of established symbolic propriety. He is on much safer ground (p. 291, n. 8) in his skepticism of Eberhard Freiherr von Bodenhausen's notion (*Gerard David und seine Schule* [Munich, 1905], pp. 180, 183) that the seven cherries are a "symbol of the Seven Joys of Mary." The number of cherries in a particular picture in fact may have significance, especially when supported by other evidence of the individual artist's interest in numerological symbolism; but the wide variation in this respect in usage of the motif (as examination of the tradition from Lorenzetti to, say, Titian's "The Madonna with Cherries" in the Kunsthistorisches Museum, Vienna, will show) surely must encourage interpretative caution. For reproduction of the Van Pannwitz painting by David, see Leo Van Puyvelde, *The Flemish Primitives* (Brussels, 1948), pl. 99.

17. Detail from central panel of triptych, Madonna and Child with Saints, by Pietro Lorenzetti [d. 1345]. Courtesy of the National Gallery of Art, Washington, D.C. (Gift of Mrs. Felix M. Warburg.)

tic accommodation of the motif, there can be no reason, given the painting's date, to suppose that the cherries are any less symbolic an attribute than those borne by the saints on the wings of the triptych. In fact, the motif spreads from the school of Siena and the large number of instances of its use, by a long line of distinguished as well as minor artists, attests to its popularity and continuing symbolic value well through the sixteenth century. I know of no native English examples but the motif must have been sufficiently available there during the fifteenth century through the influence of imported and imitated books of hours from the Lowlands and from France. Our illustration, from such a Northern French manuscript of the period (pl. 18), is an illumination representing the Adoration of the Shepherds; the Child has a cherry in his hands, and what appear to be flowering branches of cherry are borne in the beaks of the three doves on the roof of the manger.[42]

42. *Hours of the Virgin for Roman Use*, first half of the fifteenth century, apparently compiled for a man who attended the church of Peronne (Pierpont Mor-

194   Lawrence J. Ross

18. Adoration of the Shepherds. Detail from illumination in *Hours of the Virgin for Roman Use*. Northern France, first half of fifteenth century. Pierpont Morgan MS 865, fol. 62r. Courtesy of the Pierpont Morgan Library, New York.

The significance of the cherry motif in religious art has been very little explored. Elizabeth Haig remarked that "at least in the Siennese School this fruit held by the Infant Christ would seem to be the fruit of Paradise." Certainly in somewhat later German art the cherry is often used "to typify the delights of the blessed": for example, a charming Garden of Paradise by a "Master of the Middle Rhine" in the Städelsches Kunstinstitut, Frankfurt (c. 1430), depicts the garden as a *hortus conclusus* dominated by a cherry tree from which one of the blessed gathers

---

gan MS M865, fol. 62ʳ). The illuminations are those of a provincial atelier and can be shown in some instances to borrow from compositions in manuscript illuminations done for the duc de Berry. The cherry appears with notable frequency among the decorative and symbolic fruits and flowers, painted in apparent relief in association with illuminations of religious subjects, in later fifteenth-century books of hours produced in France and the Lowlands. A good example may be viewed in the Flemish *Horae*, Pierpont Morgan MS M6, fol. 72ᵛ.

Early prints may also have had a share in transmission of the motif. However, its earliest appearance in a print, as far as I know, is in one by John of Cologne, of Zwolle or Zwott (c. 1480–90), in which the Child holds two cherries in his right hand and presents a third to his mother (cited by J. D. Passavant, *Le Peintre-graveur* [Leipzig, 1860], II, 185, item 74).

the fruit.[43] An interesting feature is the association of the symbolic bird (here the goldfinch) and the cherry as "the tree in the midst" of the celestial garden. That this pairing is unlikely to have been casual is proved by later repetitions. A notable instance a century later is the tender devotional painting of the Madonna and Child (pl. 19) by the Ferrarese Il

19. Il Garofalo (Benvenuto Tisi). Virgin and Child. Collection A, Ryerson, Chicago.

Garofalo (Benvenuto Tisi). Here the Infant's concentration on the cherries and bird so emphasizes their symbolic import as attributes that we may suspect the fruit signifies, not "the delights of the blessed," but rather the paradisiac joy the Son of God sacrificially relinquished to bring mankind to heavenly bliss.[44] That the theme of the Expiation is

43. Haig, *The Floral Symbolism of the Great Masters* (London and New York, 1913), p. 243. For color reproduction of this painting, see Jacques Dupont and Cesare Gnudi, *Gothic Painting* (Skira, [1954]), p. 184.

44. The theme of the Sacrifice is further supported by the frequent association of the goldfinch (and indeed other birds with red in their markings held by the Child) with the Passion. See Friedman, p. 9.

involved in the cherry's significance is further suggested by the charade-
like action in the famous Hans Memling in the Uffizi, where the Child, a
cherry in one hand, reaches with the other to accept an apple, symbol of
the Fall, proffered by an angel.⁴⁵ Again, the substitution, in the fore-
ground of Verrocchio's Madonna and Child in the Metropolitan Museum of Art, of the cherries for the red rose of martyrdom more commonly paired with the white, urges that they too may symbolize the
Passion.⁴⁶

This symbolism may, at least in part, have resulted by a natural extension of the use of red fruits to symbolize "the fruit of the spirit is charity"
(Gal. 5:22).⁴⁷ It also appears to be a consequence of the analogizing men-
tality which saw, as expiatory counterpart for "the fruit of the tree in
the midst of the garden" of Eden, the blessed "Fruit" of the Virgin's
womb become the fruit of the roodtree (I Pet. 2:24).⁴⁸ In "The Dispute
between Mary and the Cross" (c. 1350) the Cross is given voice to make
this very point:

> Thi feire fruit on me ginneth tere;
> Thi fruit me florischeth in blod colour
> To winne the world that lay in lure;
> . . . .
> Whan Adam Goddes biddyng brak;
> He bot a bite that made vs blak,
> Til fruit werre tied on treo with tak,
> O fruit for another.⁴⁹

Garofalo did another Virgin and Child where the Virgin holds the cherries and
the Child the bird (Collection Franchetti, Ca d'Oro, Venice), reproduced in
Adolfo Venturi, *Storia dell'arte italiana*, IX, parte IV (Milan, 1929), fig. 235. The
Child has a goldfinch on his hand in a Paradisaical Garden in which cherries are
prominent in a painting of the Netherlandish School, c. 1500, in the National Gallery, London (No. 1085).

45. See Haig, p. 245. The Memling is reproduced in Van Puyvelde, pl. 88.
46. On the red rose, see e.g., Rabanus Maurus, *De Universo*, PL CXI, col. 528.
A reproduction of the Verrocchio can be seen in Harry B. Wehle, *The Metropolitan Museum of Art: A Catalogue of Italian, Spanish and Byzantine Paintings*
(New York, 1940), p. 45.

47. See, e.g., Bersuire, *Opera omnia* (Coloniae Agrippinae, 1731), IV, 230. See
also the present writer's "The Meaning of Strawberries in Shakespeare," *Studies in
the Renaissance*, 7 (1960), 225–40. The Child with strawberry in one hand and a
red-headed bird in the other occurs in a painting by Sano di Pietro in the Fogg Art
Museum (Acqu. No. 1962.284).

48. This fundamental and ubiquitous pairing of the *malilignum* and the *lignum
vitae* and its figurative elaboration in the Middle Ages are valuably discussed in
D. W. Robertson, Jr., "The Doctrine of Charity in Mediaeval Literary Gardens: A
Topical Approach through Symbolism and Allegory," *Speculum*, 26 (1951), 24–49,
and Fritz Saxl, "A Spiritual Encyclopoedia of the later Middle Ages," *Journal of
the Warburg and Courtauld Institutes*, 5 (1942), 82–134.

49. Ll. 113–15, 151–52, 417–20, in *Legends of the Holy Rood*, ed. Richard Morris,
EETS 46 (London, 1871), pp. 135, 136, 145.

In one manuscript in which a version of this poem is found it is followed by the fragment of another, on "The Festivals of the Church," in which the association of the red fruit with Christ's blood at the Passion explicitly appears in a stanza which brings together, in one context with the cherries, references to Christ as "king" and as "bird."

> . . . . that kyng was corve as a knaue,
> The briddes lymes were brode spradde.
>   On schort membre the child was schaue,
> In lowenes was that brid lad to haue
>   To kepe men fro helle cave,
>   Mannys soule to save.
> Lowness lay bynethe the sterres,
> To bye hys chaffare the child payed erres,
>   Droppes rede as ripe cherrees,
>   That fro his flesche gan lave.[50]

In sum, we should now be in a position to justify, with critical particularity, the archetypalist's expectation that "The gifts of the Shepherds (as of the three Kings) have surely some relation to the magical or otherwise rich gifts which are bestowed on a new born child or found beside an exposed child in so many folk tales and which often have to do with the ultimate recognition of his supernatural or royal origin and status."[51] The homeliness of the Wakefield shepherds' gifts is realistically appropriate to the rustic shepherds and to the poverty of the Divine Family. But, although apparently as simple as those in earlier shepherds' plays, these become, as attributes of the Christ Child, luminously significant. First, their symbolic values manifest in the Infant's presence the religious conception of Trinity in Unity. Again, their very order—a climactic arrangement of allusions to the Passion, Resurrection, and Christ "in glory and power"—suggests the spiritual history implicit in the Incarnation; for the gifts project meanings according with Christ's role to be dramatized by the cycle as a whole—the very role glorified in the "Hail Lyrics" to which the shepherds' speeches have been shown to be indebted. Above all, they designate the Child as the Christ by manifesting, as symbols of offered faith, his sacrificial manhood, spiritual primacy, and lordship and power. Their propriety as offerings looks, moreover, as well as to Christ's status, toward the shepherds as representative Christians and their life in relation to God. The gifts are, in this sense, a part of the same continuum of significance as is sustained verbally in the shepherds' speeches by such lines as "I haue holden my

---

50. Ibid., p. 217, ll. 208–20 (from leaf 133b in Royal MS 18 A x).
51. John Spiers, in *The Age of Chaucer*, ed. Boris Ford (Penguin Books, 1954), p. 169.

hetyng," "I wold drynk on thy cop," "I pray thee be nere when that I haue nede."

In symbolic method, then, as well as in number, the Wakefield shepherds' gifts appear to parallel the gifts of the Magi as traditionally interpreted; for a widely evidenced habit of mind operates in their making. For example, when Durandus discusses the propriety of poor and rich hangings in churches for the Feast of the Nativity, he writes of the latter: "Those which employ rich hangings, set forth by them the gladness arising from the Birth of a King"; but he insists on a tropological value as well: they also "teach what manner of persons we ought to be in our reception of so great a Guest."[52] Since Irenaeus in the second century, the gifts of the Magi were understood to be offered as symbols of faith in Christ as King, God, and mortal man; but, since Ambrose, they have also been understood to signify offerings owed to God in the Christian life of Everyman.[53] The application of both these modes of interpretation in the longwinded explication of the gifts in the Chester Magi play will emphasize that we are very far from dealing with recondite theological lore.[54] The similar but even more elaborate explanation of them in the *Golden Legend*[55] confirms the popular availability of those interpretive attitudes the Wakefield Master appears to have taken for granted in the conception of the multivalent gifts in his own Adoration scene.

II

At least in the Adoration scene of the *Secunda Pastorum*, then, we can claim for the Wakefield Master what has been demonstrated in the case of the early Netherlandish painters contemporary with him: namely, that his naturalism, like "the naturalism of the Master of Flémalle and his fellow painters, was not as yet wholly secular. It was still rooted in the conviction that physical objects are, to quote St. Thomas Aquinas (*Summa Theologiae*, I, qu. I, art. 9, c), 'corporeal metaphors of things spiritual' (*spiritualia sub metaphoris corporalium*); and it was not until much, much later that this conviction was rejected

52. I.iii.40 (p. 61) (see above, n. 32).
53. See the citation of these and other sources on the meaning of the gifts, Winifred Sturdevant, *The Misterio de los Reyes Magos: Its Position in the Development of the Mediaeval Legend of the Three Kings*, The Johns Hopkins University Studies in Romance Literatures and Languages, X (Baltimore and Paris, 1927), pp. 16, 65, 80–84.
54. *The Chester Plays*, pp. 178–81, ll. 37–124.
55. *The Golden Legend, or Lives of the Saints as Englished by William Caxton*, I (London, 1931), 51–52.

or forgotten."[56] The English playwright too moves through created things—the rustic characters, their speech, and homely offerings—in the representation of man's relation to spiritual mystery. His lively sense of the actual, everywhere evident in his awareness of the social scene, in his responsiveness to gesture, and in his mastery of idiom, is like the inspired meticulous observation of Van Eyck in that he also sees, and makes us perceive, that "all reality is saturated with meaning."[57] And this meaning clearly is the same kind of figural significance which Auerbach's studies have taught us to expect in the creatural contemporaneity and realism of other religious dramas of the period which were designed to lead their audiences "from the concrete, the everyday, to the hidden and the true."[58]

The inquiry we can now begin is to determine whether the long farce in the *Secunda Pastorum* is an integral part of the play because its realism actually is of the very same figural kind. Manly complains that to regard the numerous anachronistic Christian references in the "secular" part before the Nativity as mere touches of literal realism puts them in the same light, as objects presented to our view, as the shepherds' "talk of feudal landlords and their rustic gifts to the Christ Child."[59] What we may wonder is whether any of these, or other features of the play, are merely "realistic." The critical question suggested by the Adoration scene—by its fusion of affectively rendered homely realism and symbolism—is whether its modes of representation can explain the place of the long farcical action in the Nativity play as a whole.

A first condition of an affirmative answer to this question, already suggested above, is that we be prepared to see the literal data charged with symbolic import. The second condition is that we view the entire play, including the farcical part, as a Nativity play in a mystery cycle. The play is so often separately anthologized and studied in isolation that recent commentators have been compelled to remind us that it was written to be seen as part of a cycle dramatizing Christian spiritual history, that it is but one pageant in "the play called Corpus Christi." The trouble is that even some of these very commentators tend to conceive of the play linearly, as merely sequential narrative, so that the

56. Erwin Panofsky, *Early Netherlandish Painting: Its Origins and Character* (Cambridge, Mass., 1953), I, 142.

57. Ibid., I, 144.

58. See Erich Auerbach, *Mimesis* (New York, 1957), p. 135. As he makes clear, the tradition of such composition has its origin in patristic understanding that Holy Scripture itself "had created an entirely new kind of sublimity, in which the everyday and the low were included, not excluded, so that, in style as in content, it directly connected the lowest with the highest" (p. 134).

59. P. 152.

farce is related to, or "focussed" on, the Nativity only by being fore-shadowing, preparative, or prophetic. The emphatic use of so-called anachronism in the "secular" part might be enough to warn us of the probable insufficiency of such a view; and so might the probability that the staging of the play was very likely to have been "simultaneous," with all the locales present to the view of the audience from the start. In point of fact, those who refer to the farce as "burlesque," "parody," or "travesty" implicitly (or unconsciously) do assume *that the audience will be watching a Nativity Mystery while it watches the farce.* For if the action were simply "successive" then, technically, the Adoration scene would parody the farce, not the farce the Adoration. Indeed, the Adoration scene does elevatingly qualify, through parallelism, the significance of what has gone before. But the point is that one does not have to wait for the Adoration for many of the parallelisms to become realized; the referents of the parallels are there, implicit, *while* the farce is being performed.

Striking indications of this may be seen in the many aspects of the farce which obviously depend, for their full effectiveness, on the audience's awareness that it is watching a Nativity play and not an autonomous comic action. When Mak tries to keep the shepherds' search from the cradled sheep near his wife, his line, "Wyst ye how she had farne, youre hartys wold be sore" (l. 531), with its comically appropriate substitution of a word literally meaning "farrow" for "labor," would be quite as effective if the farce were simply a straightforward, literal dramatization of the folk story underlying it. But this is not entirely the case with the comic exchange when the search has failed:

2 Pastor.   I trow oure shepe be slayne. What fynde ye two?
             . . . .
3 Pastor.   Whik catell bot this, tame nor wylde,
             None, as haue I blys, as lowde as he smylde.
Vxor.   No, so God me blys, and gyf me joy of my chylde!
                                               (ll. 541, 548–50)

The full effect of this depends (however shocking it may be to modern sensibilities) on the immediate relevance of the mystery of the Incarnation, and the same is true of much else from the moment Mak lays hands on his prey, saying, "Now mendys our chere / From sorrow / A fatt shepe . . ." (ll. 290–92). Thus the emphasis on the fact that the sheep is a wether, the "child" a "knave," and thus the full comic vitality of Mak's paternal boast, "Any lord might hym haue, / This chyld, to his son" (ll. 554–56). The most striking of such passages undoubtedly are those requiring, to make their most complete sense, daring reference to the Eucharist:

Vxor.   I pray to God so mylde,
         If euer I you begyld,
         That I ete this chylde
         That lygys in this credyll.   (ll. 535–38)

Such complexities have been, however, carefully prepared for earlier. A good example of the Wakefield Master's method is provided by Mak's speech when he shows Gyll the stolen sheep.

Mak.   I am worthy my mete,
        For in a strate can I gett
        More then they that swynke and swette
        All the long day. [*Shows her the sheep*].
        Thus it fell to my lott, Gyll; I had sich grace.   (ll. 310–14)

A good part of the fun here of course is based on the comic reference to the distinction between salvation by works and by grace; but it gains its edge from the playwright's emphasis on his major theme through allusion to "the Lamb of God which taketh away the sin of the world" (John 1:29).

Comic literalization of the "Lamb of God" figure is most obviously exploited of course when Mak and Gyll try the "qwantt gawde" of hiding the stolen sheep as a swaddled child in the cradle. The out-of-tune song which Mak croons as part of his setting of a mock Nativity scene undoubtedly was meant to be one of the popular lullaby carols, for in advising him so to busy himself while she groans and cries "outt by the wall on Mary and John," Gyll had referred to a refrain familiar in these Christmas songs (ll. 441–45).[60] This alone should be enough to make us attend to the significance of the carefully emphasized swaddling of the sheep's legs ("Wyll ye see how they swedyll / His foure feytt in the medyll?" [ll. 598–99]). As remarked earlier, the "agneaux aux pattes liées," found in a literal as well as a symbolic sense in representations of the Adoration where one shepherd offers the best of his flock, symbolizes the Sacrifice of Jesus. The representational tradition, climaxed perhaps in El Greco's great painting in the Metropolitan Museum of Art (pl. 20), where the lamb is compositionally paired with the Infant to stress the point, makes it unforgettable.

Actually, the sheep with bound feet, as the most startlingly emphatic allusion, reminds us there are a number of carefully iterated references to the Crucifixion in the "farcical" part of the play. Most of these, to be sure, appear in expletive or asseverative phrases (ll. 91, 108, 118, 374, 539); but some of these are placed with such careful irony as to put their deliberateness beyond question: for example, Mak's appropriately

60. See Cawley, p. 110, and citation.

20. El Greco. Adoration of the Shepherds. Courtesy of the Metropolitan Museum of Art, New York.

garbled prayer before retiring (ll. 265–68). The propriety, in a Nativity play, of such references to the Passion, as of the references to the Eucharist, depends upon the same rationale as explains the presence of Eucharistic symbols in Nativity pictures (e.g., in the central panel of the Portinari altarpiece in the Uffizi): the sacrificial action which will culminate on the Cross and be perpetuated in the Mass begins at the mystery of the Incarnation.[61]

The audience's active awareness, within the scene, of such significance in the sheep makes infinitely more comic what follows the discovery of him in the cradle. There is, first, the comic embarrassment of the First Shepherd, who supposes the sheep is a child "merkyd amys" (l. 586). Then ensues the amusing and multiply charged doubting of Mak's stoutly claimed paternity of the oddly "hornyd lad":

MAK.   Peasse, byd I. What, lett be youre fare!
            I am he that hym gatt, and yond woman hym bare.
1 PASTOR.   What dewill shall he hatt, Mak? Lo, God, Makys ayre!
                                                        (ll. 601–4)

And this in turn prepares for Mak and Gyll's hilarious effort to maintain the fraud, even after the sheep has been recognized, by pretending that the "child" was bewitched, "taken with an elfe" and at midnight thus transformed ("forshapyn") (ll. 607–19). It is only when we have another uncanny nativity in mind that this appeal to the supernatural, to persuade the shepherds that the sheep is a child, makes high comic sense; an analogous appeal enables the play to celebrate the audience's faith that the Child is the Lamb.

Our disabling tendency is to suppose the parallelisms to be evident only through a process of critical abstraction from the completed whole. But drama is very largely an art of using prepared or given expectations, and our linear and literal approach and very different sense of the whole deny to the Wakefield Master half the possibilities available to him for exploitation. For an audience expecting a Nativity play one of whose two obligatory episodes must be the angelic Annunciation of the Birth to the shepherds in the fields, Mak's cloaked entrance, deliberately mystifying behavior, and strange speech, his attempt to pass himself off as "sond [i.e., messenger] from a greatt lordyng" (l. 202), and finally his prophetic dream of a childbirth "for to mend oure flok" (l. 388),[62]

61. See Panofsky, *Early Netherlandish Painting,* I, 333–34, 500; as he points out, the name Bethlehem ("House of Bread") inevitably was connected with "I am the bread which came down from heaven" (John 6:41). See also, M. B. McNamee, S.J., "Further Symbolism in the Portinari Altarpiece," *Art Bulletin,* 45 (1963), 142–43.

62. The immediate sense of *mend* here of course is "increase"; but the context insists on enlargement of meaning through the obvious punning sense. A very useful study deserves and has yet to be written on the Wakefield Master's use of word play. Cf. "resaue" (*Prima Pastorum,* l. 472), above in n. 14.

204 Lawrence J. Ross

were meant to win an immediately resonant response. To be sure, most of the parallels do have a preparative function, and some require, for their fullest effect, completion by the second term and our structural sense of the whole. But even quite sophisticated ones clearly are designed to have an immediate effect which alters the significance of the farce as it is being played. A very special pleasure is afforded by observing the playwright's skill in so managing his plots that in both it is the attempt to see the child and offer him gifts that manifests the infant's real nature. But "to see the Child" and "to offer him gifts" are traditional actions the audience awaits the shepherds to perform. When in the farce these actions astonish them by revealing the child really to be a sheep, the audience is witnessing a comic literal enactment of the drama it has come to see: the mystery of the Nativity of the Child who is the Lamb.

The effectiveness of much in the farce, then, obviously depends on an active sense that it is part of a Nativity play. What is far from obvious is the next step that needs to be taken if the play is to be seen as a unity: namely, a demonstration that the farcical action as a whole is a literal comic enactment of the Nativity theme, that, in fact, the heart of the Wakefield Master's symbolic design is that the two parts of his play are truly analogous actions. At this juncture, we need to come to grips with a radical limitation in Watt's view of the play's unity and in studies derived from it. Because he saw no parallel to the theft in the second part of the play, Watt considered that "In the Mak episode . . . it is not the sheep-stealing but the sheep-hiding details which are the more essential to the play, for in these latter appears a perfect burlesque of the charming Christ-child scene that concludes the play."[63] He therefore supposed the unifying theme of the play to be "the birth of a child." But this of course is to deny a good part of the farcical action a significant place in the total design of the play; and to underrate the Wakefield Master's artistry in his most mature performance. If he really knew what he was about, the unifying theme *should be* "the recovery, at the birth of a child, of what was lost." But to begin to prove that this is indeed the theme we must look again at the comic version of the theft in the play.

And this demands that we reconsider Mak as a dramatic character in the total action and not simply as a comically sharp realistic portrait of a country crook. The character obviously parallel to Mak, in his role of outsider whose entrance instigates an action resulting in the shepherds' visit to a Nativity scene, is, as we have noted, the Herald Angel. Mak has, however, another and subtler parallel or counterpart in the second

63. P. 161.

part of the play, a figure who never appears on stage yet is essential to the design of the action. This is "the feynd," "the warloo," references to whom, strategically placed at the start of both the Angel's speech and the First Shepherd's adoration of the Child, emphatically define the significance of the Incarnation in terms of the antagonist Christ will overcome, the alienator of God and man initially responsible for the loss Christ will make good.

ANGELUS.   Ryse, hyrd-men heynd, for now is he borne
            That shall take fro the feynd that Adam had lorne;
            That warloo to sheynd, this nyght is he borne.
                      . . . .
1 PASTOR.   Thou has waryd, I weyne, the warlo so wylde:
            The fals gyler of teyn, now goys he begylde.
                                        (ll. 638–40, 712–13)

Like Mak (whom Gyll sarcastically calls "Syr Gyle"), the arch- "fals gyler" also shares in a "comic" action in which he proves a "gyler . . . begylde."

From Mak's entrance, the shepherds make us see "the dewill in his ee" (l. 217), and their suspicion of him warns us to look beneath deceptive appearances: "Seldom lyys the dewyll dede by the gate" (l. 229). The diabolic references associated with the character (climaxed in his comic paternity of the "hornyd lad" with the "long snowte" [ll. 585, 601]) are too numerous to have escaped notice; and with them should be placed "the echoes of Antichrist" in his role, entirely appropriate in a Nativity play because of the widespread idea that the Antichrist will be the incarnation of the Devil.[64] Such references surely are too insistent and striking to be supposed merely moralistic "hints that Mak is of the Devil's party."[65]

VXOR EIUS. Who makys sich a bere? Now walk in the wenyand!
MAK.   A, Gyll, what chere? It is I, Mak, youre husbande.
VXOR.   Then may we se here the dewill in a bande,
            Syr Gyle!
            Lo, he commys with a lote,
            As he were holden in the throte.   (ll. 405–10)

Professor Cawley has remarked that we may "suppose that Gyll is thinking of her husband . . . as the devil whose house, she fears, is about to be entered by the shepherds in search of their lost sheep"; for under-

---

64. See W. Bousset, *The Antichrist Legend,* trans. A. H. Keane (London, 1896), pp. 139–40. See also, regarding the "hornyd lad" reference, Margaret A. Murray, *The Horned God* (London, 1931), pp. 30–34.

65. See Thompson, p. 304.

lying the passage certainly are Jesus' words in scripture (Matt. 12:28–29) about "the binding of the strong man, i.e., the devil": [66]

> But if I cast out devils by the Spirit of God, then the kingdom of God is come unto you.
> Or else how can one enter into a strong man's house, and spoil his goods, except he first bind the strong man?

"The dewill in a bande" has been noted to be a reference to the popular image of "the bound Satan," a figure frequently seen in representations of the Harrowing of Hell where Christ "spoils" the "strong man's goods": that is, "take[s] fro the feynd that Adam had lorne."[67] For poor shepherds the theft of a "fat wether" is no small misfortune; but we may be sure that when these complain "oure los is grette" (l. 507), their line *dramatically* refers to a profounder loss that has been suffered. For the sheep, the figure for spiritually graced simplicity and innocence, is not only the most common symbol of the eucharistic Victim (the Paschal Lamb being the *typus Christi incarnandi*).[68] It is also used to represent "that which was lost" which "the Son of Man is come to save" (Matt. 18:11). In the parable in Luke 15:3–7, the shepherd's placing of the found sheep upon his shoulders was glossed as Christ's assumption of human nature in order to carry the burden of human sin. And the sheep of "Rejoice with me for I have found my sheep which was lost" was interpreted, not just as the individual repentant sinner, but as all graced humanity which the Pastor restored to heaven.[69] *Periit et inventa est;* "What grace we haue fun" cry the shepherds at the close (l. 751). The Good Shepherd provides the commentary:

66. P. 110.

67. On the "bound Satan," see Augustine, in *PL* XXXIX, col. 2061, *The Golden Legend*, I, 97, *The Apocryphal Gospels*, pp. 135–36, and *The Middle English Harrowing of Hell and Gospel of Nicodemus*, ed. William Henry Hulme, EETS e.s. 100 (London, 1907), pp. 12–13.

68. See *Allegoriae*, s.v. *agnus*, col. 855: "Christus" (Exod. 7:5), (*per agnos*) "viri sancti" (Isa. 40:11), "simplices et innocentes" (John 21:16). The lamb as a symbol of the Christian deity in the earliest representations had the authority of Rev. 5:6–12, 7:2–12. On the typological symbolism of the paschal lamb, see Lactantius, in *PL* VI, cols. 530–31, and Rupert, in *PL* CLXIX, col. 1280. We should remember of course that, at the end of the *Prima Pastorum*, the shepherds sing "To the lawde of this lam" (ll. 501–2).

69. See *Glossa Ordinaria*, in *PL* CXIV, col. 311. The Good Shepherd with the sheep on his shoulders is a Christian symbol dating from the first century. For early illustration, see Charles Rufus Morey, *Early Christian Art* (Princeton, 1953), figs. 50, 171, and Louisa Twining, *Symbols and Emblems in Early and Mediaeval Christian Art* (London, 1852), pls. XIV, XV. For a print indicating the continuing vitality of the motif into the Renaissance, see the printer's device (with motto "Periit et inventa est") in Ronald B. McKerrow, *Printers' & Publishers' Devices in England & Scotland, 1485–1640* (London, 1949), no. 153.

The thief cometh not, but for to steal, and to kill, and to destroy: I am
come that they might have life, and that they might have it more abundantly.
(John 10:10)

From this background springs the significance which informs the
play's structural refrain action of sleeping and waking and allows it to
adumbrate, in its pairing of waking-to-loss and waking-to-recovery-of-
what-has-been-lost, the principle of unity in the double action. Earlier,
when Daw tells of the nightmare that has made him quake and put his
"hart . . . outt of skyn"—a dream of Mak, disguised as a wolf, stealing
a "fatt shepe" with a "gyn"—the Wakefield Master has characteristically
suggested this underlying logic of his double plot through the artful
containment of his nine-line stanza:

3 Pastor.	Me thoght he was lapt in a wolfe-skyn.
1 Pastor.	So are many hapt now, namely within.
3 Pastor.	When we had long napt, me thoght with a gyn
	A fatte shepe he trapt; bot he mayde no dyn.
2 Pastor.	Be styll!
	Thi dreme makys the woode;
	It is bot fantom, by the roode.
1 Pastor.	Now God turne all to good,
	If it be his wyll. (ll. 368–76)

Lest any of this be supposed abstruse or too recondite for use in a
play meant for a "popular" audience, it must be pointed out that the
Wakefield Master was depending on a conventional collocation of materials as commonplace as the folk plot he has used. To find already
brought together in one context the complaints about cold, hunger, and
oppression, the thief who caused Adam's loss, the shepherds' watch
against the sheep-stealing wolf, and the annunciation to them of God's
restoring through the Incarnation of the *gaudium plenum* mankind lost,
all we need do is turn to the homiletic tradition. In the medieval English
sermons on the Nativity can be found the same centuries-old background
of conventionally associated material which the Wakefield playwright
seized upon with remarkable freshness of inspiration.[70]

70. See especially *Old English Homilies of the Twelfth Century*, ed. R. Morris,
EETS 53 (London, 1873), pp. 32–37. Cf. *Middle English Sermons*, ed. Woodburn
O. Ross, EETS 209 (London, 1940), pp. 137–38, 171. On the wolf and thief, see also
Glossa ordinaria, PL CXIV, col. 397 (John 10:11) and *Allegoriae*, col. 983. Com-
mentary, from patristic times onward, of course stresses the relation between the
poor shepherds and the humble birth of the Good Shepherd whose sheep they
are, the sacrificial Lamb who brings them grace. See Bede, in *Glossa ordinaria*, PL
CXIV, col. 249 (Luke 2:8), and in PL XCIV, col. 35 (John 10); also Ambrose, on
Luke 2 in PL XV, col. 1652.

III

An important aesthetic flaw might be supposed in the design of the play suggested above, and it may usefully be considered now to enable us further to grasp the inclusiveness of the drama's vision. It may be thought that the later counterpart of the loss in the farce—what Adam lost or brought to ruin—being merely stated, is insufficiently dramatized to balance the lengthy performance of Mak's theft even though the farce be seen, on one level, as "symbolic enactment." Actually, however, "the loss" has been otherwise represented: it is dramatized in terms of the realistic consequences of Adam's fall as suffered by the contemporary audience. To accomplish this is a main function of the lengthy introductory section of the play: the complaints about their lot and their world which so deepen by contrast the joy of the shepherds—their recovery of *gaudium plenum*—at the close.

Ill-clothed, cold, hungry, and tired, overtaxed, impoverished, and so oppressed by the gentry and "maintained" men of lords that he can scarcely thrive, the First Shepherd sounds the theme of the movement—the life of the poor in a hard world suffered "in payne, anger, and wo" (l. 40)—in his numb understatement: "It is not as I wold, for I am al lappyd / In sorrow" (ll. 4–5). The Second Shepherd adds to the argument the theme of the *malmarié* in a similar tone: "These men that ar wed haue not all thare wyll" (l. 73). The Third Shepherd, young Daw, widens the perspective by sweeping reference to all "the warld" as "euer in drede and brekyll as glas," a transitory place where "all thyng writhys," and by comparison (preparative of further wonders) of the late "wyndys and ranys so rude, and stormes so keyn" to "Noe floode" (ll. 120–35). The treatment of young Daw by the elder shepherds (one of whom is his master) and his response to it (ll. 138–77), make it difficult to agree with those who characterize the shepherds, because of the Christian expletives they utter, as "pious."[71]

3 PASTOR.	A, syr, God you saue, and master myne!
	A drynk fayn wold I haue, and somwhat to dyne.
1 PASTOR.	Crystys curs, my knaue, thou art a ledyr hyne!
2 PASTOR.	What, the boy lyst raue! Abyde vnto syne . . .

(ll. 145–48)

The Wakefield Master, who shows the lot of the foot-dragging servant at the hands of "master-men" to be but an echo of their own subjection to "men that ar gretter," knew better: "Fare wordys may ther be, bot luf is ther none / this yere" (ll. 569–70). The harsh world, brightened

71. See Manly, pp. 152–53.

by his humor, which the playwright makes us glimpse through the shepherds' complaints is one in need of salvation; Mak, when he enters at
the end of this section of the play, speaks chorally when he says, "thi
will, Lorde, of me tharnys [i.e., is lacking]."

> Now wold God I were in heuen, for ther wepe no barnes
> So styll.   (ll. 191, 193–94)

It has been remarked, in comparisons of the *Prima* and *Secunda Pastorum*, that the playwright in this play offered a considerably shorter
version of the thematically necessary, but theatrically rather interrup-
tive, conventional recitation of Old Testament prophecies by the shepherds. His wry, theater-wise, comic device for securing his audience's
attention to those retained is equally worth our notice. The shepherds
have attempted—and the likelihood of their failure is remarked in advance (ll. 661–62)—to imitate the Herald Angel's singing of the *Gloria*
"right as he knakt it" (l. 659). Now Coll has to tell Gyb, who has started
a reprise, to cease his "dyn" so the prophecies can be heard (l. 674).

All such evidence (and much could be added) points to the powerful
and immediate ironic value of the play's complex sense of time. The time
references, because they run (as in the cycle as a whole) from the Creation and the Fall to the Last Judgment which the contemporary world
yet anticipates, significantly "place" the primary anachronism involved
in making Yorkshire herdsmen the shepherds addressed by the Herald
Angel outside Bethlehem at the Nativity. We dare not suppose this
anachronism—everywhere forced to the fore of our attention both by
contemporary realistic detail and innumerable Christian references—
an unconscious result of medieval naïveté.[72] The play reenacts the central event of Christian history. But the world of the shepherds—recognizably that of the audience itself—is represented as that Before Christ,
before the joyous possibilities implicit in the Incarnation are availing.
Their ensemble effect is to depict the perennial human condition before
the Incarnation, the unremedied pain of the fallen world before Corpus
Christi. It is a world still in need of rebirth, ignorant or incapable of the
grace already won for it. The Incarnation is indeed an eternally recurrent mystery—and needs to be. In the context provided by such a conception, it becomes clear why the Wakefield Master drew from the
Second Epistle of Peter (2:19) the epithet "day-starne" which his
shepherds apply both to the "barne" in the cradle and to the Infant in
Bethlehem (ll. 577, 727).

---

72. See Auerbach, pp. 136–37.

We have also a more sure word of prophecy; whereunto ye do well that ye take heed, as unto a lamp that shineth in a dark place, until the day dawn, and the day star arise in your hearts [*Et lucifer oriatur in cordibus vestris*]. . . .

It is not enough (says Bede) to interpret this "day-star" as the Lord (as in Job 37:32); in the immediate context it signifies the bright understanding (*clarus intellectus*) which should shine in every faithful Christian's mind "until the day dawn."[73]

To see that the Wakefield Master has exploited the dialectical capacities of his dramaturgy of analogical action is, perhaps, finally to be in a position to respond to Rossiter's observation, that the play's "immiscible juxtapositions" leave us "to wrestle with the uncombinable antinomies of the medieval mind." For the point, surely, is that the Wakefield Master's handling of them has made the elements juxtaposed not merely miscible but synergetic. Such a result plainly was the creatively achieved end-product of some development. Morgan has remarked how "a type of double plot emerged" in the shepherds' plays when "the significance of the central, static image" of the Nativity icon was transferred to the human drama, "bringing together the secular and sacred" in such a way that "a unity was established that depended on the *idea* and was not comprehensible apart from it."[74] But this enlarging of the religious drama by making it "include its own opposite" could really mean "a step from dramatized narrative to metaphysical drama"—and one taken "in such a way that the vigor of folk tradition and of the professional mime were added to the subtlety of the theologians"[75]—only when, as in the *Secunda Pastorum*, the mutual impact of one upon the other was artfully admitted and included. For the Wakefield Master, if he had his profound religious faith, also had no illusions. His viewpoint, while it is fundamentally Christian, shows itself everywhere incapable of ignoring what his realistic vision encompasses. That is why a simply theologic reading of the play can be no more critically adequate than celebrations of it for its farce alone or for an irreducibly obscure Gothic "ambivalence" supposedly to be found in it. To be sure, clowning and adoration, mystery and nescience and boorishness are, if not merely "laid together," nevertheless brought into the context of one vision. The effect, however, is not disjunction but something akin to the aesthetic jar produced in the Portinari altarpiece by the seeming irruption of the raw faces of the hardhanded Flemish peasants into the exquisitely charged serenity and sophisticated symbolism of the Adoration scene. A dissonance is struck; yet the Wakefield shepherds, quite as much as Van

73. See *PL* XCIII, col. 73; cf. *Allegoriae*, col. 989.
74. P. 688.
75. Ibid.

der Goes' (and undoubtedly with much less subjectivity of emotion projected in the effect), complete the picture's "composition" even as they enlarge its scope.[76] The Wakefield Master's methods, and the meaning and effect he attains with them, in fact subsume various kinds of "doubleness" by requiring them; the antinomies are combinable in a structure whose vitality springs from its effort to comprehend and ponder them. In his hands, in other words, the religious *commedia* becomes comedy by being modulated in the course of assimilating to itself "the other" comic spirit springing from the substantial earth of moral limitation—in the course of becoming a viable dramatic perspective which can renew the audience's sense of the actual in relation to the real.[77]

76. See Panofsky, *Early Netherlandish Painting*, I, 331–32, and fig. 463. Color reproduction of this central panel of the altarpiece can be seen in Jacques Lassaigne and Giulio Carlo Argan, *The Fifteenth Century from Van Eyck to Botticelli* (Skira, n.d.), p. 153.

77. [Further detail on the iconography of the gifts in Eugene B. Cantelupe and Richard Griffith, "The Gifts of the Shepherds in the Wakefield 'Secunda Pastorum,'" *Mediaeval Studies*, XXVIII (1966), 328–35, and John P. Cutts, "The Shepherds' Gifts in *The Second Shepherds' Play* and Bosch's 'Adoration of the Magi,'" *Comparative Drama*, IV (1970–71), 120–24.]

Nan Cooke Carpenter

11. Music in the *Secunda Pastorum*

To interpret the "Thre brefes to a long" passage in the *Secunda Pastorum* (c. 1450–60) as a reference to a musical figure anticipating Beethoven's immortal phrase ("Fate knocking at the door") as well as our own Morse code symbol for the letter V—an interpretation which has had at least one public expression[1]—is pleasant and facile but as truly fallacious as would be any interpretation arrived at by superimposing musical ideas and practices of a later time upon this bit of medieval criticism. Illumined by the light of its own time, however, the famous musical passage easily reveals its significance in the context as well as its part in a total overall musical pattern which characterizes the play.

That musical knowledge, of which this passage is the best-known indication, apparently formed no small part of the erudition of the fifteenth-century Wakefield Master is a fact less remarkable than is generally known, in view of the relative ease with which such knowledge might be acquired in medieval times and in view of the great emphasis upon music in the medieval schools.[2] Anyone, in fact, who went to school at all studied music, both in the grammar schools and in institutions of higher learning—cathedral schools and universities. A man destined for the clergy—and it is usually assumed that the author of the *Secunda Pastorum* was in orders—would have had even greater opportunities for musical studies, probably serving some years early in life as choirboy and thereby becoming acquainted with both musical theory and practical music—the monodic Gregorian chant, with its florid "Alleluias," and also the various forms of polyphony cultivated in the later Middle Ages. And if a university student as well—again, it is not unlikely that the Wakefield Master studied at one of the universities—

[Reprinted from *Speculum*, XXVI (1951), 696–700, by permission of the author and the publisher. Copyright 1951 by the Mediaeval Academy of America.]

1. See Robert Withington, "Thre Brefes to a Long," *Modern Language Notes*, LVIII (1943), 115–16.

2. I have treated at some length the study of music in medieval institutions of learning in a dissertation, "Music in the Medieval and Renaissance Universities," Yale University, 1948.

he not only studied music as a liberal art[3] but in all likelihood participated in its practice in his collegiate foundation.[4] In any event, this particular cleric seems to have had an especial fondness for music and to have found it especially apt for serving various functions in his play. And the three shepherds, not only musical but quite forthright in their critical approach, undoubtedly reflect the Master's interest and knowledge.

Music serves, first of all, as a structural element in the play in a way which foreshadows its use a little later in the interludes and still later in the academic comedies, the parts of which were often outlined by musical insertions. Such is the function of the three-part song discussed by the shepherds (who quite properly divide its parts, one taking the tenor, one the treble, and one the mean) which marks the end of the introductory section devoted to the shepherds alone and the entrance of Mak with the consequent beginning of the farce proper. The farce enacted by Mak, Gill, and the shepherds is again separated from the nativity story, the play within the play, by the angel's "Gloria in excelsis," which not only inspires the "Thre brefes to a long" comment but introduces a last bit of tension, as the shepherds almost postpone their journey, so eager is the *Primus pastor* to imitate immediately the celestial music—"ffor to syng vs emong / right as he knakt it, / I can."[5] But the eager songster is persuaded to save his singing for another time ("To bedlem he bad / that we shuld gang: / I am full fard / that we tary to lang")—until the end of the play, in fact; and a final strain of music marks *finis* to the play as the shepherds, having worshiped at the manger, set out on their return trip with the words "To syng ar we bun: / let take on loft" and go off singing.

Not only is music, then, an important formal element, marking off the play into symmetrical divisions—a short section at beginning and end, a long section in the middle; it is also a somewhat subtle means of

3. Although Oxford required the study of the seven liberal arts from early times, no specific mention of music occurs in any existing statute prior to 1431. Statutes of that year required, *inter alia*, "Musicam per terminum anni, videlicet Boecii": see Strickland Gibson, *Statuta antiqua Vniversitatis Oxoniensis* (Oxford, 1931), p. 234. By analogy and because the Cambridge curriculum was modeled upon that of Oxford, one assumes that the same rule applied at Cambridge. The first Cambridge statutes dealing with a course of studies date from the late fifteenth century and require music and arithmetic in the three-year curriculum to be covered by any bachelor aspiring to the *magisterium;* see *Documents relating to the University and Colleges of Cambridge* (London, 1852), I, 382, no. 136.

4. For the many musical requirements for scholars and fellows in the various colleges at Oxford and Cambridge, see *Statutes of the Colleges of Oxford* (Oxford, 1853–55) and the *Cambridge Documents.*

5. Quotations from the *Secunda Pastorum* are taken from *The Towneley Plays,* ed. George England and Alfred W. Pollard, EETS e.s. 71 (London, 1897).

pointing up the "bad" character of Mak. For the shepherds' sharp criticism of Mak's musical inabilities stresses the difference in character between him and the "good" persons in the play, the very musical shepherds. Mak's very entrance is apparently accompanied by his own off-key singing and heralded by the highly derogatory line of the *Primus pastor*, "Who is that pypys so poore?" When Gill, about to become a "mother," instructs her husband a little later,

> Com and make redy all / and syng by thyn oone;
> Syng lullay thou shall / for I must grone. . . .
> Syng lullay on fast,

Mak's response with a lullaby is evidently as poor a piece of "piping" as his earlier music—indistinguishable, indeed, from Gill's groaning; and the caustic remarks of the rustic *musici* approaching Mak's "house" once more heighten the "bad" aspects of the Scotsman's character while at the same time they underline the utter ludicrousness of the mock-nativity:

> will ye here how thay hak? / oure syre, lyst, croyne.
> hard I neu*er* none crak / so clere out of toyne.

With the sudden appearance of the angel and his singing of the "Gloria," however, the effect is just the opposite. The words of the *Primus pastor*, "This was a qwant stevyn / that eu*er* yit I hard," hint that it is the cleverly sung music which persuades the shepherds that they have indeed heard a heavenly messenger and should follow his orders. And by a technical discussion of the angel's music, the shepherds exalt and praise that music, in wonderment and awe, as perhaps they could in no other way:

> Say, what was his song? / hard ye not how he crakyd it?
> Thre brefes to a long. /
>   yee, mary, he hakt it.
> was no crochett wrong / nor no thyng that lakt it.

This discussion of the celestial music in terms of earthly practices, moreover, ties it effectively to reality and softens the transition from the very realistic sheep-stealing farce to the adoration play in which contemporary British shepherds become the worshiping herdsmen of biblical days—in which, rather, they are presumed to become biblical shepherds; actually, the final strain of music, as well as the bob of cherries, bird, and tennis ball, ineluctably preserve the contemporary British atmosphere.

The critical remarks of the shepherds reveal, too, that the quality which moves them to wonder and admiration is the speed of the music, guided exactly by rules of musical mensuration. In other words, the "Gloria's" rhythmic complexity is what the shepherds admire most.

According to the *Oxford English Dictionary* (which cites these lines in support of its definitions), both *crack* and *hack* mean to break, to split up; and *knack* is even more definite: "To 'break' (notes); to sing with trills and runs; to sing in a lively or ornate manner, to trill forth." It is the angel's melismatic, coloratura presentation which enchants the shepherds, probably because the rustic singers are more accustomed to hearing and performing music in the discant style (chiefly syllabic, chordal, *nota contra notam*), a style for which the British, with their strong penchant for sonority, had a particular fondness from early times. Originally related to *usus* rather than to *ars*, to folk practices rather than to more complex artistic practices, English discant was a type of improvisation at sight in parallel sixth chords upon a given tenor, a style which was transmitted to the Continent (especially through the work of the English composer Dunstable) and which was highly influential in shaping the style of composers of the Continental Burgundian School —Dufay and Binchois.[6] It is this type of three-part music, with its given tenor and parallel counter-melodies (improvised at sight) in the treble and mean, which the shepherds sing just before the entrance of Mak, after agreeing on their respective parts:

> *primus pastor.* lett me syng the tenory.
> *ijus pastor.* And I the tryble so hye.
> *iijus pastor.* Then the meyne fallys to me;
>   lett se how ye chauntt.

Nonetheless, the shepherds recognize soloistic artistry when they hear it, although they appear to show a certain lack of progressiveness in their attitude here. For the relation of *longa* to *brevis* (usually *modus perfectus:* one to three) had been settled by Franco of Cologne in the thirteenth century and the *ars nova* (fourteenth and fifteenth centuries) was chiefly concerned with the mensuration of smaller note values: only the tenors in masses and motets of the fifteenth century used the *modus perfectus* in their *cantus firmi* of slow-moving, long-held notes over which elaborate polyphonic structures were erected. The words of the *Tercius pastor*, "was no crochett wrong," show that his ear, at least, is attuned to quicker notes. At any rate, the shepherds are overwhelmed

---

6. There exists a group of little treatises on this characteristic English usage, written in the vernacular (indicative of a non-academic origin) and dating from the fourteenth and fifteenth centuries. These, together with a discussion of English discant, may be found in Manfred Bukofzer, *Geschichte des englischen Diskants und des Fauxbourdons nach den theoretischen Quellen* (Strassburg, 1937) and Thrasybulos Georgiades, *Englische Diskant-traktate aus der ersten Hälfte des 15. Jahrhunderts* (Munich, 1937). Three of the treatises (two of them with parallel versions in modern English) have been published by Sanford Meech, "Three Musical Treatises in English from a Fifteenth-Century Manuscript," *Speculum*, X (1935), 233–69.

by the angel's music because it represents a type of artistic, learned music more recherché than the simple polyphony in discant style which probably constituted their own performances.[7]

A glance at the shepherds' reactions to the angels' song in the *Prima Pagina Pastorum*, in which critics agree that the Wakefield Master was feeling his way toward the greater perfection of the second play, overwhelmingly confirms the shepherds' delight in a "curious" type of music with great variety in rhythmic values. The *Prima pastor* comments upon this immediately:

> A, godys dere d*omin*us! / What was that sang?
> It was wond*er* curiose / *with* small noyt*ys* emang.

And the *Tercius pastor* adds,

> It was a mery gle / sich hard I neu*er* none,
> I recorde.

After recounting at great length (in some ten stanzas, in fact) the substance of the angel's song—based, as was usual, on Old Testament prophecies and two lines from one of Virgil's eclogues cited glibly by the erudite *Primus pastor*—the shepherds leave no doubt that it is the music which convinces them of the heavenly origin of their visitor: for the *Tercius pastor* says,

> I wold that we knew / of this song so fre
>   Of the angell;
> I hard by hys steuen,
> he was send downe ffro heuen;

and the *Primus pastor* counters, "It is trouth that ye neuen, / I hard hym well spell." And, even more strikingly than in the second play, the speed of the angel's music, with its diminution of long notes, is cause for wonder, as witness the words of the *Secundus pastor*,

---

7. Even though discant was more indigenous to England than the recondite music of the *ars nova*, with its great stress upon rhythmic complexity, problems of the *ars nova* were known and understood in England as well as on the Continent. The "Quartum principale" of the *Quatuor principalia musicae*, written in 1351 by the theologian Simon Tunstede, then teaching at Oxford, is a treatise on mensural music in which problems of rhythm and notation are discussed according to Franco (*ars antiqua*) and Philip de Vitry (*ars nova*); and the *Summa super musicam continuam et discretam* of John Hanboys is a treatise of the *scholia* type on mensural music, involving imperfection, diminution, and alteration of note values from longs to semiminims. Much of the material here (especially the section dealing with Franconian theory) was, in turn, based upon an earlier *scholia* by another Englishman: Robert de Handlo's *Regule cum maximis Magistri Franconis*, 1326. All three of these treatises may be found in E. de Coussemaker, *Scriptorum de musica medii aevi nova series* (Paris, 1864–76): IV, 200–98 (Tunstede); I, 403–48 (Hanboys); and I, 383–403 (Handlo).

> Now, by god that me boght / it was a mery song;
> I dar say that he broght / foure & twenty to a long,

followed by the *Primus pastor's* more conservative but equally admiring criticism,

> In fayth I trow noght / so many he throng
>   On a heppe;
> Thay were gentyll and small,
> And well tonyd with all.

At this point, like the *Primus pastor* in the second play, the *Tercius pastor* wishes to imitate the heavenly music ("yee, bot I can thaym all, / Now lyst I lepe") to which the *Primus pastor* agrees ("Brek outt youre voce / let se as ye yelp"). But the *Tercius pastor* argues that he cannot sing alone ("I may not for the pose / but I haue help"), obviously referring to discant in three parts, the only type of music he knows; and so all three shepherds engage in a song before setting out for Bethlehem. And after they have worshiped at the manger, their final lines, spoken by the *Primus pastor,* refer not only to their song of departure which ends the play but to the discant style of this composition—improvisation at sight:

> Amen, to that worde / syng we therto
>   On hight;
> To Ioy all sam,
> With myrth and gam,
> To the lawde of this lam
> Syng we in syght.

Lavish diminution of note values, then, resulting in the highly florid, ornamental style which characterizes the celestial "Gloria," calls forth admiring comments from the chief protagonists in both the *Prima* and the *Secunda Pastorum.* But just as incidents and attitudes clearly expressed in the first play are only hinted at in the second, so there is a more concise, conservative description of the angelic music in the latter—as the twenty-four (semiminims;[8] actually the division three breves to a long is basic to this diminution also) to a long in the earlier play become the three breves to a long (a division which had been standard for centuries) in the later. And far from foreshadowing a rhythmic-melodic motif used by Beethoven or any other modern composer, the unique passages of the Wakefield Master simply reiterate the place of discant in typical English usage by distinguishing the heavenly song with a more elaborate, more elegant soloistic style.

8. Twenty-four semiminims result if the long be divided into three breves and if each breve, semibreve, and minim be equal to two notes of the next smallest value (three times two times two times two). I am indebted to Willi Apel for calling this to my attention.

Alan H. Nelson

12. The Temptation of Christ; or, The Temptation of Satan

Theologians of the medieval church agreed that the Passion of Christ was an event uniquely efficacious for man's redemption. The precise causal relationship between the death (and resurrection) of Christ and the salvation of man was a subject of some debate.[1] One of the most popular among patristic explications of this matter was the abuse-of-power theory, formulated in a well-known sermon by Pope Leo the Great:

And, dearly beloved, this very fact that Christ chose to be born of a Virgin, does it not appear to be part of the deepest design? I mean, that the devil should not be aware that Salvation had been born for the human race, and through the obscurity of that spiritual conception, when he saw Him no different to others, should believe Him born in no different way to others. For when he observed that His nature was like that of others, he thought that He had the same origin as all had: and [Satan] did not understand that He was free from the bonds of transgression because he did not find Him a stranger to the weakness of mortality. For though the true mercy of God had infinitely many schemes to hand for the restoration of mankind, it chose that particular design which put in force for destroying the devil's work, not the efficacy of might but the dictates of justice. For the pride of the ancient foe not undeservedly made good its despotic rights over all men, and with no unwarrantable supremacy tyrannized over those who had been of their own accord lured away from God's commands to be the slaves of his will. . . .

When, therefore, the merciful and almighty Savior so arranged the commencement of His human course as to hide the power of His Godhead which was inseparable from His manhood under the veil of our weakness, the crafty foe was taken off his guard and he thought that the nativity of the Child, Who was born for the salvation of mankind, was as much subject to himself as all others at their birth. . . . The unscrupulous thief and greedy robber persisted in assaulting Him Who had nothing of His own, and, in carrying out the general sentence on original sin, went beyond the bond on which he rested, and required the punishment of iniquity from Him in Whom he found no fault. And thus the malevolent terms of the deadly compact are

1. For a history of early controversies, see J. A. MacCulloch, *The Harrowing of Hell* (Edinburgh, 1930), esp. pp. 83–130 and 199–216. See also my "The Contest of Guile in the Middle English Corpus Christi Plays," Ph.D. diss., University of California, Berkeley, 1966, from which this essay has been adapted.

annulled, and through the injustice of an overcharge the whole debt is cancelled. The strong one is bound by his own chains, and every device of the evil one recoils on his own head.[2]

The Incarnation is thus a holy subterfuge designed to conceal the Godhead of Christ from Satan. In putting Christ to death, Satan oversteps the limits of his power, and thus forfeits his rights over the souls of mankind.

A vernacular sermon contemporary with the English Corpus Christi cycles uses the abuse-of-power theory to explicate the Temptation of Christ in the Desert. Satan observed Christ as he fasted for forty days: "And whan þe feende sawe þat he had so longe fastyd with-oute mete, ȝitt he was in disperre wheþur þat he was Goddes Sonne or noon. Þerfor he vente to hym and seid, 'ȝiff þou be Goddes Sonne,' he seid, 'þan commaunde þat þise stones be brede.' Oure Lord myght well a commaunded so, and he had wold, seþ þat he made all þe world of nowȝth; but he wold not, for he wold not shewe to þe feende what he was. . . . In þis maner and oþur mo tempted þe feend oure Lord for to witt wheþur þat [he] was Goddes Sonne [or] noon. But oure Lorde answerde hym so wisely þat þe feende wist not what he was."[3] In the Temptation, Satan attempts to penetrate the "disguise" of the Incarnation. So interested is this preacher in describing the general motives for Satan's conduct and Christ's, he overlooks the second and third temptations entirely.

Timothy Fry has argued that of the extant Corpus Christi plays, the theologically self-conscious *Ludus Coventriae* (N-Town) cycle is uniquely informed and unified by the abuse-of-power theory.[4] A comparative examination of the Temptation plays in the York, N-Town, and Chester cycles, however, will show that N-Town is not in fact unique in this respect. (Unfortunately, Towneley lacks a Temptation play.) Robert Longsworth has already shown that the same theory underlies much of the Cornish *Ordinalia*.[5]

In each of the three extant Temptation plays,[6] Satan begins by ex-

2. From Sermon XXII, *Letters and Sermons of Leo the Great*, in *Nicene and Post-Nicene Fathers*, 2d ser. (New York, 1895), XII, 130–31.

3. Woodburn O. Ross, ed., *Middle English Sermons*, EETS o.s. 209 (London, 1940), pp. 141–42.

4. Timothy Fry, "The Unity of the *Ludus Coventriae*," *Studies in Philology*, 48 (1951), 527–70.

5. Robert Longsworth, *The Cornish Ordinalia: Religion and Dramaturgy* (Cambridge, Mass., 1967), esp. pp. 83–89.

6. Quotations are from L. Toulmin Smith, ed., *York Plays* (Oxford, 1885); K. S. Block, ed., *Ludus Coventriae*, EETS e.s. 120 (London, 1922); and Herman Deimling and J. Matthews, eds., *Chester Plays*, EETS e.s. 62, 115 (London, 1892, 1916). I have taken the liberty to alter punctuation when it has seemed necessary.

pressing his fear that his power over mankind is in jeopardy from Christ. The York Satan, for example, broods over rumors that a "swayne" now on earth will, by his death, purchase human souls from hell:

> And certis, all þat hath ben sithen borne,
> Has comen to me, mydday and morne,
> And I haue ordayned so þam forne,
> none may þame fende;
> Þat fro all likyng ar they lorne
> withowten ende.
> And nowe sum men spekis of a swayne,
> Howe he schall come and suffre payne,
> And with his dede to blisse agayne
> Þei schulde be bought;
> But certis þis tale is but a trayne,
> I trowe it noȝt.   (ll. 13–24)

Satan affirms that the rumor is "but a trayne," only a lie which he does not believe. Nevertheless his fears lead him to tempt Christ in order to discover his identity.

The perfunctory fashion of York contrasts with the extended introduction of the N-Town Temptation. Satan summons a council in hell and reveals his doubt to his fellows:

> The dowte þat I haue it is of cryst i-wys
> borne he was in bedleem as it is seyd
> And many a man wenyth þat goddys sone he is
> born of a woman and she a clene mayd
> And all þat evyr he prechyth it is of hevyn blys
> he wyl lese oure lawe I am ryght sore afrayd
> Ffayn wold I knowe who were ffadyr his
> Ffor of þis grett dowte I am sore dysmayd
> in dede
> If þat he be goddys childe
> and born of a mayd mylde
> than be we rygh sore begylde
> and short xal ben oure spede.   (ll. 14–26)

From popular report and from the matter of his sermons, Satan begins to suspect that Christ might indeed be divine. But nothing either confirms or contradicts the rumor. If Christ has God for a father and a virgin for a mother, then Satan and his retinue will be "rygh sore begylde."

It is Belial who in N-Town proposes the plan to discover whether Christ is indeed the "kynge of blys." This will entail testing his ability to sin:

> The best wytt þat I kan say
> hym to tempte forsoth it is
> with sotyl whylys if þat þou may
> A-say to make hym to don A-mys
> If þat he synne þis is no nay
> he may nat be kynge of blys
> hym to tempte go walke þi way
> Ffor best counsell I trowe be this
> Go forth now and assay. . . .
> *Sathan:* So Afftyr ȝour wytt now wyll I werke
> I wyll no lenger here a-byde
> be he nevyr so wyse a clerke
> I xal apposyn hym with-inne A tyde.
> *Belsabub:* now louely lucyfer in helle so derke
> Kynge and lorde of synne and pryde
> with sum myst his wytts to merke
> He send þe grace to be þi gyde.   (ll. 40–60)

Belial suggests using "sotyl whylys" to make Christ reveal his true nature. Satan trusts that he can conquer no matter how "wyse" Christ proves to be. Belsabub prays to Lucifer to throw "myst" over Christ's "wytts," to dull his powers of reasoning.

The Chester Temptation begins much like the others, as Satan conceives a "gammon" to investigate a "Doseberd" now on earth:

> Now by my soveraynte I sweare
> and principalitie that I beare,
> In helle payne when I am there
> a gammon I will assay.
> There is a Doseberd I wolde dear,
> that walkes about wyde-where,
> who is his father I wot nere,
> the sooth if I shold say.
> What master man ever be this
> that in the world thus comen is?
> his mother I wot did never amisse,
> and that now marvayles me.
> his father can I not finde, I-wisse,
> for all my craft ne my quaintyce;
> it seemes he thought heaven were his,
> so stout a syre is he.   (ll. 1–16)

Satan is acquainted with Christ's mother and is troubled by her sinlessness. For all his crafty spying, however, he has been unsuccessful in determining Christ's paternity.

Satan knows that his power is in jeopardy if this is indeed God in disguise:

> My highnes aye he putis behynde,
> for in hym falte can I none finde;
> if he be god in mans kinde,
> my craft then fully fayles. . . .
> And this thing dare I soothly say:
> if that he were god veray,
> hunger shold greeue hym by no way,
> that were against reason.
> Therfore now I will assay
> with speach of bread hym to betray,
> for he hath fasted many a day,
> now meat were in season.   (ll. 41–56)

Here Satan explains his stratagem with syllogistic precision: if this person is God, then he cannot experience hunger; if he succumbs to the temptation, he is indeed hungry, and therefore not God. Hence Satan will engage Christ "with speach of bread," that is, with talk about bread. He does not suspect at this point that his first premise may be incorrect.

Satan's decision to tempt Christ first with bread is narrowly motivated. It results not from any feeling in Satan that bread has a particular moral or symbolic significance, but merely from his empirical observation that Christ is apparently suffering from hunger. Of course the Temptation is the consequence of God's design rather than Satan's, and the meaning of the event cannot be reduced to Satan's limited perception of it. But for our purposes it will be best to examine the three trials first as steps in Satan's stratagem. When this is accomplished, we will inquire into the full range of meaning in the events.

In each of the three trials, Satan's purpose is to entice Christ into some action which will definitively demonstrate that he either is or is not God. If he proves to be God, Satan will avoid putting him to death. If he is not God, Satan will take him to hell without fear. But if Satan cannot find out, he will have to put him to death and take whatever consequences ensue.

When the York Satan first confronts Christ, he slyly commends his wit:

> Þou witty man and wise of rede,
> If þou can ought of godhede,
> Byd now þat þer stones be brede,
> Betwyxte vs two;
> Þan may þei stande thy-selfe in stede,
> and othir moo.   (ll. 55–60)

Similar words are spoken in N-Town and in Chester, and the source for all is the account in the gospels.[7] The gospels are not, of course, self-

7. The Temptation is treated at length in Matthew 4:1–11, and in Luke 4:1–13. All three plays follow the order of temptations given in Matthew.

explanatory, while the precise terms of this trial require some elucidation. It is easiest, perhaps, to regard each trial separately, or all together, as an adequate test of divinity, for if the Temptation is not a real test, then any good man might prevail. Given that the test is adequate, then if Christ should submit to any trial, he would thereby prove himself to be less than God. Conversely, by refusing to submit, he proves that he is God. This converse proposition, however, is incompatible with the abuse-of-power theory.

In the sermon on the Temptation it is argued that Christ might have complied but did not, because Satan would thus be kept in doubt. It is unclear whether Christ's purpose is to hide his *innocence* or his *power* from Satan. If it is a matter of *power*, then we must contemplate three possibilities rather than two. If Christ submits to the trial and fails to perform the miracle, he is demonstrably not God; if he submits and succeeds, then he is demonstrably divine; but if he refuses to submit, he demonstrates nothing. The second alternative, submission joined with success, seems self-contradictory. It would imply that Christ is divinely powerful, since he can perform the miracle, but that he is also sinful, since he accepts the trial in the first place.

Fortunately, the trials never proceed to this point. And if they are not entirely consistent in their conception, we must remember that the particular terms of the trial were forged by demons in hell who persist in their gross ignorance of the truth. But we at least must keep in mind the implications of Satan's action and Christ's response. Satan will only be satisfied if Christ responds. If Christ does nothing, then Satan is lost. At times, as in the N-Town council, Satan contemplates the Temptation as a trial of Christ's innocence. At other times, he tempts Christ to show his power. Theoretically, the second is reducible to the first, since under the circumstances Christ cannot demonstrate power without sacrificing innocence. But this should not blind us to the possibility that frequently through the plays Satan's real interest lies in testing Christ's power. Even this, however, is merely instrumental to Satan's chief purpose, which is to discover Christ's identity.

When the York Satan experiences Christ's refusal to turn the stones into bread, he charges that Christ is only feigning hunger and invites him to mount the pinnacle for the second trial:

> A! slyke carping neuere I kende,
> Hym hungres noȝt as I wende.
> Now sen thy fadir may þe fende
> be sotill sleghte,
> Late se yf þou allone may lende
> þer vppon heghte,

> Vppon þe pynakill parfitely.
> A! ha! nowe go we wele ther-by!
> I schall assaye in vayne-glorie
> to garre hym falle.
> And if he be goddis sone myghty,
> witte I schall.   (ll. 85–96)

Here Satan names the sin of the second temptation as vain-glory. The
N-Town Satan does the same, and names the sin of the first trial,
gluttony:

> Ffor no grett hungyr þat I kan se
> In glotony þou wylt not synne
> now to þe temple com forth with me
> and þer xal I shewe þe a praty gynne
> Vp to þis pynnacle now go we
> I xal þe sett on þe hyʒest pynne
> there I preue what þat þou be
> Or þat we tweyn part a-twynne
> I xal knowe what myght þou haue
> Whan þou art sett upon þe pynnacle
> þou xalt þer pleyn a qweynt steracle
> Or ellys shewe a grett meracle
> thy-sself ffrom hurte þou saue.   (ll. 105–17)

Satan will show Christ a "praty Gynne." This is an ironic phrase. For
those who are privy to Satan's stratagems, it means a clever deceit, a trap.
But apparently Satan intends that Christ should understand it as signifying an ingenious feat.

   This second trial involves the same paradox as the first. Though he
solicits Christ's compliance in the name of a particular sin, Satan may
feel that the demonstration of Christ's true nature will lie in the outcome of the trial: if Christ is rescued by angels, then he is God's Son; if
he is not saved from hurt, then he is man. In Satan's own words: "I xal
knowe what *myght* þou haue."

   The Chester Satan maintains a double perspective, enticing Christ to
show his power, but offering "honour" as a reward:

> Very God if that thou be,
> now I shall full sone see
> for I shall ordayne honor for thee,
> or that thou wend away.
> Say, thou that sittes there so hye,
> if thou be gods sonne, be slye,
> come downe and I will say I see
> thee doe a fayre mastry.
> Thyne owne Angell mon keepe thee
> that thou hurt nether foot nor knee;
> shew thy power, now lett see,
> thou may have honour therby.   (ll. 109–20)

He admits on the one hand that his chief desire is to discover whether this man has power. On the other hand, Satan solicits Christ's desire for honor, the chief element in the sin of vainglory.

At his rebuff during the second trial, the Chester Satan is even more dismayed than before:

> Alas! woe is me to-day!
> twise haue I fayled of my pray,
> was I never rowted in such dray,
> ne so fowle reproved. (ll. 125–28)

This is typical of his reaction in the other two cycles. In N-Town he adds:

> I must now be-gynne to haue a newe travayl
> In covetyse to tempt hym it comyth now in my thought
> Ffor If I went þus A-way and shrynkyd as a snayle
> lorn were þe labore all þat I haue wrought. (ll. 146–49)

The third trial is rather more direct and distinctly less paradoxical than the first two. Its nature is most clearly defined in York:

> And sen I may noȝt in þis wise
> make hym my thrall,
> I will assaye in couetise
> to garre hym fall,
> For certis I schall noȝt leue hym ȝitt.
> Who is my souereyne, þis wolde I witte. (ll. 129–34)

Satan wants to discover whether Christ is his sovereign, as he would be if he were God, or whether Christ is his thrall, as he would be if he were merely man. Satan continues:

> My selffe ordande þe þore to sitte,
> þis wote þou wele,
> And right euen as I ordande itt,
> is done ilke dele.
> þan may þou se sen itt is soo
> þat I am souerayne of vs two.
> And ȝitt I graunte þe or I goo,
> withouten fayle,
> þat if þou woll assent me too,
> it schall avayle. . . .
> Be-halde now, ser, and þou schalt see,
> Sere kyngdomes and sere contre;
> Alle þis wile I giffe to þe
> for euer more
> And þou falle and honour me,
> as I saide are. (ll. 135–56)

Precisely the same terms apply in Chester and N-Town. In this third trial Satan asks Christ to perform an act which in itself rather than in its outcome will demonstrate subjection to Satan.

In all three cycles, Satan is sent to hell with complete ignominy. In N-Town he concedes:

> What þat he is I kan not se
> Whethyr god or man what þat he be
> I kan not telle in no degre
> Ffor sorwe I lete a crakke.   (ll. 192–95)

In Chester his departure is more prolonged:

> Out! alas! now me is woe,
> for found I never so mickle a foe,
> though I to threpe be never so thro,
> I am overcome thrye.
> Alas! my sleight now am I quitt,
> Adam I founded with a fitt,
> and hym in combrance sone I knitte
> throughe quayntice of my crafte.
> Nowe sone out of sorrow he must be shut
> and I pyned in hell pitt.
> knew I neuer none of such a witt
> as hym that I haue lafte.   (ll. 141–52)

The line, "Alas! my sleight now am I quitt," is a virtual restatement of Pope Leo's assertion that "the strong one is bound by his own chains, and every device of the evil one recoils on his own head." Satan antici-pates that the consequence of his failure will be the delivery of souls from hell. York and N-Town cycles present the episode of Pilate's wife, in which Satan, having finally realized what he was unable to discover in the Temptation, tries to put a stop to the Crucifixion. But the death of Christ is accomplished, and he makes his descent to hell. Even at the Harrowing of Hell, Satan is initially ignorant of Christ's true identity. He challenges his right to rescue the souls and learns only when it is too late that this is indeed the Son of God.

The Temptation therefore takes its place as a decisive episode in the sequential action which determines the essential dramatic structure of the cycles. But the full significance of this play is not exhausted by its literal plot. Other levels of meaning are present in all three cycles. Per-haps the simplest is the hortatory interpretation given by Christ in N-Town:

> Now All mankende exaumple take
> by these grete werkys þat þou dost se
> how þat þe devyll of helle so blake
> in synne was besy to tempte me
> Ffor all his maystryes þat he dyd make

he is ouercom and now doth ffle
all þis I suffyr ffor mannys sake
to teche þe how þou xalt rewle the
Whan þe devylle dothe the Assayle
loke þou concente nevyr to synne
For no sleytys ne for no gynne
and þan þe victory xalt þou wynne
þe devyl xal lesyn all his travayl.   (ll. 196–208)

Christ defines his purpose in undergoing the Temptation as pedagogical.

The Chester cycle concentrates on the more sophisticated typological relationships between the Temptation of Adam and the Temptation of Christ. Throughout the play Christ and Satan make explicit references to the antecedent event. The Expositor sums up:

Loe! lordinges, God's righteousnes,
as St. Gregorie makes mynde expresse,
since our forefather ouercomen was
by three thinges to doe evill:
Gluttony, vayne glorye there be twooe,
Covetousnes of highnes alsoe,
by these three thinges, without moe,
Christ hath overcome the Devill.   (ll. 161–68)

The Expositor then explains the precise significance of each of the three sins.[8]

Gluttony is the least intricate in meaning, being so obviously bound up with desire for food, the apple or the bread. Generalized, it becomes the lust of the flesh. Satan tempted Christ in vainglory, says the Expositor, "when he height [promised] hym great mastery, / to haue godhead unworthely." We are reminded of Satan's own vainglorious sin at the Creation, when, unworthily elevating himself to the throne of God, he was dashed to his destruction in hell. Christ is of course fully worthy of Godhead, but the leap from the temple would be "an unskillfull gate," an unworthy act which might win for Christ the acclaim due to a mountebank magician, but no more. In N-Town, Satan characterizes the act as a "qweynt steracle," a curious conjuror's trick. Covetousness, which is third, "Synnes not onely in riches, / but in willing of Highnes / and state, unskilfully." It is the desire for worldly power. Christ does in fact rule the world, but not as ostensible king. If he should bend the knee to Satan, Christ would concede all spiritual authority.

8. For an extended treatment of these (and other) sins, see Morton W. Bloomfield, *The Seven Deadly Sins* (East Lansing, 1952). For a comprehensive discussion of the sins involved in the Temptation, see Donald R. Howard, *The Three Temptations* (Princeton, 1966), pp. 43–56.

This specific character of the third sin is made most apparent in the N-Town play, which imitates the style of the morality tradition. Like *Mundus et Infans,* this play catalogs all the kingdoms on earth.

> ʒa and all þe wyd werde with-oute mo talys
> All þis longyth to me
> If þou wylt knele down to þe grownde
> and wurchepp me now in þis stownde
> all þis world þat is so rownd
> I xall it gyve to the.   (ll. 177–82)

Unlike Manhood, Christ declines the offer of the world. In refusing power on earth, he preserves his power in heaven. In rejecting visible authority over living men, he prepares to reestablish his authority over all souls, including those now languishing in hell.

Like other triads in the Corpus Christi cycles,[9] the gifts of the shepherds, for example, or the gifts of the three kings, the three temptations of Christ have a significance which is to be understood partly from explications presented within the play or implicit in the dialogue and partly from a wider context of theological exposition and pictorial symbol. Each trial involves an iconic bit of stage property: the stones, the pinnacle of the temple, the mountain. Christ appears in proximity to each in turn, but his passive stance declares his perfect innocence in respect to each. It is Satan who postures and gestures in desperate activity, and it is he who becomes implicated as master of the three deadly sins.

The three trials are more deeply woven into the plot of the Temptation plays and the Corpus Christi cycles than the gifts of the shepherds or kings, and must be understood not merely as variations on established themes but as necessary to dramatic structure. They contribute to the increasingly tense atmosphere of conflict. With each trial, Satan grows more desperate and tempts Christ with more heinous sin. Covetousness distinctly takes precedence over vainglory and gluttony. Each trial in turn probes more precisely into the matter in question between Satan and Christ. The first trial is a solicitation to merely private indulgence; the second an invitation to public acclaim; and the third a temptation to exchange obscure power in heaven for recognized power on earth.

But the central meaning of the Temptation lies in the action itself. This is recognized by the Chester Expositor, who concludes his homily on the three sins with a reassertion of Christ's historical victory:

9. See Timothy Fry, "The Antiquity of the Tradition of Triads in the English Cycle Plays," *American Benedictine Review,* 18 (1967), 465–81. See also Lawrence J. Ross, "Symbol and Structure in the *Secunda Pastorum,*" included in this volume.

> Thus overcome Christe in this case
> the Devill, as played was in this place,
> with those three synnes that Adam was
> of wayle into woe wayued.
> But Adam fell through his trespas,
> and Iesu withstood hym through his grace,
> for of his godhead Sathanas
> that tyme was cleane deceyved.   (ll. 201–8)

Satan's persisting ignorance is a measure of Christ's success.

This fact needs particular emphasis because the plays have been partly misunderstood by otherwise perceptive students of the Corpus Christi drama. Thus Arnold Williams writes: "The temptation in the desert is motivated in York and Ludus by Satan's uncertainty whether Jesus is the messiah or just the son of a carpenter. . . . In the temptation in the desert Satan finds out the real nature of Jesus. Later on, in York and Ludus, Satan tries to thwart the plot of Annas and Caiaphas."[10] We must now add Chester to the plays with this motivation, and assert that Satan does not in fact discover the identity of Christ during the course of this episode. Timothy Fry asserts that from his failure to tempt Christ, "Satan should have known that Christ was God."[11] The brilliance of Christ's strategy, however, is that the negative results tell Satan nothing. He has not discovered an adequate test to penetrate the disguise of the Incarnation.

Reflection upon the Temptation seen in this perspective suggests that Christ rather than Satan is the real tempter. Masking his identity from Satan, and refusing to reveal it in spite of all Satan's wiles, Christ gives him no alternative but to set out on a disastrous course which will end with the release of souls from Satan's power. Thus the antagonist and the protagonist undergo a characteristic reversal of roles. The guiler, in the course of time, must be beguiled.[12]

10. Arnold Williams, *The Drama of Medieval England* (East Lansing, Mich., 1961), pp. 109–10.
11. "Unity," p. 557. Longsworth also says of the *Ordinalia*, "The drama is at pains to emphasize that this deception is self-practiced and maintained in spite of abundant evidence to the contrary"(p. 87). This is certainly not true of the English cycles. In N-Town, for example, Jesus explains to the Doctors in the Temple the purpose of the Virgin's marriage to Joseph:
> To blynde þe devyl of his knowlache
> and my byrth from hym to hyde
> þat holy wedlock was grett stopage
> þe devyl in dowte to do A-byde.   (ll. 245–48)
12. Cf. *Second Shepherds' Play*, l. 713.

J. W. Robinson

13. The Art of the York Realist

It is almost beyond doubt that eight plays (XXVI, XXVIII–XXXIII inclusive, and XXXVI) in the York cycle of mystery plays[1] are, in the form in which they now exist, the work of one dramatist. These eight plays are all very largely written in true alliterative verse,[2] and they are all remarkable for the detailed and imaginative realism that has gone into their composition.[3] For these two reasons, they stand apart as a group and may be referred to as the work of the York Realist. His plays, all about Christ's Passion, deserve to be critically evaluated; his genius awaits a thorough estimation.[4] It is my purpose to discuss briefly the conventional aspects of his dramaturgy, and then to examine and emphasize the unique quality of his realism; in other words, to show that his realism is exceptional, but did not constitute a break with tradition.

Of course, the York Realist did not compose these eight plays from nothing. He revised plays that already existed in the cycle.[5] It is clear

[Reprinted from *Modern Philology*, LX (1962–63), 241–51, by permission of the author and the publisher. Copyright 1963 by The University of Chicago.]

1. *York Plays: The Plays Performed by the Crafts or Mysteries of York*, ed. Lucy Toulmin Smith (Oxford, 1885). Other mystery plays are cited below from *The Chester Plays*, ed. H. Deimling and Dr. Matthews, EETS e.s. 62, 115 (1892, 1916); *The Towneley Plays*, ed. George England, EETS e.s. 71 (1897); and *Ludus Coventriae*, ed. K. S. Block, EETS e.s. 120 (1922). I refer to the separate plays by number (in Roman numerals), and when convenient by title also; line numbers are given in Arabic numerals. For the *Ludus Coventriae* I give page numbers.

2. Jesse Byers Reese, "Alliterative Verse in the York Cycle," *SP*, XLVIII (1951), 649: the plays are "written in purely alliterative verse, arranged in stanzaic patterns."

3. Hardin Craig, *English Religious Drama of the Middle Ages* (Oxford, 1955), p. 228. C. M. Gayley, *Plays of Our Forefathers* (New York, 1907), p. 154, distinguishes plays XXVI, XXVIII, XXIX, XXX, XXXI, XXXIII, "and probably XXXII" as being especially realistic. E. K. Chambers, *English Literature at the Close of the Middle Ages* (Oxford, 1945), pp. 30–31, says the dramatist "whom we may also call a realist" "worked largely on the Passion."

4. Gayley gives a brief and general account of some of the qualities of these plays (pp. 154–57), and Craig does the same, going into somewhat more detail (pp. 228–32).

5. The town clerk, Roger Burton, compiled a detailed list of the plays, dated 1415. Because the eight plays ascribed to the York Realist differ in various ways

that he rewrote these plays entirely, however, and in the process made many dramatic points not in his originals. The extent of his originality will always be in doubt, but in certain important ways it can be limited. First, he was not responsible for the way in which the Passion story was divided up at York into many separate plays; that division, as is clear from Burton's list, had been organized by 1415 at the latest, and the York Realist worked mostly, if not entirely, after that date. Therefore the basic theme of, for example, play XXXI, *Trial before Herod*, cannot be ascribed to him: the play revolves around Jesus' refusal to say anything, and this, "clever"[6] as it may be, would be the natural result of devoting an entire play to the trial of Jesus by Herod, an episode of which little more is recorded, in both the Gospel (Luke 23:8–11) and—to touch the York clerics more nearly—*The Northern Passion*[7] (ll. 991–1006*b*) than that Jesus did not speak. It is not to be supposed, therefore, that in the original *Trial before Herod* at York Jesus spoke. That it was the York Realist who elaborated on the theme of Jesus' silence, however, is altogether likely. But he did not change the basic subject matter of any of the plays, and for this reason he is not to be credited with any fundamental structural work.

Second, the Passion plays at York were originally composed under the influence of *The Northern Passion*, and some of the plays also reveal the influence of the Middle English Gospel of Nicodemus.[8] *The Northern Passion* provided the bulk of the material and its arrangement, and the Middle English Gospel of Nicodemus supplied some supplementary material. As well as influencing earlier dramatists at York, there is good reason to suppose (what would in any case be expected a priori) that these narratives were known by the York Realist himself.[9] Last, certain

---

from the descriptions in Burton's list of the same eight plays, Craig concludes, very fairly, that the Realist worked over the plays some time after 1415. Burton's list is printed by Smith, pp. xviii–xxvii.

6. Craig, p. 232.

7. Ed. Frances A. Foster, EETS 145, 147 (1913, 1916). Miss Foster describes the influence of *The Northern Passion* on the York plays in her introduction, pp. 81–86. In the poem it is suggested that Herod anticipates hearing Jesus speak, and some emphasis is placed on Jesus' silence; these features are present in the play also, where the humorous and frightening elaboration is that Herod and the Jews first try to make Jesus speak, and then to account for his silence.

8. Ed. W. H. Hulme, EETS e.s. 100 (1907). The influence of this Middle English translation on the York plays is described by W. Craigie, "The *Gospel of Nicodemus* and the *York Mystery Plays*," in *An English Miscellany Presented to Dr. Furnivall* (Oxford, 1901), pp. 52–61.

9. Words and phrases from these two narratives appear in plays by the Realist: from *The Northern Passion* in plays XXVIII, XXIX, XXXI, XXXII, XXXIII, and XXXVI (Foster, pp. 84–85, and Frances H. Miller, "*The Northern Passion* and the Mysteries," *MLN*, XXXIV [1919], 89–90); from the Middle English Gospel of

dramatic features were the common property of medieval dramatists, and a number of episodes, such as boastful play openings and appeals spoken by Jesus from the cross, had rapidly become stock scenes in the fifteenth century, or even earlier; part of the York Realist's work was done on these established lines.

All this information can be put to work in the process of analyzing and appreciating the art of the eight alliterative and realistic Passion plays at York. Anything especially attractive in them must be measured against the other English mystery plays and the two or three vernacular narratives—*The Northern Passion*, the Middle English Gospel of Nicodemus, and the *Cursor Mundi*[10]—that are known to have influenced, directly or indirectly, the York compositions.

Although the York Realist's plays are especially interesting for a number of reasons, their basic affinity is to the common type of mystery play. The most obvious examples of the conventional features of his dramaturgy are the speeches addressed to the audience. Judas' soliloquies (XXVI, 127–54; XXXII, 127–49, 301–15), the Devil's soliloquy (XXX, 159–67) and the appeals spoken by Jesus to Man[11] (XXXVI, 118–30, 183–95) follow regular patterns.[12] The York Realist is here working well within the dramatic tradition, which he accepts and stamps with the mark of his approval. The openings of most of his plays are also conventional; a boastful and threatening speech delivered by a pagan character was a recognized method of beginning a play.[13] However, the York Realist's deliberate and repeated use of this method is remarkable, and, although the boastful speeches delivered by his overbearing pagans are conventional, they are distinguished from previous examples of this kind of play opening by their stylishness and vigor. This is readily apparent when the opening of, for example, Towneley IX, *Caesar Augustus*, is compared to one of the Realist's openings. The stylishness is due

---

Nicodemus in plays XXX, XXXIII, XXXVI (Craigie, pp. 53–58). These parallels could possibly be accounted for by supposing the Realist had them from his prototypes. This may sometimes have been the case; on the other hand, see Eleanor G. Clark, "The York Plays and the *Gospel of Nicodemus*," *PMLA*, XLIII (1928), 158.

10. Smith, pp. xliv–xlv.

11. These are examples of the lyrical Testament of Christ, which links the mystery plays to the Cult of Jesus, which flourished at the same time that they did. [See J. W. Robinson's later article, "The Late Medieval Cult of Jesus and the Mystery Plays," *PMLA*, LXXX (1965), 508–14, esp. p. 508, n. 3.]

12. For some of the parallel speeches, see, for Judas, York XXVII, 104–15, Chester XIV, 265–304, *Ludus Coventriae*, pp. 251–52, ll. 590–605; for the Devil, Chester II, 161–208, XII, 1–56, York XXII, 1–54; for Jesus, Towneley XXIII, 233–89, 469–79, York XXXV, 253–58, Chester XXIV, 357–436.

13. See, e.g., the openings of Chester X, York XIX, XXXVIII, Towneley VIII, IX, XIV, and three openings by the Wakefield Master—Towneley XVI, XX, XXIV.

to the genuine alliterative verse, the vigor to the abundance of masculine consonants.

His openings are not all alike; the boast is fitted to the speaker. Thus, besides such conventional factors as the boast of personal beauty (XXXII, 17–24), Pilate sets himself forward as the wisest judge, and Caiaphas adopts an attitude of sweet reasonableness, or perhaps brisk pomposity:

> Come of, do tyte, late me see
> Howe graciously I schall graunte hym his bone.
>
> (XXIX, 11–12)

The attitudes adopted by the boasters in their opening speeches continue to be held by them as the plays unfold, and thus the opening speeches, besides serving their conventional theatrical purpose of prologue and personal invitation to the audience to denounce the presumptuous pagans, serve also a dramatic function by establishing the particular emphasis to be given the character of the evil protagonist.

The earlier plays at York which the Realist had to work on may, of course, have begun in the conventional way (and so, therefore, he cannot necessarily be credited with the original connection of Caiaphas to this kind of opening),[14] but his fondness for the device is clear from the fact that he preserved it for, or introduced it to, seven of his eight plays and added it, in all probability, to a further play (XXXIV, *Christ Led Up to Calvary*), the bulk of which is not from his hand.[15] In this last instance, lacking a noble pagan among the *dramatis personae*, he has given the boastful opening speech to a common soldier, thus making (rather than simply seizing) the opportunity for it.

His one play that does not begin in this fashion, play XXVIII, *The Agony and the Betrayal*, opens with Jesus addressing his disciples. For the opening of this play the York Realist has written what may be termed an anti-boast. Jesus' fear and trembling and wise counsel to his disciples contrast pointedly with the hauteur, rashness, and presumptuous counsel of the braggarts of the other play openings. It may be noted incidentally that parallel to this anti-boast are some anti-Hail lyrics, to be found scattered in the Realist's plays: the chief example is in play XXXIII, *Second Trial before Pilate cont.; Judgment*, lines 409–20; this is a burlesque of the kind of lyric spoken in play XVII by the three Magi (ll. 253–88) which was a common literary form.[16]

14. That Caiaphas had in him the stuff for a grand opening boast may have been suggested by the *Cursor Mundi* (ed. Richard Morris, Part III, EETS 62 [1876]), ll. 14502–25.

15. Only the opening speech of this play is in true alliterative verse (Reese, *SP*, XLVIII, 649).

16. George C. Taylor, "The Relation of the English Corpus Christi Play to the Middle English Religious Lyric," *MP*, V (1907), 4–5, 18–21.

Interesting as the York Realist's frequent and particular use of conventional theatrical devices (especially play openings) is, however, the most remarkable thing about the dramaturgy of his plays is their all-pervading realism.[17] This appears at times to be something of a contrast to the stylishness and flamboyance of his chosen method of opening the plays. In order to set forth the special realism of his plays, it is proposed first to call attention to some small details of language and action, and then to work outward, as it were, to more involved incidents.

In these eight plays episodes are frequently worked out in much closer detail than is usual in the medieval drama or in analogous narrative and lyrical material. When Herod rises from his bed he says to his attendant:

> But haue here my hande, halde nowe!
> And se þat my sloppe be wele sittande.   (XXXI, 76–77)

The attention given here by the York Realist to the detail and action of the moment—the attendant giving a hand and adjusting Herod's garments—is peculiar to him. Towneley XXIV, *The Talents*, in a comparable scene, has, in contrast, two unimaginative lines:

> Bewshere, I byd the vp thou take me,
> And in my sete softly loke that thou se me sett. (ll. 196–97)

Similarly, when the soldiers seize Jesus in York XXVIII, *The Agony and the Betrayal*, one of the soldiers cries:

> ⎰ And I haue a loke on hym nowe.
> ⎱ Howe! felawes, drawe nere.   (l. 292)

There is no such detailed envisioning of the actual seizure of Christ in any of the other plays, and in *The Northern Passion* it is recorded simply that "handes sune on him þai laide" (l. 548). Another detail of the same kind may be instanced from play XXXIII, *Second Trial before Pilate cont.; Judgment*: Pilate prepares to wash his hands and his messenger approaches with these words:

> Here is all, sir, þat ʒe for sende,
> Will ʒe wasshe whill þe watir is hote?   (ll. 442–43)

Other medieval dramatists (and more learned medieval exegetes, too) would not normally concern themselves with the temperature of the water in which Pilate washed his hands—the allegorical meaning, perhaps, but not the temperature. In such cases it is clear that the York Realist has dwelt on the physical implications of each stage of a procedure and has constructed his dialogue accordingly. Thus, Pilate's servant

---

17. Craig (p. 231) mentions the dramatist's "intimate realization of the stories he tells."

helps him to his bed, remarking, "A! sir, yhe whe wele!" (XXX, 136);
and the tiredness of the disciples is felt and expressed:

PET.	My lymmys are heuy as any leede.
JOH.	And I muste slepe, doune muste I lye.
JAC.	In faithe, felawes, right so fare I,
	I may no lenger holde vppe my hede. (XXVIII, 21–24)

In other English mystery plays, although the disciples are clearly meant
to act as if they are tired, they do not speak of their tiredness, nor, indeed, do any words at all accompany their sleepy gestures.[18] Again, in
play XXXIII the determination of the strong men to hold their banners
rigid is developed realistically and imaginatively out of the oath sworn
in the Middle English Gospel of Nicodemus ("Hardily hag of his hand,"
l. 164), which, it appears, was remembered by this playwright (l. 252),
into such expressions as the first strong man's "I sall holde þis as even
as a lyne" (l. 245).

These examples suggest the realism of the York Realist; it is closely
connected to the dramatic concerns of character and atmosphere: instances given in the previous paragraph, for example, contribute to the
presentation of Herod's fastidious vanity, the soldier's bestiality, Pilate's
love of upper-class comforts, and the obsequiousness of his train. Such
pieces of dialogue, springing from a necessary chain of action, are the
York Realist's distinctive mark. This kind of realism is not found, except
in isolated instances, in other medieval English plays, where the emphasis
is usually on separate actions rather than on a process of behavior. The
York Realist works consistently on the latter principle. The difference
between his plays and other medieval English Passion plays is, in this
respect, the difference between Richardson's and Fielding's novels.

The York Realist's emphasis on processes of behavior is paralleled by
his emphasis on mental processes; this is apparent in some of the arguments and discussions in his plays. When Judas tries to persuade the
janitor, who is surly and suspicious, to give him access to Pilate and the
Jewish leaders, the janitor remains unpersuaded and obstinate until Judas
suggests that the nobles may be in some danger, at which the janitor immediately becomes more helpful. The process of persuasion (XXVI, 155–
90) is real. Similarly, Pilate has to be persuaded by the Jews to adopt an
unfavorable attitude toward Jesus. *The Northern Passion* reads as if
Pilate was finally moved to act against Jesus when the Jews insisted on
his treason against Caesar (ll. 1180–88); the York Realist took this hint,
and in several of his plays Pilate is shown to make up his mind only when
the accusations thus affect him directly—just as the janitor moves only

18. Chester XV, 264; Towneley XX, 503; *Ludus Coventriae*, p. 263, l. 925.

when Judas' suggestion affects him closely: Pilate is shown to be per-
turbed for the first time by the accusation of treason (other accusations
having left him unmoved) in plays XXVI, 117, XXX, 466, and XXXIII,
334. The real achievement in this connection, however, is the first scene
in play XXXII. The Realist is truest to his own talent when he has Pilate
remain unmoved until he is told that Jesus claims He will judge mankind; this information really disturbs Pilate because it touches him in his
professional capacity: is not *he* the great judge?

ii MILES.   He sais he schall haue vs to heuene or to hell
             To deme vs a day aftir oure dedis.
PILATE.   To deme vs! in þe deuyll name!   (ll. 85–87)[19]

The other English Passion plays do not approach this kind of realism
in which action is carefully shown to be the result of genuine decision,
and decision to be the result of genuine persuasion.

The art of realistic elaboration is applied by the York Realist to many
different characters and situations—to the characters of the priests and
the aristocrats, for example. In play XXIX, *Peter Denies Jesus; Jesus Examined by Caiaphas*, Annas and Caiaphas are distinguished as Regan and
Goneril are, the one sharp and impetuous, the other wordier but equally
cruel. It is evident from the outset that Caiaphas is intent on conducting
the trial with some surface "fayreness," but that Annas is eager for
action. In his initial boast, opening the play, Caiaphas has set himself up
as a considerate judge, and for much of the trial he is carried away by
the form of the proceedings (ll. 204–97).[20] The same feeling of self-
importance, however, that leads him to preside with such concern for
the form of the trial leads him to forget himself and his position and to
become antagonistic toward the defendant as soon as he has spoken.
From this point on, Caiaphas has to be restrained by Annas (ll. 298–354),
who, wishing to deal practically with Jesus, is also practical about the
extent of the bishops' legal rights. The opposition between the characters,
clear from the very beginning of the trial, continues even as they cross
paths; for much of the trial it is Caiaphas who is the moderating influence, and toward the end it is Annas. This interesting reversal of roles
is entirely credible and cogent, relying, as it does, on the consistent pride
and self-importance of Caiaphas and the consistently quick and practical
mind of Annas. From the point of view of the thoughts and actions of the
priests the trial before Caiaphas at York is considerably better thought

19. This effect is absent from play XXVI, l. 65, where there is an opportunity
for it. Is there some artistic self-improvement visible here?
20. Caiaphas' rather facetious concern for good form shows through his method
of saying goodnight, even—"A diew, be unte, / As þe manere is" (ll. 87–88).

out than the same scene (ll. 127–342) in Towneley XXI, *The Buffeting,*
written by the Wakefield Master. The Wakefield Master concentrates
boisterously on the broad difference between the characters of the two
priests—his Caiaphas is wildly impetuous, wishing to tear out Jesus' eyes,
and his Annas is consistently a restraining influence; they bicker and
quarrel. The Wakefield Master lacks the interest in the subtleties of
character shown by the York Realist.[21]

Three scenes in York XXIX, XXX, and XXXI are very much alike.
Caiaphas, Pilate, and Herod are in turn put to bed and awakened by, or
for, the arrival of Jesus and his captors. It is impossible to decide whether
or not the York Realist originated these scenes. However, there are no
known precedents for them in the drama (although the scenes have their
later imitators)[22] and no obvious Christian legends provided the idea.[23]
It can at least be said that the introduction of these scenes is consistent
with what may be gathered about the playwright's special interest—
for the reason why Caiaphas should be in bed when Jesus is brought to
him is a very simple one: Jesus was arrested during the night. Taking
this fact as his starting point, the playwright could have reasoned, in
his familiar way, that a bedtime and waking scene for Caiaphas should
naturally follow. Similarly, since the Devil visits Pilate's wife while she
is asleep, scenes in which both she and her husband retire to bed could
find a logical place in their play; and so, incidentally, the dramatist could
then very neatly and without forcing accommodate the mundane wishes
(whether explicit or implicit) of his patrons, who, as upholsterers and
makers of tapestry and coverlets, obviously had a vested interest in the
showing of these two episodes.[24] The presence of these scenes in two of
the plays, then, may be explained by referring to the York Realist's habit
of working out the events of the Passion story in their natural sequence
and logical detail. Liking the idea (and enjoying the irony of the scenes),
he repeated it in the third play.

Whether these scenes were original with him or not, he in any case
made them his own. The best of them is perhaps that in play XXX, *The
Dream of Pilate's Wife: Jesus before Pilate* (ll. 1–264). Here, as else-

21. Millicent Carey, in *The Wakefield Group in the Towneley Cycle* (Hesperia
Ergänzungsreihe, 11 [Göttingen and Baltimore, 1930]), writes that the Wakefield
Master's "skill in characterization in every case surpasses that found in corresponding plays" (p. 241). My comparison of Towneley XXI and York XXIX shows this
suggestion to be at least in part untenable.
22. Towneley XXIV, 65–72, 181–97. A list of plays performed at Beverley, Yorkshire, dated 1520, describes the First Trial before Pilate as "Slepinge Pilate" (E. K.
Chambers, *The Medieval Stage* [Oxford, 1903], II, 341).
23. Clark, "The York Plays," 153, n. 4.
24. Eva Freeman points out this connection between the play and its guilds in
"A Note on Play XXX of the York Cycle," *MLN,* XLV (1930), 392–94.

where, he puts his gift for realism to satirical purpose and shows himself to be a master entertainer. The play begins with Pilate pontificating and threatening (not indiscriminately, it may be noticed, but specifically demanding order in any complaints brought before him as judge); he then introduces his wife to the audience and she preens herself. Between lines 44 and 45 she obviously turns and smiles at her husband. They present stately but fond compliments to each other and proceed to dally suggestively. They are interrupted by the Beadle, and Pilate's wife begins to object to him in a most undignified fashion; the contrast between her former behavior and her sudden viciousness is calculated. Wine is next ordered in a lordly fashion,[25] and Pilate, his wife and her "damsel" drink and converse graciously, their elegant talk focused on the mechanics of drinking—a veritable piece of cup-and-saucer naturalism, but at the same time an ironic portrayal of gracious but wicked living. This scene is in fact a dramatized and satirical *voidee* (*voidees*, or ceremonious servings of wine before a company withdraws or retires at night, are frequently found in the romances). The women retire and Pilate, with much masterly fuss, is laid to rest. His wife also is seen to lie down in bed to sleep. All the characters on the stage are, it may be assumed, sleeping, and so the stage is set for the entrance of the Devil, who explains his cowardly purpose in a piece of sinister direct address to the audience and then tells his story to Pilate's sleeping wife. She awakes with a start, and addresses her son. "A!" she says, "I am drecchid with a dreme full dredfully to dowte" (l. 177). The playwright is here remembering, or taking over a memory of, the Middle English Gospel of Nicodemus, where Procula says at this point:

> I haue bene dreched with dremes swa
> þis ilk nyght als I lay.   (ll. 197–98)

However, the playwright also introduces something new here, the sloth of Procula's son. Facetiously picking up the word "drecchid," he refuses to inform Pilate of his mother's dream, exclaiming:

> Madame, for the drecchyng of heuen,
> Slyke note is newsome to neven,
> And it neghes vnto mydnyght full even.   (ll. 182–84)

The dramatist thus gives character and life to the apocryphal narrative. The scene then changes to outside the palace. The soldiers are approaching with Jesus captive. The noise of their shouting with the beadle for

25. The boastful and flamboyant pagan nobles of the medieval plays often drink and revel on the stage. In most cases their debauchery is intended to be a prelude to their fall—see, e.g., Chester VIII, 406–13, *Ludus Coventriae*, pp. 173–74, ll. 129–67. The satire in the York Realist's plays is much finer than this. See also York plays XXIX, 73–80, XXXI, 40, and XXXII, 124–26.

admittance wakes Pilate, who (of course) is furious because his rest has been disturbed—the Realist saw to it that Pilate had earlier given specific instructions that his sleep was to be undisturbed. When he is informed of the position he rises, and the trial of Jesus begins.

When, as in this scene, the playwright's elaborate realism is applied to the lives of his noble characters, it is usually satirical; it is put to work in pursuit of a novel, reserved and intelligent representation of the powers of darkness.

Another scene which the Realist introduces several times—a scene devoted to the process of gaining admission to a palace—is also a clear, logical outcome of the subject matter. In these scenes, admission is at first refused; so a debate ensues, and further instructions are sought by the gatekeeper before permission is finally granted. The procedure is more or less the same in four plays (XXVI, XXIX, XXX, and XXXI). Given the York Realist's known propensity, it is probable that he (rather than an earlier York dramatist) is here taking advantage of the opportunities afforded by the Passion story, and filling in gaps in the narrative.

To be sure, in *The Northern Passion* (ll. 153–56a), Judas "graithly to þe iews . . . gase" and finds them and their princes, but what actually happens when he arrives at their palace? How does he gain admission? By asking himself these and similar questions, the York Realist is able to introduce new but entirely acceptable matter into the Passion story (XXVI, 155–204). Again, according to *The Northern Passion*, the Jews took Jesus and "went" to Pilate (l. 816b), and Jesus was "fett" before Pilate (l. 904), and according to the Middle English Gospel of Nicodemus Christ and his accusers "gan pass" to Pilate (l. 19); no other details of their reception are given, but in play XXX the York Realist gives body to this narrative. He makes a lively and realistic scene out of their attempts to gain entrance (ll. 229–64). The case is similar for play XXXI (ll. 58–91), and for the arrival of the Jews and their captive at Caiaphas' palace in play XXIX, 176–212.

The street scenes are not simply repetitious. There is much variety in detail. For example, in play XXIX the soldiers arrive at the gate, and out of consideration for the sleeping inhabitants, their emphasis is on keeping quiet and still (ll. 176–79). Caiaphas, consequently, has to be waked by a servant. In play XXX, on the other hand, the soldiers make so much noise and bustle at the gate (ll. 229–34) that Pilate is rudely disturbed. The difference in atmosphere between the two scenes may be gauged by comparing the response of the gatekeeper in the first play—"Say who is here? Say who is here?" (l. 180)—to that of the gatekeeper in the second—"O, what javellis are ye þat jappis with gollyng?" (l. 235).

These four street scenes are interesting and entertaining in themselves. All the necessary movements of the protagonists are pondered and demonstrated. They are examples of the York Realist's predilection for discussion and argument among his characters, and they show him answering questions hitherto dramatically unthought of.[26] His elaborate realism does not here have a directly satirical effect; it contributes instead toward the lethal accumulation of the details that are to lead to the Crucifixion. Moreover, these and similar scenes in which Jesus appears without a speaking part effectively prolong the dramatic representation of *Homo paciens*. How else could his silent suffering be shown at any length theatrically?

The eight York plays so far discussed have been those which are both realistic and written in true alliterative verse. Before pursuing the discussion, a subsidiary issue may be briefly considered. There are other plays in the York cycle written in true alliterative verse (I, XVI, XL, XLV, XLVI) and still others with some realistic tendencies (especially XXXIV and XXXV). It may now be asked, not so much for the sake of establishing the "canon" of the York Realist, but for the sake of furthering the appreciation of his art, whether any of his special kind of realism may be detected in these other plays.

Of the other plays associated with the Passion, play XXV, *The Entry into Jerusalem*, and play XXVII, *The Last Supper*, contain nothing of this nature. Play XXXIV, *Christ Led Up to Calvary*, is more elaborate than these two plays, and sections of it are written realistically. However, many of the realistic details (Christ's clothes soaked in blood sticking to his skin, for example) are unoriginal and undeveloped,[27] and some episodes amenable to the special treatment of the York Realist are unmarked by his particular kind of realism: Christ, for example, is tied up almost without remark (between ll. 340 and 341), and, similarly, his face is wiped without any verbal accompaniment to the actual action (which takes place between ll. 184 and 185). The Realist usually avoids these awkward pauses. Play XXXV, *Crucifixio Cristi*, is throughout realistic, and contains lines which could have been written by the Realist (l. 190, for example).[28] Again, however, most of the realism is traditional. It is clear that none of these four nonalliterative Passion plays at York is pervaded with realism in the way that the other eight Passion plays are.[29]

26. The only parallel (and that a rather remote one) to any of these scenes in the medieval English drama is in Towneley XX, 174–205.

27. Ll. 315–16. Cf. *The Northern Passion*, ll. 1280a–1280b and 1589–90.

28. One line, 286, "And make mowes on þe mone," from play XXXV is more or less repeated in play XXXVI—"Full madly on þe mone for to mowe," l. 78.

29. Gayley (above, n. 3), however, while distinguishing six plays as especially realistic, also says that of all the York Passion plays, only XXVII, *The Last Supper*, "lacks his [i.e., the Realist's] influence" (p. 158).

In no cycle are any plays except those of the Passion elaborated in any intense detail. The special realistic detail noticed in the alliterative Passion plays is, therefore, not to be expected in play I, the alliterative *Creation, and Fall of Lucifer.* Play XL, *The Travellers to Emaus,* however, is enhanced in two places by this peculiar realism: the courtesies on entering the castle (ll. 148–55), and the apparent pause before the pilgrims notice that Jesus has vanished (l. 159) recall the style of the York Realist's Passion plays.[30] Play XLV, *The Death of Mary,* and play XLVI, *The Appearance of Our Lady to Thomas,* contain no precise realism—although in play XLVI there are two passages of debate and persuasion (ll. 150–82, 217–72, especially l. 241) reminiscent of similar passages in the Passion plays.

Clearly, different standards and methods must be applied in the criticism and appreciation of these other plays, which on the grounds of their subject matter or alliteration, might appear to have some claim to be considered in the light of the York Realist's art. And, moreover, any attempt to estimate the place of the York Realist in dramatic literature had clearly best confine itself to the eight Passion plays.

On the basis of these eight plays it is apparent that the York Realist was not in the habit of introducing into his plays anything that did not enjoy narrative—not scriptural, but narrative—warrant. That is to say, he deduced his nonscriptural material from the given portions of the Passion story. He elaborated on the given story by pursuing its matter into the places to which (with some art) it naturally led. This is not what is usually meant by "realism" on the stage. The term "realism" is applied to nineteenth-century melodrama (in which the villain drags his victim across the floor by her hair) because torture is shown—by trickery— on the stage. This is the realism of the Elizabethan stage and of the cinema. The medieval stage may also be termed "realistic," in this sense, since, for example, God takes that "Rybbe colleryd Red"[31] out of Adam's side, and Christ is stretched and nailed on the cross in full view of the audience. The crowning with a crown of thorns is done realistically;[32] in fact, the mere possibility of its performance means that medieval stagecraft is realistic. However, this is not what the York Realist

30. Cf. the apparent pause before the Virgin realizes her Son has died (XXXVI, 261–64).

31. Robert Fitch, "Norwich Pageants," *Norfolk Archaeology,* V (1859), 30. This property belonged to the guild responsible for producing the Norwich *Creation* (texts in *The Non-Cycle Mystery Plays,* ed. O. Waterhouse, EETS e.s. 104 [1909]), in which l. 13 of Text A is, "A rybbe out of mannys syde I do here take" (l. 12 of Text B is similar).

32. J. W. Robinson, "A Detail of Medieval English Staging," *Theatre Notebook,* XV (1961), 101, 102.

specializes in at all. He is, in fact, more of a naturalistic playwright than a realist, and he is misnamed. Of course, he can be realistic. His Christ is also crowned with thorns (inevitably)—but even here his special kind of realism seems to show itself; for after the crown has been stuck onto Christ's head, there seems to be *a pause before the blood begins to appear* (XXXIII, 399–402)—no other medieval English dramatist cared about details like that.[33]

Each of the York Realist's plays is self-contained. They are meant to be appreciated separately. They are mostly preparatory to the Crucifixion, but beyond this basic story they are not bound together by the development of theme or characterization. Pilate, for example, identifies himself afresh, and the Jews repeat their accusations, in several plays; in play XXVI, for example, Annas and Caiaphas make their accusations before Pilate, and then repeat them to him all over again in play XXX. Again, Pilate vacillates between siding with Christ's accusers and finding them "over cruel," and although he behaves consistently within each separate play, there is not meant to be any continuity between his frame of mind in one play and in the next; in one play he is persuaded by the arguments of the accusers, and in the next he is back again to his original skeptical position. In this respect the York Realist differs in his approach to the idea of a cycle of plays from the compiler (probably not the Wakefield Master) who worked at Wakefield at roughly the same time as he was at work, and who arranged for Pilate to be on one side throughout the Passion sequence.[34] The intention is different, the art is not less. It is difficult, if not impossible, to work out a chronologically satisfying scheme for plays XXIX–XXXI. The Realist ignores, for the time being, the implications of what he is doing in one play for what he has done or will do in adjacent plays.[35] It would clearly be unjust to consider his plays as so many acts or scenes of a larger play[36] and so to judge them lacking in the development of theme and character, and merely repetitious. His mind is on the present, and it is this concentration

33. This special realism of the York Realist has implications for the acting of his plays. Perceptive direction would have demanded some moderation of the basic stylized and ritual-like acting; I would now qualify some of the generalizations in "Medieval English Acting," *Theatre Notebook*, XIII (1959), 83–88.

34. See Arnold Williams, *The Characterization of Pilate in the Towneley Plays* (Michigan State College Studies in Language and Literature [East Lansing, Mich., 1950]), pp. 72–73.

35. Effie MacKinnon writes, "The dramatic units of the cycle are not the individual craft pageants but the groups of pageants which present any given situation" ("Notes on the Dramatic Structure of the York Cycle," *SP*, XXVIII [1931], 441). Clearly this is only true in a most general sense.

36. Eleanor Prosser, *Drama and Religion in the English Mystery Plays* (Stanford, Calif., 1961), p. 55, rightly insists that this is true generally of the mystery cycles.

that enables him to chronicle the Passion in greater detail than usual and to describe its course in a manner never successfully attempted before or since by a true artist.

However, the York Realist did repeat himself, so much so that it is clear that his genius was limited to one particular approach to the composition of Passion plays. Gayley is impressed by the fact that the materials for most of his plays are "practically the same."[37] The same might be said of the scenes of hunting and courtship in *Sir Gawain and the Green Knight*—but, of course, it is not the similarities that are impressive or telling, but the differences. The dramatist's repetition is mostly in his material itself, not so much in his manner of treating it. All the scenes he repeats—street scenes, trials, bedroom scenes, etc.—display variety in treatment, in significant detail, and in stanzaic form; in no two plays does he use the same stanzaic form.[38] The playwright rethought each episode as he composed it for the second or third time, and (like a true artist) he kept within his self-imposed limitations: nothing that did not elucidate the process of the Passion story was admissible.

From one point of view, the York Realist took to its logical conclusion a tendency inherent in the medieval drama. He did not have to break with tradition to achieve his effects. As soon as the story of Christianity began to be presented on the stage, it became necessary to link together by action and dialogue different incidents around which interest had clustered and on which dogma depended. As Émile Mâle put it—on the stage, "il fallut représenter les faits dans leur continuité."[39] As far as the Passion plays are concerned, this tendency received a decisive impetus during the fourteenth and fifteenth centuries from narrative poems and vernacular homilies about the Passion, so that in all the cycles the Passion receives more extended treatment than any other subject. Still, the Passion plays in the other cycles, and narrative poems such as *The Northern Passion*, stop well short of the "continuity" achieved by the York Realist. Like the romances, of which it is an imitation, the action of *The Northern Passion* is sudden, simple, and somewhat jerky. Relevant details are lacking, and key moments are not dwelt on. The processes of behavior are not explored and worked out in detail and in logical succession. The York Realist goes much further in his chosen direction than any other medieval English writer or dramatist who treats the Passion.

The self-imposed limitations of the York Realist mark him off sharply

37. *Plays of Our Forefathers*, p. 154.
38. Smith, pp. li–lii, has provided a convenient table of forms.
39. *L'Art religieux de la fin du moyen âge en France* (Paris, 1908), p. 29.

from the other genius working in the medieval English theater, the Wakefield Master. Their talents are different. Beyond the fact that they are both skillful metrists, both indulge in satire, and both use conventional dramatic devices in their own ways, they have little in common. The York Realist does not share the Wakefield Master's interest in extraneous invention, symbolic language and action, burlesque, deliberate contemporization, or folk humor.[40] On the other hand, the Wakefield Master has none of the subtle, careful, and extended realism of the York Realist, and little of his suggestive irony. The Wakefield Master's effects are broad, the York Realist's fine. Emphasis on the achievement of the Wakefield Master has perhaps obscured the great achievement of his contemporary, or near-contemporary.

The York Realist's work is substantial—amounting to over 3,200 lines, longer by a third than *Sir Gawain and the Green Knight*—and he should certainly be considered a major figure in Middle English letters. As a dramatist it is not simply his special kind of realism per se that is remarkable (although it is exceptional enough) but also the way in which he uses this realism to extend the Passion story and achieve a restrained yet biting portrayal of worldliness and fatuous detail undergirded by the silent but persistent figure of the suffering Christ. It is his imaginative and applied realism—a realism continually apparent in word and phrase, argument and debate, character and action, and, probably, in the introduction of whole episodes—that marks him off from the other medieval playwrights; and it is this realism that he chose, as his major undertaking, to pursue with such single-mindedness and integrity.

40. For summaries of the Wakefield Master's achievement see Carey (above, n. 21), pp. 240–44, and A. C. Cawley, ed., *The Wakefield Pageants in the Towneley Cycle* (Manchester, 1958), pp. xvii–xx, xxvii–xxx.

Hans-Jürgen Diller

14. The Craftsmanship of the Wakefield Master

The author of the *Secunda Pastorum*, conventionally regarded as the one outstanding genius of the medieval English drama, has
recently met with fainter praise.[1] Hardin Craig, though he highly commends him for his "wit" and "homely realism," condemns any predilection for the Mak episode as an aberration.[2] More recently, Eleanor
Prosser has thrown down the gauntlet with the remark: ". . . the time
has come to re-evaluate the genius of the Wakefield Master—or, rather
to place it in proper perspective."[3] J. W. Robinson, in the conclusion
of his perceptive study, believes that the broad effects of the Wakefield
Master have obscured the merits of the York Realist's finer manner.[4]
These critics are suspicious of a modernistic, and at bottom patronizing,
attitude which praises the incidental realism and humor of the medieval
plays and dismisses their central aspects as "dull," "didactic," or "merely
religious." While the basic tenets underlying those suspicions are ad-
mirable, there is a real danger of the issue becoming clouded before the
battle has actually begun. For in the older studies[5] the term "realism"

[Reprinted from *Anglia*, LXXXIII (1965), 271–88, by permission of the author
and the publisher.]
1. There is now wide agreement on the Master's canon. His six complete plays
have been edited by A. C. Cawley in *The Wakefield Pageants in the Towneley
Cycle* (Manchester, 1958). These are: *Mactacio Abel* (II); *Processus Noe cum
Filiis* (III); *Prima Pastorum* (XII); *Secunda Pastorum* (XIII); *Magnus Herodes*
(XVI); *Coliphizacio* (XXI). Cawley, p. xviii, lists further attributions, of which the
most important are: XX, st. 1–5 (Pilate's speech in *Conspiracio et Capcio Ihesu*);
XXII, st. 5–27 (main part of *Fflagellacio*); XXIV, st. 1–5, 56–59 (*Processus Talen-
torum*); XXX, st. 16–48, 68–76 (Tutiuillus, demons, in *Iudicium*). With the exception of II, for including which Cawley was criticized by Martin Stevens in
Speculum, XXXIV (1959), 453–55, the decisive criterion for attribution is the characteristic nine-line stanza. The six plays will be quoted from Cawley, all other
quotations from English mystery plays will be taken from the texts of the EETS
and from Lucy Toulmin Smith's edition of the York Plays (repr. New York, 1963).
2. *English Religious Drama of the Middle Ages* (Oxford, 1955), pp. 234, 6.
3. *Drama and Religion in the English Mystery Plays: A Re-Evaluation*, Stanford
Studies in Language and Literature, no. 23 (Stanford, 1961), p. 76.
4. "The Art of the York Realist," *MP*, LX (1962–63), 251.
5. E.g. A. W. Pollard, *English Miracle Plays*, 8th ed. (Oxford, 1927), pp. xl-

has never been closely defined as a critical concept. From this charge we cannot exclude even Millicent Carey, whose *The Wakefield Group in the Towneley Cycle*,[6] the fullest study so far published, analyzes four plays under the recurrent headings "realism," "humor," and "characterization." Surely there is no more inherent merit in merely depicting contemporary life than there is in an idealized religious scene. This fallacy, however, normally underlies the use of the word "realism" as an epithet of praise. But there is another sense in which the term can legitimately be used and which involves some of the peculiar problems of the dramatic craft. Whenever these have been mastered, there is at least a remarkable technical achievement, however debatable its integration under the ultimate purpose of the play may be. These technical problems hardly arise as long as the author treats characters, objects, and events in isolation. They involve, rather, the web of relations which ties these features together and gives the play artistic unity.

Such relations may, of course, be of the most diverse kinds. On the following pages I propose to study those prevailing between speech and action, between cause and effect, and between people. The reflection in the dramatic medium of these relations demands an awareness which is rare among Middle English playwrights and which, let it be admitted at once, is not called for by the religious conception of the earlier authors: an awareness that no two people are exactly the same, that the relation between them changes with the mood they are in, that they do not normally describe what they are feeling or doing, that one mood generates a corresponding but not necessarily identical mood in the other person. A scene does not become realistic in our sense of the word simply for a few allusions to contemporary events and customs. People are not "real" unless the atmosphere in which they move is real, unless their actions and emotions are subject to the same general laws as our own. Our realism, then, is a question of dramatic texture rather than subject matter, and the following pages are devoted to the demonstration that it is in this kind of realism that the Wakefield Master excels. With this he appropriates the dramatic medium to that interest in physical

---

xli; C. M. Gayley, *Plays of Our Forefathers* (New York, 1907), esp. pp. 135–90; John Brooks Moore, *The Comic and the Realistic in English Drama before Shakespeare* (Chicago, 1925), p. viii and passim; F. T. Wood, "The Comic Elements in the English Mystery Plays," *Neophilologus*, XXV (1939), 39–48, 194–206.

6. Hesperia Ergänzungsreihe, Heft 11 (Göttingen and Baltimore, 1930). Robinson, although he gives no definition, uses a concept of realism that has some resemblance to mine. But he scarcely considers the specific problems of dialogue as the dramatic medium.

reality which had long been developing in the mystery cycles, particularly that of York.[7]

I

At the bottom of drama lies an utterly unrealistic convention. People are made to talk almost without interruption, whereas in real life they would be engaged in actions rather than in words. Dramatic dialogue, in short, is conventionally regarded as representing action. The manner of this representation is therefore an essential question of dramatic style. Since the escape route of the modern conversation piece was not open to him, the medieval playwright had to tackle this problem squarely. It is, in fact, a commonplace among historians of the drama that the medieval audience was much more interested in lively stage business than in polished dialogue. This predominant interest seems to have influenced the development of dramatic speech in the mysteries. In such episodes as the building of the Ark or the flagellation of Christ, speech and action are normally coextensive and strictly parallel: the actor describes the work in which he happens to be engaged, the order of his phrases is directly determined by the order of his actions. The expression of emotional attitudes toward the work is limited to stock phrases such as "now I will," or the artisan's pride in good craftsmanship; it does not influence the structure of the speech. Occasionally a purely descriptive speech is followed or introduced by a general reflection. This procedure strikes the modern reader as more typical of narrative than drama. But medieval poetic theory, which grouped Virgil's first and ninth eclogues together with comedy and tragedy as "dramatic,"[8] paid no attention to the inherent aesthetic qualities of a given literary medium.

A quotation from the York *Building of the Ark* will sufficiently illustrate the type of speech indicated above:

> To hewe þis burde I will be-gynne,
> But firste I wille lygge on my lyne,
> Now bud it be alle in like thynne,
> So put it nowthyr twynne nor twyne.

---

7. On the likely influence of the so-called York Realist, the author or reviser of the York Passion plays, on the Wakefield Master, see Gayley, p. 160; Mendal G. Frampton, "The Date of the 'Wakefield Master': Bibliographical Evidence," *PMLA*, LIII (1938), 86–117; Cawley, p. xxxi.

8. This classification goes back to Diomedes' *Ars grammatica* (4th century A.D.). On the influence of Diomedes in the Middle Ages, see E. R. Curtius, *Europäische Literatur und lateinisches Mittelalter*, 2d ed. (Berne, 1954), p. 438.

þus sall I iune it with a gynn,
And sadly sette it with symonde fyne,
þus sall y wyrke it both more and mynne,
Thurgh techyng of god maister myne.
. . . .
Full trewe it is who will take tente.
Bot faste my force begynnes to fawlde,
A hundereth wyntres away is wente,
Sen I began þis werk, full grathely talde,
And in slyke trauayle for to bente,
Is harde to hym þat is þus olde.   (Y VIII, 97–104, 112–17)

The corresponding Wakefield passage runs like this:

To begyn of this tree my bonys will I bend;
I traw from the Trynyté socoure will be send.
It fayres full fayre, thynk me, this wark to my hend;
Now blissid be he that this can amend.
Lo, here the lenght,
Thre hundreth cubettys euenly;
Of breed, lo, is it fyfty;
The heght is euen thyrty
Cubettys full strenght.

Now my gowne will I cast, and wyrk in my cote;
Make will I the mast or I flyt oone foote.
A! my bak, I traw, will brast! this is a sory note!
Hit is wonder that I last, sich an old dote,
All dold,
To begyn sich a wark.
My bonys ar so stark:
No wonder if thay wark,
For I am full old.   (T III, 253–70)

Much of the conventional technique is here retained. The content of the speech is largely descriptive, but physical action and psychological reaction are much more subtly intertwined than in the York passage. Not only does the Wakefield speech depict a competent craftsman, but we catch a glimpse of the very moment when satisfaction is rising in him. Similarly, we are not simply told that he is old and tired, but we watch him getting tired by degrees: he takes his gown off, reaffirms his determination to finish the job, but cannot suppress a sigh. The Master's ability to dramatize a process rather than a static result will concern us again, especially in the discussion of Herod and Caiaphas. For the moment, suffice it to say that the Master transcends the contemporary convention of purely descriptive speech by introducing, however tentatively, a reflective element.

In transforming description into reflection, emotion clearly plays a major part. But its presence alone does not make a speech reflective. On the contrary, it is, taken by itself, just as susceptible of pure description as action. For where there is a great deal of emotion, the sequence of the words and phrases may be directly determined by the action, not by the intervening thought process. The Third Soldier in York XXIX ("Jesus Examined by Caiaphas") provides a good example when he shouts while striking Jesus:

> ... and þer is one and þer is ij;
> And ther is iij, and there is iiij.   (ll. 366–67)

This is cruelty most vivdly portrayed, and Gayley was certainly justified in dubbing the conjectural author of these lines the "York Realist."[9] But the Wakefield Master goes even beyond this:

1 Tortor.	Now sen he is blynfeld, I fall to begyn;
	And thus was I counseld the mastry to wyn.
	[*Striking Jesus.*
2 Tortor.	Nay, wrang has thou teld; thus shuld thou com in.
	[*Striking him.*
Froward.	I stode and beheld—thou towchid not the skyn
	Bot fowll.
1 Tortor.	How will thou I do?
2 Tortor.	On this manere, lo! [*Striking again.*
Froward.	Yei, that was well gone to;
	Ther start vp a cowll. (T XXI, 397–405)[10]

These torturers do not simply state that they are striking Jesus, they do not talk about their activity as such but express their personal ambition to outdo one another. The Wakefield Master, unlike his cruder predecessors in the realistic tradition, does not allow himself to be engrossed in the sensational subject matter of the scene, but concentrates on the requirements of the dramatic medium even here.

II

The exact meshing of speech and action is more than an exhibition of dramatic skill. It is above all one aspect among others of the author's insight into the psychological laws of cause and effect. As far as these involve more than one person they will have to be discussed in the next section. Here I propose to deal with motivation working on a single mind. As a type, the mystery play has very little use for motivation. If a character is evil, he will work evil: his actions do not need to be prompted by particular occasions. The characteristic tyrant's speech

9. Gayley, pp. 157–58.
10. The stage directions are Cawley's.

usually opens with a naïvely explicit statement about why the crimes in question are to be perpetrated. The evil man's motives are thus part of the exposition, never of the dramatic action.

The Wakefield Master uses an altogether different approach. With the exception of Pilate's speech, which he prefixed to the Towneley *Conspiracio* (T XX), he never begins a play with a villain's monologue. Cain and Herod are introduced by their servants, Garcio and Nuncius. The function of these is quite different from that of superficially similar figures in the Chester Plays, Expositor and Nuntius. The Chester figures remain entirely extraneous to the action and are never even noticed by the characters of the play proper; their Wakefield counterparts are engaged in dialogue with their masters. Cain's Garcio, Pikeharness, has received much praise as a forerunner of the impudent servant in English comedy,[11] but from our point of view Herod's messenger is even more skillfully employed. Like Pikeharness, he warns the audience of his master's character; but he also hints at what is, at the moment, on Herod's mind. He uses a subtler approach in trying to win the audience by a show of friendliness. Most important of all, he addresses Herod and informs him that the people (represented by the audience) "carp of a kyng" (T XVI, 78). This gives Herod a flying start for his emotional outburst and directly causes his reaction:

> Bot I shall tame thare talkyng,
> And let thame go hang thame.   (ll. 80–81)

Eight stanzas later, his rage is even further increased by the confirmation of what he had so far only suspected: the Milites bring the news that the Magi have escaped (ll. 145 ff.). After the aimless threats of the monologue (ll. 80–144) Herod is now compelled to devise a definite plan. This he does with his two Consulti (ll. 192–270), who read to him the familiar prophecies about the newborn king at Bethlehem. According to Matt. 2:4 ff., this takes place at the Magi's coming to Herod's court, not after their return by another route. By transferring the prophecies the Wakefield Master is able to demonstrate how his villain's scheme gradually gains momentum: first he learns about his prospective victim, then about the place where he may hope to find him. But even now the plan has not yet taken its final shape; contrary to all other plays on the Massacre except York, it is the counsellors who have to suggest the Slaughter. Counsellors and soldiers are thus no longer mere puppets but contribute to the development of the play.

The entire preliminary action, however, is not dissolved into dialogue. A tyrant without a long ranting speech would not have been acceptable

11. Gayley, p. 185; Carey, p. 44; Cawley, p. 91 (note on l. 37).

to a medieval audience, and the Master was too skillful a craftsman of the stage to ignore this. Here again he transforms the conventions which he inherited. The York Realist had continued a growing tendency among medieval playwrights to enrich these introductory speeches with much incidental comic material and abusive language. Caiaphas in York XXIX, Herod in York XXXI, Pilate in York XXX, XXXII and XXXIII, give a fair indication of this manner. But even here the highly colored vocabulary cannot conceal the fact that, for all their ostensible emotionalism, the speeches are surprisingly discursive and strangely uninvolved in tone. There is no progression, and therefore no motivation, in the speeches. A comparison with the much quieter opening of the Chester *Slaying of the Innocents* would show that only the details have changed, not the manner of their arrangement.

It is in the latter respect that the Wakefield Master marks a radical departure from current practices. His Herod's speech, as opposed to the York and Chester tyrants' speeches, is emotional in structure as well as in detail. The Chester Herod, the structure of whose speech is typical, pursues a very clear line of argument, the items following each other in logical order. Within individual items (which are normally coextensive with a double stanza), the connection is usually causal, thus reinforcing the rather cool, detached impression of the whole. This Herod expounds a plan which is already finished in his head and according to which the play will proceed—a plan which gradually evolves in the Towneley play. The Towneley Herod begins with a strong emotional outburst and then continues to threaten both the audience and the absent Magi, suspecting the latter of having cheated him. His first mention of them is characteristic of the associative working of his mind:

> What dewill! my thynk I brast for anger and for teyn;
> I trow thyse kyngys be past that here with me has beyn.
>
> (ll. 118–19)

The fact that he suddenly remembers them causes the exclamation "What dewill!" But before he tells us what he remembers, we see his reaction to it. Not until then do we learn about "thyse kyngys." This is the exact reverse of the Chester Herod, who merely states things but hardly ever reacts to them.

Reducing these observations to a simple formula, we may say that in Chester we observe the result, in Towneley the process, of thought. But this distinction is only the symptom of a larger one, which is a basic difference in character conception. The Chester Herod is essentially a representative of secular power opposing divine power and thus automatically an agent of evil; apart from that, he has no discernible human character. His evil disposition is merely described, it does not reveal itself. We do not know what he feels in the act of planning or doing evil. In Towneley the abstract concept of evilness is broken down into a number of subqualities which are conveyed to us by Herod's behavior: he is selfish, vengeful, treacherous, and violent. This will naturally dispose him toward evil, but he still needs to be provoked. It is these provocations which we become witnesses of in the first part of the play and which trigger off the main action. Here, then, the essence lies in the individual's character, not in his relative position to the deity.

III

In the *Magnus Herodes* we saw the protagonist as a fully developed character who at a particular moment is subject to particular influences, who not only dominates the figures around him, but also reacts to them. But the relationship is still one-sided. Herod finds no partners who could react to him in the same way. The Wakefield Master does not stop here. In the two shepherds plays and the *Coliphizacio*, as well as in occasional passages in the other pageants, he shows that subtle shading of interpersonal relationships which is one of his main claims to excellence.

The normal mystery play reduces personal relations to the simple dichotomy of good and evil. Occasional exceptions grow out of such basic human relations as father-and-son, husband-and-wife. The latter are usually created in humorous scenes without biblical authority, especially in the Noah plays or the scene of Pilate and Percula (Y XXX). These remain largely incidental without affecting the texture of the play as a whole. The chief example of the former group, the Brome Abraham play, shows a similar wealth of personal relations to that of the Wakefield Pageants, but is much more lyrical in tone and appears to be entirely unconnected with the northern realistic tradition.[12]

The Wakefield Master not only gives emotional expression to personal relations but provides them with a firm foundation in the physical sphere, betraying a keen eye for scenic possibilities. Thus Slawpace, the Third Shepherd in the *Prima Pastorum*, while pointing the moral of his fellows' foolish quarrel, gives them exact indications where to stand and how to move (T XII, 164–69). Nor is this the only example. Mak, in the

---

12. Cf. Carrie A. Harper, "A Comparison between the Brome and Chester Plays of Abraham and Isaac," *Studies in English and Comparative Literature, presented to Agnes Irwin*, Radcliffe College Monographs, no. 15 (Boston, 1910), pp. 51–73; J. Burke Severs, "The Relationship between the Brome and Chester Play of 'Abraham and Isaac,' " *MP*, XLII (1945), 137–51.

Secunda Pastorum, is made to lie down to sleep between the shepherds. In the *Coliphizacio* the first two torturers lead, the last follows, Jesus (T XXI, 428–32). The most charming instance is provided by the shepherds just before they enter Mak's cottage. They hear him "crak . . . clere out of toyne" (T XIII, 477). Instead of having to picture them vaguely on their way to Mak,[13] we know that they are already within earshot of him. Space, which in the older religious drama was of purely symbolic significance, becomes here an object of physical experience.

This interest in physical space may even lead to the reinterpretation of a theological topos. The stool on which Jesus is traditionally seated during the buffeting is of course a mocking reference to the throne which is properly his. It is given a practical justification by the Wakefield Master:

> If he stode vpon loft, we must hop and dawnse
> As cokys in a croft.   (XXI, 354–55)

If the traditional handling of this motif may be called a cruel parody of Christ's divinity, the Wakefield Master makes the torturers debase him as a human being. The relevance of the stool lies no longer in its extrinsic reference to religious belief but is intrinsically bound up with the context of the play and the physical appearance of the actor.[14]

These are small things, and yet they can become dramatically most effective, as when Caiaphas, according to Cawley's plausible conjecture, "strikes at Jesus and misses him," exclaiming:

> Fy on hym and war! I am out of my gate[15]).
> Say, why standys he so far?   (XXI, 298–99)

By placing his actors adroitly on the pageant-wagon, the author heightens the impression of the impotent fury of Christ's adversary. This playwright is obviously able to enlist even the most trivial-seeming details for his overall dramatic purpose.

The last-quoted instance is an example of the intensifying effect of spatial relations on emotional ones. While an increasing interest in emotions is common to the realistic tradition, the Wakefield Master is original in the dramatic rendering of them. Since the trial of Jesus by Caiaphas is perhaps the most striking emotional collision in all the mystery cycles, I propose to deal with it somewhat more fully. Cawley

---

13. This convention of "on-the-way" scenes is still current in Elizabethan plays. Cf. Muriel C. Bradbrook, *Themes and Conventions of Elizabethan Tragedy* (Cambridge, 1935), p. 9.

14. For the suggestion that the part of Christ was acted by a tall man, see Cawley, note on ll. 354–55.

15. I.e. "I'm not within striking distance of Christ" (Cawley, note).

comments on the contrast between the silent Christ and the raging Caiaphas,[16] but he does not mention the small details which support and build up this major effect. Caiaphas begins (ll. 129 ff.) with a cunning mixture of rude threats and vague promises, which betrays a certain strategy in dealing with Jesus. This is punctuated by aptly varied attempts at eliciting a reply. As these attempts grow more insistent (ll. 134, 137, 141, 168, 172), personal references to his victim (ll. 145 ff., 165 ff.) become more and more insulting, and his whole approach loses its original polite cleverness. In his last stanza (ll. 172–80) he forgets all self-control and so calls forth the intervention of the more sedate Annas. Thus we have not isolated moments of rage, but a very clear line of development. Compressed within little more than fifty lines, this emotional climax is particularly effective; but a similar development can be traced in the *Mactacio Abel*[17] and in the purely humorous quarrels.[18] These scenes, and especially the Trial, are remarkable not only for their dramatic intensity. What distinguishes them most clearly from their counterparts in other cycles is the continuity and, as its corollary, the structure with which even the smallest dramatic units are informed.

Of all human relationships, those between enemies (or, at least, opponents) lend themselves most easily to vivid dramatization. But the Wakefield author's vision of life is too complex for him to be satisfied with that. He is careful to distinguish members of one group from one another, to set off the First Shepherd against the Second, etc. The distinguishing qualities which he employs are usually simple but clearly noticeable and therefore dramatically effective; they can be both social and personal. Thus the third member of such a group is often cast as a servant and has to obey the others. The first two are distinguished in a more subtle way. *Secundus Tortor* in the *Coliphizacio*, for instance, complains repeatedly of the trouble they had to undergo (ll. 10 ff., 39 ff., 48 ff.), whereas *Primus Tortor* is much more preoccupied with threatening and insulting Jesus. In addition to his greater aggressiveness he shows more initiative. It is he who addresses the High Priests and, reporting the

16. Cawley, p. xxvii.

17. Cain's language is rude from his first entrance (T II, 25 ff.); he insults Abel immediately after his arrival (l. 59), then violently abuses the institution of the tithe (which probably got him some sympathy from the audience [ll. 108 ff.]). The last stage before the murder is reached with open blasphemy ("God is out of hys wit!" [l. 300]).

18. In *Processus Noe* the attempts to urge the reluctant Uxor on board become increasingly insistent (T III, 354, 355, 357, 367 ff.). In *Prima Pastorum* the fight over the imaginary sheep is prepared by a careful delineation of characters, about which more will have to be said below.

capture, claims all the credit for himself (ll. 68–71). Characteristically, this story is accepted without a word of protest by his indolent colleague.[19] None of this contrast, however, is maintained in the buffeting scene proper (ll. 343–414). It has served its purpose and is abandoned in favor of the more obvious opposition between the first two torturers and their servant Froward.

In the *Prima Pastorum* such differentiation becomes the supporting pattern of the entire play. Millicent Carey has a useful survey on conventions of character-drawing in French and English shepherds plays.[20] But the truly astounding thing is the significance which even the minutest details acquire in the light of the speakers' characters. The First Shepherd complains about the general state of affairs (ll. 1 ff.) and his own misfortunes (ll. 19 ff.), then mentions the cause of his distress: the loss of his sheep (ll. 24 ff.). From this he proceeds to his plan:

> To the fare will I me,
> To by shepe, perdé, . . .   (ll. 42–43)

This logical, discursive structure of the monologue corresponds with the details: the conditions of the shepherd's life are conceived of in the abstract, his style is conceptual and antithetical, occasionally supported by alliteration and anaphora. There is only one address to the audience (l. 19), and that a faintly didactic one. Every single utterance is that of a thoughtful, serious, somewhat self-centered man.[21]

The Second Shepherd's speech is the exact opposite. He establishes contact with the audience at once:

> Bensté, bensté, be vs emang, . . .   (l. 46)

The "vs" is in marked contrast to the other man's "ye" (l. 19) and is characteristic of the speaker's attitude throughout. The monologue is full of concrete details which appeal to the common experience of speaker and audience. There are no generalities; all the evils are seen as caused by human beings, some of whom are vividly described as social types (ll. 64–72). Alliteration and anaphora (ll. 51–53) have a cumulative effect, not a disjunctive one as with the First Shepherd. The

---

19. Considering the Master's usually excellent stagecraft, it is tempting to think that this psychological distinction found some reflection in the actors' appearance: perhaps a lean, wiry man as First Torturer, and a fat one as Second.

20. Carey, pp. 187–90.

21. Superficially this analysis may resemble that of the Chester Herod. But it should be noted that this shepherd's utterances are not mere statements but reactions to his difficult situation and therefore a direct expression of his own self. They are, moreover, informed by his personal style, in which he differs from his fellows, whereas the Chester Herod speaks in the same vein as his *entourage*.

sequence is no longer logical but spontaneously associative. The speaker shows himself a sanguine extrovert.

It is only apposite that the Second Shepherd should first discover his friend, address him, and pick a quarrel with him.[22] Character portrayal is thus not limited to the monologues but is extended into the quarrel and even beyond. For throughout the remainder of the play we find the First Shepherd the most sedate, thoughtful and reasonable of the three.[23] During the meal he calms the occasionally excited spirits of the other two (ll. 202, 252, 275). He gently mocks the Third for his "gramery" (l. 242) and later on displays the greatest learning about the prophecies of Christ (ll. 332 f., 386 ff.).[24] In worshipping the Child, he alone maintains a reverent attitude, with no trace of "lytyll tyn mop" (l. 467), "swetyng," "praty mytyng" (ll. 476 ff.).

These shepherds are not passive recipients of the good news draped with a few shreds of real life. They are human beings betraying their individual characteristics and reactions in front of the manger as they did out in the fields. Certainly these characteristics are not very obtrusive, but they are consistently present and strong enough to contradict Miss Carey's dictum that "there is no attempt even in Towneley XII at consistent character development."[25]

The introductory monologues of the *Secunda* reveal none of the clear-cut distinctions of the *Prima* (abstract vs. concrete, logical vs. as-

22. The method of having the second character address the first is popular with the Wakefield Master but unusual in the mystery plays as a whole. The Master's technique helps to reduce the ceremonious stiffness of the opening. The congruence between the characters and their parts in the quarrel has been hinted at by Carey, p. 191.

23. This view contradicts, of course, Cawley's interpretation of the scene in "Iak Garcio of the *Prima Pastorum*," *MLN*, LXVIII (1953), 169–72, where he comes to the conclusion that Iak is not a separate character but identical with the Third Shepherd. His main argument for this attractive proposition is (1) that such a skillful dramatist as the Wakefield Master would hardly introduce a character for a mere eleven lines, (2) that the Third Shepherd is no fool and Iak has no right to call him so. The main objections to his theory he sees in l. 179, where Garcio calls the others "foles all sam," and l. 186 ("Ye thre bere the bell"). "All sam," he admits, suggests more than two people, but he finds counter-evidence in the Master's own *Processus Noe*, where *Secundus Filius* addresses his two brothers with "Brether, sam" (l. 320). But here, as Cawley agrees in the glossary of his edition, *sam* does not mean "together," but is derived from OE *samnian* "to collect." On balance, it seems more likely that we have to accept the incongruity of a very short part, which may even have been introduced as a mouthpiece to qualify all three shepherds as equally foolish. Moreover, there is no other evidence in the play that the author regards the pouring of the meal on the ground as less foolish than the quarrel over imaginary sheep, even though it points the moral.

24. I cannot agree with Carey that he is "unmercifully chaffed by the others" (p. 91). John Horne's good-natured taunt (ll. 388–92) is certainly not meant as ridicule; it is silenced the moment Gyb provides a translation.

25. Carey, p. 191.

sociative, self-centered vs. extrovert). It is true that the henpecked husband is described in more detail than in the *Prima*,[26] but his actions and manner of speech do not make it so clear that he is the sort of man that could be henpecked. The three shepherds are now treated as a group rather than as individual types,[27] and as a group they become the opponents of Mak.

The character of the sheep-stealer is too famous to need comment. The only important thing in this connection is the complete change in the method of characterization. For Mak nothing so simple as the usual contrasting would do. Such a technique would have put his adversaries on a par with him. He is the first figure in the history of English drama to reveal his character entirely through action and dialogue: as a born actor and schemer he is always on top of the situation (except when alone with his wife); the shepherds never catch him off his guard, and even when the truth is out he enjoys his "act" so much that he cannot give it up.

For the most effective use of character contrast we have to return to the *Coliphizacio*. The joint trial by the two high priests is common property of many popular medieval versions of the Passion, both narrative and dramatic. The author of the York play of *Jesus Examined by Caiaphas* (**XXIX**) even attempted some differentiation between the characters.[28] But the Wakefield Master is the only English playwright to distinguish the two characters consistently and to give this distinction a dramatic function. Thus when Caiaphas is interrupted by Annas (T XXI, 181), there follows a long and stormy dialogue (ll. 181–243), in which Annas seeks to restrain Caiaphas. Jesus, who remains silent, is the constant object of their violent exchange, thus providing an additional contrast, and, more important still, staying in the focus of dramatic interest.[29]

This scene from the *Coliphizacio* is a good instance of its author's craftsmanship in that it demonstrates that his mastery of character-drawing is in fact inseparable from his skill in plot-construction. As a

26. Cf. XII, 96–99, with XIII, 64–108.

27. This is borne out by a curious but probably significant fact: throughout the play the speaking order of the shepherds (omitting Mak and his wife) is, with very few exceptions, 1–2–3: their relations remain constant. In Towneley XII the order changes with the phases of the action.

28. There is, however, a strange confusion: Caiaphas is sometimes the more choleric (XXIX, 336–39), sometimes the more diplomatic of the two (ibid., 245 f., 288 f.). Robinson (p. 246), in a somewhat strained argument, interprets this reversal of attitudes as a particularly subtle point of character portrayal.

29. That the difficulty of conveying silence in the dramatic medium perplexed the medieval playwrights may be inferred from such stage directions as "nihil respondet" (Ch XVI, 184); similarly in L.C. XXX, 412.

comic playwright he is not so much interested in the conflicts and passions of the individual as in the enrichment of the action by individual characteristics; in many respects this technique resembles that of Chaucer in some of his comic tales, especially in the *Miller's Tale* and the *Reeve's Tale*. The Wakefield Master keeps his distinctions between individuals consistent, but they must remain subservient to the plot. Thus it is entirely possible to give up a contrast in the course of a play, as we have seen in the *Coliphizacio*. This underlying principle of "plot over character" explains, too, why in the maturest play, the *Secunda Pastorum*, we find actually less character differentiation than in its presumable forerunner, the *Prima Pastorum*.[30]

IV

The preceding pages have offered, I hope, sufficient proof that the Wakefield Master was not just someone who hit upon the Mak story by a stroke of luck or even unaccountable genius, but a conscious craftsman who knew how to make his characters "live." If we now try, as Prosser demands, to place his genius "in proper perspective,"[31] one question has to be asked: is he still to be regarded as a religious dramatist? His strong interest in, and obvious mastery of, the physical sphere with its spatial, causal, and psychological aspects reduces the transcendent quality that is so predominant in the older parts of the York cycle and in the bulk of the very conservative Chester Plays. Anne Righter believes that to the medieval audience the matter represented in the cycles was more "real" than their own lives.[32] Such an attitude, if it was consistently maintained, would preclude any interest in the manner of representation and would above all deny the plays any degree of aesthetic autonomy. But although this was apparently the opinion of the ecclesiastical authorities,[33] it is difficult to believe that the interest of the medieval public was limited to the plays' religious function in this narrow sense. Not only does the constant increase of realistic detail,

30. This is not a correction, but at best a modification, of Arnold Williams's view that the York and Towneley plays betray more interest in character whereas *Coventry* and *Ludus Coventriae* devote more space to plot (*The Drama of Medieval England* [East Lansing, Mich., 1961], pp. 107–8). My contention is merely that the Wakefield Master shows the most skillful combination of the two. Williams is, of course, speaking of the cycles in general.

31. See above, n. 3.

32. *Shakespeare and the Idea of the Play* (London, 1962), pp. 14–15.

33. We find it reflected, e.g., in the granting of a pardon to the audience of the Chester Plays. For the fullest discussion of this tradition, together with careful reprints of the relevant documents, see Frederick M. Salter, *Medieval Drama in Chester* (Toronto, 1955), pp. 32ff.

most noticeable in York but by no means absent even from Chester, witness against such a view, but the very origin of the vernacular Corpus Christi plays results from a reaction by the church to popular religious tendencies of the thirteenth and early fourteenth centuries. These tendencies, which originated among the rising bourgeoisie of the prospering cities and were institutionalized in the Friars, the Feast of Corpus Christi, and a renewed emphasis on preaching, contained a grain of realism from the very beginning. The plays are concerned with the humanity of the suffering Christ no less than the poetry of the Franciscans is. Their rougher, earthier tone does not make them irreligious.

David J. Leigh

15. The Doomsday Mystery Play: An Eschatological Morality

The four English mystery cycles conclude with a Last Judgment play that has raised fewer problems for critics than it deserves. Several critics have remarked on its sources, date of origin, and staging techniques, but none has faced up to the unique features which mark the play off from all the others in the mystery cycles.[1] And no critic, to my knowledge, has explored the basis for these distinctive features and their implications for the development of dramatic form.

In this paper I shall show that the Doomsday play exhibits five distinctive features that make it problematic for the historian of drama. At the root of these five characteristics I find its eschatological subject, its symbolic techniques, and its ambivalent time and audience relationships. By comparing the five distinctive features with similar aspects of early morality plays, I propose the Doomsday play as a possible key to the still unsettled problems of defining and finding sources for the English moralities.

PROBLEMATIC FEATURES OF THE DOOMSDAY PLAY

The first and most obvious feature of the Doomsday plays is their nonhistorical setting: they attempt to represent an event which is beyond historical time and space, on the margin of eternity. Although purportedly taking place on earth, the Judgment transcends any particular place by various methods used in each of the plays. The Chester play spectacularly unites heaven and earth by mechanically lowering Christ on a cloud from which he judges the souls of persons gathering

[Reprinted from *Modern Philology*, LXVII (1969–70), 211–23, by permission of the author and the publisher. Copyright by The University of Chicago.]
1. For discussion of the origin and date of cycle Doomsday plays, cf. Hardin Craig, *English Religious Drama in the Middle Ages* (Oxford, 1955), pp. 130 ff.; V. A. Kolve, *The Play Called Corpus Christi* (Stanford, 1966), pp. 98–102; G. R. Owst, *Literature and Pulpit in Medieval England* (New York, 1933), pp. 539 ff. Staging of the play is treated by Martial Rose, ed., *The Wakefield Mystery Plays* (New York, 1962), pp. 551–52.

from earth, heaven, and hell to reunite with their bodies (Chester, l. 356).[2] The York play gives no clear indication of place but presents Christ seating himself and his apostles on judgment seats (York, l. 177 ff.). The souls are called by two trumpeting angels and separated by a third angel. Demons apparently run up from Hellsmouth to lead away their victims (York, l. 227). The Wakefield play, with its truncated opening, provides no special clues to its setting except the overall situation of some place where heaven, hell, and earth come together. The 130 lines of the *Ludus Coventriae* play also lack significant place details.

More important however is the fact that the Judgment plays depict events on the tangent of eternity. The problem of nonrepresentative time arises in several other mystery plays, but all of them (with the exception of the Creation and the Parliament of Heaven) have some basis in linear historical time insofar as they attempt to dramatize a historical past event.[3] Only the Doomsday play portrays an event at the end of time, on the "Last Day," which according to the more progressive movement in traditional theology transcends the normal human experience of time.[4] But the Judgment raises problems not merely because it is at the margin of eternity but also because in it are summed up all the events of historical time. Every incident of salvation history (as recalled by Christ's speech on his passion) and of the lives of individual men is somehow present in the instant of Judgment represented on stage. In addition, the whole of eternity is related to temporal events by the presence of God. This is most sharply drawn in the opening lines of the York cycle, in which God solemnly recalls his motives for creating and now terminating the world (ll. 1–80). Also stressing the parallel with the creation is

2. All references to the mystery plays in this essay will be to the following texts: *The Chester Plays*, ed. for EETS by Hermann Deimling and Dr. Matthews, pt. 1 (London, 1892), pt. 2 (London, 1916); *Ludus Coventriae*, ed. for EETS by K. S. Block (London, 1922); *The Towneley Plays*, re-ed. for EETS by George England (London, 1897); *York Plays*, ed. by Lucy Toulmin Smith (Oxford, 1885). Non-cyclic or morality plays referred to are from the following texts: *The Macro Plays*, ed. for EETS by F. J. Furnivall and Alfred W. Pollard (London, 1904); *The Non-Cycle Mystery Plays*, re-ed. for EETS by Osborn Waterhouse (London, 1909); *Two Coventry Corpus Christi Plays*, ed. for EETS by Hardin Craig (London, 1902). I follow Martial Rose in calling the above manuscript "Wakefield" rather than "Towneley," but refer to the Hegge manuscript or N-Town plays as *Ludus Coventriae*.

3. I shall mention later some of the devices used in other mystery plays to deal with nonrepresentative time. The problem of the medieval notion of the historicity of the early books of the Old Testament is beyond the scope of this paper, but it seems unlikely that the dramas were written with any insinuation that Adam, Cain and Abel, and Noah were not strictly historical personages.

4. For a brief summary of medieval opinions on the suprahistorical nature of the judgment, cf. the Appendix to the present article.

the Chester play, which presents God as an active character and explicitly points up his divine eternal presence by his "Alpha and Omega" speech (ll. 1–24).

The nonhistorical situation portrayed in the Doomsday plays demands a type of dramatic action that is the second distinctive feature of these plays. All the main actions on stage—the descent of Christ, the physical separation of good and bad souls, the descent into hell and ascent into heaven, the tribunal action of Christ, and so forth—all are types of action not to be taken in a literal representative sense. Again, such nonrepresentative action also occurs in other mystery plays, but these others are still primarily concerned with actions that have some historical basis beneath their literal external representation, even if their basic historicity was fictionally expanded by the author or possessed of various figurative meanings. In the Judgment plays no action can be taken literally. In the terminology of medieval exegetes, the "literal" sense of the scriptural events portrayed in these plays is identical with their "anagogic" sense, for they represent eschatological actions which are beyond the grasp of present human experience except through the medium of nonrepresentative symbolic action.

It is enlightening to focus on the various methods used by each of the four cycles to portray symbolically the action of the Last Day. The York play very starkly presents God delivering a long speech on the history of salvation (ll. 1–80), followed by the call and separation of good from bad souls by three angels (ll. 81–176). Next Christ seats himself and his apostles for the Judgment, an incident interrupted by a song and the arrival of two devils (ll. 177–228). The play comes to its climax in an address by Christ in which he recalls his sufferings for them, and then he rewards and punishes on the basis of works of mercy (ll. 229–380). Thus the York play is little more than a direct, solemn dramatization of Matthew 25:31–46.

The Chester Last Judgment expands the action to include a series of characters representing various classes of men who deliver self-incriminating or self-vindicating speeches (the latter mainly pleas for mercy). The Chester play also adds the physical descent of Christ on a cloud ("si fieri poterit," according to stage directions), sensationalizes Christ's passion speech by a literal emission of blood (l. 420), and portrays the central Judgment event as a legal conflict in which the demons parade the damned souls and offer scriptural arguments to Christ that he is obliged to condemn them (ll. 509–676).[5] After the demons lead the souls off to hell, the four evangelists deliver sermons of warning to the audience (ll. 677–708).

5. Kolve, *Play Called Corpus Christi*, pp. 101 ff.

The Wakefield play contains the basic Doomsday structure—the calling of souls, separation of good from bad, descent and judgment of Christ, and departures to heaven and hell. But the fragmented opening dialogue among four evil souls provides a detailed analysis of the history and reactions of the damned (ll. 1–70). The activities of the demons is likewise highly developed in a long section in which they discuss their methods and victims (ll. 142–243). Tutivillus's "Welcome to hell" speech adds a description of the lost souls involving satire aimed at medieval social and religious abuses, and contains hints of the use of personification in pantomime of the seven deadly sins (ll. 305–49). Christ's judgment is given in the form of the scriptural dialogue in which he identifies himself with the recipients of the souls' mercy or disdain. Throughout the play, and especially in the descent to hell, the touch of the Wakefield Master betrays itself as the demons act out their roles in comic terms providing satire and even slapstick.

The brief extant section of the *Ludus Coventriae* play adds only one unique method in its portrayal of the eschatological action: the reading of the condemnation written in black letters on the foreheads of the damned. In all the cycles, however, besides these varieties in plot structure, properties of all sorts were no doubt used to signify the final incineration and renewal of the world. For instance, evidence from property lists for a lost Doomsday play at Coventry indicates that barrels were set on fire to symbolize the consummation of the world.[6]

Despite these various methods of concretizing the end-time action, the basic event of the Judgment in all the cycles is in the form of a symbolic trial judged by Christ. The conflict in and around the trial occurs on various levels: between the angels and demons for the souls of the risen; within the souls by way of narration of their past struggles now present in effect; between the demons and the resisting damned souls; and, most basically, between Christ as merciful judge and the demons demanding "justice."[7]

A third distinctive aspect of the Judgment plays is their largely non-historical representation of character. The only person who occurs in all the plays in a form similar to his historical image is Christ. Yet, as risen and glorified in body, even he somehow transcends the ordinary limits of time and space, according to scholastic theology. Peter appears briefly in the *Ludus Coventriae* play to lead in the saved, and the apostles are seated by Christ at the Judgment in the York drama, but none of

---

6. *Two Coventry Corpus Christi Plays*, pp. 98–99. Cf. also M. Dormer Harris, "The 'World' in the Doomsday Mystery Play," *Notes and Queries* 149 (1925), 243.

7. The struggle between Christ and the demons is evident in Chester, York, and *Ludus Coventriae;* the demons' conflict with angels and lost souls is clearest in Wakefield; the inner struggle accounts are primarily in the Chester speeches.

them is given lines to speak. Four devices seem to have been used in these plays to deal with the nonliteral portrayal of character. First, as in other mystery plays, God and spirits are anthropomorphized.[8] Second, the human race is presented in the form of anonymous crowds of "good" or "evil" souls. Third, parts of the human race are represented by universal types of major classes familiar to the audience. Finally, there is incipient use of personification, in narration and probably in pantomime.

The characterization of God was probably done by means of the medieval figure of an old man. In the Chester play he speaks only twenty-four lines and is addressed primarily as "Lord." The York Doomsday allots more than the first fifth of its text to God's paternal speech reviewing the history of the world and presenting a series of motives for ending history. God does not appear in either of the partial texts of the other cycles.[9]

The process of characterization of angels and devils offered little difficulty to the medieval dramatists with their highly developed speculations on the nature of spirits common among the schoolmen, and with the medieval nonhistorical approach to scriptural exegesis. In the Judgment plays, however, the only specifically named spirits are Gabriel and Michael in the *Ludus Coventriae* play, and Tutivillus in the Wakefield play. The rest of the supernatural world is portrayed anthropomorphically by means of universal types, the same technique used to depict the human race. But the distinctive feature of the angels and devils in the Doomsday play (apart from their large number and important structural function) is their direct relationship to all mankind. In the other mystery plays they relate only to specific persons and incidents in history, whereas in the Last Judgment they are directly concerned with the actions of the human race as a whole. This feature is brought out by the forensics of the Chester play and the comic narrations and mockeries of the Wakefield demons. The spirits are closely joined with the personal lives of the souls to be judged—as past tempters, present accusers, or future tormenters.

Far more distinctive of the Doomsday play than the portrayal of the suprahuman world is the nonliteral representation of the human race. For only in this play does the audience find itself on stage. The means of representation is through an anonymous crowd (York, Wakefield)

8. God appears as a character in thirty-five of the cycle plays, most often as addressing man in scriptural terms at the beginning of the play or at crucial moments.

9. Kolve points out that the late (1609) Banns to the Chester cycle promise that the part of God will be portrayed by a hidden voice. *Play Called Corpus Christi*, p. 30.

or through universal social types, either narrated *(Ludus Coventriae)* or acted out (Chester). As Kolve notes, this is the only mystery play in which types are used consistently instead of historical or imaginary personages.[10] There is also an incipient use of personification in two of the four Doomsday plays. In the *Ludus Coventriae* play, the devils read aloud the ways in which the seven deadly sins opposed the works of mercy and helped damn the souls (ll. 92–126). Also in the same cycle, the damned have their sins inscribed on their foreheads, perhaps the predominant vice visible in large letters to the audience. In the Wakefield drama, Tutivillus speaks of the seven deadly sins in terms that make it clear that certain ones of the lost souls were to act in pantomime the role of each sin (ll. 305 ff.).[11]

This nonhistorical representation of character raises the question of the fourth distinctive feature of the Judgment plays: how did they relate to their audience? The other cycle plays portrayed the past historical events as past but with present relevance because of various theological links between the Old and New Testaments, between Christ's life-death-resurrection and the life of the church and its members (e.g., connections of typology, ritual, moral relevance, doctrines of universal redemption, personal incorporation in the church and in Christ, etc.). They used various sorts of anachronisms and homiletic speeches to stress these connections, especially for moral and satirical purposes. But in the Doomsday play the audience views the future as present, their own lives and those of all men concentrated into the moments of stage time. This identification of audience and stage is achieved primarily by the nonliteral use of anonymous crowds and of universal social types. The audience involvement is heightened by the direct address of God and Christ and the demons to the audience. The narrations of the saved and damned types in the Chester plays are an explicit call for repentance and hope; the criterion of judgment by Christ is an implicit appeal for works of mercy by the audience. One of the Wakefield demons, as G. R. Owst notes, directly refers to the warnings about this Day so common in late medieval sermons:

> Alle this was token domysday to drede,
> Full oft was it spoken, full few toke hede.
> (Wakefield, ll. 197–98)[12]

10. Ibid., p. 224.
11. W. Roy Mackenzie first mentioned the probability of the use of personification: *The English Moralities from the Point of View of Allegory* (Boston, 1914), pp. 32 ff.
12. Owst, *Literature and Pulpit*, p. 520.

As Kolve points out, the Doomsday play was necessary to the cycles because it alone gave complete meaning to the present time, the time of the audience. For in the light of the Last Judgment, all human history since the time of Christ is, for popular medieval theology, principally a time for repentance and preparation for the day of doom.[13] The fact that Christ as judge repeatedly mentions that the "time of mercy" is over is a direct appeal to the audience to repent before it is too late.

Social satire also plays a part in the Chester and Wakefield Doomsday plays to make them more relevant to the audience. Several dramatic problems arise from this use of satire. For instance, the roles of the merchant and judge in the Chester play are puzzling. Both are damned but have no saved counterparts as do the pope, emperor, king, and queen. In fact, the merchant and judge seem structurally to have been added on but not integrated into the play. Furthermore the lack of ordinary persons among the types represented in this play raises various interesting speculations about audience response. In the Wakefield play, the abundant social satire and humor add greatly to the "realism" of the drama but perhaps threaten to dissolve the ultimate seriousness of the play, a fact that has led one critic to consider similar plays in the same cycle dramatic failures.[14]

The fifth distinctive feature of the Doomsday play is its explicit narration of the history of salvation to make it relevant to the present time, both the "present" of Doomsday and the "present" of the audience. In York, as was previously noted, God recounts the history of redemption in a long address describing Creation, Paradise, the Fall, Redemption, Christ's example and effect, and the reasons for ending history. Later in the play, Christ himself recalls his own sufferings and death motivated by love for men as the center of history (ll. 229 ff.). The Chester and Wakefield plays present no long description of the history of God's relations with man, but both contain Christ's personal narration of his death for man as the key to the Judgment of human history (Chester, ll. 357–432; Wakefield, ll. 402–33).

THE BASIS OF THE DISTINCTIVE FEATURES OF THE DOOMSDAY PLAY

These five distinctive elements show that the Doomsday play is radically different, in subject matter, structure, and dramatic

13. Kolve, pp. 101 ff. See also Eleanor Prosser, *Drama and Religion in the English Mystery Plays* (Stanford, 1961), pp. 19–39. Prosser's thesis is that the doctrine of repentance, as preached in the fourteenth century, was the key to the theology behind most of the cycle plays.
14. Prosser, p. 80. She is dealing specifically with the Killing of Abel.

techniques, from the other mystery plays. Its nonhistorical situation, its totally symbolic action, its special use of types and incipient personifications, its unique audience-stage relationship, and its explicit narration of the history of redemption—all these indicate that the play is trying to be something quite different from the historical cycle plays that led up to it.

What is at the root of these differences? I believe that the Doomsday play is basically an attempt to represent an eschatological event by means of symbolic techniques drawn from scripture, sermons, and perhaps other cycle plays. It is thereby trying to relate this transhistorical event to both salvation history as past and the audience as present. The primary reason for the uniqueness of this play is, then, the subject matter, the eschatological action of the general judgment. The nonhistorical nature of such an event plus its mysterious relationship to history and the audience required a symbolism of a quite different order from that used in the earlier cycle plays. Even the medieval theological explanations of the Judgment tended to conceal more than they revealed.[15] All the cycle Doomsday plays start with the symbols used in Scripture— the trial, separation, judgment, rewards, and punishment—and modify them in the various ways listed above.

It is difficult to define the precise literary genre of this play. Perhaps the closest description would be to call the Judgment an *apocalyptic allegory* involving symbols, types, and personifications. As an allegory, it sets up a structure within which the elements take on a nonliteral, suprahistorical meaning to be determined by the basic theology underlying the action, in this case medieval eschatology. Following Bernard Spivack, we could distinguish the symbolic elements in the play (the judgment, separation, God-as-an-old-man, angels, time, place, etc.) from the incipient personification elements (deadly sins) and the universal types (good and bad souls, social types).[16] Because the allegory is apocalyptic, representing events at the breakup of the universe on the verge of transformation into eternity, the symbols are ultimately inadequate. The drama inevitably strains to portray the nonhistorical historically, the transcendent by limited means, the absolute by the relative. But the attempt is not pure fantasy, for, as Erich Auerbach has said with regard to Dante's use of allegory in a similar, if far more sophisticated, manner:

Dante, then, took over earthly historicity into his beyond. . . . But earthly existence remains always manifest, for it is always the basis of God's judgment

15. See the Appendix to the present essay for a description of the medieval symbolic interpretation of eschatological statements, especially as deriving from Origen.
16. Bernard Spivack, *Shakespeare and the Allegory of Evil* (New York, 1950), p. 67.

and hence of the eternal condition of the soul. . . . For it is precisely the absolute realization of a particular earthly personality in the place definitively assigned to it, which constitutes the Divine Judgment.[17]

The Doomsday play, of course, is the principal but not the only play in the mystery cycles that deals primarily with nonhistorical representation of transcendent realities. The most obvious example is the *Ludus Coventriae* Parliament of Heaven play, in which Psalm 84 is dramatized into a debate among Mercy, Truth, Righteousness, and Peace to convince God how to act toward the human predicament. This unusual example of a complete allegory of personification in the four cycles, though probably late, is not unrelated to the distinctive features found in the Doomsday play. The Parliament involves its own nonhistorical setting, symbolic action, nonliteral characters, and a transtemporal relation to the history of salvation. More specifically, it is based on a conflict between Mercy and other forces, as is the Last Judgment; and it carries out in terms of personifications what is portrayed in terms of God, Christ, and spirits in the Doomsday play.

Another play in which the nonhistorical element breaks in abruptly is the drama of the Death of Herod in the *Ludus Coventriae* cycle, in which Death enters on stage as a personification, not of an internal quality but of an external event. Death performs the function for Herod of the trumpeting angel in the Last Judgment play for those still on earth. In other *Ludus Coventriae* plays, personifications interrupt the historical events occasionally, but with little significance. The only characters remotely resembling anyone in the Doomsday play are the two demonic accusers in the Trial of Joseph and Mary, and the deadly sins renamed by Lucifer in the Council of the Jews.[18]

THE DOOMSDAY PLAY AND EARLY MORALITIES: SOME IMPLICATIONS

Even a cursory comparison of the Last Judgment play with the early morality plays reveals striking resemblances precisely in the five features found to mark off the Doomsday drama from the rest of the mystery cycle. The early moralities, especially *The Pride of Life, The Castle of Perseverance, Mankind,* and *Everyman,* present nonhistorical events by various forms of symbolic action conveyed by type and personified characters. All these moralities manage to relate their events to salvation history by direct narration, and all involve their

17. Erich Auerbach, *Mimesis: The Representation of Reality in Western Literature* (New York, 1953), pp. 168–69.
18. Mackenzie, *The English Moralities*, pp. 30 ff.

audience by means of identification and moralizing similar to those used in the Last Judgment play.

The early moralities, as Spivack points out in contrasting them with later moralities, focus on Christian eschatology, on the *unum necessarium*, and thus transcend both the salvation history plays that preceded them and the secular history plays that follow.[19] The setting of these moralities is nowhere and yet everywhere, at no particular time yet every instant of time is involved. Always in the present time, they are eternally relevant. Although not directly portraying the final, general judgment, all implicitly foreshadow the particular judgment, and one, *Castle of Perseverance*, explicitly treats of it (ll. 3130 ff.).[20] Of course they are more intricate in their use of time than the Doomsday play, but in their basic nonliteral, nonhistorical setting they are attempting to depict an analogous dramatic situation.

In such a setting, the action of the moralities is clearly not literal historical representation, however selectively modified. They deal in symbolic terms with thematic actions common in the nondramatic art of the Middle Ages—the dance of death, the debate of the soul and the body, the debate of the virtues after death—and with the basic conflict of soul to emerge as their dominant structure in the sixteenth century, the psychomachia. In fact, in working out these themes, the moralities seem to be developing several modes of symbolic action mentioned above as distinctive of the Doomsday play. The mystery play, for instance, in summoning mankind to give testimony before the tribunal of God is the second half of a Dance of Death morality play. As the "wicked soul" says in the York Doomsday:

> What schall we wrecchis do for drede?
> Or whedir for ferdnes may we flee,
> When we may bringe forthe no goode dede
> Before hym that oure juge schall be?
> To aske mercy us is no nede,
> For wele I wotte dampned be we.   (ll. 121–26)

This seems to be the negative side of the key passage near the death of Everyman:

19. Spivack, *Shakespeare*, p. 62. Spivack holds that the change in morality plays from the fifteenth to the sixteenth century "is essentially a shift of emphasis from spiritual to secular values—that is, from Christian eschatology, with its contempt for the world and its concentration on the post-mortem destiny of the soul, to consideration of human life in its own terms of success or failure." In my conclusion I will discuss the possible grounds for this transition.

20. The lost ending of *The Pride of Life*, according to indications from the prologue, consisted of the pleading of the Virgin Mary for the salvation of the King after death, an aspect of the judgment omitted in *The Castle of Perseverance*. See *The Non-Cycle Mystery Plays*, pp. 88 ff.

GOOD DEEDS.   All fleeth saue Good Dedes, and that am I.
EVERYMAN.   Haue mercy on me, God moost myghty,
And stande by me, thou moder and mayde, Holy Mary!

Another example would be the legal debate in the Chester Doomsday play between Christ and the demons—perhaps a form of the debate of the virtues. The separation process carried out by angels and devils, not to mention the discussion and lamentation of lost souls over their sins, has within it the remnants of a psychomachia.[21] However, the important element in this comparison of thematic action in the Doomsday and early moralities is not their identity (for the differences are marked), but their underlying similarity in using symbolic action in analogous ways to deal with nonhistorical events in their eschatological implications.

The symbolic action of the moralities embodies characters that were seen to be distinctive features of the Doomsday play—universal types and personifications. The latter, of course, are highly developed in the moralities, while barely extant in the mysteries. But the representative type plays a remarkably similar role in the Doomsday and early moralities. If, as Arnold Williams claims, the morality can be defined by its use of a "dramatic individual capable of general application," then the Doomsday use of the anonymous crowd, good and bad souls, and social types is closely related to it.[22] The moralities as allegories are a blend of personified abstractions and representative types. And their history seems to have consisted, in part, of the development of the types into historical individuals and the disappearance of the personifications. In the Doomsday play, on the other hand, the personifications are just emerging, and the types have faint traces of past historical characters (e.g., pope, emperor). The early moralities, moreover, still retain traces of the anthropomorphizing of the suprahuman world.[23]

These similarities in character portrayal lead to what is perhaps the key to most of the parallels between the Last Judgment and the early moralities—the relation of the play to the audience. In both the Doomsday play and the moralities, the audience is called to identify itself in a unique way with the center of action on stage, with the Human Race, Everyman, the crowd of souls. This identification process is not, as in

21. Spivack, *Shakespeare*, p. 72. Spivack thinks that the psychomachia was the central factor in all the moralities, even the earliest. My suggestion is that the Last Judgment is an eschatological psychomachia in symbolic form.

22. Arnold Williams, *The Drama of Medieval England* (East Lansing, Mich., 1961), p. 145.

23. God and angels appear in *Castle of Perseverance*, only angels in *Pride of Life*.

the historical mysteries, by means of theologically meaningful anachronisms or faith in the historical efficaciousness of past salvation history, but an identification with the central characters in the ever-present situation symbolically portrayed on stage, the struggle between the forces of grace and sin for the eternal destiny of the person. As previous analysis showed, the Doomsday play is implicitly a play of the present time, of the lifetime of every man in its ultimate terms. Likewise, the early moralities are complex workings-out in various symbolic forms of the same lifetime, with less emphasis on the eschatological judgment and more on the basis for that judgment in the life of each man. Both focus on the same fundamental lesson of repentance.

The moralities, of course, do not preach repentance completely cut off from the history of redemption. In fact, they use the same devices as the Doomsday plays—direct narration and recurrent allusion—to make the audience alert to the relevance of the history of salvation to the story of every man. Mankind spends the first forty-four lines reviewing divine history. Later in the same play, when Mercy alludes explicitly to redemption by Christ, she immediately links it with the final Judgment:

> How may yt be excusyde be-for the Iustyce of all
> When for eury ydyll worde we must yelde a reson?
> They haue grett ease; ther-for thei wyll take no thought.
> But how then, when the angell of hewyn xall blow the trumpe,
> Ande sey to the transgressors that wykkydly hath wrought,
> "Cum forth on-to yowur juge, and yelde yowur a-cownte!"
>
> (ll. 167–72)

Everyman shortens the historical references and expands the sacramental (ll. 28 ff., 711 ff.). *The Pride of Life* alludes several times to the redemptive force of Christ's death on the cross. *The Castle of Perseverance* contains several references to Christ's death, his example, and the sacramental consequences (ll. 335–39, 351–63, 1329 ff., 3150 ff.), but explicitly recounts the relation of Christ's Passion to man's sin, the fall of Lucifer, and the Last Judgment. The conclusion of this comes in the speech spoken by Pax:

> We [Pax and Misericordia] schal devoutly pray
> At dredful domysday,
> & I schal for us say
> that Mankynde schal have grace.   (ll. 3545–48)[24]

24. *Castle of Perseverance* goes on to recount in detail Christ's passion (ll. 3549–61). Allusions to Christ's death in *Pride of Life* are scattered (ll. 112, 383–90, 404).

CONCLUSIONS

This remarkable similarity in five elements between the Doomsday and early morality plays is hardly mere coincidence. The resemblance implies two basic conclusions that may help toward the solution of two major problems in the history of late medieval drama:

1. The first and most obvious conclusion is that the Doomsday and early moralities were fundamentally attempting to cope with analogous forms of the same problem—the symbolic representation by means of allegory of nonhistorical events directly related to the moral lives of their audience. The primary focus in the Doomsday was on explicitly eschatological events and thus produced what I have called apocalyptic allegory; the center of attention in the early moralities was on implicitly eschatological psychic events, thus producing what has come to be known as moralities, or moral allegories in dramatic form.

2. The second conclusion, much more speculative, is that the Doomsday play contained within it the grounds and conditions for the possibility of a transition from salvation-history events to psychological-moral events, and that the morality play carried out these possibilities by first portraying psychic actions overtly related to the eschaton, and later by translating these into nonsacral terms for depicting other psychic and political struggles of merely secular interest.[25]

The difficulty with these conclusions, of course, is the lack of evidence available to bolster them by showing causal relationships among external factors in late medieval drama in England. If more manuscripts and extrinsic evidence were available, it would be far easier to show the relevance of these conclusions to the solution of two major problems concerning English moralities: their very definition and their dramatic sources.

The definition problem is not settled yet. For widely varying reasons, critics have considered one or more of the following elements essential to the English morality play: dramatic allegory, moral lesson, abstractions, representative types, personifications, psychomachia, ethical choice, and focus on the individual Christian.[26] Perhaps these attempts

25. A third conclusion, also hypothetical, could be drawn regarding character development: that the Doomsday play developed by means of anonymous crowds and representative types the universal character (Everyman) that the moralities were to continue until his typicality was to be overshadowed by the particularity of other characters in the moralities. This same character eventually disappeared (along with personifications) into sixteenth-century political allegory and historical drama. See Spivack, *Shakespeare*, pp. 62–63, 93–94.

26. Mackenzie tried to eliminate all inadequate definitions suggested in his day. For instance, he opposed E. K. Chambers's contention that all morality characters

at "essential" definition, in trying to differentiate moralities from mysteries so sharply, have overlooked the morality impulse latent within the Doomsday play. If such a tendency exists, providing a link between mystery and morality, then a radical differentiation will be not only difficult but fundamentally impossible because of an intrinsic connection (by way of eschatology) between the external history of redemption and the psychological history of moral struggle. The basic distinction, therefore, would have to be based on the historicity or nonhistoricity of the situation, events, and characters represented in the drama. The only other ground for a distinction, then, would be purely formal, thus providing for a more abstract but perhaps more adequate definition.[27]

The other problem, the question of the sources of morality plays, is more directly relevant to our conclusions. There is no question of a lack of nondramatic influences on the moralities. Critics point to influences from medieval sermons, the Dance of Death, literary allegories, folk origins, scholastic philosophy, etc.[28] An interesting fact appears, however, when the manner of influence of medieval sermons is examined. According to Owst,[29] the sermon influenced the morality tradition in three ways—in the use of allegory, in dramatic treatment of death, and in the function of dramatized debate between abstract, supernatural,

---

were abstractions. He also disagreed with A. W. Ward's notion that morality characters are "personified abstractions . . . enforcing a moral truth." Mackenzie also rejected J. P. Collier's claim that such "characters are allegorical, abstract, or symbolical." His own definition discounts God, angels, and individuals as characters in moralities; it runs as follows: "A Morality is a play, allegorical in structure, which has for its main object the teaching of some lesson for the guidance of life, and in which the principal characters are personified abstractions or highly universalized types" (*The English Moralities*, pp. 2–9). Craig claims the essential of a morality is "dramatized allegory," but does not clarify what this means (*English Religious Drama*, p. 338). Spivack stresses the role of the psychomachia as the essence of English moralities, *Shakespeare*, pp. 72–73. F. M. Salter in his *Medieval Drama in Chester* (Toronto, 1955) describes a morality as a "play in which all the characters are abstractions" (p. 10). David Bevington tries to capture the genre with his description: "The genre was characterized primarily by the use of allegory to convey a moral lesson about religious or civil conduct, presented through the medium of abstractions or representative social characters" (*From Mankind to Marlowe* [Cambridge, Mass., 1962], p. 9). Kolve gives no definition but distinguishes moralities from mysteries by the focus of the former on "ethical choice" and the use of representative type characters (*Play Called Corpus Christi*, pp. 3, 224).

27. In this light, Mackenzie's and Bevington's definitions seem most satisfactory, as long as "religious conduct" and "guidance of life" are wide enough to include the eschatological dimension.

28. See Owst, *Literature and Pulpit*, pp. 526–45; Craig, *English Religious Drama*, p. 342; A. P. Rossiter, *English Drama from Early Times to the Elizabethans* (New York, 1950), pp. 81 ff.; Salter, *Medieval Drama in Chester*, pp. 10–11; Williams, *Drama of Medieval England*, pp. 42 ff.

29. Owst, pp. 526–27, 537–40, 544.

or representative characters. Yet these three ways of influence are identical with the key features distinctive of the Doomsday play, the very features that mark it off from the preceding mystery plays. Thus it seems clear that both the Doomsday play and the early moralities were influenced by the same source (medieval sermons) in the same three ways. This seems more than a hint that they are basically the same type of play.

But within dramatic tradition itself, critics are strangely silent about the dramatic sources of morality plays. Some point to a twelfth-century Latin *Antichristus* play with a few personifications (and no extant consequences) or to lost Paternoster plays that a leading critic has claimed were actually miracle plays.[30]

If the five elements of the Doomsday play are as clearly distinctive as I have tried to show (and the influences from sermons corroborates the evidence), then the puzzle about dramatic sources for the moralities is not as mysterious as critics say. Not that we would be able to prove by documents chronological causality, but our conclusions merely show that the eschatological allegory of the Last Judgment as performed in the fourteenth and fifteenth centuries held within itself the conditions for the development of a full-fledged morality play. These became actualized within the cycles themselves in the *Ludus Coventriae* and outside them in the early moralities. But grounding the transition was the play of the Last Judgment, the ultimate in English morality drama.

APPENDIX: The General Judgment in Medieval Theology

It is important for understanding the thesis of this essay to see the two schools of medieval theology, in their interpretation of the Last Judgment, as elements in the overall development of Christian understanding of eschatological statements. Theologians in the early church, accepting the Day of Judgment without much reflection on its nature, generally assumed it would take place as literally described

30. Craig, *English Religious Drama*, p. 342. Even if it could be shown that the Tegernsee *Antichristus* play or the Limoges *Sponsus* influenced English moralities by means of their use of personification, it would still fit in with my general thesis. For both the *Sponsus* and the *Antichristus* are eschatological plays. The *Sponsus* dramatizes a scene from Matthew 25:1–13 which is a symbolic variant on the resurrection-judgment process; the *Antichristus*, as Karl Young notes, is based on the "general speculative notion of a battle between God and the devil at the end of time" (*The Drama of the Medieval Church* [Oxford, 1933], p. 369). The Antichrist is a familiar apocalyptic figure who was given many interpretations, both historical and nonhistorical, in Jewish and Christian theology.

in the imaginative apocalyptic chapters of Scripture.[31] In the third century, exegetes, aware of the many contradictions in the imaginative accounts and influenced by neo-Platonism and allegorical hermeneutics, became divided in their interpretation of such passages as Matthew 25:31–46.

One school continued to reaffirm the imaginative cosmological account as literal history (e.g., Hippolytus, Tertullian, Lactantius).This literalist strand continued unreflectively with very little development in the works of many theologians, except for the gradual reinterpretation of the more obvious contradictions by resorting to nonliteral explanations (e.g., the general rejection of Lactantius' chiliastic thousand-year judgment process). This literalist strand continued on through the Middle Ages with theologians tending to mix literalist-imaginative interpretations, especially of the place of Judgment, with symbolic interpretation of the Judgment process described in Scripture.

The other school sprang from the Alexandrian theologian Origen (A.D. 185–253). In accord with his "spiritualizing" hermeneutics, he held that the General Resurrection and Judgment, although one real event, would not take place in time or in a particular place (any more than creation took place in time and place). The Judgment was to be completely the work of divine power, take place instantaneously within the consciences of men, and be a "gathering" only in the sense that all men would pay homage to Christ's authority.[32] The apocalyptic details, such as clouds, angels, trumpets, seats, books, etc., were all to be understood allegorically. Origen's symbolization of Matthew 25 was never condemned, as were several of his opinions, but began the major strand of eschatology that has led by development (and reaction) to most modern symbolic interpretations of the Scriptural "last things."

The course of this symbolic tradition continued in chapter 20 of Augustine's *City of God*, in which he interprets the Last Judgment procedures as a divinely produced, instantaneous "intuition" by each person of his own and others' sins and sentences. This mental judgment process was a subject of debate among theologians, with Peter Lombard

---

31. For an excellent treatise on the growth of theological insight into the particular and general judgments, see J. Rivière, "Jugement," *Dictionnaire de théologie catholique*, vol. 8 (Paris, 1925), cols. 1722–1828.

32. Origen, *Commentary on Matthew* 14:9, 24:30 ff., 25:31 ff., ed. and trans. from the Latin by Erich Klostermann, in *Die Griechischen Christlichen Schriftsteller*, vol. 11, Commentarium Series, 50, 51, 70 (Leipzig, 1933). Cf. R. P. C. Hanson, *Allegory and Event: A Study of the Sources and Significance of Origen's Interpretation of Scripture* (Richmond, Va., 1959), pp. 333–58; Henri de Lubac, *Histoire et esprit* (Paris, 1950), p. 199; Origen, *Contra Celsum*, trans. Henry Chadwick (Cambridge, 1953), p. 376 n.

(1095–1160) summarizing the positions in his *IV Sentences*, d. 47–48, but not taking a position himself. Lombard also collected the other symbolic interpretations that had become part of the patristic tradition (e.g., the renovating unearthly "fire" before the Judgment; the uncertainty of the cosmology at the last day; the meaning of "Josaphat" from Joel 3:2 as not a literal place but simply the Hebrew for "judgment of the Lord"). In regard to the place of Judgment, Lombard upholds the tradition in favor of an elevated congregation in the air near Mount Olivet (based on I Thess. 4:7).

Richard of Saint Victor (d. 1173) reaffirmed the Origen-Augustine position on the instantaneous judgment process within the conscience caused by the "light of divine wisdom."[33] Bonaventure (1217–74) agrees with the symbolic interpretation of the signs preceding the Last Judgment (angelic voice, command, trumpet, etc.), and of the judgment process from the Book of Life as an instantaneous awareness not involving historical time. His position on the place of the Judgment is more literal, but he grants that if necessary the whole assembly will take place in the air by means of divine power.[34] Albertus Magnus, the teacher of Aquinas, clearly held for a symbolic interpretation of the Judgment procedures *(mentalis non vocalis)* and of the trumpet, the fire, and other matters leading into the Judgment.[35] He defends the use of imaginative language *(corporalis similitudo)* in apocalyptic descriptions as suitable for the uneducated audience of the gospels. Regarding the entire question of place as a waste of time, he agrees that Mount Olivet would be "more appropriate" than other suggestions.[36]

Thomas Aquinas shows in his own thought a recapitulation of the entire development up to his day. In his early works (c. 1256), he held the "mixed" position of Albert: the signs preceding the Judgment are allegorized; the Judgment process, both examination and sentencing *(totum illud iudicium)* is mental and instantaneous rather than historical.[37] He hesitates before the problem of place. On the one hand he

---

33. *De Iudicaria Potestate, PL* 196, cols. 1181–86.
34. *In IV Sent.*, d. 43, q. 2, a. 1–3; d. 48, *dubia* I.
35. *In IV Sent.*, d. 47, q. 1.
36. Ibid., d. 48, q. 6.
37. Thomas Aquinas, *In IV Sent.*, d. 47, q. 1, a. 1, q. 2: "Videtur quod illa sententia et totum iudicium mentaliter expleatur"; this is repeated in the *Supplementum*, which consists of excerpts from his commentary on the *Sentences* attached to the *Summa Theologiae* to complete the latter when it was left unfinished by Aquinas, q. 88, a. 1, q. 2c: "Procerto definiri non potest, tamen probabilius aestimatur quod totum illud iudicium, et quoad discussionem, et quoad accusationem malorum et commendationem bonorum, et quoad sententiam de utrisque, mentaliter perficiatur." This nonliteral interpretation is repeated in the undated *Responsio ad Magistrum Joannem de Vercellis, Opusc.* IX, a. 27, where Aquinas says: "Probabilius

allegorizes some of the place details (e.g., clouds, right hand), but on the other he admits as "probable" that "it can be gathered from Scripture" that Christ will return near Mount Olivet.[38] However, because he had admitted earlier that the entire experience of space and time will be different after the *renovatio mundi*, which precedes the Judgment, he is forced to go into a long cosmological word game to account for the nature of the suprahistorical "new earth."[39] In addition, Aquinas clearly asserts that Christ as Judge will appear as glorified with his risen body, which is not limited by the normal experiences of time and space.[40] In brief, the early Aquinas did not work out the consequences of holding a "mixed" position in which certain historical elements were transcended (especially temporal process), but other elements remained as before.

In a later work, his commentary on St. Matthew's gospel, written sometime after 1259, Aquinas shows that he has been explicitly influenced by Origen's spiritualizing interpretations.[41] Quoting Augustine against Lactantius, he reaffirms the procedures described in Matthew 25 as an *interior instinctus* produced by the power of God, and not a temporal process. He then takes up the question of location: first, in the same commentary, he follows Origen's allegorizing of the *sedes* to mean the saints and angels who are the media of promulgating instantaneously the *interior instinctus;* second, he presents both the literal or semiliteral interpretation of the separation of good men from evil *(potest dici,* as he puts it), but then gives Origen's spiritualizing of this "separation" to mean merely the final remuneration itself; third, he allows that "we can understand" the gathering as an event in a particular place, but then presents Origen's position that the whole affair will be a *congregatio spiritualis.*[42]

Unfortunately, Aquinas never finished the *Summa*, leaving us with no final word on eschatology beyond this scriptural commentary of his middle period. However, it is clear that he had moved from a

---

videtur quod [sententia iudicis] sit spiritualis, quia et alia quae tunc, spiritualiter divina virtute agentur." His discussion of the "signs" occurs in *In IV Sent.*, d. 47, q. 1, a. 1; d. 48, q. 1, a. 4.

38. *In IV Sent.*, d. 48, q. 1, a. 4, q. 4; *Supplementum*, q. 88, a. 4.

39. Ibid., d. 48, a. 2.

40. *In IV Sent.*, d. 47, q. 1, a. 2, q. 3.

41. *In Matt.* 25; see also ibid., 19. Aquinas refers to Origen by name several times in this section, apparently making use of the quotations he had collected in his *Catena Aurea* from Origen's *Tract 34*.

42. Loc. cit. In his *Catena Aurea*, Aquinas had collected Origen's words that the Judgment will not involve a local assembly: "non localiter intelligamus quod congregabuntur ante eum omnes gentes . . . non enim in aliquo loco apparebit [divinitas Christi]." The *Catena* is dated around 1264. See *Catena Aurea, In Matt.* 25:31.

mixed toward a pure "Origenistic" position on the suprahistorical nature of the Last Judgment. Almost all traces of historical time and space as experienced by men in their present state have been eliminated from his interpretation of Matthew 25. In the commentary on the gospel, the Judgment is an eschatological event in which the *virtus divina* enters to transform the world and transcend the limits of historical space and time. Like the creation event which "began" time, the "end of time" is an event essentially different from the occurrences in chronological salvation history. The account from Jewish apocalyptic literature was recognized for what it was, an imaginative presentation in historical terms of a suprahistorical event.

The medieval theologians, of course, did not work out the consequences of many of their symbolical interpretations of this event. Most of their explanation was negative, denying the imaginative details as literally true. It was left for later thinkers to present various explanations of the positive meaning of the Last Judgment in terms of existentialist philosophy, historical realization, and so on.[43]

It is sufficient, however, for establishing the thesis of this essay on the Doomsday play to be aware that the theological tradition from Origen onward contained a definite trend toward symbolic interpretations of the general Judgment. Thus the first feature mentioned in the essay—the suprahistorical situation—had a foundation in the theological background of the age, and implicitly conveyed itself to the audience as something other than literal history. The other four "problem features" are merely functions of this symbolic event: the actions, characters, audience relationship, and use of narration. Because the fundamental nature of the Judgment event was suprahistorical, the components of the dramatization of the event are basically different from those in plays representing actions with some basis in the linear chronology of salvation history.

43. See Karl Rahner, "The Hermeneutics of Eschatological Assertions," *Theological Investigations* (Baltimore, 1966), IV, 323–46; Neill Q. Hamilton, "The Last Things in the Last Decade," *Interpretation*, XIV (1960), 131–42.

Edgar T. Schell

16. On the Imitation of Life's Pilgrimage in *The Castle of Perseverance*

Ever since Creizenach compared the allegory in the morality drama with Prudentius's fourth-century *Psychomachia* there has been relative unanimity among scholars in seeing such plays as *The Castle of Perseverance, Everyman,* and *Mankind* as dramatic versions of the Prudentian allegory.[1] Indeed this conception of the plays is so firmly established that a recent book on medieval drama could describe *Everyman* as "an ethical debate between personified Virtues and Vices"[2] without raising a murmur of critical dissent—in spite of the fact that the Vices, if there are any in *Everyman,* do not even meet the Virtues, let alone engage them in ethical debate. Of course a case might be made for seeing Everyman's progress to salvation as the consequence of an internal debate,[3] but it is nonetheless true that the progress and not the debate is dramatized by the play. *Everyman* offers, then, a rather special example of the violence necessary to fit at least one dramatic fact under this critical formula; and perhaps its reluctance to slide into place justifies us in asking how easily other plays may be made to fit.

Let me hasten to make clear that I do not propose to reject a formula which has received such widespread critical support. There is ample

[Reprinted from the *Journal of English and Germanic Philology,* LXVII (1968), 235–48, by permission of the author and the publisher.]

1. Wilhelm Creizenach, *Geschichte des neuren Dramas* (Halle, 1893), II, 463. Cf. E. K. Chambers, *The Medieval Stage* (Oxford, 1903), II, 154; W. Roy Mackenzie, *The English Moralities from the Point of View of Allegory* (Boston, 1914), p. ix, et passim; Robert Lee Ramsay, ed., Skelton's *Magnyfycence,* EETS e.s. 98 (London, 1908), p. cxlix, et passim; Bernard Spivack, *Shakespeare and the Allegory of Evil* (New York, 1958), passim; and David Bevington, *From "Mankind" to Marlowe* (Cambridge, Mass., 1962), passim.

2. Glynne Wickham, *Early English Stages, 1300–1600* (London, 1959), I, 234. Wickham's description actually applies to the whole of the morality drama, and it is perhaps a measure of the extent to which "morality" calls up "conflict" or "Psychomachia" that he should have chosen *Everyman,* perhaps the least likely play, as his sole example.

3. Cf. Thomas van Laan, "*Everyman:* A Structural Analysis," *PMLA,* LXXVIII (1963), 471. Van Laan finds a "subdued version of the Psychomachia" in *Everyman* because at the end of the play Everyman is presented with a series of specific *remedia* for the sins with which he had been associated at the beginning.

evidence in almost every morality play of the importance of the psychomachia metaphor in its most general sense to the vision of human experience which informs the plays. But there is, I think, room for a readjustment of critical emphasis when we consider the plays as single and organic imitations of action rather than collections of more or less discrete homiletic episodes.

If we think in terms of individual episodes we have no difficulty in multiplying examples of the Conflict of Vice and Virtue—the siege of the Castle of Perseverance is closest in form to the battle in Prudentius's poem. But those who have argued most vigorously that the moralities are from first to last dramatizations of the psychomachia have been forced to bring in supplementary metaphors to account for the action of an entire play, that synthesis of episodes around the central figure of Mankind which affords each play its beginning, middle, and end. Thus, while Robert Lee Ramsay defines the moralities as dramatizations of the "conflict allegory," the formula he uses to describe the morality pattern of action—Innocence, Temptation, Life in Sin, Repentance, and Salvation—is finally grounded in a supplementary allegory of "Humanity with his fall into sin and subsequent repentance."[4] And the situation has not changed very much in the sixty years since Ramsay's seminal essay first appeared. Bernard Spivack finds it necessary to supplement the "image of moral conflict," which he argues is "the basic metaphor of the morality drama," with the "image of moral sequence," which binds together the episodes of conflict into a coherent whole.

Spivack goes on to observe that "outside the drama the natural image for such a sequence is the allegorical journey," but "such a journey governs the structure of only three plays, the relatively late 'wit' moralities. Otherwise it is absent from the morality drama."[5] Taking Spivack's hint that the natural form of this structural metaphor is the allegorical journey, I would like to approach our earliest and most inclusive morality, *The Castle of Perseverance*, just the other way around: to argue that what has been taken to be a supplementary metaphor is really the primary metaphor, that the *Castle* may be read as an imitation of the action of life's pilgrimage as that action was formulated in a number of allegorical poems written during the late Middle Ages, but an imitation in peculiarly dramatic terms. In brief, I intend to argue that the *Castle* does not differ from a poem like Deguilleville's *Le Pèlerinage de la vie humaine* (c. 1330) in the action which it imitates, but merely in the means through which it imitates that action.

4. Ramsay, pp. cxlix–cliii. Ramsay goes on to suggest that the *Castle* is made up of two allegories which "might even be separated," the Psychomachia and the allegory of Humanity (p. cliv).

5. Spivack, pp. 100–101.

I

In speaking of the *Castle* and *Le Pèlerinage* as imitations of action I am taking what I assume to be Aristotle's meaning of the phrase in his definition of the narrative arts; that is, I am assuming that the imitation of an action is a rendering in the "language" appropriate to a particular narrative medium, whether music, drama, or poetry, of that synthesizing principle which distinguishes plot from a series of casually related episodes, that principle which subsumes the episodes under an intelligible pattern with a beginning, a middle, and an end. It is this principle of intelligibility, this perception of the relationships among discrete episodes, which lies behind plot, informing its order and emphasis. And it is this perception of an essential unity in events which plot imitates in sensuous form.

Aristotle defines the quality of that perception in the most neutral terms, characterizing the best plots as those held together by necessity or probability. Clearly, however, events appear necessary or probable only in a defining context; and in fortunate times events may cohere in necessary or probable patterns which are not determined solely by reason or literal experience, but rather by a cultural unity manifested in myth or ritual. Such a defining mythic pattern was developed in the literature of life's pilgrimage, where events were so organized as to reveal the archetypal shape of Mankind's developing moral life in conformity with Christian doctrine.

One difficulty in talking about the literature of the pilgrimage, however, is that the term "pilgrimage" itself is ambiguous. It may refer either to the defining perception of the nature of man's life as a journey toward eternity, manifested in a variety of travel images, or it may refer to the extended form of the pilgrimage metaphor, the narrative motif in which that defining perception is customarily imitated. These two meanings most often work together; and thus in such works as Deguilleville's *Le Pèlerinage* and Bunyan's *Pilgrim's Progress* (1678) the narrative journeys give objective and consistent form to the belief that man in the world is "but in exile and wilderness, out of his kyndely contre,"[6] and that the process of "man's whole life is a pilgrimage, either from God, as Cain's, or from himself, as Abel's."[7] But the fictional journey of a pilgrim through a symbolic landscape is itself only an imitation of the action of the pilgrimage in terms appropriate to narrative poetry; and theoretically at least we might have analogous imitations of the

---

6. *Myroure for Lewde Men,* quoted in G. R. Owst, *Literature and the Pulpit in Medieval England* (Cambridge, 1933), p. 103.

7. Samuel Purchas, *Hakluytus Posthumus, or Purchas, His Pilgrimes* (Glasgow, 1905–7), I, 138. While Purchas's book was relatively late, the attitude is medieval.

soul's journey toward God in music or drama which would take different forms, using "languages" appropriate to those media. We might say that a work belongs to the literature of the pilgrimage primarily, then, because it imitates the metaphorical journey of life, and only secondarily because of the way in which it imitates that journey.

I realize that such a definition slides almost imperceptibly into universality, drawing thereby any work concerned with spiritual development under the heading of the pilgrimage, at least analogically. But it is sufficiently limited for the purpose I have in mind: that is, to point in a general way to the necessity of maintaining a distinction between plot and action. And the elasticity in the definition is checked in the works with which I am concerned because they share a common model of the shape and rhythm of life's journey. Such poems as *Le Pèlerinage, Reason and Sensuality* (translated by Lydgate in 1412 from *Les Echecs amoreux*), *The Voyage of the Wandering Knight* (1581, translated by William Goodyear from the French of Jean Cartigny), and Book I of *The Faerie Queene* tend to follow the same sequence of action in presenting the spiritual lives of their central characters. The narrative journeys in these poems serve to imitate that spiritual sequence in particular plot forms, each quite different from the others but all demonstrably related to the same stock. If we can find the same sequence at the heart of *The Castle of Perseverance*, we can conclude that the *Castle* imitates the same mode of human experience, and we can assign the differences in the mode of imitation to the different demands made by the theater and the different opportunities it offers.

The model of experience to which all of these works refer is defined explicitly at the end of a parable assigned, perhaps falsely, to Saint Bernard of Clairvaux. In the parable itself the character of life's pilgrim is merged with the biblical Prodigal Son in the figure of Filius Regis, and the parable records his wandering from the Paradise of Good Conscience into regions of sin, and thence, in company with the heavenly guides Fear and Hope, to the Castle of Sapience, where he is prepared for reunion with God. This symbolic journey is reduced at the end of the parable to a single moral formula expressing in four stages the course of man's spiritual development:

Primo enim est egens et insipiens: postea, praeceps et temerarius in prosperis; deinde, trepidus et pusillanimus in adversis: postremo, providus, et eruditus, et perfectus in regno charitatis.[8]

That formula is in turn reflected in the most extended treatment of

8. Bernard of Clairvaux, "Parabola I," *Opera genuina* (Paris, 1839), III, 446.

life's pilgrimage, Deguilleville's *Le Pèlerinage de la vie humaine,* written a half-century before *The Castle of Perseverance* appeared.

The action of Deguilleville's poem proceeds through three closely intertwined journeys: first, the pilgrim's temporal journey from birth to death; second, the pilgrim's spiritual progress from a state of flawed innocence to salvation; and finally the journey of the plot, the pilgrim's physical journey through a symbolic landscape, by means of which the temporal and spiritual journeys are given sensuous form. The motif of the physical journey provides a certain narrative tension in each of the encounters between the pilgrim and the personified vices and virtues, but by far the greater part of the burden of the poem is carried by long passages of dialogue between the pilgrim and the moral personifications who instruct him in their signification and in the consequences of the mode of life they represent. Dialogue is, of course, a form of action, as dramatists know; and the action which all parts of *Le Pèlerinage* are designed to reveal is the developing shape of the moral life of mankind, the metaphorical journey of the soul of the pilgrim through the land of its exile. That journey provides the basic structural pattern of the poem, and that pattern reflects in turn the pattern of the Bernardine parable.

Briefly, the pattern is composed of four spiritual states or stages of action. During the first, the state of flawed Innocence, the pilgrim is, like Filius Regis, "egens et insipiens." He wants to travel to the New Jerusalem, but he casts off the armor with which Grace Dieu has clothed him because he believes that he can protect himself from life's dangers. At the crossroads of Idleness and Industry his essential weakness is revealed and he enters the second stage of his journey, his Fall from Innocence. Under the guidance of his Youth he passes beyond the hedge of penance and into a nightmarish land of sin, where he remains for some time living his Life in Sin. The monastic Deguilleville conceives this third stage of man's spiritual journey as a series of assaults on the pilgrim. Venus and Gluttony tie him to the tail of a swine; Sloth binds him with her cords; he is harried by the hounds of Conspiracyon and beaten by Worldly Gladness. Finally, after a series of grotesque adventures, the pilgrim is driven to take refuge on a rock in the Sea of the World. And there, lost and frightened as Filius Regis is "trepidus et pusillanimus in adversis," he prays to God to "brynge me throgh thy grete myght, / Into the wey I may go ryght."[9] Immediately upon this evidence of his repentance Grace Dieu appears in the Ship of the Church to carry him off to the "Castle" of the Cistercians,

9. I have used Lydgate's translation (1426), published as *The Pilgrimage of the Life of Man,* EETS e.s. 77, 83, 92 (London, 1899–1904), ll. 21699–700.

the monastic order to which Deguilleville himself belonged. Inside the castle he is set to penitential disciplines, bound in the cords of Obedience, introduced to Charity, and instructed by Lady Lesson. Like Filius Regis in the Castle of Sapience, he is there prepared to enter into the New Jerusalem.

That sequence—Innocence, Temptation and Fall, Life in Sin, Realization and Repentance leading to salvation—is one of the patterns of action of life's pilgrimage; the spiritual progress of the pilgrim through that sequence is one form of the action of life's pilgrimage; and a narrative journey like that in Le Pèlerinage is one way of imitating that action. With sufficient leisure we might trace that pattern through series of late medieval and Renaissance poems which provide almost a continuum of less transparent imitations of life's pilgrimage, poems such as Reason and Sensuality, The Faerie Queene, and Gavin Douglas's King Hart in which the narrative surface becomes more opaque, the terms of reference become more secular, and finally the narrative journey drops away altogether, leaving its trace in the use of place as an index of moral state.[10] What unites these poems is that they share a common model of action. And it is chiefly in sharing the same model that The Castle of Perseverance imitates the action of the pilgrimage of life.

II

The playing area for which the Castle was written, the area represented in the well-known diagram of a circular platea with mansions set at fixed points around its perimeter and the castle standing in the center, realizes in theatrical terms the moral landscapes of the narrative pilgrimages.[11] As the play develops, the mansions take on moral qualities, if they do not have them at the beginning through symbolic

10. I refer to an aesthetic rather than a chronological development. One of Bunyan's nineteenth-century editors, Adam Clarke, constructed a genealogy of the Pilgrim's Progress, demonstrably false in its particulars, but right, I think, in its feeling for an essential similarity among the plays and poems: "John Bunyan seems to have borrowed his Pilgrim's Progress from Bernard's Isle of Man; Bernard his Isle of Man from Fletcher's Purple Island; Fletcher took his plan from Spenser's Faery Queen; Spenser his Faery Queen from Gavin Douglas' King Hart; and Douglas his plan from the old mysteries and moralities which prevailed in his time." Quoted in James Blanton Wharey, A Study of the Sources of Bunyan's Allegories (Baltimore, 1904), p. 79.

11. In a rather different way the plans of the Lucerne Mysteries and the Valenciennes stage do the same thing: see Richard Southern, The Seven Ages of the Theater (New York, 1964), pp. 105, 107. All three plans are of course consequences of a single and fixed playing area as opposed to the multiple and mobile stages of the pageant wagons.

decoration or the symbology of their arrangement, and throughout the play they serve, like the Valley of Despair, the Castle of Obedience, or the Castle of Alma, as physical indices of Mankind's moral state. The *platea* itself, the neutral ground between, is the place of moral change where the first stirrings of the spirit toward God or the world are given physical form in movements toward the symbolic scaffolds.

As Shakespeare, by opening *Macbeth* with the weird sisters, defines one dimension of the moral world of the play, so the anonymous author of the *Castle*, by opening with the vaunts of the World, the Flesh, and the Devil, defines one dimension of the moral world through which Mankind must make his journey. In spectacle, diction, and thought these characters imitate in the Aristotelian sense a mode of life open to Mankind. They are physical manifestations of the mode of life— World, with his banners under which "bryth basnetis be bateryd, and backys ar schent,"[12] and Flesh, standing as a "brod brustun gutte on these touris" (l. 209). And they reveal to the audience the full quality of that life, "with lystys and lykinge i-lent" (l. 238), and the end to which it leads, "tyl thei be dyth to dethys dent" (l. 169). For the moment the issue is the Psychomachia in its eternal and cosmic sense, the timeless opposition between good and evil, between soul and body, focused in and on all of mankind. That opposition remains throughout the play as the palpable atmosphere in which the action takes place: good and evil are its lateral coordinates as heaven and hell are its vertical coordinates. And for the moment the character of Mankind is simply irrelevant. We are concerned with timeless, impersonal conflict, and timeless force. But with the entrance of Mankind we are thrust very quickly into time. The focus of the play narrows to the movements of a representative human soul between the poles of good and evil, toward the goals of heaven and hell; and thenceforth the central action imitated in the play by all of the resources of drama is the development of the intelligible shape of Mankind's moral life.

At his entrance Mankind begins almost at once to speak of the processes of his life in metaphors of travel, and throughout the scene of his temptation the language of travel persists as a way of manifesting the moral process at issue.[13] He alludes first in a telescoping metaphor to the temporal journey which has brought him to that moment of discretion when he must choose his way of life:

12. Ll. 161–62 in *The Macro Plays*, ed. Frederick Furnivall and Alfred Pollard, EETS e.s. 91 (London, 1904). Further citations in my text are to this edition.
13. Cf. Henry Medwall's *Nature* (1490–1501), *John the Evangelist* (1517–18), and *Lusty Juventus* (1547–53), in each of which an extended travel metaphor is used in the same way.

> This nyth I was of my moder born,
> Fro my moder I walke, I wende.
> Ful feynt and febyl I fare you biforn.
> . . . .
> I not wedyr to gon ne to lende,
> To help my-self mydday nyn morn.   (ll. 276–82)

And then he turns to define his moral state. Flanked by the Good and Bad Angels, who would draw him in different directions, Mankind, like Deguilleville's pilgrim, would "folwe be strete and stalle, / The aungyl that cam fro heven trone" (ll. 316–17). But the course offered by the Bad Angel tempts him, and he quickly finds himself at a moral crossroad:

> Whom to folwe, wetyn I ne may!
> I stonde and stodye, and gynne to rave.
> I wolde be ryche in gret a-ray,
> And fayn I wolde my soule save!
> As wynde in watyr I wave.
> Thou woldest to the Werld I me toke;
> And he wolde that I it forsoke.   (ll. 376–82)

The issue is literally travel in both the physical and moral senses. "Cum on, Man," the Bad Angel cries, "Where-of hast thou care? / Go we to the Werld, I rede thee, blyve" (ll. 385–86). And as Mankind turns to follow him, the Good Angel calls, "A! nay, Man! For cristis blod, / Cum agayn be strete and style!" (ll. 403–4). But just as Deguilleville's pilgrim is led from the proper path by the personification of his youth, so Mankind is led off by the Bad Angel's specious arguments on the opportunities of youth: "With the Werld thou mayst be bold / Tyl thou be sexty wynter hold. / Wanne thy nose waxit cold, / Thanne mayst thou drawe to goode" (ll. 418–21). Thus the scene of temptation turns on the same mode of travel with which it began. The physical weakness of Mankind's youth translates itself into moral weakness; and for all his yearning for "heven trone" Mankind is revealed to be, like Filius Regis, "egens et insipiens."

That scene is played entirely in the neutral space surrounding the castle, which has not yet assumed its symbolic meaning. No journey to a particular place is postulated for Mankind in the plot—the Good Angel's offering is remarkably vague. Nor is Mankind explicitly identified as the pilgrim of life. But his situation in the opening scene is precisely that of Deguilleville's pilgrim at the beginning of his journey; and the action imitated in that brief scene is essentially the action of the first 12,000 lines of *Le Pèlerinage*, stripped of Deguilleville's compendium of doctrine and presented dramatically in the temptation of

Mankind rather than under the figure of an allegorical journey. Mankind has a spiritual goal to which he aspires, a goal as yet beyond his range but represented for the audience in the Deus scaffold. And the Bad Angel leads him from that goal toward the World and death. The sustained physical journey of the narrative poems is not used in the *Castle* as a plot motif in part because the physical representation of action onstage enforces a stricter separation of modes of being than the imaginative representations of narrative poetry, which take place in the more elastic theater of the mind, and in part because a sustained journey is at best awkwardly represented on stage. It is part of the "language" of narrative poetry. Nevertheless the sense of the journey of life is sustained throughout the scene in the metaphors of travel. And at the end of the scene, as at important moments throughout the play, the underlying action is manifested in physical movement, as Mankind and the Bad Angel set off for the Mundus scaffold, weaving a wandering path as symbol of a long journey.[14]

Throughout the middle section of the play the major stages of the action are marked by physical movement, and the playing area becomes a moral landscape as clear as that in *Le Pèlerinage*. The scaffolds as well as those who act upon them objectify Mankind's moral state. As he leaves one or another behind in the course of his journey, we are made to see the successive stages of the moral life, just as we are made aware of similar stages through the articulated landscapes of the poems. The journey to the Mundus scaffold initiates Mankind's spiritual journey into sin. He arrives with visions of pleasure, although he retains the comforting thought that he can repent when his nose grows cold. Thus at the base of the scaffold he is met by Folly, to whom he pledges his friendship. When he meets the World, however, he is ready to forgo heaven entirely for worldy pleasure: "Of my soule I have non rewthe. / What schulde I recken of domysday, / So that I be ryche and of gret a-ray?" (ll. 609–11). And consequently, to signal this advance, "ascendit Humanum Genus ad Mundum." Enlisted in the service of the World and symbolically dressed in "robes ryve / With ryche a-ray," Mankind is sent back across the *platea* in the company of Backbiter, symbolic of the way to get on in the world, to the scaffold of Covetous, who will henceforth be his chief guide. There his general self-indulgence sharpens to more aggressive, more particular sins, as he vows under the influence of Covetous that "I

14. That action is not indicated in the text. I am following the suggestion of Richard Southern, who argues that the action is necessary because of the long speeches on and about the Mundus scaffold before Mankind reaches it (*The Medieval Theater in the Round* [London, 1957], p. 156).

schal never begger bede / Mete nyn drynke, ne hevene blys; / Rather
or I schulde hym clothe or fede, / He schulde sterve and stynke, i-wis"
(ll. 874–77). Through Covetous, Mankind is introduced to the rest of
the Seven Deadly Sins. But he does not travel to meet them as he
might in a narrative poem, for the stage does not offer an infinite
number of places as does an imagined landscape. Theatrical economy
rather turns the journey around. Covetous calls them forth from their
places on the other scaffolds, and they come in procession across the
platea to be counsellors of Mankind. Under their instruction Mankind's spiritual journey continues step by step toward the pit. Like
Filius Regis, he has become "praeceps et temerarius in prosperis," and
with a glance at the preacher who lies behind every morality play he is
careful to point out for the audience whence he has come and where he
is going:

> Mankynde I am called by kynde,
> With cursydnesse in costis knet;
> In sowre swettenesse my syth I sende,
> With seven synnes sadde be-set.
> Mekyl myrthes I move in mynde,
> With melody at my mowthis met.
> My prowde pouer schal I not pende
> Tyl I be put in peynys pyt,
> To helle hent fro hens.   (ll. 1241–49)

At this point the focus of the play widens again, and we are made
to see the drama of Mankind's life in terms of the cosmic drama it
briefly realizes. For a moment Mankind becomes merely a pawn in the
conflict between Vice and Virtue, as the Good Angel calls for Shrift
and Penance to halt Mankind's evil course. This first of the play's
peripeteias is in some measure dramatically incoherent, for Mankind's
repentance does not grow out of the developing line of the action; it is
rather imposed upon him by characters who in effect descend from the
machine. Mankind repents because Penance touches him with his
lance, and only that magical moment intervenes between Mankind's
denial of his conscience and his acknowledgment that "a seed of sorrow is in me set" (l. 1406). The logic of the scene is thus mythic rather
than dramatic, a response to the model of life's journey rather than to
the particular reality of Mankind's state of mind or his situation.
Mankind's resolute march to hell is arrested by the forces of virtue,
just as the pilgrim's wandering in the regions of sin is ended by the
appearance of Grace Dieu; but unlike the pilgrim, Mankind is saved in
spite of himself—as if the model were stronger than any single em-
bodiment of it. And just as Filius Regis is sent off to the Castle of

Sapience and the pilgrim to the Castle of the Cistercians, so Mankind is sent off by Shrift and Penance to the Castle of Perseverance, there to be instructed by the Seven Moral Virtues and to be prepared for salvation.

The sermons of the Virtues, like the instructions of the Deadly Sins, are not homiletic intrusions into the play. They are literally action, unclothed by plot. Each sermon serves as a *remedium* for the lessons of the appropriate vice, and together they bring Mankind step by step back from his deviant moral journey to a state in which he can receive God's grace—if he perseveres. Thus when Mankind enters the Castle, Humilitas observes that he is there to continue his spiritual pilgrimage in another form: "He hauntyth now hevene halle / þat schal bryngyn hym to hevene" (ll. 1712–13).

Mankind has now passed through the four stages of the pilgrimage pattern of action, Innocence, Temptation and Fall, Life in Sin, and Realization and Repentance. When Filius Regis reaches a similar point in the Bernardine parable and is installed in the Castle of Sapience, the castle is attacked by the enemies of man. After Deguilleville's pilgrim reaches the Castle of the Cistercians, the Castle is invaded by Fals Envye, Treason, and Detraction, along with Scilla and her hounds. The full-scale military Psychomachia enacted at the center of the *Castle*, then, does not fix the entire play as a dramatization of the Psychomachia metaphor any more than military conflicts or battles of various sorts in the poems fix them as imitations of the Psychomachia.[15] The siege of the Castle of Perseverance by the forces of the World, the Flesh, and the Devil is merely an incident in the pilgrimage of Mankind's life. As we saw in considering the opening scenes, the focus of the *Castle* alternates between the cosmic and human levels of action, depending upon which most clearly illuminates the central action of Mankind's moral pilgrimage. Thus we may see Mankind from time to time as a partially blind seeker after the good for himself, as he is in his first few scenes, or as the passive prey of contending forces, as he is here in the battle scene. But both views merely imitate from different perspectives the rhythm and developing shape of his moral life. Thus the timeless conflict between good and evil enacted in the siege is at last contained in the particular time of Mankind's life. The successful defense of the castle by the Moral Virtues takes place dur-

15. Mankind's absence from the stage during this, the fullest version of the Psychomachia in the morality drama, is interesting in light of Spivack's observation that "in the logic of the Psychomachia metaphor man himself cannot appear as a figure in the action because he is the battleground on and for which the battle is fought or the castle besieged and defended" (p. 92). Spivack explains the appearance of the Mankind figure as a "convention" of the drama (p. 93).

ing his vigorous middle years; but after the battle, when Mankind is "a party wel in age" and his moral resolution has been colored by the fears attendant on the weakness of age, he is easy prey for the temptations of Covetous. The self-indulgent youth, who had remained securely in the Castle of Perseverance during his manhood, now becomes an avaricious miser, heaping up treasure against a time "whan so þe wynde blowe." And this moral change is signaled, as we might expect, by a journey to Covetous' "castel cage."

Following the battle, the pattern of Temptation and Fall, Life in Sin, and Realization and Repentance is repeated by way of enforcing the particular homiletic concerns of the play: the precariousness of virtue and the necessity of perseverance. In the course of this second movement of the action several of the stock motifs of medieval literature appear, as Mankind is summoned by Death, his body and soul engage in a truncated debate, and the Four Daughters of God debate whether he should be granted mercy or held to the strict rigors of justice. Like the Psychomachiae enacted along the way, these "allegories" imitate stages in Mankind's moral journey. The homiletic intention of the play demands that Mankind be saved at the last moment, as it were, in order to make his failure in perseverance most harrowing for the audience. Thus he persists in covetousness until he is summoned by Death; and then, "trepidus et pusillanimis in adversis," he cries for mercy. His dying cry initiates the debate between Mercy and Justice. And it is only in consequence of that debate that he is granted the goal of Life's pilgrimage, salvation with God. This shift to the cosmic perspective bridges, a bit undramatically perhaps, the gap between the predicament of Mankind in a homily of perseverance and the action of life's pilgrimage which informs the shape and rhythm of the play. But like all of the other shifts in perspective and variations in motif in the play, it too serves to realize the skeletal action of the pilgrimage of life.

III

The proposition that *The Castle of Perseverance* imitates the action of life's pilgrimage rests upon two points of similarity between the play and poems such as *Le Pèlerinage:* the pattern of action which both share, and the tendency of each to use place as an index of moral state and movements through space as indices of moral progress. Clearly neither similarity would support the proposition if "imitation" were intended in a restricted sense, as the conscious adoption of a model, for the similarities are not reflected in similar plot motifs. Indeed in that sense one might rather see the *Castle* as an imitation of the *Psychomachia*, since the plots of the two works run parallel for roughly a thousand lines. What those similarities do suggest, however, is a relationship through Aristotle's sense of the imitation of action; for the play and the poems refer independently to a common model of the shape of the life of the spirit, a model identified for convenience's sake as the pilgrimage because outside of drama it is most often imitated in a narrative journey. While the nature of the stage militates against that mode of imitation, it provides equally effective modes of its own. The isolated mansions of the *Castle* reflect spiritual growth as effectively as the continuous space of *Le Pèlerinage*, and the physical and psychological representations of an actor reveal it as clearly as and more dramatically than an allegorical journey.

It is for this reason that the motif of the journey is progressively submerged and finally drops out altogether in the three versions of Wit's pilgrimage, which Spivack sees as the only moralities to imitate the pilgrimage metaphor. Because the indebtedness of the two later plays to Redford's *Wit and Science* (c. 1535) is so clear, the plays provide together a classical example of the stage's adaptation of a useful but awkward metaphor, and thus throw retrospective light upon the *Castle*. The allegorical journey is an oblique literary device, which the stage finds not only physically difficult but also unnecessarily indirect. Hence *Wit and Science*, the play in which the motif is clearest, merely suggests the journey of Wit to Mount Parnassus and concentrates instead on the direct encounters between Wit and the humanistic Vices and Virtues who hinder and aid him. In the relatively more literal, more urban settings of *The Marriage of Wit and Science* (1568–70) and *The Marriage between Wit and Wisdom* (1579), the journey of the plot is abandoned and the motif of the journey is absorbed into the language, to appear in defining metaphors just as it does in the *Castle*. The nature of the imitation of action in *The Castle of Perseverance* suggests that the stage—or at least the popular stage—prefers direct and concrete representation.

Natalie Crohn Schmitt

17. Was There a Medieval Theatre in the Round? A Re-examination of the Evidence

Richard Southern's reconstruction of a medieval theatre in the round[1] based primarily on the drawing accompanying the morality play *The Castell of Perseverance* (c. 1425) has, since its presentation in 1957, come to be accepted as fact. I would like to challenge that reconstruction, to offer instead an alternative explanation of the drawing, and then finally to bring into question the other evidence which has been put forth, by Southern and others, in corroboration of the argument from the drawing that there was such a structure as a medieval theatre in the round.[2]

I

A reproduction of the original drawing accompanying *The Castell of Perseverance*, apparently in the same hand as the manuscript of the play, appears in plate 8.[3] Various words in the legend about the drawing are not used in modern English: *Caro* means Flesh; *Mundus* means World; *Belyal* is Devil; *lettynge* is hindrance. Southern explains that a *styteler* was a man who controlled the crowd, part of which moved about during the course of the play to secure better vantage points as the location of action changed. *Copboard* is cupboard.[4]

[Reprinted from *Theatre Notebook*, XXIII (1968–69), 130–42, and XXIV (1969–70), 18–25, by permission of the author and the publisher.]
1. Richard Southern, *The Medieval Theatre in the Round* (London, 1957).
2. I am indebted throughout to the guidance and encouragement of V. A. Kolve and Eleanor Prosser, and to the considerable help of Anthony Graham-White.
3. Play and drawing in *The Macro Plays*, EETS e.s. 91, ed. F. J. Furnivall and Alfred Pollard (London, 1904).
4. Southern is puzzled that "Coveytyse copbord" is at the foot of Mankind's bed. That is puzzling indeed. I can only suggest that perhaps the cupboard does not belong specifically to the figure of Covetousness but is rather the cupboard of covetousness, the cupboard where Mankind, in his covetousness, thinks to keep his money. This idea is suggested by lines 2749 ff., in which Mankind wishes he had castle walls to protect his money; perhaps, then, Mankind does actually hide his money within the castle in the cupboard, as in Hieronymus Bosch's *Death and the Miser* (pl. 21).

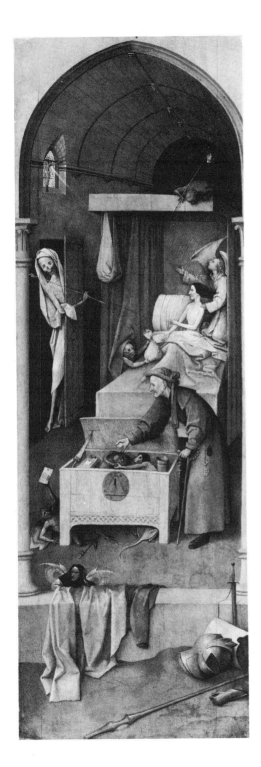

21. Hieronymus Bosch.
Death and the Miser. Courtesy
of the National Gallery of Art,
Washington, D.C.
(Samuel H. Kress Collection.)

The drawing indicates some circular, or roughly circular, playing area along the outside of which are scaffolds or *sedes*[5] for the various important characters. There is considerable evidence to suggest that there were other medieval plays done in the round and with such scaffolds. Of particular relevance is the evidence that the Digby *Mary Magdalene* and some of the plays in the N-Town cycle were staged in this way for it is conjectured that these plays and *The Castell of Perseverance* are all from the same place—Lincoln.[6]

The warning on the drawing that no man should sit in the midst of the place for "lettynge of syt" suggests that the audience was to be within the circular area or place but not "in the midst of the place." Much of Southern's elaboration upon this fact and upon the observation that the playing area was circular and surrounded by *sedes* is very good. But I challenge Southern's basic tenet that the drawing of the Castle of Perseverance is a drawing of a medieval theatre in the round and as such constitutes one of the most important documents of medieval theatre. It seems to me that for all the evidence the drawing provides, the play might have been done in a theatre by professionals as Southern argues, or it might have been done by amateurs in an open field or on the town green; for I do not believe that this is a drawing of a theatre but merely a set-design and that the ditch in the drawing is not a trench round the outside of a theatre, as in Southern's theoretical reconstruction (pl. 22), but merely the moat round the castle.[7]

5. For a morality play *sedes* are not only raised seats or stages for the various characters who figure importantly in the life of the main character but also stages on the way of life of the central character.

6. Jacob Bennett, " 'The Castell of Perseverance': Redactions, Place and Date," *Mediaeval Studies*, XXIV (1962), 141–52; Harry Ritchie, "A Suggested Location for the Digby 'Mary Magdalene,' " *Theatre Survey*, IV (1963), 51–58; Kenneth Cameron and Stanley J. Kahrl, "Staging the N-Town Cycle," *Theatre Notebook*, XXI (1967), 122–38, 152–65. For other examples of medieval drama staged in the round, see Martial Rose, *The Wakefield Mystery Plays* (London, 1961), pp. 33–40.

7. See, for example, the picture reproduced in Raimond Van Marle, *Iconographie de l'art profane au moyen-âge et à la renaissance* (The Hague, 1932), II, 425.

22. Reconstruction of the set for *The Castell of Perseverance*. Reproduced from Richard Southern, *The Medieval Theater in the Round* (London: Faber & Faber, 1957).

Moat is the second most common meaning given for the word "ditch" in the *Middle English Dictionary*, half a column of examples of its use being given.[8] Certainly the presence of water in a medieval play would not have been unusual. We know, for instance, that water was to have been used in the outdoor production of *Ane Satyre of the Thrie Estaitis* and in the Digby *Mary Magdalene*.[9] And the conjecture that the ditch is a moat far more easily fits the drawing than Southern's trench and it eliminates the problems which arise concerning the construction of Southern's theatre.

Southern moves the ditch, placing it external to the scaffolds which on the drawing are indicated as outside the ditch. While the drawing is admittedly crude there seems no reason why, if the artist had so intended, he might not have shown the scaffolds as within the ditch. The writing within the inner circle might just as well have been placed outside it. Even with the writing within the inner circle, where it is, there is also room to indicate that the scaffolds are within. It must also be noticed that the word "scaffold," a word which suggests something on raised legs, is used and that it is the ditch and not Southern's mound of earth which is represented and referred to in the legend around the picture. In Southern's reconstruction the ditch is secondary; it is the hole out of which the earth is taken to make the mound of earth which encloses his theatre. But the mound, which could have been no higher or wider than the ditch, would have been no more difficult to represent in the view of it the artist has taken than the ditch. If we assume that the drawing is a plan for a theatre we must wonder why the castle is drawn in relatively greater detail than the theatre or the other scaffolds. If, however, we assume that the drawing is a set-design, the especial parts of which are the castle and the moat, then we can understand why the drawing and accompanying description have the focus they do. The placement of the scaffolds on the circle need not be explained as having some complex relationship to the entrance into the theatre as in Southern's plan. It seems to me sufficient explanation of the arrangement of the scaffolds to point out, as Southern does (p. 12), that the division of major roles is not systematic—that Covetousness is not of the same order of magnitude as God or the Devil and that therefore his scaffold is not on a primary axis.

If we assume that the ditch is a moat around the castle, the size of the ditch and the size of the castle as shown in the drawing bear some appropriate relationship. Southern assumes that the ditch was very

8. Hans Kurath, ed. (Ann Arbor, Mich., 1956–).
9. For more plays in which water was used, see Gustave Cohen, *Histoire de la mise en scène dans le théâtre religieux française du moyen âge* (Paris, 1906), pp. 100–102.

much larger in relation to the castle than is shown. On the basis of this assumption Southern writes (p. 50), "the plan of *The Castle* has in fact an important omission": namely, the large amount of dirt which must come out of a trench the size Southern imagines. But unless one is intent on constructing Southern's mound there is no reason to think that either the ditch or the castle was very large. As part of a set they may only have served to suggest strength and grandeur. What dirt would have had to be removed for a moat could either have been carted off or used to build a slight rise upon which to place the castle.

Southern objects (p. 47) that there could have been no ditch between the castle and the audience or extended playing space because no bridge is indicated in the drawing. That is true, but the large bridge needed for entry into his theatre is not indicated either. There are medieval paintings which show small ditches over which split logs have been thrown as crossings. Certainly the script allows plenty of time for the staging that a bridge over a moat would entail. Indeed, the bridge would better motivate the circular movement which, Southern suggests, accounts for the repetitiousness of certain portions of the play: the actor would have to walk around the outside of the moat to get to his destination outside the castle area. The allegorical figures might have required no realistic means of crossing over the ditch.

Southern's assumption of a ditch large enough, filled with water, to prohibit crossing and free entrance into the theatre, and large enough to make a mound for the *sedes* to be set upon, entails a very great earthwork. Ryan, the only one I know to have taken objection to Southern's theory in print, has calculated that Southern's plan necessitates the removal of 20,000 cubic feet of earth and, to fill the ditch, 150,000 gallons of water.[10] With simple equipment that would have meant no small labour and since Southern apparently believes that the theatres were constructed specially for each performance the labour to fill the trench back up again should also be figured in. Regardless of how low the cost of labour might have been, it would have been cheaper to hire enough men to patrol outside the ditch than to fill it with water. If, however, the ditch is a moat around the castle, the drawing gives us no indication that the audience paid and that such an earthwork was needed to keep out those who did not.

If the ditch was a moat round the castle, then we can understand why, as the legend on the picture suggests, it was to be preferred to a strong barring about. Even if the wall were very low and, as I assume the

10. P. M. Ryan's review of Southern's book is in *Quarterly Journal of Speech*, XLIV (1958). Ryan makes these calculations on the basis of a theatre 110 feet in circumference—much smaller than any theatre Southern imagines.

moat to have been, primarily a symbolic barrier, the moat would still have afforded greater visibility. And an action with water, imaginary or real, would have been more amusing. Southern does not suggest why, in his view, a ditch would have been preferable. If, as I have suggested, the play might have been done on the town green, then we may understand why a ditch could not always have been dug.

It follows from my understanding of the word "ditch," different from Southern's, that my understanding of some other words is also different: namely, of the words "place" and "about." I understand the word "place" to mean the flat playing area as distinguished from the scaffolds and, in this case, defined at the perimeter by the scaffolds. I take "the midst of the place" to mean that area bounded by the moat. I do not take the word "place," as Southern does, to mean an area bounded by a theatre. In both our views the use of the word "about" (in "this is the water about the place") is somewhat problematical. In Southern's view the water surrounds the place but—and this contradicts his definition of the word "place"—it also necessarily surrounds the mound and the scaffolds. In my view the water surrounds not the whole playing area or place but only that part of it which immediately surrounds the castle. I can only point out in both my defence and Southern's, as those critics who have argued against Hotson's reconstruction of the Globe Theatre have pointed out, that the medieval and renaissance use of the word "about" was at least as vague as our own.

II

Strong support for the theory that the ditch surrounding the Castle of Perseverance is a moat comes from other medieval allegories of the castle. Owst tells us that the allegorical castle was no less than a commonplace of the medieval pulpit.[11] Roberta Cornelius, who devoted a dissertation to the medieval allegorical castle, traces interest in it back to at least the ninth century; but, she tells us, the allegorical castle did not really become important until the twelfth and thirteenth centuries when the real castle became the centre of medieval life.[12] The allegorical castle could represent a number of different things and could serve in a variety of allegories. It could, for instance, be the devil's castle, or the castle of the Blessed Virgin, or the castle of the body. It could be the object of a pilgrimage, or a way station on it, or it might, like the Castle

11. G. R. Owst, *Literature and Pulpit in Medieval England* (New York, 1961), p. 84.
12. *The Figurative Castle* (Bryn Mawr, Penn., 1930), p. 13. Most of the information in this paragraph is from this dissertation.

of Perseverance, be the object of a siege. Elaboration of the parts of the castle might constitute the main part of an allegory; or, as in *The Castell of Perseverance*, the castle might be central to the story, while not itself particularly elaborated; or the castle might figure merely as an element of design in some other kind of allegory. There is among allegories much overlapping of elements, much intertwining of themes. Thus in some allegories of Mary as a castle she is at the same time a fountain—of baptism or of life or rebirth—and the source of the four rivers running in the garden of paradise: "ffour fair stremes in hit out of a well springe / ffro myddes the hegh tour, thai fille the dykinges."[13] While it is of course useful to make distinctions between the kinds of allegories, it is clear that one must not insist that these distinctions be, by our standards, rigorous.

The first thing of note about these castles and relevant to my argument is that when the details of the castle are elaborated, the primary part of that elaboration is the fortification of the castle. The essential characteristic of the castle is that it is a place of protection. Sometimes the castle is walled or surrounded by towers; sometimes it is built on a high rock; in the majority of instances there is a moat and often this moat constitutes the most important part of the fortification. Owst gives us examples of castles with moats: "The depe diche of stondyng watir that compaceth about this castel mai wel be the foule unordynat love that thei hav in her evele"; or in another, "The moat surrounding the fort is Avarice. . . . The water which flows in it around the fort is of great quantity, foul and perilous; and it is the water of Carnal Lust." In yet another example the frogs croaking in the "filthy water" of the castle moat are the gluttons, the lustful, and other ribalds. Into the moat tumble a large part of the invading host sent to capture the fortress, there to be miserably drowned.[14]

The Castle of Perseverance, however, is clearly a castle of goodness, a castle in which the soul is protected, and we must focus our attention on such castles and particularly on castles of the Virgin—for there is indication to suggest that the Castle of Perseverance is of this type:

CONFESSION	þat castel is a precyous place,	1558
	fful of vertu & of grace:	
	Who-so leuyth þere, his lyuys space,	
	no synne schal hym schende. . . .	
CHASTITY	Mankynde! take kepe of chastyte,	1631
	& moue þee to maydyn Marye.	

13. A Sawley monk's version of Grosseteste's "Castle of Love," in *Minor Poems of the Vernon MS.*, pt. 1, ed. Carl Horstmann, EETS 98 (London, 1892), p. 418.
14. Owst, pp. 79, 82–83.

> fleschly foly, loke þou fle,
> at þe reuerense of oure Ladye.
> þat curteys qwene, what dyd sche?
> Kepte hyr clene & stedfastly,
> & in here was trussyd þe trin[i]te
> þorwe gostly grace she was worthy,
> & al for sche was chaste.
> who-so kepyt hym chast, & wyl not syynne,
> whanne he is beryed in bankis brynne,
> al hys joye is to begynne:
> þerefore, to me take taste!

After these lines from *The Castell*, Mirk's homily on the castle as the Virgin Mary (c. 1500) seems familiar.[15] The homily tells us that Mary was the castle that Jesus entered into; "for just as a castle has various properties that belong to a castle that is big and strong, so had our lady various virtues that made her able before all women to receive Christ.... Our lady was as strong as a castle, and resisted the assault of the fiend's machinations." And the homily continues, "just as a castle has a deep ditch to strengthen it, so has our lady a ditch of meekness so deep down into the earth of her heart, that no man can go over it.... If the ditch be full of water, it adds even more strength to the castle; this water is compassion that a man has for his own guilt or for any other man's diseases. This water had our lady, when she wept for her son's passion and for his death so much, that when she had wept all the water that was in her eyes, she wept blood over this ditch, like a drawbridge that shall be drawn up against enemies, and let down to friends that will keep this castle. By this bridge ye shall understand discrete obedience."

The most widely known of all the castle allegories was one of the castle of the Virgin, Grosseteste's *Le Château d'Amour* (c. 1230). It was several times translated into English and widely imitated. Below is a passage from an English version of *Le Château d'Amour*[16] roughly rendered. The passage suggests a dramatic action which bears striking resemblance to that in *The Castell of Perseverance*.

> Gentle lady of this castle,
> Let me my mischief to thee tell.
> Mother of mercy and queen of pity,
> To sinful man thou art ever avowed:
> Therefore at thy gates now I lie,
> Thy help and mercy for to cry;

15. John Mirk, *Mirk's Festial: A Collection of Homilies*, ed. Theodore Erbe, EETS e.s. 96 (London, 1905), pp. 228–29. The date of composition of this homily is given by Kurath, in the *Middle English Dictionary*, as approximately eighty-five years earlier.

16. *Minor Poems* (above, n. 13), pp. 420–21.

Mercy shall I fast cry before this lovely tower,
Ever 'till I find some of thy succor.
Hope of help made me hither flee
When three great enemies fast pursued me:
One is the foul fiend with all his company,
That puts forth pride and wrath and great envy;
The second is the false world with many shrewd guises;
That always shoots at me sharply with all covetousness;
The third is my own flesh, to me a great enemy,
That pricks me with lechery, sloth, and gluttony.
Well of mercy, I will soon be dead and destroyed
Unless a stream of thy grace comes to me soon.
Lady, let me lie in thy castle dike
And wash me well there as thy servant:
Then, if mine enemies will me assail,
In trust of thy good help I will take up that battle.
In this castle Jesus Christ took of thee mankind:
Therefore hope I ever here succor to find.

The *Cursor Mundi* (c. 1400),[17] said to be derived from *The Castle of Love*, contains a passage which even more nearly suggests the action concerning the ditch which I conjecture for *The Castell of Perseverance*. As in *The Castle of Love*, man comes to the castle of the Virgin and beseeches entrance and thereby escape from his enemies—the devil, the world, his flesh, and their various assistants. He implores: "Do [let] me to passe these diches ouer / there the castle stondeth stabul."

J. M. Manly suggested that *The Castell of Perseverance* was influenced by *The Castle of Love*.[18] The preceding passage from *The Castle of Love* and that from a successor to it, *Cursor Mundi*, describe an action so similar to that of *The Castell* that some influence is certainly suggested. Furthermore it would seem that the author of *The Castell* based some of his personifications on the attributes of *The Castle of Love*. *The Castle of Love* has seven barbicans which are in fact the seven virtues. In *The Castell of Perseverance* the seven virtues which guard Mary's castle are female figures. The castle of Love is painted in four colours: red, blue, green, and white. White is the pure heart of Our Lady, green her truth, blue her hope, and red her love. If the Castle of Love did serve as a model for the Castle of Perseverance, then we can perhaps understand why the colours of the mantles of the four daughters (also characters in *The Castle of Love*) are specified on the

17. *Cursor Mundi*, EETS 59, ed. R. Morris (London, 1875), Trinity version, pp. 581, 583.

18. This suggestion is mentioned and discussed by F. J. Furnivall in "Afterwords" to *The Macro Plays*, pp. xxxix–xli and is further discussed by Cornelius in *The Figurative Castle*, pp. 63–65.

castle plan whereas no other costumes or colours are mentioned. The author may have associated the colours of their clothing with the colours specified for the Castle of Love. If *The Castle of Love* did influence *The Castell of Perseverance* and if that influence was fairly direct, that would constitute extremely strong evidence for the theory that the ditch in the plan is a moat. But the relationship between the two allegories has not been definitely established and perhaps cannot be.

The allegories also provide evidence of a different sort to suggest that the ditch in the plan may have been a moat. In *The Castle of Love* it is said that the water in the ditch is of the four streams which come from the fountain of Mary in the castle. In some of the allegories of the castle we find that the castle is reached, not by crossing a ditch, but by crossing a river. In *The Castell of Pleasure* (1518) the aspirants must cross a river the source of which is Mary, "the mother water of vertues" and which is called the stream of humility.[19] The characters wait by the river in patient humility until the tide recedes and then they cross on the stones of steadfastness. It is said that those who deal in doubleness or those who are proud of heart are quickly drowned in the waves and rising tide. The Abbey of the Holy Ghost, in an allegory said to be related to *The Castle of Love*,[20] is also founded on a "good river," the river of tears "which cleans God's seat, that is man's soul."[21]

There are also some castles which can be reached only by crossing both a river and a ditch. To get to the Castle of Truth in *The Vision of William concerning Piers Plowman* (1393) one must cross a brook called "be-seemly-of-speech" by a ford called "honour-your-fathers": "Thenne shaltou come to a Court Cleer as the Sonne, / the Mot is of Merci the Maner is al abouten."[22] Seven virtues also guard this castle. (Furnivall believes that *The Castell of Perseverance* was influenced by *Piers Plowman*.)[23] *The Court of Sapience* (c. 1475) also has a castle in which the seven virtues live.[24] To reach it one must first cross the river of Quiet (the water, rocks, plants, and fish of which are detailed for some twenty pages of the text) and then one must cross the "dyke" which is also filled with the water of Quiet. In *The Book of Vices and Virtues* (four-

19. William Nevill, *The Castell of Pleasure*, ed. by Roberta Cornelius, EETS 179 (London, 1930), pp. 82–83.

20. See *Minor Poems of the Vernon MS.*, p. 355 n.

21. "The Abbey of the Holy Ghost" (c. 1440), in *Religious Pieces*, ed. G. G. Perry, EETS 26 A (London, 1889), p. 50.

22. William Langland, *The Vision of William concerning Piers Plowman*, ed. Walter Skeat, EETS 28 (London, 1867), pp. 70–71.

23. See "Afterwords," Furnivall, *The Macro Plays*, p. xxxix.

24. John Lydgate, "The Court of Sapience," ed. Robert Spindler, *Beiträge zur englischen Philologie*, VI (Leipzig, 1927), 124–216. This piece is also thought to be closely related to *The Castle of Love*; see *Minor Poems of the Vernon MS.*, p. 355 n.

teenth century) there is no castle but there is the well of grace which
feeds the seven rivers watering the garden of the tree of life.[25]

All these examples tend to suggest that the river and, by association,
the water in the ditch, were important not merely as fortification for the
castle, but in their own right. Water is a symbol of cleansing and puri-
fying. In this sense it is used in the sacrament of baptism, symbolizing
the washing away of sin and the rising to newness of life. It also denotes
innocence.[26] What is suggested, then, is that crossing over the water in
The Castell of Perseverance signifies a transformation of the soul. If that
is so, we can further understand why the ditch was to be preferred to
the wall and why it is the single means of fortification indicated in the
drawing.

III

The text of the play offers some confirmation of my
view and also raises objections to it. The following references to a hill
seem quite literal and my hypothesis provides no explanation of them:[27]

þer-for, on hylle, syttyth all stylle, & seth wyth good wylle oure ryche a-ray.	271
Wonder hyȝe howtis, on hyll, herd I houte:	909
Howtyth hye up-on ȝene hyll, ȝe traytours in ȝoure trumpys!	1898
Now, now! now, go now! on hye hyllys lete us howte—	1927

On the other hand there is evidence for my view which Southern has
not taken into account. The references to the *sedes* as "towers" (ll. 235
and 239) or "bowers" (ll. 886 and 2705) support the impression made by
the word "scaffold," on the drawing, of stages raised above ground.

If, as Southern believes, the word "green" as well as the word "place"
bears special reference to the flat playing space within his theatre, then
the reference to the location of performance given in the banns is
puzzling:

25. *The Book of Vices and Virtues,* ed. W. Nelson Francis, EETS 217 (London,
1942), p. 96.
26. See George Ferguson, *Signs and Symbols in Christian Art* (New York, 1966),
p. 45.
27. In the Chester *Adoration of the Shepherds* a pageant wagon is used and
referred to as a "hill." Something resembling a hill may have been built on top of
the wagon, however.

þis day seuenenyt, be-fore ȝou in syth,   133
  A*t* [*name of town*] on þe grene, in ryall a-ray.

If the company to which the speaker belonged was, at the time of his speaking, building a theatre on the outskirts of town, why does not the speaker refer to the theatre? It seems, rather, that he is saying that the play will be performed on the town green.

On the theory that there is a moat surrounding the castle, the editors' conjecture that the play opens "on the Castle-Green," that is to say, in the midst of the place, seems a good one. If Mankind is in an area set off as belonging to the castle, he begins his life in an area clearly free from sin. His departure then toward the world with the Bad Angel is very dramatic. I imagine that this departure takes place, over the moat, during the course of the following lines:

Now go we forth, swythe a-non!
to þe Werld us must gon;
& ber*e* þee manly eu*ere* a-mong,
  Wha*n*ne þou comy*st* out or Inne.   439

HUMANU*m* GEN*us*. ȝys, & ellys haue þou my necke,
  but I be manly be downe & dyche;
& þou I be fals, I ne recke,
  wit*h* so þ*at* I be lord [i-]lyche,   443
    I folwe þee as I can.
þ*ou* schalt be my bote of bale;
for, wer*e* I ryche of holt & hale,
Þa*n*ne wolde I ȝeue neu*ere* tale
  of God ne of good man.   448
    [*Exeunt* MAL. ANG. *and* HUM. GEN.]

From the time of their departure until they come to the World, at line 565, I imagine that Mankind and the Bad Angel are circling about outside the moat toward their destination. Southern also postulates a circular journey at this point; the moat, with a particular crossing place, would enforce this circularity and make dramatic sense of it.

Following line 448 (above) is the direction [*Exeunt* MAL. ANG. *and* HUM. GEN.]. Southern says of this direction, "it looks most authentic with its abbreviations but it is not justified at all. It would raise the question: Where do the Bad Angel and Mankind exeunt to?" And he discounts this direction and all other directions to exit and enter as of a later date "because, as we begin to see, there is very little 'going-out' or 'coming-in' in this [his] circular method of presentation" (pp. 160–61). He does not tell us whether the script clearly shows such directions to be of a later hand, or whether they just must be because they do not accord with his idea of a theatre. While the direction to exit (above) makes clear sense on my theory, I cannot make sense of all the directions to exit and enter either and so am willing to accept Southern's word that they are of a later hand. However, in general I do not find the various entrances and exits nearly so problematical as Southern does. His theatre has but one entrance, and entry or exit through that cannot be made unobtrusively. On an open place entrances and exits might have been made at any number of points and need not have been occasions. Thus I am not troubled, for instance, as Southern is, that no mention is made of Backbiter's exit following l. 829, of the exit of Shrift and Penance following l. 1604, or of the exit of the vices after their defeat.

In the passage below, the references to "ȝone castle" suggest that the castle is at some distance from the speaker:

> In-to þe Castel of Perséueraunce.   1552
> If þou wylt to heuene wynne,
> & kepe þee fro werldyly dystaunce,
> goo ȝone Castel, & kepe þee þer-Inne,
> For [it] is strenger þanne any in Fraunce: 1556
> to ȝone castel I þee seende.

It seems unlikely that the castle was at any real distance. The production was, I believe, fairly intimate; and in the lines almost immediately following those above Mankind says that the castle is "but at hand":

> HUMANUM GENUS. a, Schryfte! blessyd mote þou be!   1562
> þis castel is here but at honde;

It seems possible that the suggestion of distance was to be created by some barrier, namely, by a moat or a wall. The reference to the strength of the castle (l. 1556, above) also suggests that the castle was fortified. Reference to "ȝone castle" appears again at lines 1762 and 1773; and what is especially interesting is that in the context of these lines it is also said by one of the vices the virtues are upon "ȝone plane," that is, it seems, upon a plain other than the one he is on, presumably the one in the midst of the place. Preparing to attack the castle, the forces of evil continually speak of the castle as if it were at some distance:

> BELYAL. I here trumpys trebelen al of tene:
> þe worþi Werld walkyth to werre,
> for to clyuyn ȝone Castel clene,
> þe maydnys meyndys for to merre.   1903
> sprede my penon up on a prene,
> & stryke we forthe now vndyr sterre!
> schapyth now ȝoure scheldys schene,
> ȝene skallyd skoutis for to skerre   1907
> up-on ȝone grenë grese!

make ȝou redy, allë þre,   1913
    boldë battyl for to bede!
to ȝone feld[ë] lete us fle,
    & bere my baner forthe on brede!   1916
to ȝone castel wyl I te;
    þo mamerynge modrys schul haue here mede.
but þei ȝeld[yn] up to me,
    with byttyr balys þei schul blede;   1920
    of here reste I schal hem reue.
    In woful watrys I schal hem wasche.
    haue don, felaus! & take ȝoure trasche,
    & wendo we þedyr on a rasche,
        þat castel for to cleue.   1925

with care o ȝone castel to crachen & to crase   1946
    in Flode.
help we, Mankynde fro ȝone castel to keuere!   1955

The reference at line 1908 may once again suggest the midst of the
place. The reference at line 1946 is particularly interesting because it
definitely associates getting to "ȝone castle" with a river (Flode). In
light of that association the reference to "woful waters" (l. 1922) may
be significant, for we shall see later (l. 2330) that the water in the ditch
is referred to as the water of grace, i.e., Mary's tears.

At lines 2016, 2158, and 2318 there are references to "castle town."
It seems clear that something more than the castle proper is implied in
these references. At line 2318, for instance, Lechery is definitely not
within the castle:

CHASTITY. þerfor go fro þis castel toun,   2318
    Lechery, now I þee rede;

He is outside the castle in some specific area associated with the castle.
He is, I believe, within the area surrounded by the moat.

When Mankind gives up his life of sin and returns to the castle, it
seems that the virtues come down out of the castle to greet him. It would
be far more meaningful if the virtues were standing then, not just in the
place, as in Southern's view, but rather in the midst of the place, in that
special area surrounding the castle and, like the castle, clearly defined as
the area of goodness. Unfortunately the crucial evidence in this argument is missing. At the point where Mankind enters into the castle area
a leaf of the manuscript is missing.

Shortly after Mankind's return it is clear that he and at least some of
the virtues enter and go aloft in the castle. Southern believes that all the
virtues go aloft within the castle. Certainly it would be more dramatic
if they did not, if some of the virtues remained down in the midst of the
place. There follows a rather long verbal exchange between the vices

and the virtues. If in this exchange some vices and virtues taunted one another across the moat it would be more interesting than if all the virtues were removed within the castle. Out on the green the interchange between vices and virtues could be expressed physically as well as verbally. Similarly if in the actual battle all the virtues were not always merely enclosed within the castle but, instead, engaged in real encounters—sallying forth to chase vices, forcing them into the moat, etc.—the play would have had a truly theatrical centre; it would have been a spectacle worthy of an audience's attention.

In fact, it is very difficult to reconstruct the battle from the text. But there is indication that the battle did indeed have some vigour. In other medieval allegories of the castle, we have seen that the castle is often Mary, mother of Christ, and that the water in the ditch around the castle is related to her. In this case it seems that the water is Mary's grace and that in the course of the battle Chastity throws Lechery into it:

> Madyn Marye, well of grace,
>   schal qwenche þat fowle hete.   2304
> Luxuria. Out on Chastyte, be þe rode!
>   Sche hathe dayschyd & so drenchyd.
> ȝyt haue sche þe curs of God,
>   for al my fere þe qwene hath qwenchyd;   2391

One might think that Chastity and Lechery are merely speaking metaphorically, except that in the same place in the text Sloth clearly speaks of the ditch. He is determined not to be treated in the way that Lechery has been and he is resolved to make access to the castle easier:

> Accidia. Ware, war! I delue with a spade;
>   men calle me þe 'lord syr Slowe.'
> gostly grace I spylle & schade;
>   fro þe watyr of grace, þe dyche I fowe;   2330
> ȝe schulyn com ryth I-nowe
>   be þis dyche drye, be bankys brede.

Sloth, Accidia (spiritual dryness), says that he is digging in order to divert the water from the ditch. He cleans the ditch by draining it (*fowe* means "clean"). Industry then comments upon Sloth's action:

> þerfor he makyth þis dyke drye,
>   to puttyn Mankynde to dystresse;
> he makyth dedly synne a redy weye
>   In-to þe Castel of Goodnesse;   2356

On the assumption that there is a moat around the castle we can make sense of the fact that when Mankind is again beguiled from the castle, this time by Covetousness, he makes what appear to be two exits, one at line 2557 and another at line 2648:

GOOD ANGEL   he goth fro þis worthi woɳnynge.
            Coueytyse, a-wey ʒe chace;
                & schyttyth Mankynde suɱ-wherɇ herɇ-Inne,   2552
                    in ʒoure worþi wyse!
                    ow, wrechyd man! þou schalt be wroth,
                    þat syɳne schal be þee ful loth.
                    a, swete ladys, helpe! he goth   2556
                        a-wey *with* Coueytyse. [tunc descendit ad Auariciaɱ
                                                        Humanum Genus].
GENEROSITY   þou Mankynde fro þis castel fle:
                wyte it Coueytyse!   2648
BAD ANGEL   ʒa! go forthe, & lete þe qwenys cakle!

The first departure may be from the castle proper, the second from the castle green or midst of the place.

The final indication of the use of the ditch may be in line 2914. Here World's Boy threatens to "lift" Mankind "into a lake." "Does this mean," queries Southern (p. 209), "that he will throw his body into the Ditch?" The question is inevitable, especially since the action is promised by the flag-bearer in line 99: "Deth comyth foul dolfully, & loggyth hym in a lake ful lowe." Southern lets the question pass, I assume because it would hardly be meaningful for the Boy to suggest throwing Mankind into Southern's ditch, not visible to the audience and not part of the established acting area. But he could understandably throw Mankind into the castle moat.

IV

My principal intent has been to suggest an interpretation for the drawing of the Castle of Perseverance which, in effect, disallows Southern's interpretation of it as the primary evidence of a medieval theatre in the round. However, so entrenched has the idea of the existence of a medieval theatre in the round become that it is necessary, further, to re-examine the ancillary evidence for such a theatre.

A. The Cornish Rounds[28]

There are remains of prehistoric rounds, probably forts, in many places in England.[29] In Cornwall in medieval times it seems that indeed plays were at least sometimes given in these rounds. There is no evidence to suggest that plays were given in these rounds outside

28. I am largely indebted to Anthony Graham-White's unpublished research in this area.

29. See Christopher Hawkes, "Hillforts," *Antiquity*, V (1931), 60–97; and Jacquetta Hawkes, *A Guide to the Prehistoric and Roman Monuments* (London, 1951).

Cornwall; and it would seem unlikely that they were: in Saxon times most of the English population moved out of the uplands, away from the rounds. In Cornwall, however, the people continued to live near where the rounds had been built.

There is only one source, Richard Carew, writing in 1603, to suggest that Cornish rounds were specially raised for theatrical performance.[30] Since the prehistoric rounds have lasted very plentifully in Cornwall to this day,[31] it would be surprising if the miracle players constructed fresh rounds for each performance. There is some reason to doubt Carew's reliability as a historian of medieval theatre. Carew wrote: "the state of our country hath undergone so many alterations since I first began these scribblings that in the reviewing I was driven either likewise to vary my report or else speak against my knowledge."[32] We might dismiss this remark as mere humility. But it must be taken into account that Carew was born in 1555; thus in 1570 when miracle plays were still being produced, but only sporadically, he was just fifteen, and by the year of his book, 1602, the miracle plays were no longer to be seen.[33] If, however, Carew's account is trustworthy we should observe that the rounds of which he speaks were quite small—forty or fifty feet across. If the account is reliable, then the fresh rounds were most likely modelled on those which already existed nearby as modern day rounds constructed in Cornwall are said to be.[34]

The other evidence Southern puts forth concerning the Cornish rounds is likewise doubtful or plainly incorrect. The wall he mentions, around the outside of one of the rounds, was constructed in the mid-nineteenth century.[35] The description of stone seats in one of the rounds, given by the eighteenth-century antiquarian Borlase, may reveal more influence of some lines he quotes from Ovid than direct observation;[36] as Treve Holman points out, Borlase's bent was generally romantic and his accounts otherwise inaccurate.[37] Treve Holman also tells us that the faint impression of tiered seats in an existing earthen round is likely to have been made by the footsteps of those who for

30. F. E. Halliday, *Richard Carew of Antony* (London, 1953), p. 144.

31. J. B. Cornish, "Ancient Earthworks," *The Victoria History of the Counties of England: A History of County Cornwall*, ed. by Wm. Page, I (London, 1906), 464–70 for a list of defensive earthworks with single banks.

32. Halliday, p. 48.

33. These observations are made by William Tribby in "The Medieval Prompter: A Reinterpretation," *Theatre Survey*, V (1964), 71–76.

34. Cornish, p. 457.

35. Ibid., p. 473.

36. William Borlase, quoted by William Morris in *Ancient Cornish Dramas* (Oxford, 1859), II, 454.

37. Treve Holman, "Cornish Plays and Playing Places," *Theatre Notebook*, IV (1950), 52–53.

centuries have climbed the round.[38] The evidence then, for Cornish *plen an gwaries* as distinct from forts, and specially constructed for theatrical performance rather than just adopted for that use, is dubious.

B. *The Picture from the Terence Manuscript, c. 1400* (pl. 23)[39]

Mary H. Marshall provides us with considerable information relevant to the understanding of the theatre shown in this miniature.[40] It is a Roman theatre in which a recitation of one of Terence's plays is taking place. The rendering of it conforms rather strictly to contemporary medieval antiquarian ideas concerning the presentation of Terence plays.

The structure at the centre of the theatre, the *scena*, was thought to be a booth. Marshall carefully traces the gradual corruption of the word *scena*, written on the booth in the illumination. In 620, Isidore of Seville explained the *scena* "as a place within the theatre constructed in the form of a house with a raised platform, the orchestra, where comic and tragic performers sang, and actors and mimes danced." The Greek *skene* he interpreted as house, booth or tent ("domus," "domicilium") (p. 9). By the tenth century it was thought that a single man stood within the *scena* and from there recited the plays of Terence. Here the man is Calliopius, a supposed friend of Terence. Either he or the poet himself was commonly represented in pictures such as this. The recitation, it was believed, was accompanied by miming by several mute actors. The functions, then, of poet singing or reciting the words and actors performing the gestures became clearly separated in this description. Marshall believes it possible that the influence of the ubiquitous contemporary mimes may have affected the description, although she provides etymological explanations as well (p. 17). The dictionary most influential for the later Middle Ages was written at the end of the twelfth century by Hugutio of Pisa. "Orchestra" did not have for Hugutio the Isidorian associations with the stage. "He defined orchestra according to Juvenal as a platform or seat for nobles apart from the people. Juvenal was alluding to customs of the first century A.D. when the senators occupied seats in the orchestra . . . , but Hugutio, apparently using quotations without context, made no such connection" (p. 24). Marshall tells us that Hugutio sometimes produced "fantastic etymologies by free association" (p. 23) and it seems likely that his alter-

38. Ibid., pp. 52–53.
39. From Southern, *A Medieval Theatre in the Round*, n. 1, frontispiece.
40. Mary H. Marshall, "Theatre in the Middle Ages: Evidence from Dictionaries and Glosses," *Symposium*, IV (1950), 1–39, 366–89. Page references in this section of my paper refer to this article.

23. Illumination from the *Térence des Ducs*. MS Arsenal 664, fol. lv. Courtesy of the Bibliothèque Nationale, Paris.

ations in the traditional description of the *scena* reflect contemporary theatre practice as much as careful scholarship. The poet's booth, he said, was covered by posts and curtains like the booth of a contemporary merchant. He evidently thought the *scena* was quite small. And, he adds, masked actors retired to and made entrances from this booth (pp. 23–25).[41]

In the picture, the theatre building itself appears to be in the centre of town and made of stone like a Roman theatre or amphitheatre. No medieval stone theatres are known to exist. Tiered seats are indicated: the audience sits with their hands in their laps. No information is provided concerning the supposed size of such a theatre; none of the buildings in the picture is shown to size. Such a theatre as Terence's plays were thought to have been recited in was generally described as semicircular (p. 369). The picture Southern offers pretty surely shows a circular theatre. The circularity of the theatre, as the one apparent deviation from standard description may, as Southern believes, reveal contemporary staging practices; on the other hand, the distinction between Roman theatres and amphitheatres was not generally made at that time (p. 375) and amphitheatres were described as round.

Southern hints that the use of the word *theatrum* on the painting may reveal medieval usage of the word. Marshall is quite clear on this subject: while the antiquarian knew the word *theatrum* to have had as one of its meanings a structure for dramatic use, the "notion of theatre in contemporary use, distinguished from the antiquarian . . . [was] any public place where sights were to be seen" (p. 372) and often to this definition was added specifically "public square" or "marketplace" (pp. 378–81).

Some of the errors about ancient theatre made by medieval antiquarians very likely reveal medieval practice or inclination. However, Marshall does not lead us to conclude that the antiquarians simply interpreted classical theatre in accord with contemporary practice, as Southern would like to suggest. On the contrary, she believes that antiquarian scholarship resulted in descriptions of the classical theatre so alien that the medieval dramatist did not know how to make use of them:

The main mediaeval error was in interpreting the method of representing Roman plays as a form of recitation, sometimes with accompanying miming, as we have seen. Creizenach and other historians of the drama have emphasized the seriousness of this mistake, because it meant that the plays of Terence which were known did not in general, aside from Hrotsvitha's unique crea-

41. What is suggested, perhaps, is that the lower portion of medieval scaffolds, enclosed, might have served as dressing rooms. See Marshall, p. 28.

tions in the tenth century, serve as effective dramatic models. But the error is understandable when one considers the strange vagaries of the Roman theatre of mime and farce, pantomime and recitation, after the death of formal drama, of which glimmers came to the men of the middle ages, as to us, through scattered references in Roman writers, and church fathers like Jerome and Augustine (p. 375).

C. Jean Fouquet's "The Martyrdom of Saint Apollonia"

The French miniature painting "The Martyrdom of Saint Apollonia" from about 1455 appears to be a representation of a theatrical performance on a *platea* with scaffolds close together at the back and extending round the sides (see pl. 1). Some of the scaffolds seem to hold spectators, others performers.[42] Southern believes that this painting offers strong supportive evidence for his reconstruction of a medieval theatre in the round based on the drawing from *The Castell of Perseverance*. He believes that the area at back bounded by the scaffolds is semicircular, that in fact what is shown at the rear is half of a theatre in the round, and that the front portion of the theatre—which is strongly barred about—is represented by the wall at the bottom of the picture. On this view Saint Apollonia appears at front centre of the picture but she is, in actuality, in the midst of the place. Fouquet has merely eliminated the crowd on this side of the picture (that crowd which would have had its back to us) and then foreshortened the front so as better to enable us to see the action. Southern believes that otherwise the picture contains no distortion.

I would agree that this is probably a painting of a performance done in a more or less round playing area (the enclosed area at the back appears to be more polygonal than strictly round). The picture seems to contain more distortion than Southern allows, and he should be grateful for that. The arrangement of the actors is strongly frontal. If this were an accurate representation of performance, the audience shown—half the total audience by Southern's reckoning—could see nothing whatever of what seems to be the play's most dramatic moment. The frontal arrangement must be pictorial convention, not theatrical fact. If there is no space compression, then the audience is so crowded together it could not move. In any case the audience seated down front would prohibit significant audience movement.

Southern's interpretation of this miniature in relation to the drawing

---

42. Marshall supplies evidence which is in keeping with Southern's idea of scaffolds for the spectators. Relevant perhaps to Southern's intent of establishing theatre performed in the round is one passage which she takes to suggest that the raised seats for the audience at one thirteenth-century spectacle were in wedge-shaped sections (pp. 372–73).

from *The Castell of Perseverance* is more seriously challenged by comparison of this miniature with other Fouquet miniatures. Many of the other miniatures show the central action as on a raised plane (see pl. 24).[43] Sometimes the vertical at front of the raised plane is made of natural materials, stone or earth, sometimes it is man-made, often looking like a raised proscenium stage. I do not think that this suggests that all these minatures represent performances on raised stages, but rather that the central action in each of these pictures is presented as raised as a matter of pictorial convention. Comparison of "The Martyrdom of Saint Apollonia" with the other pictures certainly suggests the possibility that the painting is in accord with this convention and that the wall at front is a retaining wall, not a wall which forbids entrance except at the gate as in Southern's theory.

D. Thomas Churchyard's "The Worthiness of Wales"

Arthur Freeman has brought to attention evidence of performance in the round in Shrewsbury, Shropshire.[44] In 1587 Thomas Churchyard, a native of Shrewsbury, wrote the following description in *The Worthiness of Wales:*

> I had such haste, in hope to be but briefe,
> That monuments, in churches were forgot:
> And somewhat more, behind the walles as chiefe,
> Where playes have bin, which is most worthie note.
> There is a ground, newe made theator wise,
> Both deepe and hye, in goodly aunctient guise:
> Where well may sit, ten thousand men at ease,
> And yet the one, the other not displease.
>
> A space below, to bayt both bull and beare,
> For players too, great roume and place at will.
> And in the same, a cocke pit wondrous feare,
> Besides where men, may wrastle in their fill.
> A ground most apt, and they that sits above,
> At once in vewe, all this may see for love:
> At Aston's play, who had beheld this then,
> Might well have seene, there twenty thousand men.

Freeman assumes that the word *auncient* does not mean Roman but traditional and "traditional in and around Shrewsbury," and that accordingly "deepe and hye" refers to Southern's ditch and wall. He assumes that "newe made theator wise," means a newly constructed

---

43. See also Paul Wescher, *Jean Fouquet and His Time* (New York, 1947), pls. 1, 8, 9, 10, 11, 13, 21, and 23.

44. Arthur Freeman, "A 'Round' Outside Cornwall," *Theatre Notebook*, XVI (1961), 10–11.

24. Jean Fouquet. The Conversion of Saint Paul. From *Le Livre d'heures d'Etienne Chevalier*. Courtesy of the Musée Condé, Chantilly. (Photo: Giraudon, Paris.)

theatre rather than ground newly adapted for theatrical performance. Either way there is evidence to suggest that Churchyard is not to be relied upon. Freeman tells us that:

the area Churchyard describes, "Behind-the-walls," was known by that name in the sixteenth century, and thereafter as "the Quarry." In Churchyard's time, evidently, "the Quarry" was the name given to the amphitheatre itself, for we have a record of the lease of the whole area *excepting* the theatre in 1570: "1570. July 8: Lease to be granted to three persons for ten years of a certain pasture called 'Behind the walls,' excepting the Quarrell where the plases have bine accustomyd to be used."

Despite Freeman's explanation that the theatre was called the Quarry, the wording of the lease suggests that the plays were given in a real quarry. Chambers tells us that there is record of plays having been given in this quarry in 1495, 1516, and 1533, as well as by Thomas Ashton, mentioned in the poem.[45] Freeman reports that Ashton died in 1578 and that the last record of his having produced a play is 1568. Thus Churchyard writes of a performance given about twenty years prior to his writing, in something that was in use as a theatre at least ninety-two years prior to his writing, which was by other records a quarry. The one other mention of location of a performance in Shrewsbury Chambers gives is a churchyard, 1542. Evidently plays were not given in this quarry as a matter of course. Nonetheless it is interesting that they were given in a quarry and that, if Churchyard's description has any relationship to truth whatever, some thousands of people watched a performance at one time. . . .[46]

The ancillary evidence put forth by Southern and by Freeman is interesting but certainly questionable. I have presented reason to interpret the primary evidence, the drawing of *The Castell of Perseverance*, as other than a drawing of a medieval theatre in the round. This does not prove that there were no specially constructed medieval theatres in the round. It is not unreasonable to think that there were. The fact that Churchyard and Carew both speak of such theatres suggests that they did not seem implausible at the end of the sixteenth century either. But the bulk of the evidence so far seems to me to suggest more flexible and intimate playing areas and productions which were less formalized than such specially constructed theatres would allow.

45. E. K. Chambers, *The Medieval Stage* (Oxford, 1903), II, p. 394.
46. [Omitted here is a detailed critique of Merle Fifield, *The Castle in the Circle*, Ball State Monographs, no. 6 (Muncie, Ind., 1967); a more recent study by Fifield is "The Arena Theatres in Vienna Codices 2535 and 2536," *Comparative Drama*, II (1968), 259–82.]

V. A. Kolve

18. *Everyman* and the Parable
of the Talents

Many scholars at work over several decades have done much to discover the sources of *Everyman*. We have learned that it owes something to the traditions of the Dance of Death, to confessional manuals, to treatises on the art of holy dying, to a medieval schema that divides all human endowments into gifts of Nature, Fortune, and Grace; and most important of all, we have been shown its likeness to a testing-of-friends story (Buddhist in origin) that appears first shaped to a Christian moral in the Greek *Barlaam and Ioasaph* of the eleventh century. A. C. Cawley, in his edition of the play, summarized and significantly extended those enquiries.[1] Though I shall propose in this paper a new and more inclusive way of describing the play's central concerns, I have no wish to forsake any of this genealogy of relationship already established. The literary kindred of the play called *Everyman* are as numerous as the centrality of its subject would suggest. That subject is nothing less than man's dying and doom.

But there remain a number of things unexplained and unaccounted for. Scholarship has passed over in silence some facts that bulk very large. Consider, for example, the way the title page names the central action:

Here begynneth a treatyse how the hye Fader of heuen sendeth Dethe to somon euery creature to come and gyue a-counte of theyr lyues in this worlde / and is in maner of a morall playe.

Notice that the play is *not* entitled "A treatyse how a man shulde lerne dye," or ". . . how a man his trewe frendes may knowe," or ". . . what

[Reprinted from Sandro Sticca, ed., *The Medieval Drama* (Albany: State University of New York Press, 1971), by permission of author and publisher. Copyright 1971 by the State University of New York Press.]
1. *Everyman*, ed. A. C. Cawley (Manchester, 1961); hereafter cited as "Cawley." All references to the play are to this edition. The possible priority of the Dutch *Elckerlijc* over the English *Everyman* is of no real consequence to this paper, and I have not thought it necessary to rehearse that problem here. If *Everyman* is indeed a translation from the Dutch, it is a fully achieved translation; its audiences would not have been aware they were watching a foreign play. I am concerned with the meaning of the action and the words which describe it for an English audience.

be yiftes of Kynde, Fortune, and Grace," though such formulas are what a careful reading of the scholarship surrounding the play might lead one to expect. The audience will of course learn something about all three subjects—as titles, none would be wholly misleading—but they were not what the printer or the dramatist thought the play was about: that they defined instead as a summons to ready and render accounts.

The playing-text indeed makes necessary that description. The words "reckoning" and "account" occur (in varying grammatical forms) more than twenty-five times in the play, often together, and always at moments of high urgency, where most meaning is being gathered in fewest words.[2] I propose to give them some close attention, and wish to begin with two summary foreclosures. First of all, we must not ascribe this language to the dramatist's unique invention, to the particular poetry of his play; as will be seen, it is language very common in relation to the Doom.[3] And more important, we must not confuse this summons to an accounting with the sublime image of Revelations 20:12, 15:

And I saw the dead, great and small, standing in the presence of the throne. And the books were opened; and another book was opened, which was the book of life. And the dead were judged by those things which were written in the books, according to their works. . . . And whosoever was not found written in the book of life was cast into the pool of fire.

(Douay translation)

We must not confuse these images, though I suspect many have. These books are kept in heaven, they are part of a mystery. Everyman, in strong contrast, must bring with him his own account book—it is a literal stage property—and his urgent task is to ready and "clere" it. His greatest concern is, in terms of sources, in no way indebted to the high mystery of Apocalypse, but is instead a thing smaller, humbler, more precise.[4] God orders Everyman to *"bring with hym* a sure rekenynge" (l. 70).

2. For "rekenynge" see lines 20, 70, 99, 106, 113, 137, 147, 160, 333, 375, 419, 511, 529, 652, 865, 914; for "accounte," lines 244, 336, 376, 406, 420, 493, 551, 580, 916. And cf. "my wrytynge" in line 187.

3. Cawley's note to line 104 (p. 31) relates such language to the verses on the bailiff in Lydgate's translation of the French *Dance of Death* poem. But there, terms such as "assise," "sommended," "to yefe a-comptes" are used simply as a witty play on the bailiff's own profession. It is too particular, and too late in date, to offer a source for this kind of language. See *The Dance of Death*, ed. Florence Warren, with an introduction by Beatrice White, EETS e.s. 181 (London, 1931), p. 36 (Ellesmere MS version).

4. Minor devils were sometimes thought of as recording man's sins, sometimes in a slightly comic context, as in the Doomsday pageant of *The Towneley Plays*, ed. George England and Alfred W. Pollard, EETS e.s. 71 (London, 1897), esp. pp. 371–79, or in exempla concerning Saint Brice (for several references, see V. A. Kolve, *The Play Called Corpus Christi* [Stanford, 1966], pp. 140 and 299, n. 43). More often, this is treated gravely, as in the *ars moriendi* block-book illustration of

The search for a possible source for this action will be made easier if
we note how closely it is related to another recurring theme of the
play: the notion that life and goods are "lent," not given. Everyman is
forced to confront that sad truth at several crucial moments of loss,[5] in
exchanges like the following:

DETHE.   What, wenest thou thy lyue is gyuen the,
              And thy worldely gooddes also?
EVERYMAN.   I had wende so, veryle.
DETHE.   Nay, nay, it was but lende the. . . .   (ll. 161–64)

Later, as his understanding grows, Everyman will recount his duty in
that same way:

        Of all my workes I must shewe
        How I haue lyued and my dayes spent;
        Also of yll dedes that I haue vsed
        In my tyme, syth lyfe was me lent. . . .   (ll. 338–44)

Words like "reckoning," "account-making," "lending," and "spending,"
compose the essential verbal matrix of the play; and the account book
Everyman brings with him is the emblem of their interrelationship. It
is what the play most urgently concerns.

A fifteenth-century English poet in the act of contemplating the
nearness of his own death offers evidence that such an association of ideas
is not novel and can furnish a clue to its ultimate source. John Lydgate,
in his *Testament*, writes:

        Age is crope In, calleth me to my grave,
        To make rekenyng how I my tyme haue spent,
        Baryne of vertu, allas, who shall me saue,
        Fro fendes daunger tacounte for my talent,
        But Iesu be my staf and my potent,
        Ouerstreite audite is like tencombre me,
        Or dome be youen, but mercy be present
        To all that knele to Iesu on ther kne.[6]

---

how dying men may be tempted to despair. It shows a devil at the deathbed, holding up a large bill-of-writing and a scroll which says *Ecce peccata tua*. See the
facsimile *Ars moriendi*, ed. W. Harry Rylands, Holbein Society (London, 1881).
The drama's Everyman must present his own account book; it is a different tradition altogether.

5. See also ll. 57, 437–41. Words signifying something "lent" occasionally occur
in connection with the fifth temptation named by the *ars moriendi*, that of family
and temporal things. See, for instance, *Ratis Raving and Other Moral and Religious
Pieces*, ed. J. Rawson Lumby, EETS 43 (London, 1870), pp. 5–6. But this most
probably derives from the parable of the talents, and should not be regarded as an
ultimately independent source.

6. *The Minor Poems of John Lydgate*, ed. Henry Noble MacCracken, pt. 1,
EETS e.s. 107 (London, 1911), p. 337 (ll. 217–24).

The only important word in this verse not found in *Everyman*, other than those suggesting an advanced old age, is the word "talent." But where that word occurs, these others occur also. And where these others occur but the word "talent" is missing, it is, I shall argue, the necessary explanation of them. The parable which gives meaning to Lydgate's verse furnishes for *Everyman* also an intellectual structure just below the surface of the play, and from it many of the play's characters, the most distinctive part of its language, and the logic of its total action derive. It is less a new "source" for *Everyman*, than the source behind the sources: the covered logic of an action that made that action coherent and inevitable. Interrelationships between medieval texts are sometimes so complex that it is possible to name those nearest and most like without having looked at the most important of all.

Because it will be our steady concern in what follows, I wish to set out here the parable of the talents, entire, as it is found in Matthew 25:14–30:

For even as a man going into a far country called his servants and delivered to them his goods;

And to one he gave five talents, and to another two, and to another one, to everyone according to his proper ability; and immediately he took his journey.

And he that had received five talents went his way and traded with the same and gained other five.

And in like manner he that had received the two gained other two.

But he that had received the one, going his way, digged into the earth and hid his lord's money.

But after a long time the lord of those servants came and reckoned with them.

And he that had received the five talents, coming, brought other five talents, saying: Lord, thou didst deliver to me five talents. Behold, I have gained other five over and above.

His lord said to him: Well done, good and faithful servant, because thou hast been faithful over a few things, I will place thee over many things. Enter thou into the joy of thy lord.

And he also that had received the two talents came and said: Lord, thou deliveredst two talents to me. Behold, I have gained other two.

His lord said to him: Well done, good and faithful servant, because thou hast been faithful over a few things, I will place thee over many things. Enter thou into the joy of thy lord.

But he that had received the one talent came and said: Lord, I know that thou art a hard man; thou reapest where thou hast not sown and gatherest where thou has not strewed.

And, being afraid, I went and hid thy talent in the earth. Behold, here thou hast that which is thine.

And his lord answering said to him: Wicked and slothful servant, thou knewest that I reap where I sow not and gather where I have not strewed.

Thou oughtest therefore to have committed my money to the bankers; and at my coming I should have received my own with usury.

Take ye away therefore the talent from him and give it him that hath ten talents.

For to everyone that hath shall be given, and he shall abound: but, from him that hath not, that also which he seemeth to have shall be taken away.

And the unprofitable servant cast ye out into the exterior darkness. There shall be weeping and gnashing of teeth.   (Douay translation)

Any modern commentator will tell you that a talent was originally a unit of weight which became also a unit of monetary value, its precise worth depending on the metal it measured. But that clarifies only the literal sense of the parable. The talents are obviously used here as a figure of speech, as a way of talking about something else. Indeed, it is only because Christ used them to talk about something else that the word "talent" is current still. Its present signification descends from the glosses of the Fathers concerning Christ's real subject, and therefore stands now for natural endowment, ability, capacity. It does so in French, Italian, Spanish, and English.

Though this text from Matthew will be our chief concern, it is not possible to separate it entirely from two other parables which also concern talents loaned or placed in trust—not possible, because medieval writers and preachers did not always distinguish between them. One is the version offered by Luke 19:12–27, differing in some details but clearly an alternate account of the same teaching. The other is found in Matthew 18, beginning at the twenty-third verse:

Therefore is the kingdom of heaven likened to a king who would take an account of his servants.

And, when he had begun to take the account, one was brought to him that owed him ten thousand talents.

And, as he had not wherewith to pay it, his lord commanded that he should be sold, and his wife and children and all that he had, and payment to be made.

But that servant falling down besought him, saying: Have patience with me and I will pay thee all.

The king has pity and releases him from his debt. The servant later chances to meet a man who owes him a hundred pence in turn. He demands an immediate settlement, and when the other pleads his inability to pay, the king's servant has him thrown into prison. The king, hearing of this, summons his servant again, charges him with his failure to forgive as he himself had been forgiven, and delivers him to torturers until the debt be paid.

This parable is entirely separate from the other two, but I mention it now because it also bears an important relationship to *Everyman*, and because the word "talent" links all three parables in ways medieval authors were not always concerned to keep separate. The parable from Matthew 25, however, is much the most important—for its narrative power, its richer detail, the greater significance of its surrounding matter (the wise and foolish virgins precede it, the corporal deeds of mercy follow), and perhaps as a result of all the above, the greater patristic attention paid it over the course of several centuries. It would be worth our present attention if only to explain the play's central figure, a man summoned to render account of goods lent him for a time and now recalled. But in fact its importance for *Everyman* is far more extensive in ways patristic commentary on the parable alone can make clear. I wish to suggest some of those ways, one instance at a time.

Let me begin with the desertions—that movement-into-aloneness generic to tragedy which is here represented by the betrayals of Felawship, Kynrede, and Goodes, and later by the departure of Beaute, Strength, Dyscrecion, and V. Wyttes. The tale of the man who has three friends, two of whom betray him in his greatest need (a tale existing in numerous versions and many languages, deriving ultimately from *Barlaam and Ioasaph*), has long been recognized as a source of this action. Everyman does test his friends and some of them bear names deriving from prose moralizations of that story. The first friend is most frequently explained as standing for Riches, or the World; the second as figuring Wife and Kindred (sometimes including Friends); and the third friend, too little loved but alone faithful, is named Good Deeds, or Charity, or Christ. The relationship is close and vital. But on its own it is not enough. These analogues offer no help in accounting for the second set of desertions, the second tragic movement of the play. For those, we are accustomed to refer to the *ars moriendi*, which does indeed concern the experience of death, but in ways a good deal less physical and interior than the play's second part.[7] The *ars*, it is true, does speak of wife and children and riches as temptations to a dying man, for he is likely to turn to them for help, uselessly, and in ways ultimately dangerous to his soul. But, in terms of literary genetics, that is merely to account again for some features already provided by the three-friends story. The subject of the *ars moriendi* is emphatically *not* the physical process of dying: it insists that in the moment of extremity only spiritual matters are worth attention. In short, these two sources between them can account for Felawship, Kynrede, Cosyn, Goodes, Good Dedes. A great deal, but not all. The parable of the talents and patristic commen-

7. For an introduction and bibliographical guide to the literature of the *ars moriendi*, see Sister Mary Catharine O'Connor, *The Art of Dying Well* (New York, 1942).

tary upon it, in strong contrast, can furnish us not only with the central figure of a man summoned to a reckoning, and with the characters just named, but also with those characters excluded so far: Beaute, Strength, Dyscrecion, V. Wyttes, Knowledge, and even Confessyon. It does so in two different ways.

The first way, and the more generally inclusive, is developed by those commentaries that work from the idea of talents per se, ignoring (as does the Gospel of Luke) the 5-2-1 numerology of Matthew. This tradition goes back at least as far as Saint John Chrysostom in the fourth century,[8] but I shall quote from the vastly more influential statement of it made by Gregory the Great at the end of his brilliant homily on the parable—a version incorporated by Rabanus Maurus into his own eight-book commentary on Matthew written some two centuries later.[9] Gregory writes:

> There is no-one who can truly say: I have received no talent at all, there is nothing about which I can be required to give a reckoning. For even the very smallest of gifts will be charged as a talent to the account of every poor man. For one man has received understanding [*intelligentia*] and owes the ministry of preaching by reason of that talent. Another has received earthly goods, and owes alms-giving from his talent, out of his property. Another has received neither understanding of inner things [*internorum intelligentia*] nor wealth of worldly goods [*rerum affluentia*], but he has learned an art or skill by which he lives, and this very skill is charged to his account as the receiving of a talent. Another has acquired none of these things, but nevertheless has perhaps come to be on terms of friendship [*familiaritas*] with a rich man; he has therefore received the talent of friendship. So if he does not speak to him on behalf of the poor, he is condemned for not using his talent . . . [etc.].[10]

Already this could suggest to a dramatist the characters Knowledge, Goodes, Felawship. And in his insistence that the very smallest of gifts—those common even to the poor—must be recognized as talents and put out to use, Gregory may be taken to imply that humbler inventory that Chrysostom had named earlier:

> For the talents here are each person's ability, whether in the way of protection, or in money, or in teaching, or in what thing soever of the kind. . . .

8. See *The Homilies of S. John Chrysostom . . . on the Gospel of St. Matthew*, trans. Sir George Prevost (London, 1885), pt. III, pp. 1041–42; see also pp. 1027–28. Chrysostom died in 407.

9. In *Patrologiae cursus completus: Patrologia Latina*, ed. J. P. Migne, 221 vols. (Paris, 1844–64); hereafter cited as P.L. For Rabanus Maurus, *Commentariorum in Matthaeum* (written c. 822–26), see vol. 107, col. 1095.

10. Gregory the Great (c. 540–604), *XL Homiliarum in Evangelia*, P.L. 76, col. 1109.

For this end God gave us speech, and hands, and feet, and strength of body, and mind, and understanding. . . .[11]

Here Strength makes a separate appearance, and Dyscrecion [mind] as well, to single out only those not already named in the passage from Gregory. A commentary long attributed to the Venerable Bede, but actually based on Rabanus, concludes its exposition of the parable by emphasizing this same kind of open-ended applicability, as I suppose any of us would if we were asked (without preparation) to suggest its general meaning: "These things may be interpreted in many ways as concerning charity, ability and knowledge." The *Glossa ordinaria* instructs in a similar mode: "Note that what is given to each one in worldly or spiritual things is charged to his account, as the talent for which he will have to give a reckoning when the Lord returns."[12]

But patristic tradition can offer further and more particular help, for the numbers in Matthew also invited theological speculation. A 5-2-1 progression, with its multiples, necessarily exercised the imagination of a culture that thought numbers one of the hidden languages of God. Because no number in Scripture could be without spiritual meaning, however enigmatic, several explanations were made over the course of centuries. The earliest known to me, that of Saint Hilary of Poitiers from the mid-fourth century, is especially concerned with how the Gentiles won the inheritance promised the Jews. The servant who received five talents is read as a figure for those people of the Law who received the five books of Moses and who doubled that trust by the faith of the Gospel, recognizing the sacraments as having been foreshadowed in the Law. Because those persons thereby fulfill the commandments in a new way, they are justified by both Law and faith. These are, I take it, the Jews who accept Christ, of whom the apostles themselves stand as first exemplars.

Hilary interprets the servant who received two talents as standing for those people of the Gentiles who have faith in their heart and confess by their mouth that Christ is Lord—a capacity for inner faith and public witness are the two talents, which they double by good works, authenticating their faith through action. It is with reference to them that the unprofitable servant charges his master with reaping where he has not sown, for the final harvest is here foreseen to be mostly of the Gentiles,

---

11. *Chrysostom*, pp. 1041–42.

12. For the pseudo-Bede, see *In Matthaei Evangelium Expositio*, P.L. 92, col. 109. Paul the Deacon (c. 720–800) in his *Homiliarius*, P.L. 95, cols. 1554–55, lays distinctive emphasis on skills in the various arts and crafts. For the *Glossa ordinaria*, see P.L. 114, col. 166.

instead of the seed of Abraham, to whom the Messiah was promised. The first servant offers works doubled by faith; the second servant, faith doubled by deeds.

And the third servant, it follows, must typify the Jews still living in darkness, rejecting Christ and his Gospel, carnal in their understanding, thinking to be justified by the Law alone. The teaching of Christ they hid in the earth, neither using it themselves nor wishing others to use it. And their fate will be terrible: "For to them that have the use of the Gospels, even the honor of the Law is given; but from him that has not the faith of Christ, even the honor which he seems to have of the Law will be taken away."[13]

This early version of the parable's meaning is without consequence for *Everyman*, as is part of another tradition, rather closely allied, summarized by Rabanus Maurus so: "The first servant, in being given five talents, received the five books of the Law, which, by the doctrine and fulfillment of the ten commandments, he increased. The second, in being given the two talents, received the two Testaments, and these, in a moral and mystical sense, he doubled by piously spreading their teaching abroad. The third, in the likeness of one talent, received the gift of grace, but he hid it in earthly pleasures, and was therefore cast into hell, for he produced no profit from it."[14] Such a reading of the two talents is not uncommon, and the interpretation of the single talent as grace buried in earthly pleasures has some obvious bearing on *Everyman*. But a tradition descending from Saint Jerome is another matter altogether, more useful to preachers concerned with the moral lives of their parishioners, more widely disseminated and influential, and more steadily illuminating for our play. In his longer commentary on Matthew, Jerome explains that the five talents are to be understood as the five senses—sight, hearing, taste, smell, touch—which are exactly equivalent to the character V. Wyttes in *Everyman*; that the two talents are to be understood as *intelligentia et opera*, which almost as certainly furnish us the characters Knowledge and Good Dedes (his context suggests an affirmative, not neutral, meaning for both terms); and that the one talent is to be understood as *ratio* alone, which I take to be synonymous with the character Dyscrecion. This version of the numbers was transmitted by Isidore of Seville in his *Allegoriae quaedam sacrae scripturae* and thence by Rabanus Maurus in his *De universo*.[15]

13. Hilary of Poitiers (c. 315–67), *Commentarius in Matthaeum*, P.L. 9, cols. 1061–63.

14. Rabanus Maurus, *De Universo* (c. 844), P.L. 111, col. 79.

15. Saint Jerome (c. 342–420), *Commentaria in Evangelium S. Matthaei*, P.L. 26, col. 186. In the pseudo-Jerome *Expositio Quatuor Evangeliorum: Matthaeus*, P.L.

One of the identifications I have just made demands fuller and more careful statement, for it addresses one of the most difficult questions in *Everyman* scholarship. Namely, is the character Knowledge to be understood in something like our modern sense of that term [*scientia, intelligentia*]? Or does it stand instead for the even then rarer, and now archaic, medieval sense of "acknowledge," naming that part of the sacrament of penance which concerns a full confession of sins? The latter sense was first proposed in 1947 by H. de Vocht, and has since been skillfully supported by several others. It is an attractive idea, and I was once persuaded by it; but close attention to the morphology of the word in our text, where it occurs only as a noun, never as a verb, and—more to the present point—evidence from patristic commentary on the parable of the talents, both suggest the older and simpler answer is probably correct.[16] Good Dedes and Knowledge are linked in the play as intimately as are *opera* and *intelligentia* in explanations of the two talents given the second servant. Indeed, the tradition just named, that of Jerome, Isidore, and Rabanus, can help a good deal in clarifying the relationship of certain allegorical characters in the play to others closely allied. The gift of the five senses (V. Wyttes) is defined by them as a knowledge of external things, that is, the receiving of sense data. Reason (Dyscrecion) separates us from the beasts, and comprises the ability to interpret such data. And Knowledge in its turn is the product of reason working perfectly upon sense data: reason not blinded by earthly concerns, not stupidly tenacious of the literal, but seeking instead the spiritual truth that lies hidden within all phenomena.[17] In *Everyman* it is clear, I think, that Knowledge exemplifies this deepest kind of understanding. As a character, she has knowledge of Confession and its effi-

---

30, col. 559, the endowments are distinguished less clearly: *quinque sensus, intellectus et operatio, intellectus* alone. For Isidore (c. 560–636), see P.L. 83, col. 124, and for Rabanus, see P.L. 111, col. 79. They both offer the Five Books–Two Testaments–Grace interpretation as well.

16. Lawrence V. Ryan, in a distinguished essay, "Doctrine and Dramatic Structure in Everyman," *Speculum*, XXXII (1957), 722–35, discusses this question among others, and makes a strong case for the "acknowledge" interpretation. But I take the fact that the word appears only as a noun or proper name to be crucial; in that form, and in the absence of contextual limitation, it is unlikely to have been understood as "acknowledgment." Note too that Knowledge is introduced to Everyman in response to his request for "counseyll" (l. 516); later he asks to be given "cognycyon" (l. 538) about where to go to Confession. Knowledge is the answer to both, and would seem to be synonymous with them. See Helen S. Thomas, "The Meaning of the Character Knowledge in 'Everyman,'" *Mississippi Quarterly*, XIV (1961), 3–13, for a summary (with full references) of scholarship devoted to this problem, and a useful contribution to it. She also concludes, for reasons other than those outlined above, that Knowledge is a "Wisdom-figure."

17. See ll. 732, 737–39, on the need to go beyond sense evidence.

cacy, and is a useful guide to it; but she speaks many other truths as well.

The parable of the talents, then, can explain the figure of Everyman as a man summoned to render accounts; and, better than the more immediately proximate sources, it offers a comprehensive rationale for the other *dramatis personae*, both interior and exterior, whom he confronts in the course of this action. It also offers help in what must be always one of the crucial tasks of criticism: the attempt to define with maximum precision what happens within a work of art.

For instance, there is another group of words closely associated in the play, and nearly as insistently central as those concerned with "accounts" and "reckoning." More than twenty-five times, the words "pylgrymage," "vyage," or "iourney" occur, and these, too, despite their linguistic weight, have never had any close attention.[18] Perhaps this is because the idea of pilgrimage as a figure for all human life was so common in the Middle Ages; even now it seems to require no glossing. Besides, Everyman goes on a journey before our eyes, from one friend to another and finally into the grave. But again, as with Everyman's account book, if that *is* the explanation of the scholarly silence, then I think that we have mistaken the matter, conflating two metaphors allied but separate, only one of which is really at the center of the play. The pilgrimage in question is not that "of human life"—in the manner of *The Canterbury Tales* or *The Castle of Perseverance* or Deguilleville's *Le Pèlerinage de la vie humaine*. That pilgrimage has been underway since Everyman's birth and is hardly spoken of here. It does not add up to news, or require a message of command. The errand assigned to Dethe,

> Go thou to Eueryman
> And shewe hym, in my name,
> A pylgrymage he must on hym take,   (ll. 66–68)

employs a different metaphor, and concerns a new contingency in a life already at the full. In the pilgrimage of life, Everyman's friends have been his constant companions, but in this new and "longe" journey, their constancy is at an end. The latter is, quite simply, the death-journey of the soul to Judgment—Deguilleville's *Le Pèlerinage de l'âme*—and most of the play is devoted to showing the soul freeing itself from earth so that it can depart. That brief and final action—a swift and simple journey upwards—alone is the pilgrimage suddenly ordained and so inadequately prepared for. The angel describes it so:

18. For "pylgrymage" see ll. 68, 146, 331, 550, 565, 629, 673, 784, 818; for "iourney," ll. 103, 141, 242, 247, 259, 268, 279, 295, 363, 464, 495, 641; for "vyage," ll. 415, 674, 782. At l. 566, Penance is described briefly as "this vyage," and an awkward parallel construction at ll. 141–42 can be easily misread; but the subject everywhere else is unequivocally the soul-journey.

Come, excellente electe spouse, to Iesu!
Here aboue thou shalte go

. . . .

Now shalte thou in to the heuenly spere,
Vnto the whiche all ye shall come
That lyueth well before the daye of dome.   (ll. 894–901)

That journey was first made by Christ in his ascension, and to it the
parable of the talents was always understood to refer in its opening
words: *Sicut enim homo peregre proficiscens . . .* (Matthew) or *Homo
quidam nobilis abiit in regionem longinquam . . .* (Luke)—(Englished
by the Wyclif Bible, "Sothely as a man goynge fer in pilgrimage," and
"Sum noble man wente in to a fer cuntree . . .").[19] According to the
Fathers, Christ used the terms *peregre* and *in regionem longinquam* because he was foretelling his ascension in the flesh. The mystery of the
Incarnation, in which God united himself with man's kind forever, made
his long journey also a pilgrimage, for that word, in the Bible as well as
in countless medieval texts, has about it always the suggestion of exile,
of finding oneself in a country foreign and potentially hostile. The soul's
true home is heaven, but the flesh will go there a stranger and afraid.

I would not wish to claim, in the absence of these other relationships,
that *Everyman*'s use of pilgrimage as a metaphor for the soul-journey
need be explained by reference to the parable of the talents. It was
available in many other places. But the fact is that the parable, which
is necessary on other grounds, does make those words available, uses
them as a part of its vital meaning, and may therefore help account for
their great frequency and importance in the play: the pilgrimage of
Everyman's soul recapitulates the first of Christ's journeys in the parable.
What can easily seem to us the "longe journey"—all those desperate
wanderings in the *platea*, the search for companionship into the grave—
is really born of the allegorical mode itself, that same formal and artistic
necessity that also fragments a man's personality and experience of life
into two sets of "friends." Its purpose is merely to disentangle, to make
consecutive, spatial, and linear, the extremely complex process of how
a man dies. Each stage of human dying—that mysterious transition from
being to apparent nonbeing—is rendered as a separate event, but its real-
life referent may of course be much shorter or much longer. The duration of the play need represent barely more than the moment of death
itself, when light and life fade together, though it must be long
enough for a motion of contrition within the soul and for the receiving

19. *The Holy Bible . . . made from the Latin Vulgate by John Wycliffe and his
Followers*, 4 vols., ed. Rev. Josiah Forshall and Sir Frederic Madden (Oxford, 1850),
IV, 70–71, 210–11.

of sacraments on one's deathbed. The desertions—friends, kin, goods, beauty, strength, the five senses—are in some sense simultaneous, for none of these is utterly and irretrievably lost until they are lost altogether, at the moment of extinction. To separate them is simply to make the totality of that loss more readily apprehensible by the mind and the imagination. But the Everyman specific to this play is possibly youthful and certainly no more than in his prime ("O Dethe, thou comest whan I had thee leest in mynde"), and this division into parts, native to allegory, is also meant to image another kind of dying: that which comes to the old, who do lose these things slowly, remorselessly. The frenzied movement here and there that we see in the *platea* is ultimately that of the soul of any man, whatever his age, as it struggles to free itself from man's body and world's time in order to mount to eternity. That ascent alone is the pilgrimage named so often in this play.

Patristic commentary on the master's journey can help explain another aspect of the play that exhibits a parallel richness of meaning. The action's place in historical time is allegorically as ambiguous as is the duration of the dying, and the play's movement from a double to a single time is one of its finest artistic strategies. Because the play concerns a single figure called Everyman—printed by Cawley, quite properly, as one word with a capital E—it speaks of death as it may come to any one of us, individually, at any time. The play's historical moment is in that sense a perpetual present, not tied down to history. But simultaneously a specific historical time is also addressed which is nothing less than Doomsday, the general death that will befall all those still living at the end of the world. We are implicated collectively as well as individually, for there is a steady, sustained ambivalence of pronoun in God's opening speech: Everyman is spoken of as both singular and plural in number.[20] I shall italicize the alternation:

> *Euery man* lyueth so after *his owne* pleasure,
> And yet of *theyr* lyfe *they* be nothynge sure.
> I se the more that I *them* forbere
> The worse *they* be fro yere to yere.
> *All that lyueth* appayreth faste;
> Therfore I wyll, in all the haste,
> Haue a rekenynge of *euery mannes* persone;
> For, and I leue *the people* thus alone
> In *theyr* lyfe and wycked tempestes,
> Veryly *they* will become moche worse than beestes,
> For now *one* wolde by enuy *another* vp ete;
> Charyte *they* do all clene forgete.
> I hoped well that *euery man*

20. R. W. Zandvoort, "Everyman—Elckerlijc," in *Études Anglaises*, VI (1953), 1–15, has briefly remarked on this fact (see p. 3).

> In my glory sholde make *his* mansyon,
> And therto I had *them* all electe . . .   (ll. 40–54)

When God gives his order to Dethe:

> Go thou to *Eueryman*
> And shewe *hym,* in my name,
> A pylgrymage *he* must on *hym* take,   (ll. 66–68)

we seem to be safely back in the singular; but Dethe's answer again allows no one to escape:

> Lorde, I wyll in the worlde go renne ouer-all
> And cruelly out-serche *bothe grete and small.*   (ll. 72–73)

The ambiguity is present even earlier in the opening speech of the Messenger, which denies the audience any certainty about the kind of death-and-judgment play they will see:

> For ye shall here how our Heuen Kynge
> Calleth Eueryman to a generall rekenynge.   (ll. 19–20)

A listening audience cannot tell whether "Everyman" is written as one word or two, just as the word "general" can mean both "comprehensive" (a man giving a full account of his life) and "collective" (all men, the general) brought to judgment. The ambiguity is no accident: *I* do not know when I will die: *we* do not know when, as a race, we will have exceeded the patience of God.

The text provides for—indeed, subtly ensures—a kind of staging that will carry this meaning. The Messenger calls out from the *platea:* give audience to the play, hear what God has to say. God appears above to talk about what he sees—"euery man" in his sin; and for the first part of his speech at least, it seems clear that a character called Everyman should not be evident or distinguishable from the rest of the audience. The audience itself is the first "euery man" that God names: it is what is in his view, and what therefore he must be understood to order Dethe to summon. When Dethe cries "Loo, yonder I se Eueryman walkynge," "Eueryman, stande styll" (ll. 80, 85) the leading actor is designated, but until then he belongs in the audience, anonymous, unexceptional. The actor might well be directed to begin making his way easily and gracefully toward an exit just before the summons comes, for we live as though such matters hold no interest, cannot concern our own life. Only when Death names us directly do we take any notice, and then, like Everyman, bewildered and unready, it is in the broken rhythms of "What, sente to me?" Reluctantly Everyman will acknowledge that summons—up to this point ambiguous—in the name of us all, for he is at once our likeness and our brother.

Neither the *ars moriendi* nor the faithful-friend analogues can offer any explanation for this doubled pronoun of address, this dual sense of time. They concern a man's death, that is all. But the parable of the talents does exhibit this same allegorical doubling of significance. The man gone on a pilgrimage to a far country is Christ, and the parable speaks of what will be required when he returns, at the Second Coming, which is Doomsday. Gregory explains it so:

> For when the judge will come, he will ask from each of us as much as he gave. Therefore, so that each one may be sure of giving a reckoning when the Lord returns, he should think fearfully every day of what he has received. For, lo, the day is near when he who went on a journey to a far land will return. For he who left this earth on which he was born did indeed as it were go away to a far country; but he will surely return, and demand a reckoning for the talents.[21]

This understanding of the parable's "moment" must be the source of the darker, more apocalyptic overtones of God's opening speech in the play. Until the very last of its forty-two lines there is no mention of death, or of pilgrimage or journey, nor is any clear priority given the singular pronoun. We hear instead about sin and justice and a general reckoning. It is the language of the master returned. Only in the command given Dethe, at line 68, is it clear this play will concern a rehearsal of the Final Day, that its subject is that individual judgment at any individual death which will be formally recapitulated at the Day of Doom.[22]

These, then, are some ways in which attention to the parable can enable a closer and more accurate description of certain aspects of the play than has perhaps been readily available before. Let me choose just one more instance, last in my sequence, but far from least: the character and function of Good Dedes.

The problem is not one of any substantial misunderstanding. We see Good Dedes go into the grave with Everyman; we honor the fact that she alone does not desert him; and, in a general sense, we understand why. But the parable of the talents can allow us to name that reason with greater precision. It seems likely Jerome's use of *opera* furnished her name, Good Dedes, but her specific function in the play derives from another part of the parable. She is the crucial part of the reckoning Everyman must make, the spiritual profit, the increase, which God demands of his servants when he calls back the talents and hears the accounts. The reckoning concerns *lucrum spirituale*, and the servant

---

21. Gregory the Great, P.L. 76, col. 1109.
22. See Cawley's note to l. 885. Lines 259–61 confirm that Doomsday is not yet, but to come.

cast into exterior darkness is he who hides his talent in the earth, becoming thereby unprofitable in the economy of God's love and man's salvation. Good Dedes in the play, we may say simply and surely, is the profit on Everyman's total endowment: on his beauty, strength, reason, senses, friends, kindred, goods.

And in a manner again intrinsic to the parable, which speaks as though literal riches were its subject, the play creates a special relationship between Goodes and Good Dedes. There is on the one hand, however peculiar to the English language, the close verbal link between their names. And there is also a close emblematic relationship. Both are initially discovered prostrate and unable to move: Goodes because it is stacked, trussed, locked in chests, sacked in bags (ll. 393–97), as a talent hoarded and hidden rather than put out for use; and Good Dedes because she is buried in earth ("Here I lye, colde in the grounde") and fettered by sin (ll. 486–88). These parallels suggest what the Fathers declare explicitly and what the play itself will later make clear: that the one must become the other; that goods (here standing in for all of the talents) must become good deeds.[23] Dethe, in his opening summary of what we will see, offers one of those synonyms so oddly characteristic of this play, giving a character a name other than that he ordinarily bears. Everyman will dwell in hell forever, he tells us, "Excepte that almes be his good frende" (l. 78). Later, the play will explore in action the logic of that oblique naming. After Everyman has returned from Confession, he makes of his last will and testament his best Good Deed, adding to (and defining the nature of) those few earlier good deeds his penance has set free to walk again:

> Now herken, all that be here,
> For I wyll make my testament
> Here before you all present:
> In almes / halfe my good I wyll gyue with my handes twayne
> In the way of charyte with good entent,
> And the other halfe styll shall remayne
> In queth, to be retourned there it ought to be.   (ll. 696–702)

What is rightfully his—one half of his goods—he leaves to the poor in alms. What he has gained wrongfully—the other half—he will have restored to those he took from. He makes restitution, and he performs through his "almesse" the seven works of charity—those actions which alone can insure man's salvation at the Day of Doom and which are named by Christ in the verses that immediately follow the parable of the talents in Matthew 25. They are those good deeds to the poor and

23. See especially ll. 431–34. Cf. "A Poem of Goods," ed. A. G. Rigg, *A Glastonbury Miscellany of the Fifteenth Century* (Oxford, 1968), pp. 65–66.

wretched which cannot be done generously without doing them to
Christ: "To fede the hungry; to gyf the thirsty drynke; to clethe the
nakyd; herber the howsles; to viset the seke; to viset prisonners; bery the
ded."[24] Those deeds are the medieval meaning of "almesse," whether
accomplished by one's own hand or by a legacy to the church. "As long
as you did it to one of these my least brethren, you did it to me" (Matt.
25:31–46). Everyman has come a long spiritual way from that earlier
attempt to put his Goodes to use, when he sought to buy off Dethe for
"a thousande pounde" (l. 122).

This same passage affords a second instance of the way the parable of
the talents, within medieval tradition, seems to have gathered to itself
many like or nearby things. Everyman's last will and testament derives
almost word for word from Saint Luke's story of Zacheus, a rich man
of Jericho and a sinner, in whose house Jesus announces he will stay.
The respectable people murmur against it:

But Zacheus, standing, said to the Lord: Behold, Lord, the half of my
goods I give to the poor; and if I have wronged any man of any thing, I restore him fourfold.
Jesus said to him: This day is salvation come to this house, because he also
is a son of Abraham.
For the Son of man is come to seek and to save that which was lost.

(Luke 19:8–10)

The speech of Zacheus above must be the ultimate source of Everyman's almsgiving and restitution, whatever medieval handbooks for
priests may stand between. This ultimate indebtedness, so far as I know,
has never been noted; but more interesting from our present point of
view is the fact that Luke's version of the talents follows immediately.

Although in this play Confession is initially spoken of as a "clensynge
ryuere," a "gloryous fountayne" that can wash away sin (ll. 536, 545),
the dialogue soon moves from that imagery into a long prayer spoken
by Everyman, rehearsing his sins and asking mercy (ll. 581–618). At
the end of it, Good Dedes is at last enabled to move. *The Book of Vices
and Virtues*, a fourteenth-century English translation of the immensely
influential *Somme le Roi*, discusses the sacrament of penance in ways
helpful here and very closely related to the parable of the talents. It says
that man should think of his Holy Confessor as God's Bailiff, conducting
(and, through the sacrament, clearing) a preliminary rendering of ac-

24. British Museum MS Add. 37049, fol. 55 (an English miscellany from the first
half of the fifteenth century), names them so on a tree of the works of mercy. The
Doomsday plays of the Corpus Christi cycles stage an inquiry into these deeds as
their major action.

counts, of all of our "receites" and "dispences."[25] Good Dedes, free to move, will carry the account book, for she is what it records:

EVERYMAN   Good Dedes, haue we clere our rekenynge?
GOOD DEDES   Ye, in dede, I haue it here.   (ll. 652–53)

It is now clarified by penance of all *except* good deeds—the spiritual profit he will present as evidence of an (ultimately) faithful stewardship of talents entrusted for a time and now recalled. And in his own hand, with equal symbolic force, Everyman bears the cross—the sign of that one good deed man could not accomplish on his own, sufficient to remedy Adam's sin. In two of the *Gesta Romanorum* versions of the faithful friend story, the third friend (more commonly identified as Good Deeds or Charity) is Christ himself, the friend willing to die to prevent his friend's dying.[26] Without the sacrifice, no account books kept on earth could ever win grace. V. Wyttes notes this crucial fact after Everyman's visit to Priesthode for the sacraments:

Peas! For yonder I se Eueryman come,
Whiche hath made true satysfaccyon.   (ll. 769–70)

It names the change as though Everyman were its agent; but of course the facts are otherwise. Christ alone could make true satisfaction for sin —He is the great restitution—but it is available to any man through the sacrament of the altar. Everyman makes satisfaction in the only way possible for man fallen and forlorn: he satisfies justice by accepting Christ's body into his own. That assent and mystical incorporation win him heaven at the end. The third chapter of *The Boke of the Craft of Dying* advises as a medicine against despair that the dying man be helped to say:

The deth of oure lord Ihesu Crist I put betwene me and all myn euell meritis, and the merite of this worthi passione I offre for the merite that I shuld haue had and alas I haue it not; Sey also: Lord put the deth of oure lord Ihesu Criste be-twene me and thi ryghtwysnes.[27]

From this medieval Christian truth derives the power of the penultimate stage action: Good Dedes and the account book, Everyman and the cross

25. *The Book of Vices and Virtues*, ed. W. Nelson Francis, EETS 217 (London, 1942), p. 174. Also of interest are pp. 68–92, 212–15.

26. *The Early English Versions of the Gesta Romanorum*, ed. S. J. H. Herrtage, EETS e.s. 33 (London, 1879), pp. 131, 132. Lines 778–80 make it clear that Everyman now bears in his hands a cross.

27. "The Boke of the Craft of Dying," in *Yorkshire Writers: Richard Rolle . . . and His Followers*, 2 vols., ed. Carl Horstmann (London, 1895, 1896), II, 413.

of Christ. The union is emblematic. They go into the grave together, for the lack of either would destroy the hope of heaven. Having learned *to wish* to die, Everyman has learned the highest lesson of the art of dying well: "I go before there I wolde be. God be our gyde" (l. 780). The play now moves swiftly to its end as all except Good Dedes fall away at the grave's edge. Everyman commends his soul to God, asks to be saved at the Day of Doom, and is received above to the sound of heavenly singing. An angel speaks to him, "Come, excellente electe spous, to Iesu!" It is equivalent to the parable's "Enter thou into the joy of thy lord."

All this would seem to indicate that some knowledge of the parable of the talents, and the commentary that grew up around it, can offer important help to our understanding of the play. For certain central facts, it has claim to be the necessary cause; and if that is granted, it becomes (in the technical sense) an adequate cause for other characters, events, and actions of the play. But the question of external probability remains. Evidence is needed that this Death-and-Doomsday subject was elsewhere and in important places conceived in terms of the parable of the talents: that the conjunction of the two would have seemed natural to a late fifteenth-century dramatist and readily comprehensible to some reasonable portion of his audience.

If space were available to sketch the history of the parable and its influence on medieval vernacular literature, one might begin by looking at the bestiary of Guillaume le Clerc, written in Anglo-Norman in 1210 or thereabouts, which uses the parable significantly; or at that same author's *Le Besant de Dieu*, where the talents provide the governing idea for the entire poem.[28] But later evidence will serve our present purposes better. The most important link between Doomsday and the parable of the talents in popular medieval tradition is the *Speculum humanae salvationis*—one of the most important books of the later Middle Ages, and, along with the *Biblia pauperum*, one of the two most popular versions of sacred history read as a series of typologically related events. The *Speculum* was written in 1324, and was so widely disseminated that no census has ever been attempted of all of its sur-

28. For the *Bestiaire*, see the edition by Robert Reinsch (Leipzig, 1890), p. 374 (ll. 3469 ff.), or the translation by George Claridge Druce (Ashford, Kent, 1936), pp. 94 ff. For the *Besant de Dieu*, see the edition by Ernest E. Martin (Halle, 1869). "Besant" derives from the Latin *bysantium*, meaning a Byzantine coin; the Wycliffe Bible uses it as an English synonym for "talent" as well. On these works by Guillaume, see M. Dominica Legge, *Anglo-Norman Literature and Its Background* (Oxford, 1963), pp. 207–8, 228–29.

viving examples. (Lutz and Perdrizet, whose two-volume study[29] remains the most important work on the subject, knew of 205 Latin and Latin-German manuscripts, nearly 80 of them fully illustrated.) The text was translated into German, French, English, Dutch, and Czech. It became one of the most popular block books, again with extant examples beyond numbering. Granted the close relationship that existed between *Everyman* and *Elckerlijc,* we might note the fact of translation into both English and Dutch; and we might recall as well that the Netherlands was a great center of block-book printing.

The *Speculum* concerns us because in it, the Last Judgment is prefigured by (1) the parable of the talents, (2) the parable of the wise and foolish virgins, and (3) the writing on the wall at Belshazzar's feast. In the block books and the illuminated manuscripts, the four are most often depicted in a series spread across two pages, with their texts below, and the Last Judgment at the extreme left.[30] Christ is seated on an arc in the heavens, displaying his wounds, the lily and a two-edged sword emerging from his mouth; Mary and John kneel on either side of him, and the dead arise from their graves below. Directly alongside this picture is shown the parable of the talents, with the reckoning completed and the unprofitable servant bound or being led out to torture.[31] The influence of this work upon the visual arts was very considerable; it would have made the relationship I postulate between parable and play one that would have been more easily accessible to contemporary audiences (even the illiterate) than it is to us now. My evidence from the Fathers indicated that the parable was understood in terms of Doomsday.

29. *Speculum humanae salvationis,* 2 vols., ed. J. Lutz and P. Perdrizet (Mulhouse, 1907–9). They name Matthew 25 as the text most important to the passage, while noting that "dans Luc les talents deviennent des mines. C'est de mines que parle le *Speculum*" (I, 233). For the Latin text, see I, 82; for the French translation made by Jean Mielot in 1448, see I, 156–57. On the Dutch translations, see I, 104. A fifteenth-century English translation was edited by Alfred H. Huth for the Roxburghe Club, vol. 118 (London, 1888), as *The Miroure of Mans Salvacionne;* see pp. 137–38. M. R. James and Bernhard Berenson edited a facsimile volume of a fourteenth-century Italian manuscript, *Speculum humanae salvationis* (Oxford, 1926), with valuable introductions. Other facsimile editions have been made by J. P. Berjeau (London, 1861) and by Ernst Kloss, 2 vols. (Munich, 1925).

30. See the Kloss facsimile, p. 62.

31. Its text is based on the Luke version of the parable, but it has on either side of it pictures and texts that name Matthew 25 as their source; and sometimes, as in Pierpont Morgan MS 385, a fifteenth-century Dutch manuscript, Matthew 25 and Luke 19 are both named as sources to the talents picture. Elsewhere, as in the Dutch block book edited in facsimile by Kloss, Matthew 18, Matthew 25, and Apocalypse 20 are named as sources to the first two pictures, without Luke 19 being named at all. Luke is correctly cited more often than not, but this is evidence again of all three parables being treated almost as though they were one.

The present evidence makes it clear that the converse was also true, and via the block books well into the sixteenth century, Doomsday was thought of in terms of the parable of the talents.

There are intermediate works that should be looked at in detail but here can only be mentioned. A late fifteenth-century Scots poem, "The Thrie Tailes of the Thrie Priests of Peblis," offers evidence closely contemporary with *Everyman* that the talents version of the crisis survived, even though many of the analogues in between name it only in a generalized way as "being in peril of death." The Scots poem, like these others, never uses the word "talents," but it does specify the precise reckoning required by the King of Kings (identified so in the tale's second line):

> Thus but [i.e., without] delay befoir him to compeir.
> And with him count and give reckning of all
> He had of him al tyme baith grit and small.[32]

And from the fourteenth century in England, there is a remarkable example of all these traditions flourishing together, clustered around the idea of the talents. In one of the Middle English sermons edited by Ross, there is narrated a version of the faithful-friend story that has never been formally noticed in *Everyman* criticism.[33] It is used as an exemplum on the theme *Redde quod debes*—"Yelde that thou owest"— but between the first statement of the text and the narration of the story there intervenes a most elaborate development of theme, subsidiary theme, and illustration. It demonstrates most vividly how the idea of the talents as such subsumed material from all three parables I spoke of earlier. One hears first of the unmerciful servant of Matthew 18, who owed a debt of ten thousand talents, after which the other parable of the talents is narrated. Luke is the version cited—quite properly, for the synonym "besauntes" is used for talents, and the unprofitable servant hides his talent in a napkin rather than in the ground—but it details an unequal distribution of talents, using the 5-2-1 sequence Matthew's gospel alone provides. The preacher then goes on to quote the speech of Zacheus (again from Luke) that furnishes Everyman his last will and testament. He generalizes from it: "than it semeth well here-by that

32. In David Laing, *Early Popular Poetry of Scotland and the Northern Border*, ed. W. C. Hazlitt (London, 1895), I, 159 (ll. 1032–34); see also ll. 1104–5 and 1179–80. For later uses of the talents in poetry, see, e.g., Milton's sonnet on his blindness, and Dr. Johnson's verses "On the Death of Mr. Robert Levet."

33. Cawley, p. xix, discusses one analogue in *Middle English Sermons*, ed. W. O. Ross, EETS 209 (London, 1940), pp. 86 ff., but not the one on pp. 36 ff., which I describe here. Ross's list of analogues is in a note to this first version, and since Cawley directs the reader to that list, it seems unlikely he overlooked it entirely.

euery man is bondon to peye is dette of the goodes that God hath sende hym," and after speaking of alms-deeds and their necessity, he names Christ as man's ultimate and only way of settling his debt with God. The preacher then—and only then—goes on to narrate the story of the three friends, one of whom alone is faithful. There is no other text I know that shares so many of the materials the dramatist of *Everyman* used in his turn.

These intermediate links testify to the continuity of the tradition; and some later proof, of an oddly circumstantial kind, can take us further into the sixteenth century. Our text of *Everyman* depends chiefly upon two early editions printed by John Skot which survive complete. Two other editions, printed by Richard Pynson, are extant only in fragmentary form, one of them dated about 1510–25 and the other about 1525–30. The year 1525 links both guesses,[34] though guesses, of course, they remain. But it is interesting to find Pynson, in the following year, 1526, publishing a treatise called *The Pylgrimage of Perfection*, whose seventh chapter of the first book concerns God's gifts to man:

god wyll / that such gyftes and graces that he hath frely and without de-seruyng gyuen to men / should nat be taken in vayn: but whan he cometh to the yeres of discrecion / & hath the vse of reason / he shuld labour and exercise hymselfe in them: for *they be the talentes* that god hath *lent* to man in this lyfe: of the whiche he wyll aske moste *streyt accounte* in the *daye of iudgement.* . . .[35]

We have here what I called earlier the essential verbal matrix of the play of *Everyman;* and, as with the Lydgate verses quoted then, one further word, "talents," which is the explanation of the rest. If *Everyman* was indeed written in the 1480s, this treatise is later by some forty years: but the printed editions (which are all that remain) testify at the very least to its popularity in the early decades of the sixteenth century. This evidence suggests that Richard Pynson, or anyone reading both of these works from his press, would surely have understood the parable of the talents to be the scriptural text underlying *Everyman*. On the basis of evidence already put forward, they would almost equally surely not have been the first to do so.

I have one final reason, perhaps stronger than all the others, for thinking that. As noted before, *Barlaam and Ioasaph*, a Greek work of the eleventh century, has long been recognized as the earliest source of the (Christianized) faithful-friend story, but since there are many inter-

34. See Cawley, p. ix.
35. *The Pylgrimage of Perfection,* printed by Richard Pynson (1526), S.T.C. 3277, p. 20v; italics mine. Wynkyn de Worde also published the work, in 1531, S.T.C. 3278, pp. 12–12v.

mediate versions of the same, *Everyman* scholarship has tended to concern itself with those that are later in time and nearer in place. This is quite proper: no one would wish to claim for the dramatist direct knowledge of an early Greek original. It was, indeed, the last version I turned to in my research. But it offers a most striking confirmation of the reading I had reached, and have so far been putting forward, on other grounds. For the Fifth Apologue of that work, the ultimate source of our story, names the crisis confronting the man who had three friends in this way:

Now one day he was apprehended by certain dread and strange soldiers, that made speed to hale him to the king, there to render account for a debt of ten thousand talents [ταλάντων].

In the end it is only the neglected third friend,

the company of good deeds,—faith, hope, charity, alms, kindliness, and the whole band of virtues, that can go before us, when we quit the body, and may plead with the Lord on our behalf, and deliver us from our enemies and dread creditors, who urge that strict rendering of account in the air.[36]

In short, the story which gives to *Everyman* its most distinctive action and shape—the testing of friends—in its earliest Christian version explicitly works from the idea of the talents. The Greek author takes the figure ten thousand from Matthew 18: it makes a striking beginning, and all preliminaries can be avoided by simply announcing a call to repay a huge debt. But Matthew 18 contributes nothing except that specific number. For the rest, we are dealing with the meaning of the talents as defined by those several centuries of patristic commentary on Matthew 25 that preceded this eleventh-century narrative. Without that implicit understanding of what the debt involves, "the company of good deeds" and "the whole band of virtues" would make no sense as a way of explaining the third and faithful friend.

Should there be any doubt that the scriptural sense of "talent" is alive in his pages, the author's introduction to the whole work can put it to rest:

So I too . . . heedful of the danger hanging over that servant who, having received of his lord the talent, buried it in the earth, and hid out of use that which was given him to trade withal, will in no wise pass over in silence the edifying story that hath come to me. . . . It readeth thus.[37]

36. [St. John Damascene], *Barlaam and Ioasaph*, ed. and trans. G. R. Woodward and H. Mattingly (Loeb Classical Library, 1914) reprinted with an introduction by David Marshall Lang (1967), pp. 192–99. The attribution of authorship to Saint John Damascene has been discredited. For a detailed study of the history of this facinating work, see Lang's introduction to his translation of a Georgian version of the same name, *The Wisdom of Balahvar* (London, 1957), pp. 11–65.
37. *Barlaam and Ioasaph*, p. 5.

The Jesuit scholar, Jean Sonet, in a two-volume study of *Barlaam and Ioasaph* and its transmission, names a normative medieval Latin version, of which sixty-two manuscripts are known to him: its features include both the debt of ten thousand talents and praise of the third friend as returning *with usury* (that is, with spiritual profit) such small kindness as had been shown him.[38] Again, the second of these details makes sense only in relation to the later parable. It cannot derive from Matthew 18.

Whether the talents survive as an explicit detail in any given version, or whether they have gone underground, as in the *Golden Legend*, here translated by Caxton, "And it happed so that this man was in grete perylle of his lyf and was somoned tofore the kynge,"[39] in either case it seems clear that this parable continued to be the explanation of that action and its deepest controlling logic, from the eleventh century well into the sixteenth.

What happens on stage in no way looks like visual representations of the parable as they are found, say, in the *Speculum humanae salvationis*, where it is usual for two servants to be shown presenting coins or purses, while the third is bound and punished.[40] Instead the stage is occupied by allegorical personages who are explicitly, denotatively, what those coins signify, with Everyman and his account books at their center. He is engaged in a different literal action—the testing of friends—with the result that the symbols and referents of the parable have perforce been recombined, shaped into something new, and no single patristic commentary has been used with perfect consistency or as a whole. But Everyman offers in reckoning still his Good Dedes and the cross of Christ. We know that the first Christian redactor of that testing-of-friends story had the talents in mind; they were his reason for telling it, and determined its moral. When a version of that story, probably not much longer than its original, came into the hands of a fifteenth-century dramatist, the parable and its commentaries seem once again to have provided clues and indications as to how that brief exemplum might be expanded into a rich and complex work of art. His procedures were eclectic, certainly. His concern was to make a play potent to move a popular audience, not to transmit lecture notes on the Fathers, and so

38. *Le Roman de Barlaam et Josaphat*, 2 vols. (Namur and Paris, 1949, 1950), I, 37–40, 74–88.
39. Quoted by Cawley, p. xviii.
40. The works cited in note 29 name or reproduce a good many illustrations to the parable. Some others seen in manuscript are perhaps worth listing: Bodley MS Laud Misc. 165, fol. 399v and fol. 460v (William of Nottingham's Commentary on the Gospels); Bodley MS Douce 204, fol. 40 (a *Speculum*); British Museum MS Royal 15 D. v., fol. 173 (Gregory's Homilies); and four MSS of the *Speculum* at the Pierpont Morgan Library: MS M.140, fol. 42v; MS M.385, fol. 42v; MS M.766, fol. 61v; MS M.782, fol. 74.

he used what seemed useful, governed only by the need to make of those old materials something strong and stageable and new, at once dramatically coherent and doctrinally correct.

We do not see the parable staged, but unless we would ignore the fact that ideas have histories and that drama involves words spoken— uses words because it is interested in ideas more complex than dumb shows can manage—then we may find that the text that lies behind this play is like the soil beneath a rich carpet of green grass: it has a great deal to do with everything we do see that is substantial, pleasing, and alive. And it can help us see it better, for it invites a closer attention to the actual language of the play, permits a more precise definition of what is underway at any given moment, and—not least—allows us to apprehend more clearly the play's essential unity of action.

For modern audiences, *Everyman* is perhaps most moving, most successful, in its "tragic" action—its imitation of how a man dies. We are more than ever in search of an *ars moriendi*, having abandoned the medieval kind. But the other part of the play, its rising action—that which moves toward joy and reconciliation and salvation—has its own power and special conviction still, if only because once that was where the deepest truth was known to reside. For a medieval audience this "play of holy dying" was most urgently a play about holy living, an *ars vivendi atque moriendi*. The parable of the talents in no small part was responsible for that.

Index

Memling, Hans, 196
Menchen, Jehan, 93
Meredith, George, 158
Metrical Paraphrase (A Middle English Paraphrase of the Old Testament), 161, 161 n.6
Meyer, Wilhelm, 44 n.3
Mézières, Philippe de, 106–13
Michel, Jean, *Passion* by, 82–83, 89
Milet, Jacques, 113–15
Mirk, John, 163–64, 299
Mistaire et vie de Sainct Christofle, Le, 96–97
Mistère du Viel Testament, Le, 171–76
Mithou, Maître, (Jean Daniel), 93
Moëlles, Jacques, 81
Mone, F. J., 66 n.3
Mons, *Passion* of (1501), 82, 86, 87, 88, 89
Montbéliard, *Jeu de Monseigneur Sainct Sebastien* at, 89–90; *Jeux de Mgr. Saint Maintbeuf* at, 89
Monte Cassino Passion play, 33
Montferrand, *Passion* of (1477), 89
Moore, J. B., 160
Morality plays, 17, 23–26, 32, 268 ff., *279–91, 292–307, 316–40*; characters in, 264–65, 271–72, 267–68, 271, *279–91, 316–40*; dramatic sources, 274; nondramatic sources and influences, 273, 280 ff., 316, 322, 323, 332–39; poetic analogues, 280 ff., 317 n.3, 318, 326, 331, 336; similarity to Doomsday plays, *260–78*, 317 n.4. *See also* Allegory; Symbolism; Theology, use of, in drama; Typology
Morgan, Margery M., 179, 180, 210
Mount Olivet, 134–35, 137, 276–77
Mouton, Jean, 93
Müller, l'Abbé Eugène, 57
Mundus et Infans, 228
Muris, Jean de, 85
Murray, Gilbert, 29
Music: Burgundian school of, 215; in French history plays, 18; Gregorian, monophonic, 45–63, 64–80, 84 (*see also* Trope); instrumental, 81, 84, 86, 88–93, 95, 97; in liturgical plays, 15, 15 n.22, 30, 39, 57, 81; in liturgy, 45–46, 49, 50–53, 64–80; musical interludes, 81, 87; in mystères and miracles, 81–97; polyphony, 83, 84, 86; professionally supplied, 88–96 passim; in Second Shepherds' Play (Wakefield cycle), 21, *212–17;* vocal, 81 ff., 87, 91 ff.
Music-drama, *28–43, 64–80;* and divine office, 47, 48, 50–53, 62–63; history of, 2, 28, 29–30, 46–47; modern productions, 7 n.13; symbolism in, 9, 10, 18, 52. *See also* Beauvais, *Daniel;* Benedictbeuern, manuscript from monastery of (plays in); Drama, history of: dialogue form in matins lections and responsories; Fleury Playbook (plays from)
Mystère d'Adam, 14, 53–55, 56, 58 n.57, 60, 155
Mystère de Jules César, 113
Mystère de la Nativité, 92
Mystère de la Passion. See Montferrand
Mystère de la vengeance de Jhesus-Christ, 91
Mystère de S. Louis, 113
Mystère de Saint Martin, 90
Mystère des trois doms. See Romans, *Mystère des trois doms* at
Myth, mythic drama, 11, 23, 29, 30, 33–36, 148 ff., 159 ff., 281

Narbonne, Easter play of, 38
Naturalism, 20, 22, 198, 241–42. *See also* Realism
Nelson, Alan H., 5, 19–20, 21–22, 23–24, *116–47*, 149 n.5, *218–29*
Nicoll, Allardyce, 137
Northern Passion, The, 231–32, 235, 239, 243
Norwich, Grocers' cart of, 118, 120
Notker Balbulus, 57
N-Town cycle (Hegge cycle, *Ludus Coventriae*), 19–20, 21–22, 23, 131–47, 156, 164–71 passim, 219–29 passim, 235, 238 n.25, 257 n.29, 260–66 passim, 268, 274, 294